WITHDRAWN

RECENT CONSERVATIVE POLITICAL THOUGHT:
American Perspectives

Russell G. Fryer

University Press of America™

5551.3

Copyright © 1979 by

University Press of America, Inc.™

4710 Auth Place, S.E., Washington D.C. 20023

All rights reserved

Printed in the United States of America

ISBN: 0-8191-0694-1

Library of Congress Catalog Card Number: 78-68568

UK
271
.F7

To Eleanor

CONTENTS

ACKNOWLEDGMENTS

I am indebted to my niece, Christine Fryer, for invaluable editorial assistance in the preparation of this manuscript.

I would also like to express my gratitude to a colleague, Elizabeth Apetz, for the editorial help she provided in an early draft of this book.

AUTHORS WHOSE WRITINGS ARE ANALYZED IN THIS STUDY

Hannah Arendt
Edward C. Banfield
Daniel Bell
Raoul Berger
Alexander M. Bickel
William F. Buckley, Jr.
James Burnham
Peter F. Drucker
Jacques Ellul
M. Stanton Evans
Milton Friedman
Nathan Glazer
Barry Goldwater
Friedrich A. Hayek
Sidney Hook
Bertrand de Jouvenel
Willmoore Kendall
George F. Kennan
Russell Kirk
Irving Kristol

Walter Lippmann
Seymour Martin Lipset
Frank S. Meyer
Hans J. Morgenthau
Daniel P. Moynihan
Reinhold Niebuhr
Robert Nisbet
Robert Nozick
Michael Oakeshott
Jose Ortega y Gasset
Kevin P. Philipps
Ayn Rand
Murray A. Rothbard
George Santayana
William A. Simon
Leo Strauss
Peter Viereck
Eric Voegelin
Robert Welch
James Q. Wilson

The role and meaning of ideology in political science is surely one of the areas of greatest disagreement and uncertainty. If there was some way of dispensing with the terms liberalism, conservatism, and radicalism, I am sure there would be considerable sentiment in favor of such a development. These ideological concepts are so slippery, so open to diverse interpretations, and so subjective in usage, that it would be better if they were not so frequently associated with political discourse. Yet it is also the case that the assumptions, values, and policy-preferences which count so heavily in one's attitude toward politics cannot really be dealt with except in reference to these ideological stances and predispositions.

In recent years, there has been an astonishing amount of scholarly exegesis designed especially to define and evaluate liberalism and radicalism in American thought. Much less attention has been paid to conservatism, and what there is has largely been written by conservatives in defense of their professed values, or by those who start out quite unsympathetic toward all aspects of conservative doctrine. This study, therefore, is an attempt to avoid both these extremes while exploring the complex convolutions of conservative ideas, movements, and thought during the better part of this century.

One very real difficulty I encountered throughout innumerable outlines for this book was deciding who qualified as a conservative thinker. As my own understanding of conservatism changed in the course of this research, I saw the need to expand the original list, and even then there is considerable ambiguity in classifying such people as Reinhold Niebuhr and Sidney Hook as conservative, not to mention those individuals that I refer to in chapter 8 as liberal-conservatives, who indeed may well be part of an emergent neo-liberalism or neo-conservatism, the latter being the more common designation. In the course of this study, I do give reasons for the particular labels I attach to different varieties of conservative political thought.

The main purpose of this book is to evaluate recent conservative political thought in relation to the contributions of some key thinkers to an authentic conservative tradition. Although I do not pretend to provide a thorough, comprehensive treatment of such thinkers, I have tried to reveal the essence of their political philosophies from a close reading of their various writings, and I have provided sufficient direct quotations to enable the reader to judge for herself/himself just how relevant each is for a better understanding of conservative theory and practice. Since conservatism means little unless it can be related to institutional developments and historical forces, this also has been a major concern throughout the analysis.

Part I, "Conservative Perspectives," touches upon the unique relationship of conservative to liberal thought in America; the ups and downs of conservatism in recent times; the continuities, as well as discontinuities, between 18th-19th century conservatism and recent conservatism; the ideological ambiguity represented by two of the most influential writers of the age—Reinhold Niebuhr and Sidney Hook; then in chapters 4 and 5 the two main strands of 20th century conservative thought, traditionalist and libertarian, are analyzed from the perspectives of leading advocates of these quite divergent approaches to conservative thought.

Part II, "Contemporary Critiques of Liberalism," identifies those writers who have been most concerned with the relationship between policy and politics in American political life in chapters 6 through 8, underscoring the considerable variations in the ideological content of their contributions to conservative thought. Chapter 9 is something of a departure, for it focuses upon five leading European conservative thinkers; their inclusion here is for the purpose of highlighting some important differences between American and European conservatism, as well as identifying conservative thinkers whose books are widely read and available in the United States at the present time.

Part III, "Ideological versus Non-Ideological Conservatism," seeks to relate recent conservative thought to the American political culture; briefly review some recent contributions to conservative thought, including studies by the late Alexander M. Bickel and George F. Kennan, that may portend both a new direction and greater popular acceptance of conservatism; and finally, a concluding analysis which evaluates conservatism in reference to contemporary aspects of liberal and radical thought, the American mind, and the politics of conservatism. Although the approach to conservatism is critical throughout this book, I have tried to be appreciative of those elements of conservative thought that do have objective merit.

There is no substitute for a direct, systematic, and all-inclusive personal encounter with the original writings of important thinkers, regardless of their ideological proclivities. At the same time, for those readers who desire to save time and still gain a familiarity with noted thinkers there is need for studies that summarize and extract significance from ideological movements. This book has been written to that purpose and in that spirit.

INTRODUCTION

As one looks back on the course of American history, the nation's political mood has seemed to shift periodically a- long a conservative-liberal axis; a relatively moderate yet significant liberal reform phase, lasting perhaps a decade or so, is inevitably succeeded by an equally indeterminate per- iod of relative consolidation and conservative reaction. Too much should not be made of this cyclical tendency, however, since such an ideological designation for historical periods is fraught with considerable imprecision and inconsistency. What this does suggest is the possibility that political ide- ology, as it relates to periodic national mood swings, does play an important role in determining the outcome of public policy, whether or not other aspects of change may be even more decisive.

A brief retrospective glance over the past three-quar- ters of a century seems to confirm this hypothesis. The ear- ly years of the century were marked politically by a liberal movement away from a late nineteenth century conservatism highlighted by Social Darwinism and economic laissez-faire. The Populist-Progressive Age of Protest and Reform culminated in Woodrow Wilson's first administration's enactment of a sub- stantial amount of reform legislation, including railroad reg- ulation, a new Federal banking system, direct election of U.S. senators, anti-trust laws, and various experiments in extend- ing popular democracy, such as the initiative, referendum, recall, and party primaries. Although World War I intervened to bring a premature end to the new liberalism, and Wilson's own version of liberalism was quite ambiguous, the result was a major transformation of the traditional Lockean-Jeffersonian least-government-the-best liberalism into a new liberal com- mitment to strong government and state welfarism.* The 1920's witnessed another pendulum swing to economic conservatism and non-activist government under the Republican Party aegis of Warren G. Harding, Calvin Coolidge, and Herbert Hoover, al- though the latter was a much more activist president than his two predecessors, and if it had not been for the stock market crash of 1929 and the onset of severe economic depression, Hoover could easily have gone down in history as a successful, rather than failed, leader.[1]

The financial-economic collapse of the early 1930's ush- ered in Franklin D. Roosevelt's New Deal, a swing toward lib- eral reform and government interventionism on a scale hither- to unknown in American history. Although historians are di- vided as to the extent and significance of the reform impulse under FDR, there is no question that the nation did experience a decided shift during the 1930's toward so-called mixed capi- talism and the welfare state.

Then, after World War II, despite Harry Truman's efforts to keep the reform impulse alive, the anticipated reaction set in, and the 1950's were noted as an era of political con-

* See Appendix I

1

servatism marked by the popular Dwight Eisenhower's eight
years of Republican Party retrenchment and by the rise and
fall of McCarthyism. The paper-thin triumph of Senator John
Kennedy over Vice President Richard Nixon in the 1960 election
heralded another decade or so of liberal ascendancy, until the
tragic assassination of the two Kennedy brothers and civil
rights leader Martin Luther King and America's ill-fated involvement in the Vietnam war paved the way for the rise of a
"new radicalism" and for the embattled presidency of Lyndon
Johnson. So by the late 60's, the country's mood was again
shifting toward conservatism, and it has continued this way
through the 1970's under the successive presidencies of Richard Nixon, Gerald Ford, and Jimmy Carter. Even as a liberal-
oriented Democratic Party seemed to dominate both Congress
and the White House, there was increasing evidence of an anti-
government, anti-taxation, anti-egalitarian groundswell across
the land, making it difficult for politicians of either party
or ideological persuasion to give coherent direction and leadership to the country.

More than anything else, the late 1970's seemed to reveal a reform-oriented liberalism in considerable dissaray
and obviously on the defensive; a neo-radicalism all but dead
and buried as far as practical politics was concerned, even
if this is not quite the case in the intellectual arena; a
conservative intellectual movement experiencing something of
a popular revival, yet mired in internal splits and without
any broad-based constituency.* At the same time, if this be
true, there is even more reason to seek to unravel the tan-
gled web of dissonent meanings and uncertain analysis that
seems to enshroud the use of such terms as liberalism and conservatism in political discourse. Although this particular
study focuses upon conservatism, in an attempt to identify
and survey leading spokesmen and thinkers representative of
this ideological outlook in the context of twentieth century
politics and thought, one cannot completely disregard the
fact that one needs to consider the relationship to conservative thought of liberal and even radical outlooks, including
the complex of ideas and policy-views that can be associated
with these viewpoints. So before proceeding to a systematic
study of conservative ideas and thinkers in contemporary America, it may be advisable to contrast liberalism and conservatism as ideological predispositions in reference to the recent past and the present of the American political culture.

Historically, the major assumption that divides conservatives and liberals in America has to do with the matter of
authority versus the individual. The conservative looks for
constraint on the excesses of human behavior in external authority; the liberal rejects external authority and makes an
absolute out of the individual conscience, human will, and
self-regulation. Only self-imposed restraints are permissible to the liberal; the conservative finds this both inadequate and unrealistic.

*See Appendix II (a) and (b)

Could this be the hidden flaw in democratic theory? Does authority come from within (i.e., man's conscience) or from without (i.e., society or government)? The liberal claims that the former is the case; the conservative maintains the latter is how it should be. Who is right? Or is neither totally correct?

In America, there is little doubt that the liberal view has predominated. Even as the contemporary liberal embraces the idea of positive government, he retains his individualistic, anti-authority premises; and the contemporary conservative, who claims to be the real protector of individual freedom, has lost confidence in the authority of government. Both liberals and conservatives, in other words, are caught up in major theoretical and practical contradictions.

Like the Marxist, the contemporary conservative tends to feel that politics largely derives from economic arrangements and the distribution of power, whereas the liberal seeks to separate economics and politics, believing that the latter should be in a better position to control the former.

Paradoxically, the traditional liberal was the great advocate of limited government and individual liberty; and the traditional conservative was the chief advocate of social constraint and strong government. Now it is the contemporary liberal who looks to government as the instrument of greater equality, even if this means the individual sometimes has to take a back-seat to society's so-called greater good; while the contemporary conservative wishes to reduce government intervention and to erect strong bulwarks for the protection of individual rights, especially the right to do what one wishes with one's property and the incentive promoting virtue of socio-economic inequality.

The overriding goal of liberalism has always been to maximize individual autonomy and freedom of choice. Contemporary conditions create endless roadblocks to this as the individual becomes more and more a creature dependent on consumerism and on a pervasive organizational, or collective, life; this situation instills a profound sense of powerlessness, if not alienation, in conservatives and liberals alike.

Conservatism also postulates this goal of maximizing individual autonomy, but looks in a different direction for a solution to the problem. Paradoxically, the conservative wants less government and greater respect for institutionalized authority. The liberal is equally paradoxical: he is willing to accept greater government activism in the interests of expanded social justice, but also desires greater individual freedom from social constraints. Either way, the ideal of maximized individual autonomy gets short shrift. Neither political philosophy can resolve its respective contradictions. The conservative distrusts political power, but is quite willing to see the state, through its legal and moral sanctions, expand its social power over individual life. The liberal, in contrast,

3

is willing to see political power expand, while seeking a drastic contraction of social power. The contradictions are real and pervasive.

There is no way to bridge the gulf between theory and practice in this reversal of roles and policy-orientations. At best, one can only take note of what has been happening, and try to clear away the debris that clutters the roadway.

Yet it should be brought out that people (including the elites) will be quite ambivalent regarding their political, social, and economic values. For example, most Americans are opposed to welfarism per se, but are in favor of public assistance to specific groups, such as the seriously handicapped, unemployables, etc. They are for improved economic opportunities respecting discriminated against minorities, but are strongly against busing or affirmative action "quotas" as a means of "correcting" disadvantaged status.

Everyone can be more or less identified in terms of a conservative-liberal-radical political spectrum; the difficulty comes in clarifying such elusive and controversial terms. Although ideological consistency vis à vis differing political issues varies among individuals, and this itself has a bearing on certain forms of collective action, any attempt to clarify ideological orientations must necessarily draw heavily upon contemporary thinkers who have provided the qualitative analyses that illuminate the theory-practice dilemma.

There is no clear-cut dichotomy which shows consistent liberalism or conservatism for elites or the general public in the United States. On the other hand, there is considerable evidence that liberalism versus conservatism becomes a divisive matter when basic underlying assumptions are at issue, including attitudes toward the nature of man, society, and government.*

Private property accumulation is the driving force of capitalistic liberal democracies; this creates an insoluble contradiction between private wants and public need, whereby the latter becomes irremediably dependent upon the former, creating a severe crisis for capitalistic-pluralist democracies. As the political sector continues its subordinate relationship to the corporate economic structure, and as the latter becomes more dependent upon state activity, a crisis of legitimacy is inevitable. Constitutional democracy cannot long survive in the absence of a legitimized consensus behind the basic institutional processes. Elite power eventually undermines democratic controls.

Both democratic radicalism and neo-liberalism require an activist and politically conscious public in order to achieve necessary institutional change and to shift power away from the private to the public sectors. Democratic conservatism, on the other hand, opposes both majority rule and unrestricted popular democracy, placing its trust instead in an enlightened meritocracy and in a minimum of government control over the

*See Appendix III

4

private sector. Given the continuous growth of bureaucratic-organizational power in post-industrial modern societies, is it not possible that none of the major ideological movements of our time has a satisfactory and effective answer to the growing threat an expanding bureaucratic-organizational society poses to democratic values and practices? Ironically, it now looks as though Max Weber, not Karl Marx, was the true prophet of advanced industrialized societies. It is not irremediable class conflict that will determine the future, but the ability of modern man to tame and rationalize huge bureaucratic power structures. In this respect, contemporary liberal, conservative, and radical thought all fail the test equally, and one seems no better than another in measuring up to the challenge.

Normally, America tends to experience cycles of moderate liberalism and moderate conservatism, and the Presidency is the main reflector of this fluctuating national mood. This may still be the case. But national problems are not solved, nor are needs satisfactorily met, on this basis. Interest-group pluralism is a stronger influence on public policy today than is any particular institution or agency of American government. The maintenance of American democracy depends upon a legitimate means of mediating conflicts of interests and values in an extremely heterogeneous society, where there is basic agreement on the fundamentals of the constitutional order, but little agreement over means.

Any political party or leader which claims to speak for all Americans in behalf of a particular vision of the public good poses a major threat to the stability and legitimacy of democratic politics. This is why the two major political parties are loose, temporary coalitions of diverse voting blocs, and why leaders have to appear to be more or less ideologically centrist, only slightly to the left or right on the political spectrum. Otherwise, they are perceived by most voters as too "radical," and thus dangerous to the basic stability of the system.

Equality, liberty, and consent (or participation) are the three great ideals of American democracy. But there is little or no agreement as to which takes precedence when progress in one area may mean retrogression in another.

Can liberalism accommodate itself to the rise of the technostructure which requires an elitist meritocracy rather than egalitarianism and participatory democracy?

Can equality be advanced without loss of liberty and a trade-off in reverse discrimination?

Can greater equality be achieved by democratic means, and without too high a price in bureaucratization and political coercion?

America has been conservative in social thought and liberal in political thought. In other words, a conservative outlook and values have dominated the institutional, cultural, and social level, with the Puritan-Protestant ethic, nativism, anti-radicalism, and moralism being the main historical manifestations of this development; at the same time, in politics, a liberal-moderate reform outlook has generally prevailed, embodied by the Jacksonian—Populist-Progressive—New Deal—Fair Deal—New Frontier—Great Society tradition. But the fact remains, these two traditions co-exist in uneasy tension, and many would conclude that the results have been generally less than satisfactory.

The dilemma of American liberalism and conservatism is that on economic issues (welfarism and social security), the majority of the people are left of center, and on social issues (distributive justice and social structure change), they are right of center, while increasingly, on political issues, they are largely complacent and apathetic, if not completely alienated from an increasingly bureaucratic system.

At the present time, all political ideologies are being placed under great strain because of the ceaseless demands of technological change, which seems to have a force all its own that both transcends and is disrespectful of all ideologies.

In America, liberalism has been essentially conservative in nature, while conservatism has had to accommodate itself to a dynamic society.

In America, liberalism reflects the basic national consensus in regard to the importance of restraints on the exercise of power reconciled to the need for sufficient change to maintain stable progress. Unfortunately, these two needs are frequently in conflict with one another.

Conservatives tend to defend such values as community, responsibility, duty, and tradition. Liberals tend to espouse such values as individual rights, equality (at least legal, if not always social, equality) and the inherent opposition between self and society.

In America, the working class has been one of the main supports of liberalism, at least since the New Deal, but only on economic issues; when it comes to democratic values, such as equality and tolerance of dissent, the working class is paradoxically quite illiberal.

Liberalism (political) and conservatism (social) have been the cement that has kept American society together and forged a consensus on fundamentals. Will a protracted economic deterioration (i.e., inflation) severely weaken this consensus? And even if America should avoid prolonged economic decline, will there not still be a widening gap between the "have mores" and the "have less"? In other words, which of the two versions of the dominant American ideology—liberalism or conservatism—is most likely to aid the American public in sorting through these immense contradictions and uncertainties so that ideology can strengthen, not weaken, the nation's commitment to effective democracy? This book does not pretend to answer this essential question, but it does seek to clarify the possibilities, and in respect to conservatism, render a judgment as to what might be expected from a revival of conservative ideas and thinking.

The attempt to understand how ideological mood, attitudes, and values relate to other historical factors is difficult under the best of circumstances, since liberalism and conservatism are concepts that have always resisted clear definition and consensual agreement in American thought and practice. I do not pretend to have succeeded where so many others have failed. The only claim that I can make to having achieved a modicum of objectivity and fairness in this study of recent conservative political thought is that I initially took on this assignment for the sole reason of finding out for myself why there was so much one-sidedness and subjectivity in the treatment of conservatism, and to see if I could not find a better answer to the question: What is conservatism?[2]

In the course of this research, I found that I was quite critical of certain aspects of conservative thinking and ideology; but somewhat to my surprise, discovered much more to commend and appreciate than I had believed I would when I embarked upon the study. Above all, I concluded that conservative ideas and values deserve to be given consideration equal to that given to the dominant liberal tradition that so often monopolizes our attention; for contrary to the conventional liberal view of conservatism, there is much more substance and historical importance to conservative thought than is usually attributed to it. This study has not made me more conservative in my own ideological attachment, but it has caused me to be more critical of what I do think and believe about the nature of the American democratic experiment. In a time of notable institutional weakness and intolerable discrepancies between democratic ideals and practices, conservative political thinkers need to be listened to with great care and respect. One must especially bear in mind that there are many varieties of conservatism, and they are not of equal merit. One of the purposes of this book is to review this situation and to indicate why some thinkers and aspects of conservative political thought stand out over others.

Two other purposes govern the format of this book. One is to identify and analyze the leading ideas of those twentieth century political theorists and philosophers who can be loosely tied to a conservative, liberal-conservative, or radical-conservative ideological orientation. In some instances, there may be a tendency to imply greater cohesiveness and interrelatedness among disparate thinkers than is justified under a "conservative" rubric. In these cases, it is my aim to convey both the significance and the invalidity of such designations. The second purpose of the book is to analyze the relationship of conservative ideas and values to a theory of American democracy. Ultimately, the appeal and importance of

7

conservative political thought must be judged on whether it does or does not contribute to a better understanding of American democratic norms and practices. Nothing is more paradoxical about conservatism than that it professes values that are inadequately represented in the political and social systems, and at the same time seeks to preserve that which is threatened by advocates of reform. Conservatives would like to see American democracy function in closer conformity to conservative than to liberal or radical values. What these values are, however, can only be determined by a careful study of thinkers who have argued the case for conservative values in politics.

One of the more tantalizing questions which arises in confronting conservative political thought is whether or not conservative values are truly compatible with the main thrust and tenets of democracy itself. If democracy is defined as unlimited popular participation in government, majority rule, and a belief that the liberty advanced by political democracy depends finally upon an expansion of socio-economic democracy and equality, then most conservatives are anti-democratic. If democracy is defined mainly as individual rights, private enterprise capitalism, limited government, and a belief that the main threat to liberty is an unchecked egalitarianism, then most conservatives are surely democratic. There is a sense in which conservatives are more means-oriented than ends-oriented. Only radical-conservatives, including those thinkers analyzed in chapter 5, would be the exception here. The question is not whether conservatives are basically unsympathetic to democratic norms, but rather, which particular democratic norms they believe should be acclaimed and advanced as a matter of priority. There may indeed be problems with conservative ideas in respect to democratic norms as we investigate the matter throughout this book, but it is a good thing to remind ourselves that there is more than one version of democracy to be considered. Liberals do not have a monopoly on democratic norms.

It would appear, therefore, that the bias of most treatments of conservatism in American thought has been pronounced, and there has been practically no agreement concerning the question of whether there really has been a viable, definable, and significant conservative tradition linking a succession of thinkers and intellectual movements throughout the course of American historical development. In addition, there has been little agreement among commentators and historians as to what constitutes a conservative political philosophy or stance or ideology. This is not unusual, for there is nothing more slippery and elusive in intellectual history than the attempt to clarify and evaluate the role of ideas in shaping history. Ralph Ketchum is surely correct when he observes: "Ideas are not separate from reality: they are part of it."[3]

Every human action is a reflection of an individual's unique perception of reality, and of his value choices. At

At the same time, a conservatism/liberalism dichotomy is one of the more persistent realities in politics. However much inconsistency and uncertainty there may be on a subjective level regarding the intensity, efficacy, and self-awareness of an ideological orientation to political and social reality, the fact remains that everyone can be identified somewhere on the ideological spectrum. The difficulty comes in defining that spectrum objectively—perhaps an impossible expectation. The best we can hope for is an approximation that offers sufficient insight for a better appreciation of the complex interrelatedness of ideas, interests, and conditions in the shaping of institutions and policy choices.

PART I CONSERVATIVE PERSPECTIVES

"Politics will, to the end of history, be
an area where conscience and power meet,
where the ethical and coercive factors of
human life will interpenetrate and work
out their tentative and uneasy compromise."

—Reinhold Niebuhr

"What may appear progressive or even revolutionary under certain conditions is
part of the established order under
others."

—Eugen Weber

"The ironic flaw in American liberalism
lies in the fact that we have never had
a real conservative tradition."

—Louis Hartz

"The most important difference between
liberals and conservatives...is to be
found in the interest groups they identify with."

—Theodore J. Lowi

CHAPTER 1

THE REVIVAL OF CONSERVATISM IN RECENT AMERICAN THOUGHT

The American Political Tradition

Unlike liberalism, conservatism has not enjoyed an honored place in the evolution of American political thought, although there is good reason to conclude that on a practical level it has done remarkably well.[1] This paradox is a unique legacy of American political history. As an ideological stance or movement, conservatism has not fared well. A dominant liberal tradition has so monopolized the ideological consensus that neither conservative nor radical thought has ever managed to establish itself as a viable alternative to a diluted and vague liberalism.[2] Most Americans have preferred pragmatic experimentation to ideological orthodoxy.[3] A country blessed from the beginning by an abundance of land, resources, and favorable climate nurtured an optimistic faith in the good life for the many and not just the few. So conservatism, which emphasizes quality over quantity, the disadvantages rather than the hoped for advantages of change, and restrictive rather than unrestrictive democracy, has never taken root in the American soil. Yet Americans are more attuned to means than ends. And so there is a paradox that lies at the heart of the American political experience: America has been a change oriented country whose ideological faith has been profoundly liberal, but it has been a liberalism marked by strong conservative overtones.[4]

The implications of this central paradox of American thought can be viewed from contrasting perspectives. The consensus seems to hold that America has enjoyed considerable success because the libertarian tradition of the pre-revolutionary, revolutionary, and constitutional periods continues to mold the American mind in the interests of a broadening liberty, equality, and justice.[5] Despite ups and downs, and some notable failures, such as slavery and racism, this view suggests that a close approximation exists between ideology and practice. Means and ends have conjoined around a firm commitment to a democratic-libertarian creed. This creed stresses liberty <u>and</u> equality <u>and</u> opportunity as the birthright of the masses, not just of the few. At the same time, however, a handful of intellectuals and thinkers have periodically challenged this prevailing view from either a conservative or a radical perspective. Instead of essential harmony, they see pernicious weakness, and even failure, in an ideology that partakes more of myth than substance, permitting an intolerable discrepancy between abstract ideals and operating realities.[6] From these unorthodox perspectives, there is more evidence of failure than success in the ability of American institutions to improve the quality

13

of life, even though Right and Left have quite different notions of what values and changes should be substituted for liberal orthodoxy. It is only recently, however, that the basic legitimacy of the liberal creed has endured systematic review and attack from both radical and conservative perspectives.[7] Whether this development should be looked upon favorably or unfavorably may be the single most divisive question facing the American people today.

Before the liberal creed can be cemented back together again as the consensual basis of the American value system, it will have to confront more realistically the gap between promise and performance. A notable contribution of both the conservative and radical-left traditions has been the spotlight they have directed at the underside of an American liberal mind that masks the frequent failures of liberalism in practicing what it preaches. But both conservatism and left-radicalism have been severely handicapped in selling their various messages to the American public. Neither presents an alternative that is acceptable to a public that has for so long looked benevolently upon a marriage of conservative means and liberal ends.

The liberal value system has long been a mirror image of an economic system that seemingly advanced the welfare of the many, if not of all. It is only now that the price of economic strength and political weakness seems higher than it should have been, both in respect to environmental depredation and economic injustice.[8] The recent revival of conservative ideology in the United States is a counterpoint to the "crisis of liberalism" that has been so evident in the wake of serious institutional breakdowns.[9] It remains to be seen whether conservatism itself can successfully fill the void left by a declining liberal consensus.[10]

In order to accomplish this historic reversal, however, conservatism has much to answer for and many obstacles to overcome. At its best, conservative political thought seeks to raise the level of civility and morality in political behavior by emphasizing man's social, not just individualist, nature. Too often, this commendable end has been subverted by what Samuel DuBois Cook has called the "moral myopia" of an ideology which seeks the "ought" in the "is" and "was"; and which, consequently, tends to rationalize and perpetuate injustices that a democratic society should not countenance.[11] More important, liberal and conservative values were so intermixed during the formative period of American politics that a conservative-liberal political outlook coalesced around Lockean individualism, fusing, rather than demarcating, these potentially alternative conceptions of democracy. The result is well expressed by Sheldon S. Wolin:

> While this confluence of liberals and conservatives produced a 'mainstream' of American politics, it left conservatism in something like a permanent

14

identity crisis, without a distinctive idiom
or vision. The occasional efforts of such figures as Fisher Ames, Noah Webster, or Calhoun to
stake out a conservative preserve in defense of
privilege, talent, racial inequality, and regionalism had little effect on a society where
badges of distinction were resented, property
easily available, and opportunities too plen-
tiful.[12]

Many commentators have pointed to the fact that the
absence of an aristocratic tradition and the limited socio-economic stratification have been the main stumbling
blocks to an authentic conservative tradition in America.[13]
In marked contrast to the European experience, American
society has never created the obstacles to social mobility
that arose elsewhere; and this lack of a supporting institutional hierarchy deprived conservatism of its most important ingredient.[14] The traditionalism which conservatives wish to restore is suffused with a bourgeois ethos
that has given remarkable stability to the political structure. The one classical political thinker who commands
near universal respect among conservatives, Edmund Burke,
would be a poor guide in the American political context,
for the conservative values he upholds—custom, hierarchy,
order, exclusiveness, and a pessimistic view of human nature—are inimical to the mainstream liberal commitment to
progress, equality, opportunity, and expanded democracy.[15]
Thus conservatism assumes a radical coloration in American
politics—mainly because it favors the politics of ideology
over the politics of consensus—and this immediately limits
its potential appeal to the average voter. Once again,
the conservative dilemma arises from the incompatibility
of conservatism with a liberal consensus, and from the
lack of a conservative tradition to feed upon.[16]

This being the case, Harry K. Girvetz may be correct
when he views the situation with something less than approval:

> The weakness of an authentic conservative tra-
> dition in this country is a great tragedy. Conser-
> vatism is a useful and important counterpart to lib-
> eralism. We need conservatives to alert us to the
> continuity of history and the role of tradition in
> human affairs. We need them to remind us of what
> the liberal and old-style radical often ignore;
> that man is not a completely rational animal and
> that we must address ourselves to his heart as
> well as his head, and reckon with his feelings
> as well as his cool, calm calculation of conse-
> quences. We need conservatives to warn us, also,
> that in human affairs the consequences are not
> easily calculated and often wholly unexpected, so
> that a known present should not be lightly dis-
> carded for a precarious future.[17]

No word seems to be used more frequently in describing and evaluating the American political system than ambiguity.[18] The capacity to reconcile contradictory principles and values seems to be the most characteristic feature of the American political tradition. Whether it is Jefferson versus Hamilton, or judicial self-restraint versus judicial activism, or states' rights versus national supremacy, or liberty versus equality, these contradictory tendencies permeate the norms and functioning of American government. The trouble arises when considering whether this has facilitated or retarded the ability of the system to integrate responsive, effective, and accountable government. Liberalism has tended to defend and even glorify this unique quality of the system. Essentially, the liberal assumes that Americans have had the best of both worlds, centralization and decentralization of power; and for this reason alone, it is better to commend this all-pervasive ambiguity than to seek to displace it with a more consistent alternative that favors one set of values over its opposite. The radical-left response to this crucial element of the American system is generally to argue that ambiguity slides into a perennial complacency and into resistance to the changes necessary to close the gulf between democratic rhetoric and inadequate performance. Ultimately, the evils of capitalism become self-perpetuating and ineradicable.

The conservative response to ambiguity is a bit more subtle. While sanctioning the superiority of capitalism and the bourgeois ethos, conservatives deplore the ascendancy of a mass culture, egalitarianism, and the erosion of moral standards that conservatives attribute to the liberal's preference for equality over liberty, and secularism over religiosity. In the conservative's view, ambiguity is too high a price to pay for misplaced values. So the conservative directs his fire at the liberal hegemony and dismisses the radical-left as an alien force in a country where there seems no real possibility that capitalism will be replaced by some form of socialism. To the liberal, ambiguity is the chief strength of the system; to the radical-leftist it is the system's chief weakness; to the conservative, ambiguity is not something to be either sanctioned or eliminated but superceded. Only when liberal democracy is replaced by conservative democracy will this happen.

The major problem with regard to conservatism, however, is defining the role it has placed in the American political tradition. As Samuel P. Huntington has indicated, the only two political developments in American history which reflected a consistent conservative ideology were the Federalist party and pro-slavery defenders of the ante-bellum South; and neither of these had significant long-term consequence. "The great political controversies of American history with a few exceptions have been between two or more varieties of liberalism."[19]

16

Coupled with the absence of a viable radical tradition, the effect of this situation for American political thought has been to weaken and compromise liberalism, for the price of consensus is the emasculation of ideas, the muting of debate over policies and issues, and the introduction of an enduring note of complacence in respect to the institutional structure.[20] That the dominant liberal ideology has undergone so many mutations, and has assimilated to itself such a heavy dose of conservatism in the process, seems to have suited the American temperament; but it has not been without cost. American statesmen are adept at posing stark policy alternatives and then rejecting either "extreme" for what appears to be a sounder, more reasonable, and much less risky moderate course which in effect usually means doing little or nothing of substance to resolve a pressing foreign or domestic problem.

Whether this approach is the better one, whether it usually serves the public interest, is not easily evaluated, because there is no way of knowing whether the American people would accept any other approach; and it is doubtful whether the consequences can be objectively assessed to determine the viability of alternative approaches. The one time that political compromise failed completely and it became a case of either/or, the country suffered the anguish of civil war. Yet the persistent inability of Americans to allow their leaders to consider alternative courses of action that may require a greater departure from existing patterns of conduct and a stronger commitment to a particular end makes it difficult to perceive reality objectively, to subject basic assumptions to careful scrutiny, or to do justice to a course of action that may be effective in the long run, despite the seductiveness of short-run expediency.

A political tradition which persists in seeking the middle way, the moderate position, the safer course, will probably enjoy political stability; however, there will be occasions when the inability to think clearly about a wide range of ideas and choices will act as a trap that lurks in the underbrush, ready to be sprung if the quarry should inadvertently take the wrong path. The Vietnam war situation is a case in point. Such over-reliance on safe and habitual patterns of thought invites a preference for illusion over reality.[21] All of this leads to the conclusion that the political culture itself, rather than any failure of conservatism as an ideological or philosophical world-view, has been the main impediment to the development of a strong and consistent conservatism.[22]

The conservative political tradition has not always offered realistic solutions to national problems; this has undoubtedly been as much the fault of conservative thinkers as of the defensive stance conservatives have been forced to adopt in the American context.[23] But the persistent weakness and ineffectuality of conservatism in providing a significant alternative to mainstream liberalism is worth

17

examining, especially since such an examination may help us to understand better the contemporary crisis of liberalism that so many commentators have alluded to.[24]

Despite a notable achievement in the establishment of political democracy, liberalism has failed tragically, in the view of a rising chorus of critics, in achieving necessary and sufficient progress in the establishment of socio-economic democracy. As Harry S. Kariel has suggested: "Today it is doubtful that political stability, not to say maturity, can be maintained despite social and economic inequalities. An awareness of inequality (or of a merely sluggish movement toward equality) creates the very discontents which doom politics."[25] Or, as Robert Paul Wolff argues: "The most significant fact about the distribution of power in America is not who makes such decisions as are made, but rather how many matters of the greatest importance are not objects of anyone's decision at all."[26] And as Theodore J. Lowi has observed: "As capitalist society galloped into the twentieth century its intellectual weakness strained belief. At some undetermined point capitalism ceased to constitute the public philosophy, although it remains a strong ideological force."[27]

Of course, these writers are criticizing aspects of liberalism from a moderately radical, rather than a conservative, perspective. But the crisis of liberalism also represents an unprecedented concern, on the part of many Americans, about the health and continuing viability of American political institutions, particularly the presidency and the party system. Conservatism has always been in crisis within the American political tradition, although crisis is a relatively new phenomenon for liberalism. In many respects, the conservative political tradition lacks coherence and substance. To some extent, it has acted more as an on-going critique of liberalism than as an attractive alternative to the existing institutional structure. The built-in negativism of much conservative thought, wherein it makes a louder noise when it is against something rather than for something, seems to be its main defect and the reason why it tends to have such a limited appeal for the general public.[28]

One question that has perplexed scholars and critics of conservative political thought is whether conservatism really qualifies as an ideology. In one of the most frequently cited essays on contemporary conservatism, Samuel P. Huntington distinguishes conservatism from all other ideologies except radicalism because "it lacks what might be termed a substantive ideal."[29] If it is one of the common characteristics of any political ideology to project a vision of a better society than one presently in evidence,[30] conservatives seem preoccupied with defending an existing status quo and resisting change, rather than proposing an alternate conception of the political order. But Professor Huntington and those who agree with this view of conservatism fail to consider that conservative thinkers do prefer certain values to others and that they define democracy in qualitative, rather than quantitative terms; for example, the Good Society versus the Great Society. In effect, what matters most to the conservative is leadership by a meritocracy unhindered by excessive egalitarian and social welfare demands of the many.

Conservatives advocate restrictions on popular control of government because they generally feel that democracy is best served by enabling "qualified" individuals to run things, even if this approach sanctions a hierarchical and elitist structure. There may be uncertainty regarding the "qualifications" desired for rulership, but the real thrust of conservative thought is as much positive as it is negative. This is seen in the fact that conservative values are in constant opposition to liberal values in policy matters, and each position can be just as ideological as the other. On a higher philosophical level, conservatives distrust ideology and rationality to the extent that these concepts entail imposing a set of ideas or changes on existing institutional structures. On the other hand, conservative thinkers have indeed found a traditional ideal which inspires their trust in a better political order.31 In most cases, this ideal is none other than liberty; but unlike the liberal's commitment to liberty, the conservative's value concept is one of personal freedom purged of egalitarianism. As Jasper B. Shannon has argued quite relevantly: "The American conservative has found in the doctrine of liberty a defense against equality."32

The Crisis of Liberalism

The one topic that seems a hot item for political columnists, intellectual journals of opinion, and news magazines these days is the decline and fall of contemporary liberalism.33 Even though one encounters more heat than light in much of this material, there is good reason to believe that contemporary liberalism is experiencing some sort of crisis. The sheer volume of critical analysis is either tuned in to something important, or it has become a self-fulfilling prophecy based upon flimsy data. Usually, "contemporary liberalism" refers to the New Deal tradition of positive government and expanded welfarism. Disillusionment and withdrawal have set in as a result of apparent failures in dealing with pressing social problems over the past few decades despite huge allotments of federal funds. Certainly, the performance record regarding recent federal efforts to alleviate, if not remedy, poverty, housing, health, welfare, and related issues, has not been impressive. And since the liberal camp, once upon a time, promised substantial progress in establishing a greater degree of social justice in America if liberal policies were given sufficient funding and public support, the bewildered middle-class public, as it contemplates rising inflation, taxes, and corruption, can be excused for suddenly realizing it

19

has been had, as the saying goes.[34]

Interestingly, despite stirrings of hope and anticipation, advocates of conservatism have yet to capitalize upon liberal failures, and the prospects are less-than-even that this situation will change in the near future. Although it is true that books, articles, and media attention in the 1970's seem much more hospitable than ever before to conservative causes, ideas, and publications, there is overwhelming evidence that the conservative movement has not been able to adequately fill the vacuum created by a wounded and vulnerable liberalism. The Republican Party, bastion of political conservatism and a necessary vehicle for effective conservative politics, attracts the allegiance of slightly more than 20 per cent of affiliated voters, and continues to be racked by internal ideological warfare on all levels of organizational politics. In addition, the conservative movement generally lacks a unifying center and the symbolic leadership that might lift it high in public awareness and esteem. Although the National Review has a stable of skillful publicists and a celebrity star in William F. Buckley, Jr., less ideologically-motivated conservatives feel uncomfortable under such an umbrella. An aging Barry Goldwater, Gerald Ford, and Ronald Reagan still attract attention, and the presidential hopes of Ford and Reagan are still alive as this is written; but time is the omnipresent handicap here. Conservative organizations sprout up in ever greater proliferation; and the prestigious "think tanks," such as the Hoover Institute at Stanford University, the Georgetown Center for Strategic Studies, and the American Enterprise Institute, provide havens for conservative scholars as well as occasional financial subsidies for their articles and books. There is no disputing that conservatism is today alive and well in America. Yet it is still quite uncertain whether the trees will bear a heavy harvest of fruit. Even in crisis, liberalism has a broad-based constituency that conservatism lacks and may not be able to command for reasons that will be analyzed fully in this book.[35]

A sampling of recent scholarly studies confirms the seriousness of liberal disenchantment, since many of the critics are themselves certified liberals who find themselves becoming radicalized or simply remaining in the liberal fold, while exhibiting a notable loss of confidence in the liberal approach to current problems. In The Politics of Disorder, Theodore J. Lowi continues his critique of interest-group liberalism begun in a much better book, The End of Liberalism. Among other things, he criticizes the tendency of liberals to join with conservatives in a futile embrace of the benefits of decentralization; in Lowi's view, any attempts to decentralize power in America, either by shifting greater responsibility to lower levels of government or by reducing the scope of federal responsibility, "tend to plug government into the interest group system. Thus, during a time of great change like the present, decentralization, in effect, commits government to system maintenance just when it is trying to be...on the side of change."[36]

20

Lowi presents a convincing portrait of duplicity in the uses of power whereby liberals have long been guilty of trading incremental expediency for needed structural changes in the system.

After a careful and thoughtful survey of the multi-billion dollar U.S. foreign aid program that began with President Truman's "Point-Four" recommendations in 1949, Robert A. Packenham (<u>Liberal America and the Third World</u>) concludes as follows: "The United States can do better in regard to Third World political developments by doing less...than by attempting to do more."[37] He finds more evidence of failure than of success in American foreign aid programs during the past three decades, and blames this on a liberal illusion, rooted in the American ideological tradition of judging other nations by our standards and values instead of assessing more realistically what can and should be accomplished through American aid abroad.

In a flawed but arresting examination of the liberal tradition, Paul N. Goldstene (<u>The Collapse of Liberal Empire</u>) sees evidence of liberal decline in the failure to keep the political and economic systems separate in the manner envisioned by the Founders.[38] The older concept of balanced interests and limited power has been destroyed, according to Professor Goldstene, by a capitalistic system sanctioned by liberals that can no longer promote democratic welfare or make a viable contribution to the public good. The author's indictment is much too sweeping and disorganized to merit high praise, and his vague alternative of science and technology as the road to salvation hints at exchanging liberal values for "the politics of a scientific civilization"—whatever this may mean. Ultimately, what Professor Goldstene seeks is a revived liberalism capable of taming the corporate economic structure and of redistributing wealth in a way that would substitute a society of abundance for the principle of scarcity which now operates. As one might expect, however, there is no realistic analysis showing how this might feasibly happen under contemporary conditions.

A common complaint of leftist critics is that liberalism has not so much failed as succeeded too well: that is, liberals have learned to compromise so successfully with the inequities of the system that liberals have lost all credibility where it matters most. In the words of Jack Newfield: "The New Deal has become the status quo; the old solution has become the new problem."[39] Irving Louis Horowitz maintains that, by not holding steadily to liberal principles, "...liberalism's pragmatic and pluralistic character only serves to polarize further the ideological framework in American life."[40] And in the view of Michael Harrington, liberalism's downfall began when Lyndon Johnson's pseudo-consensus version of liberalism became "the official national ideology of the United States of America."[41] This development deprived liberalism of its adversary role in the culture, weakened responsible radicalism and conservatism, and thus paved the way for the Great Society debacle. William Pfaff agrees with Harrington that liberalism has allowed itself to become too tame and has been co-opted into the system, while the so-called New Politics of the Left, which was aimed at revitalizing Democratic Party politics, has since revealed its true conservative colors.[42]

The critique of liberalism from within is best exemplified by the historian Otis L. Graham, Jr., and by former Kennedy aid Richard N. Goodwin. In The American Condition, Goodwin analyzes the rise of the "bureaucratic state" as one of the unintentional consequences of the liberal era.[43] Otis Graham argues that liberalism sacrificed a golden opportunity to the politics of expediency by identifying itself with the "broker state" theory of incremental change and piecemeal reform, instead of with a planning system which would have allowed the political sector to dominate the economic power structure.[44] Toward a Planned Society is surely one of the most rewarding studies of the failures and successes of a liberal society since early New Deal days to be published. It may be that the author expects too much from a single solution, a better national planning system, but he does provide a perceptive historical analysis that gives equal attention to both the possibilities and the weaknesses of the liberal tradition.

The conservative critique of liberalism will be dealt with in fuller detail later in this book. The main charge can be briefly noted: the true dimensions of liberalism's failures are big government, unresponsive bureaucracies, and a dangerous weakening of the national security system. By placing such a heavy burden on government as problem-solver, liberals have fallen into the trap of raising false expectations, while causing the inevitable ignominy of poor performance and undelivered promises.

Even within the liberal camp, there is a clear indication that problem-solving optimism has slipped away and has been replaced by discouragement and confusion. Perhaps the late Senator Philip A. Hart said it best when he was interviewed following his retirement from the Senate in 1975:

> Senator and Mrs. Philip A. Hart of Michigan said today that the optimism they brought to Washington 17 years ago—the belief that liberalism could change the world—had given way to discouragement bordering on dismay. "I think that it is correct to say that the optimism which we brought with us in 1958—that whatever the problem was we could get a handle on it—we don't have that kind of optimism any more," Mr. Hart said. Mr. Hart said that the mood of the time—the feeling that government could solve most problems—may have marked a peak for liberalism.[45]

It need only be added that Senator Hart was one of the most highly respected liberal senators of his generation, and fought many a good fight for liberal policies and principles. His parting remarks provide a poignant epitaph for the liberal legacy, although he was not without hope that a more realistic liberal revival was in the offing.

It may be, however, that the real problem lies not so much with a failure of the liberal tradition per se as it does in conditions of social change which offer too great a burden for any ideological perspective--liberal, conservative or radical. It may be appropriate to conclude this section by quoting from Peter Clecak's recent survey of contemporary ideological movements, Crooked Paths. It offers a perspective on the "crisis of liberalism" that elevates it above partisanship:

> We are, it seems evident, in the midst of a realignment of political ideas and political sensibilities. It is not merely the deepening of the ideas of social equality that subverts previous ideological convictions and political coalitions, but also rising demands on the part of most citizens for fuller personal development and expression. New conceptions of self imply changing valuations of self-interest. Bound by the discipline of the work ethic, the idea of individualism that animated various factions of the New Deal coalition did not include the expectation of happiness, the assumption that private life would consist of progressively more--and more satisfying—leisure. These were mere hopes, consistent with Jeffersonian ideals. Now, nearly everyone expects not only a freer life, but a more satisfying one, made felicitous by some combination of more income, less work, and better public services (roughly in this order of importance). But we have as yet no full philosophical rationale or ideological consensus on how to integrate new conceptions of individualism into the framework of a workable public philosophy. And so, the content of the notion of self-interest expands and deepens. Everyone expects to have more and be more. But the political realities of interest group democracy force awkward divisions of personal interest: equality is pursued by categories of age, race, and gender that often do not match individual profiles. In the absence of a balanced social component, then, the only widely accepted ideological mold—the old, individualist liberal capitalist one—leads many to regard the heightened expectations of others as excessive or unjust, and their own as unfulfilled. It may be, then, that as the expectation of happiness grows, the hope of it wanes.[46]

The Changing Face of Contemporary Conservatism

The peaks and valleys of twentieth century conservative thought can be roughly sketched as follows: prior to the end of World War II, an individual author or book occasionally surfaced to create interest in conservative ideas within a limited circle of disciples; but no discernible intellectual movement could be identified until the so-called neo-conservative flurry of activity focusing upon Peter Viereck's books developed in the 1950's. After this, William F. Buckley, Jr., rose to prominence following his graduation from Yale University and his precocious attack upon the "liberal establishment," God and Man at Yale, published in 1951; the inauguration of a bi-monthly conservative news magazine, National Review, provided a home base for many intellectual conservatives; Barry Goldwater's capture of the 1964 Republican Party presidential nomination, and his subsequent lop-sided loss to Lyndon Johnson in the election of that year momentarily revivified political conservatism. Since the mid-1970's, conservatism has enjoyed its strongest and most sustained resurrection in a newly dubbed "neo-conservatism," spearheaded by a group of highly respected scholars, politicians, journalists, and editors, including such names as Daniel Moynihan, Nathan Glazer, Irving Kristol, Daniel Bell, James Q. Wilson, George F. Will, Robert Nisbet, and Norman Podhoretz—the vanguard of a major effort to replace the reigning liberal orthodoxy as the nation's foremost intellectual elite.

In the early years of this century, both as a statesman and as a publicist for American individualism and private enterprise capitalism, Herbert Hoover gave conservatism high respectability and a grip on the nation's levers of power. Hoover shined brightly in a succession of important national positions, beginning with international food relief during World War I, continuing as a cabinet-level member of the Harding-Coolidge administrations, and finally as President from 1929 to 1933. But the economic breakdown that accompanied the decade-long depression of the 1930's served to discredit Hoover's leadership and reputation, especially in the light of President Roosevelt's twelve years of popular leadership. Although there is now growing evidence of scholarly revisionism regarding Hoover's historical role which has successfully upgraded his presidential performance, conservatism sustained almost a knock-out punch as a result of a tendency to place all the blame for the nation's economic troubles on his seemingly out-moded laissez-faire economic and political policies. It is only in a broader historical perspective that it has become easier to see that New Deal "positive government" interventionism was not so sharp a break with the past as it was portrayed at the time, and that real economic recovery was more the result of World War II mobilization than of New Deal policies.[47]

Two individuals who deserve a brief mention as oases in the desert of mid-century conservative thought are Albert Jay

Nock and John Chamberlain. In a small volume of historical and contemporary analysis published in 1935 and later reprinted, Our Enemy, The State, Albert Jay Nock picked up where Herbert Spencer, the English sociologist-political philosopher who advanced the cause of Social Darwinism in the late 19th and early 20th centuries, left off, warning of the dangers to socio-economic-political democracy as the role of government continued to expand unchecked by traditional constitutional limitations.[48] In other books, including his autobiography, The Memoirs of a Superfluous Man, Nock won a small but dedicated following for his eloquent defense of individual self-reliance and non-dependence upon government.[49]

John Chamberlain, a long-time writer for Fortune magazine and other business-related publications, and a teacher at the Columbia University School of Journalism, carried the torch for conservatism in numerous books and articles during a period when conservatism had few defenders within the intelligentsia. One of his more popular studies, The Roots of Capitalism, drew heavily upon John Locke, Adam Smith, and Ludwig von Mises to show that the bases of liberty were the protection of property rights and an unregulated private enterprise capitalism.[50] His prescription for the future health of a society based upon democratic principles was to return all welfare responsibilities back to the private sector, to repudiate Keynesian economic theory, which sanctioned deficit spending, to tame labor union power, and to sharply curtail governmental interference in the average citizen's life.

Even though these ideas failed to find much support against the rising tide of service-state liberalism, Albert Jay Nock and John Chamberlain were among a handful of contemporary thinkers who managed to keep the conservative faith during inhospitable times. In addition, two heavyweights in the conservative arena, the economist Milton Friedman and the political philosopher, Friedrich von Hayek, began to attract attention and provide a rallying point for intellectual conservatism. It is probably correct to say that Milton Friedman and Friedrich von Hayek, over a span of more than three decades, which began with Hayek's The Road to Serfdom and Friedman's articles in wide-circulation publications, have been the strongest voices in conservative thought; both have won Nobel Prize recognition for their writings.

Some mention should be made of the late Robert A. Taft, Ohio Senator from 1939 to 1953, who political reporter Richard H. Rovere has referred to as "the most thoughtful and articulate political spokesman for American conservatism in this century."[51] Taft was an early and lonely critic of the post-war shift in American foreign policy away from non-interventionism toward globalism. With some exceptions, such as federal aid to housing and education, he fought against the extension of federal power in many areas formerly left to state-local and private-sector jurisdiction. And as Mr. Rovere points out, his opposition to government was based upon the acute observation that in a country as large, diversified, and heavily populated as the United States, the ability of government to perform well and to escape the evils of excessive bureaucratization required a slower expansion than was the present trend. As Rovere comments wistfully: "...a solid case can be made that the federal government is today, as Taft held it to be several decades ago, an incompetent and overextended agency promoting public policies for a nation that has grown too large and diverse for its own well-being."[52] When he was alive, Taft's views were heavily criticized and frequently derided in an ideological climate dominated by New Deal liberalism; but today, Robert Taft looks like an honorable and prescient prophet to increasing numbers of Americans plagued by the very evils he predicted would come to pass.

Among the rapid changes which marked post-war America were a phenomenal birth-rate rise, internal mass migrations (mostly white lower-middle and middle-class moving to suburbia, and blacks leaving the rural South for Northern urban centers), technological advances that accelerated the trend toward mixed public-private capitalism, and East-West Cold War conflicts that fueled the expanding defense establishment. Liberals certainly profited from these and other developments, while conservatives could only view with deepening dismay the onset of statism and its threat to individualism, older values, and a past that looked more and more like the golden age of American history.

Two thinkers who refused to sit still and watch the worst happen without a protest were Russell Kirk and Peter Viereck. They soon became the center of a revival of conservative thought that for a time, was widely referred to as "neo-conservatism," probably to contrast it with the more individualist, laissez-faire, business-oriented older conservatism.[53] The three main elements of the neo-conservative critique were an all-out attack upon socialism-collectivism, condemnation of an overly materialistic and consumption-oriented society, and resistance to the growing signs of a new popular acceptance of public policies geared to egalitarian democracy. Above all, neo-conservatism was a cry for principle over pragmatism and for an organic society based upon traditional conservative values, instead of amoral pluralist relativism.[54] Ultimately, neo-conservatives managed only a small splash in a large pond; their contributions to literature and scholarship were more enduring than their impact upon politics.

The decade of the 1960's was a generally bad time for conservatism. Caught between relatively prosperous economic conditions, which won over a good proportion of the public to liberal social and economic policies, and the sometimes violent war protest movement which was reinforced by a countercultural radicalism, conservatives found few converts in the general public. Recent memories of McCarthy-era repression and anti-democratic extremism of the Far Right did not help either.[55] Barry Goldwater's dismal showing in the 1964 election further hurt the cause. But by 1968, things were surely looking up. The election of Richard Nixon brought renewed hope and expectation, while the liberal establishment, after licking its wounds from its full-scale implication in the Southeast Asia foreign policy failures, began to experience the backlash from rising costs, wasteful government, and social disorder. Then Nixon betrayed conservatism in a manner which few had predicted, and no one quite expected: despite his addiction to conservative rhetoric, Nixon's activist leadership invariably produced the opposite of what conservative values demanded. His administration precipitated a quantum jump in the White House bureaucracy, temporary wage and price controls, huge budget deficits, and complete failure in forging a New Republican Party Majority. In the end, which was Watergate, conservatives were as perplexed and disheartened as everyone else.[56]

But just at the moment when things looked darkest, the sun came out and has been shining ever since. Conservatives suddenly discovered in the 1970's that the national mood was moving in their direction, and an unprecedented historic opportunity loomed for conservative thought and politics, provided that reality conformed to appearances—perhaps an illusory hope even for conservatives.

Resurgent Conservatism

The opinion polls reveal it; various surveys reinforce it; news magazines report it; book publications confirm it: conservatism is now respectable.[57] More than this, it looks as though the worlds of scholarship and public opinion are flirting with some form of neo-conservatism. No matter how difficult it may be to sort through the disparate writings that are now grouped around the neo-conservative label, there can be no doubt that an ideological predisposition that, only a short time ago, held few claims to public attention now promises to dominate future discourse, and will help to shape the climate of the times. Yet, despite conservative euphoria, some important questions remain to be answered:

(1) Can conservatives achieve sufficient unity of purpose or will much good effort be dissipated because conservatism, like socialism, has suffered from internal fragmentation throughout its recent history?

(2) Can conservative thought be translated into effective political action, particularly in respect to the Republican Party or a new third party political movement, or will the public continue to prefer a modified version of Democratic Party welfare statism, even as it rejects increased government expenditures that raise the tax rate?

(3) Can conservatives develop new solutions to recalcitrant problems and new ideas that offer positive leadership prospects, or will anti-liberal polemics take the place of programmatic substance and leave the public once again hold-

ing an empty hand?

At the moment, these questions are rhetorical and await answers. It will be a testing time for ideas as well as for politics. As this is written, there are some straws in the wind that provide some indication of what might be expected in the way of a resurgent conservatism. Four books, in particular, are worth considering as justification for the notion of a "resurgent conservatism," since they provide a glimpse showing how social, economic, political, and judicial thought may be influenced by a revitalized conservatism.

Murray A. Rothbard is an economic historian who has written a series of scholarly studies of considerable merit. In recent years, he has also become a leading spokesman for and active participant in a "new libertarian movement." Rejecting both statist liberalism and big business-dominated conservatism, he advocates a major assault on all aspects of big government as the means of liberating individuals from all forms of social, political, and economic control over their lives. The movement's avowed manifesto is Rothbard's 1973 book, For A New Liberty.[58]

"Libertarianism" is an old box newly packaged, along with some new "goodies" placed in the box. While it rests on the old box of laissez-faire capitalism and the free market economy, it also contains elements of Marxist "withering away of state power" and of anarchist freedom from all social constraints. The task at hand is to take away from government most of its present-day social welfare responsibilities, to reduce drastically the military establishment, and to break up all large corporations into smaller units. All current aspects of government coercion, and denial of individual choice and welfare, need dismantling. The individual matters, not some abstract meaningless entity called "society." What is left is the following:

> The central core of the libertarian creed, then, is to establish the absolute right to private property of every man: first, in his own body, and second, in the previous unused natural resources which he first transforms by his labor. These two axions, the right of self-ownership and the right to 'homestead,' establish the complete set of principles of the libertarian system. The entire libertarian doctrine then becomes the spinning out and the application of all the implication of this central doctrine.[59]

Government, according to Rothbard, is by its nature man's enemy, and is predisposed to commit aggression at the individual's expense at every opportunity. "The entire tax system is a form of involuntary servitude," and is therefore immoral.[60] In fact, commitment to mental institutions, jury duty, many labor union practices, and all regulatory actions of government represent serious and indefensible infringements upon individual rights. Unlike most other conservatives,

Rothbard would extend protection of these rights to the realm of "legislating morality," and believes that even weak censorship controls are wrong, since "the libertarian holds that it is not the business of the law—the use of retaliatory violence—to enforce anyone's concept of morality."[61] This includes all attempts to restrict pornographic displays, because "prohibition of pornography is an invasion of property right, or the right to produce, sell, buy, and own."[62] A woman's right to have an abortion is an absolute right. All laws designed to regulate gambling are also unjustified. Furthermore, where harmful drug use is concerned, an individual has an absolute right to harm himself if he wishes, and should not be prevented by government edict from obtaining drugs.

Public education is a form of covert ideological "brainwashing," mainly because it is compulsory; therefore, the burden of schooling should devolve upon the private sector, and all public schools should eventually be phased out. As for welfarism, "the libertarian position calls for the complete abolition of governmental welfare and reliance on private charitable aid."[63] Public sector responsibilities should be kept to the minimum, including police, firemen, laws, and the courts. The private sector can do everything that government now does, and can do it better—so why not follow the logic of this position to its obvious application? Rothbard is convinced there is nothing utopian or unfeasible about his "libertarian" principles.[64] All that is lacking is the will to put them into practice.

Granting the possibilities of libertarian principles as set forth in For A New Liberty, there remains these questions:

(1) Will it reduce or increase social unfairness and inequity?

(2) Are all forms of "coercion" necessarily bad; is it not likely that human beings need a certain amount of structure, authority, and coercion for their total well-being?

(3) Can human selfishness be transformed into sufficient human cooperativeness to make a libertarian system work to everyone's mutual advantage?

The reader can decide these questions for himself. The value of Rothbard's book, and of the political action movement it has inspired, is that it sets forth a consistent and appealing vision of how to go about drastically reducing, if not totally eliminating, governmental responsibilities and controls over individual life. The problem that it leaves unresolved is the underlying radicalism of its major preoccupations and its unqualified trust in human benevolence. This, needless to add, is the exact opposite of what most conservative thinkers have always believed.

He was born in the dingy industrial city, Paterson, New Jersey. His mother died when he was eight; his father was in the insurance business, and he learned early in life that hard work, self-discipline, and honest application were the road to success. Despite mediocre grades in his early years of schooling, he graduated from Lafayette College, a small liberal arts institution, and became a $75-a-week Wall Street management trainee for a securities company. He married his childhood sweetheart and fathered seven children. He prides himself on being a "workaholic." Within three years, he had become an assistant vice-president and manager of one of the company's departments. In another dozen years he had occupied a vice-presidency and a senior partnership with two other Wall Street firms, sharing in the last firm's profits. He got involved in public affairs by participating in business advisory committees, which placed him in contact with New York City and Treasury Department officials. He contributed money and actively supported Richard Nixon's successful 1968 presidential bid, and was duly offered a position in the new administration as Deputy Assistant to the Treasury Secretary. Within two years, the Secretary had resigned and he was selected to become the next Secretary of the Treasury. He continued in this position through the latter part of the Nixon and the full Ford presidency. As Treasury Secretary, he gained both notoriety and criticism from liberals as a neanderthal preacher of old-style political fundamentalism—the superior virtues of political and economic laissez-faire. His names is William E. Simon.

Mr. Simon returned to a high-paying position in the private business world after leaving government service, but he has not lost his strong conviction that America is on a collision course with disaster if it does not soon change its ways and give up its over-dependence upon government as The Great Problem Solver. In 1978, William E. Simon published a book, A Time For Truth, which contained a preface by Milton Friedman and a forward by F.A. Hayek.[65] It is a book which many conservatives will clutch tightly to their chests and applaud as that rare book in political economy that "tells it like it is" and offers a blueprint for "turning things around." On the surface, the book seems to have a shallow and dubious thesis: What's good for big business is good for the country; excessive government regulation of the business sector is the chief reason why the country is in so much trouble today. Yet there is more to it than this. Mr. Simon is a perceptive critic of current political and economic policies and just possibly, successfully riding a big wave coming in off the ocean: deregulation, de-bureaucratization, and de-governmentalization may prove to be the shape of things to come.

To begin with, Simon equates economic and political freedom; any weakness in the former sector is bound to affect adversely the latter sector. So far, the United States has escaped the worst dangers of the current world trend toward greater statism and totalitarianism; but it has not completely avoided these threats, and has certainly ventured far out onto very thin ice. Over-taxed democracies are threats to individualist democracy. As organized labor grows in power it too

threatens economic stability. And contrary to liberal mythology, mixed capitalism is neither necessary nor desirable,
since even a semi-planned economy poses a real danger to democratic societies. What is more, "In the United States a population accustomed to historically unprecedented liberty is
now ruled, almost exclusively, by a political-social-intellec-
tual elite that is committed to the belief that government can
control our complex marketplace by fiat better than the people
can by individual choice and that is ideologically committed
to social democracy or democratic socialism."[66] If America
continues its headlong pursuit of socio-economic democracy
much longer, disaster is inevitable.

Mr. Simon then goes on to explain how the gas shortage
emergency resulting from the Arab boycott in 1973 was mis-
handled: the culprit, of course, was bureaucratic power plays,
not business interests. Discussing his dealings with Congress
during his years in office, Mr. Simon has only contempt for an
almost universal "constituency myopia" that prevents any real
concern for the true public good.[67] The fact that Democratic
Party liberalism has ostensibly controlled the legislative
power system for all but four of the past forty-odd years gets
strong emphasis; this may be news to liberals, who question
the reality of liberal dominance and conservative impotence.
He defines liberalism as follows: "A hash of statism, collectivism, egalitarianism, and anti-capitalism. This murky conceptual mess renders even the most innately brilliant of men
stupid."[68]

With all due fairness, Mr. Simon can be equally sharp in
his criticism of fellow Republicans:

> But for forty years those free enterprise values
> that made America a lusty, inventive giant have
> been discredited. And after decades of function-
> ing as a minority in a philosophically inimical
> atmosphere, the Republican—with notable excep-
> tions—has lost his moorings. To survive polit-
> ically, he has often felt obligated to modify,
> compromise, abandon, and betray many of his own
> standards.[69]

Slipping productivity, horrendous yearly federal deficits,
irresponsible government spending policies, uncontrolled inflation and burdensome taxation, over-regulation, high unemployment—these are conditions which distrub Mr. Simon a
good deal, and cause him to be alarmed about the present
state of the nation. The blame for all this is easily ascertained: "The wall of economic ignorance which surrounds
so much of the liberal world like a moat...a half century
of irrational and unrealistic policies."[70] A chapter on
how New York City recently committed economic suicide and
near bankruptcy is entitled "Disaster in Microcosm," hint-
ing at what lies down the road for the rest of the nation
if present policies are not dramatically reversed.[71]

The litany of error, misjudgment, and stupidity, accord-

ing to Mr. Simon, need not continue. A solution is at hand.
Stop all government interference in the magical, powerful, and
workable free market-private enterprise system. Get rid of
the unlawful, unconstitutional, and largely ineffective regulatory agencies. Convince the country's responsible business
community that it is wrong to accept the system as it is, and
that businessmen are wrong in continuing to fall over themselves accommodating collectivist policies and tendencies.
Restore faith in competition, incentive, and efficiency. Join
the fight against those who reject capitalist principles, whatever the ideological motivation.

One thing is for sure: it is not as easy as it once may
have been to deplore, deride, and dismiss such ideas as either
simplistic, outmoded, or unrealistic. The fact is, William E.
Simon's diagnosis of policy failures echoes throughout the system. The question is, does he give an adequate explanation of
why it has happened and of what kind of solution is both desirable and feasible? Neither the historical record nor empirical
evidence supports his blind faith in a restored private enterprise, free-market, laissez-faire capitalism, even if this
were still possible: economic power is so great these days
that one can only wonder what might happen if it were to be
completely unleashed to go its own way and find its own level
of performance. Some would maintain that American democracy
is in better health today than ever before in our history, in
spite of the very substantial policy failures and poor governmental performance Mr. Simon takes such pains to describe in
A Time For Truth.

Finally, principles are not self-explanatory. The principles Mr. Simon cherishes may merit respect, but there is
danger to a democratic system of government when any individual or group thinks it can impose its own conception of principle on a majority still struggling to make up its mind. One
can only hope that William Simon and his growing army of supporters respect this deeper principle of democratic politics.

Accompanying the apparent swing toward the right by the
general public during the 1970's, has been a movement to center stage of a group of intellectuals who are commonly referred to as "neo-conservatives." They write books and articles in great profusion, and are generally highly respected
for their literary skills and their scholarship. They include
sociologists, political scientists, economists, and political
philosophers. Two influential journals of opinion, The Public
Interest and Commentary, provide regular opportunities for the
expression of the neo-conservative outlook on society and politics. And despite very real differences among them, neo-conservatives are more often than not grouped together as representatives of a particular ideological movement that has been
gathering momentum in recent years, and promises to become
even more significant in the future. Nearly all the writers
now classified as neo-conservative were at one time in their
earlier careers either democratic socialists or liberals. They

are equally uncomfortable with ideological conservatism. Perhaps the most apt description might be "disillusioned liberal," but "liberal-conservative" will be the term employed as synonomous with "neo-conservative" in this book. Chapter 8 is devoted entirely to this new school of thought—if this is a valid designation—but it might be helpful at this point to preview what comes later by discussing Irving Kristol's new book, Two Cheers For Capitalism, as a notable example of the genre.[72]

The characteristic which comes through strongest in a book like Two Cheers For Capitalism is a "new realism" that seeks to slow down change rather than to encourage it, mainly in the interests of better governmental performance. Capitalism, whatever its deficiencies, hardly deserves the devastating criticism it has endured from both liberals and the radical-left in recent years, according to Mr. Kristol. It is the only instrument available for improving general welfare and preserving political democracy. What bothers Kristol the most, however, is the growing power of a "new class," consisting of "scientists, lawyers, city planners, social workers, educators, criminologists, sociologists, public health doctors, etc.—a substantial number of whom find their careers in the expanding public sector rather than the private."[73] What they have in common is a firm conviction that public sector socialism is preferable to private sector capitalism, although they might not put it in such terms. At the very least, Kristol argues, they are anti-capitalist. Their intentions are good; they want to see a fairer, more egalitarian, and libertarian society. But the results are opposite from what is desired: bureaucratization, dependency, and inadequate economic growth. In addition, their anti-growth, anti-technology bias is simply wrong-headed and self-defeating, since it substitutes an illusion of abundance for the reality of scarcity.

Irving Kristol believes there is no substitute for the incentive motive. Whatever discourages incentive is bad; whatever inspires it is good. Bad economics does not produce good solutions to national socio-economic problems, and this is the common failing of all leftists. Since human wants are insatiable, liberals err in thinking egalitarianism can save democracy from its own excesses. Without a strong restraining force—which religion once provided—a hedonistic ethic can know no limits; and in a predominantly secular age, this spells the death of a liberal civilization. However, Kristol is far from being an apologist for business-as-usual. He feels that the corporate world can do much better in matters of business ethics and social responsibility—in fact, this is a must if capitalism is to perform its rightful role in maintaining and advancing a democratic society. One fact is often overlooked: measured by its effect upon people other than just their employees, the modern large corporation is a quasi-public institution. This implies reciprocal rights and responsibilities, not either without the other. Of course, Kristol finds much more to commend than to disapprove of regarding the performance of American capitalism. Liberalism is doomed because it cannot escape its optimistic-utopian temperament, but traditional conservatism will need to do much better in the area of practical politics if it expects to shape the future.

At bottom, the source of contemporary difficulty and failure lies in changes in the social structure that are bound to frustrate liberal and conservative ideals equally. Here is a sample of Kristol's reasoning on this vital point:

> The transformation of the bourgeois citizen into the bourgeois consumer has dissolved that liberal-individualist framework which held the utopian impulses of modern society under control. One used to be encouraged to control one's appetites; now one is encouraged to satisfy them without delay. The inference is that one has a right to satisfy one's appetites without delay, and when this 'right' is frustrated, as it always is in some way or other, an irritated populace turns to the state to do something about it. All this is but another way of saying that 20th-century capitalism itself, in its heedless emphasis on economic growth and ever increasing prosperty, incites ever more unreasonable expectations, in comparison with which the actuality of the real world appears ever more drab and disconcerting. It doesn't matter what economic growth is actually achieved, or what improvements are effected—they are all less than satisfying. Ours is a world of promises, promises—and in such a world, everyone, to some degree or another, automatically feels deprived.[74]

What can be done to reverse these nefarious tendencies? Kristol has difficulty rising above an innate pessimism, but he does suggest that improvement would occur if public policies were to reflect liberty rather than equality, the "new class" of professional bureaucrats and media intellectuals could be reduced and diverted from their blind distrust of capitalist values, and government could adopt a supportive rather than adversarial role toward the corporate world. In addition, there should be less concern about pseudo-inequities of income and more attention paid to the needs of the working-class as distinct from the welfare-class; economic growth will do more to improve general conditions than all the misconceived efforts of liberals to "redistribute income by fiat."[75] Kristol approves of reform, and unlike libertarian conservatives, like Rothbard and Simon, he accepts the need for a certain amount of government interventionism: what he looks for is "some combination of the reforming spirit with the conservative ideal."[76]

How important is this so-called neo-conservatism? What is its relationship to established liberalism and conservatism? Will it attract broad-based popular support? Is it the wave of the future, or just another stream flowing into the river? Is it a "cop-out," as one writer has phrased it, or "the most vital and perceptive theorizing that America has seen for decades," in the words of Philip Abbott of Wayne State University.[77] None of these questions are yet answerable. The following summary of neo-conservative policy views that appeared in _Newsweek_ magazine deserves quoting:

> The neo-conservatives now want to rely more on market mechanisms and less on government agencies to solve social problems. They tend to favor giving housing vouchers to the poor instead of building government housing projects. They would rather establish pollution taxes than cumbersome environmental regulations. And they want a negative income tax for the poor instead of a welfare bureaucracy. Such market-oriented solutions, they contend, would get the job done more efficiently and allow poor people some measure of choice about how to spend their money or where to live. Liberals are not necessarily opposed to such ideas, but with little experience to go on, they question whether the market would work as well as the conservatives say. Besides emphasizing market efficiency and the primacy of individual freedom, the neo-conservatives also seek something of a return to traditional values...[78]

But as Amitai Etzioni suggests, it may not be so easy for neo-conservatives to persuade the general public to support policy options that are derived from their political and social philosophies:

> The sense that one is quite familiar with these positions quickly gives way when one ponders the political dilemma of neoconservatives: how is an ideology which openly embraces elites rather than masses, achievements rather than entitlements, 'lids' rather than what comes naturally, to be sold to the masses? To put it differently, approximately 30 per cent of Americans see themselves as conservatives; they need not be sold; they already subscribe to these values...But how is one to get to those attracted to the nearly 42 per cent who see themselves as middle-of-the-roaders, and 20 per cent who consider themselves liberals.[79]

In chapter 8, we will take this matter up in greater detail.

Of the various political institutions and centers of power in America, none has elicited more consternation and criticism for failure to live up to historic democratic norms and ideals, as conservatives would define them, than the Supreme Court of the United States. This has been especially true in regard to the fifteen years of Warren Court liberalism (1953-1968); but conservatives are by and large united in their feeling that all levels of the judicial system, and especially the Supreme Court, have repeatedly usurped constitutional authority and have tilted the system away from the proper functioning of a democratic judiciary. While liberals tend to either approve or disapprove of Court decisions depending upon whether or not they were made in accordance with liberal values, conservatives go a step further and question the legitimacy of what they consider to be excessive abuse of judicial power in recent times.

Few thinkers have gone as far as Raoul Berger in his recent explosive study of the historical origins and development of the Fourteenth Amendment in the matter of constitutional interpretation, and no one has taken such a strong stand against the Court's present status. Since Professor Berger has previously written three historical studies—on executive privilege, impeachment, and the relationship between Congress and the Supreme Court—that were well received, especially in liberal quarters, it is surprising that he should become so controversial for harboring such apparently "reactionary" views.[80]

It is no secret that the most ambiguous, unresolved, and debatable feature of the American constitutional system is the proper scope of judicial power and authority. Most conservatives feel that contemporary courts have been too ready, willing, and able to transcend normal limits of judicial decision-making and to impose unwarranted political solutions that sometimes have a revolutionary impact on American society.[81] When a judicial body of nine individuals, given life tenure by successive presidents after Senate confirmation, can become the top policy-making organ of government, one must pause and reflect upon the contradiction this creates for a democratic polity. This may not happen often, but it has happened at regular and sometimes critical periods in American history. Sometimes the results have received wide public approval, as did the 1954 Brown v. Board of Education school desegregation decision; and sometimes they have not, as happened in the 1857 Dred Scott decision that helped precipitate civil war. Either way, however, the conservative is likely to criticize and deplore as a matter of principle such an exercise of political, as opposed to judicial, power; the liberal, more often than not, welcomes the Court's activist role as a counterweight to a frequently stalemated and weak-willed Congress or President.[82]

Raoul Berger, it should be said, sees no mystery in the situation. He wrote Government by Judiciary as an indictment of those who would betray the intentions of the Founders and subvert the constitutional system in the name of two false gods: judicial activism and judicial supremacy.[83] The Fourteenth Amendment, part of a three-amendment sequence which was an integral feature of post civil-war Reconstruction policy, has become, in the eyes of many, virtually a constitution within itself, since the "due process" and "equal protection" clauses have been used so often in subsequent Supreme Court opinion as a justification for major policy decisions and incursions into what long have been considered state prerogatives.

36

In Berger's view, the only legitimate means for initiating basic structural changes envisioned by the Founding Fathers is the amending process, not judicial interpretation. Although Warren Court decision-making has not been the only example of such "abuse of power," it was responsible for a great deal of damage to the system of checks and balances, damage which still threatens to undermine democracy in America.[84] According to Berger, it is illegitimate for the Court to substitute its authority for that of the properly-constituted popular branches of government. Whenever it does so, the results are bound to be contrary to the original intention of the Framers. And what the architects of any part of the Constitution intended, for Raoul Berger, is sacrosanct; this is what endows a constitution with legitimacy: "Judges are appointed to 'defend the Constitution,' not revise it."[85] Berger notes how vociferously liberals comdemned the Social Darwinist-dominated Court that proved so unsympathetic to Franklin Roosevelt's early New Deal legislation, and how quickly they praised the later Warren Court for doing much the same thing; the difference was that the Warren Court transformed liberal values into highly prejudicial jurisprudence.

But Berger's main concern in <u>Government by Judiciary</u> is to demonstrate, with painstaking historical scholarship, how the Fourteenth Amendment has been bent out of shape and distorted, in violation of the real purpose and intent of those who drew it up and passed it in the 1860's. Protecting the ex-slaves' rights was one thing; establishing social and political equality was another, and was not a legitimate exercise of judicial power either then or now, according to Berger. Whenever a limited objective is given constitutional sanction, later Court majorities have no authority to go beyond it simply because circumstances have changed, and a later generation of jurists seize an opportunity to rewrite the Constitution.

A matter which especially concerns Berger is the late Justice Hugo Black's success in persuading a Court majority to abrogate states' rights under our constitutional system by extending to the federal government powers it formerly did not have and should not have in respect to the constitutional Bill of Rights and federalism. This opened a whole Pandora's Box of constitutional revisionism. The series of Court mandated redistricting decisions beginning with the 1962 <u>Baker v. Carr</u> was another instance of massive and illegitimate infringement on "state sovereignty." An "open-ended" constitutional interpretation is tantamount to destroying the integrity of a democratic constitution. And though he recognizes the necessity for some government action to desegregate the schools at mid-century, Berger feels strongly that the Warren Court set a very bad example by manipulating the situation to insure a unanimous opinion; in this, as well as in so many other recent instances, it should properly have been the two popular branches of government, not the Court, which shouldered this responsibility. A carefully limited "equal protection" clause, originally designed to give Negroes the same protection as whites under the law was later converted into a blanket permission, under which egalitarian policies would acquire constitutional sanctioning. Similarly, the "due process" clause of the Fifth and Fourteenth Amendments were not meant to substitute substantive for procedural due process, as has often happened. "The Court, in short, was not empowered to substitute its policy choices for those of the framers."[86]

As is well known, the establishment of judicial review by John Marshall in **Marbury v. Madison** (1803) and other subsequent decisions gave to the Supreme Court an extraordinary grant of power that no other judicial system enjoys anywhere even to this day. Combined with the unique features of a separation of powers governmental structure, judicial review became the means by which the Supreme Court could, from time to time, influence the distribution of power within the system. Berger approves of judicial review, but he deplores the fact that a limited constitutional principle has so frequently been employed almost as though there were no limits to the extent of judicial power and authority. The result has been periods in which judicial supremacy has all but demolished the integrity of the constitutional system: "No power to revise the Constitution under the guise of 'interpretation' was conferred on the Court; it does so only because the people have not grasped the reality: an unsafe foundation for power in government by consent."[87]

As so many commentators before him, Berger maintains that the only safeguard against judicial abuse of power is judicial self-restraint. Furthermore, whenever the judiciary assumes "policy-making" prerogatives, the separation of powers principle is in dire jeopardy. In effect, only strict, narrow, limited constitutional interpretation is legitimate in a democracy; broad, permissive, unlimited constitutional authority at all times and under all circumstances poses a direct threat to democratic principles. Berger's view, unlike that of most critics, is unqualified and unambiguous: "To thrust aside the dead hand of the Framers is to thrust aside the Constitution. The argument that new meanings may be given to words employed by the Framers aborts their design; it reduces the Constitution to an empty shell into which each shifting judicial majority pours its own preferences."[88]

Berger's book had a mixed reception: liberals hate it and conservatives love it and there is little in-between. Any fair-minded person has to respect the author's careful scholarship and his thought-provoking analysis; it is his conclusions that elicit this acceptance-rejection reaction.

Two things need emphasizing: starting with Jeffersonian "strict construction" and Hamiltonian "broad construction," there has been no resolution throughout American history of this issue, usually referred to as judicial self-restraint versus judicial activism as representing the two diametrically opposed views regarding the proper limits and extent of judicial power; and in addition, the consequences for both the constitutional system and public policy whenever either view has prevailed continues to be incalculable. If Berger is right, then this ambiguous constitutional legacy needs to be resolved, once and for all, in favor of judicial self-restraint, or else we will eventually sacrifice democracy itself. If he is wrong, and the constitutional system is better served by sanctioning and perpetuating this very ambiguity, then the conservative position, even if it is stated in a less extreme form than that found in <u>Government by Judiciary</u>, can be safely rejected. Elliott Abrams has expressed this latter verdict quite well in his review of the Berger book:

> Berger, then, is blind to the role played by the tension between the restraints of the Constitution and the shifting will of the people—a tension which is at the very heart of America's constitutional system, and which has much to do with its success in preserving our liberty for over two centuries. In the arduous task we set our judges, to strike a delicate balance between the duty of judgment and the duty of restraint...Berger offers no assistance.[89]

Whatever one's view of the value and relevance of these four authors' restatements of conservative political, social, economic, and judicial philosophy, and with all due recognition that their differences are as important as their similarities, such books as these, as well as others which are analyzed later in this study, provide strong testimony that a "resurgent conservatism" is a very real and significant aspect of recent developments in American thought. In fact, one would have to conclude that neither liberalism nor radicalism can now lay claim to an equal share of public attention. As long as this continues to be the case, conservatism is probably responding to some deeper changes and needs being experienced by the country-at-large.

THE CONSERVATIVE TRADITION IN AMERICAN THOUGHT

Few would question the fact there is a mainstream liberal tradition in American political thought that has its
origins in Lockean-Jeffersonianism.[1] When it comes to a
conservative tradition, however, there is substantial disagreement that any such development can be identified in
the course of American political history. Although it is
generally felt that one of the two major parties has been
more conservative than the other party in its main policy
orientation, at least since the Jacksonian era, there is
too much ambiguity in the role and function of political
parties within the American political system to clearly distinguish policy differences between the major parties. We
have already mentioned the way liberalism has frequently
functioned in a conservative manner. Conservative statesmen and thinkers, when they do appear on the scene, tend
to operate within a liberal consensus that does not provide much leeway for the emergence of an authentic conservative ideology. If this were all there was to it, then one
would have to discard any reference to a conservative tradition that had distinctive features to it. But this approach
has its own built-in bias which may do an injustice to important facets of the American historical experience.

The recent debate over whether consensus or conflict
best characterizes American thought is a case in point. If
one stresses consensus, the recurrent pattern of ideological warfare in America is conveniently neglected; if one
stresses a conflict theme, there is a tendency to underes-
timate the underlying value consensus that has channeled
most conflict in a moderate direction and clipped the wings
of an inconclusive radicalism.[2] There is no easy solution
to this problem, but it does suggest the possibility that
ideological conflict has performed a notable function in
American history despite the consensual nature of American
politics. There is also ample evidence that conservative
ideas have not only contributed to this liberal consensus,
but have, from time to time, proposed an alternate model
for democratic theory.

The reason the conservative strand of American political thought seems less important and distinctive than the
liberal strand is due to the consensual character of the
ideological legacy of the Revolutionary-Constitutional period. Three distinctive traditions in the history of Western
political theory, going back to Ancient Greek and Roman sources, fused together, providing an underlying value consensus
that cushioned the shock of potential ideological divergence.
These were the Natural Law, Natural Rights, and Limited Government traditions that flowed through Hobbes, Locke, and
Montesquieu into the consciousness of the colonial leadership, uniting them on the key issues of popular sovereignty
and the virtues of limited government. Despite very real

difference of interest, section, and ideology, the Founders were able to agree on the most basic features of the governmental system: separation of powers, checks and balances, and federalism.[3] It was only _after_ the system was instituted and the 1787 constitutional document was ratified, that there soon erupted major ideological disagreement as to how the system should be implemented, and what interests would benefit most from its operation. A liberal/conservative dichotomy emerged the moment the Constitution went into effect, and the early struggles between Jefferson's and Hamilton's views on the scope and limits of national power and elite rule mirrored this growing ideological cleavage.[4]

For conservative thought, the Constitution of 1787 was the high point of its influence in American history. Three leading conservative statesmen—George Washington, John Adams, and Alexander Hamilton—left their mark on the institutional structure that derived from that event, while the more liberal-oriented James Madison also performed a notable role in mediating the conflicts of interest and value which necessitated the "compromises" that characterized the actual designing of a constitutional structure for the American nation.

Although not a thinker in the usual sense of the word, Washington certainly had a powerful imprint upon the system as it went into effect after its ratification in 1789. His charisma, in the eyes of his fellow countrymen, was authentic tribute to the statesman-like wisdom he embodied—and his judicious handling of the executive authority during the first eight years of the Republic went a long way toward reconciling, at least temporarily, partisan passions and ideological differences. Without Washington as a focal point of common hopes and principles, the prospects for even a modicum of national unity might easily have foundered.[5]

John Adams may have faltered as a national leader after becoming the nation's second president, but he performed an invaluable service in laying the groundwork for framing a constitution, first as the main architect of the influential Massachusetts State Constitution, and later as the author of A Defense of the Constitution of Government of the United States, published on the eve of the 1787 Constitutional Convention, which included a highly persuasive analysis of the virtues of "balanced government."[6]

Alexander Hamilton may have had little direct influence upon the final document, since his rather pronounced affection for the British monarchy made many of his ideas unacceptable to the other constitutionalists. However, his eloquent and incisive analysis of the new governmental system in a series of articles that later became part of The Federalist Papers; his leadership role as Washington's first Secretary of the Treasury; and his authorship of the first blueprint for the nation's early economic policies—a series of reports presented to the Congress of the United States—left an indelible stamp on the conservative side of the ledger during the early national period.[7]

Despite the obvious coalescence of conservatism and liberalism during this crucial phase of the nation-building process, the importance of the conservative strand should not be overlooked. Above all, it contributed to a sense of common purpose that could not be duplicated under other circumstances.

America did not escape the disillusionment that invariably sets in when the great expectations surrounding such a liberating event as successful de-colonization confronted the harsh demands of reality.[8] Despite continuing leadership of a reasonably high order, the United States experienced unprecedented dislocation and social malaise during the early decades of the nineteenth century. Although they were united in neither ideology or vested interest, the so-called Federalists enjoyed a monopoly of power in national government until 1801, when the Jeffersonian Republicans succeeded in capturing control of both the White House and Congress. Political change, at least in regard to the transfer of power, came remarkably peacefully, but this did not camouflage the serious disturbances that threatened the fragile fabric woven by the Constitutionalists. Political partisanship was only part of the trouble; a vision of "republican" excellence was being denied to those who had fought so hard and invested so much in the struggle to overthrow autocracy. To the Federalists, Jefferson's assumption of power symbolized a change for the worse; to the Republicans, the Federalists were none other than the "enemy," pretending to be democrats but garbed in monarchical clothes, posing a serious threat to the Revolutionary legacy of liberty _and_ equality.[9]

Once again, it was not so much conservative privilege confronting democratic aspirations, as privilege competing against privilege, or to put it more kindly, different elites vying with each other for a lion's share of the available power. "A manufacturing-commercial elite versus a plantation-landed gentry elite" describes the situation aptly. Nevertheless, it was not only a matter of competing interests, for the conservative ideal of an orderly universe conflicted with the liberal ideal of progress; and as the conservative camp lost political control, the liberal camp compromised its principles in order to enhance its own position of power and privilege. Thus, Jefferson violated his view of constitutional legitimacy in order to buy the vast Louisiana territory from Napoleon—and the nation had reason to be grateful to him ever after.[10] In the same spirit, that arch Federalist, John Marshall, transposed his conservative principles into an activist's assertion of national authority in a series of earth-shaking Supreme Court decisions that defended the rights of property while also advancing the democratic ideal of popular sovereignty. Out of this complex matrix of theory/practice discontinuity a conservative/liberal dichotomy began to live a life of its own.[11]

Yet there is little doubt that circumstances favored a future-oriented liberal ideal over a past-oriented con-

servative ideal. The entire first half of the nineteenth
century—until the Civil War erupted—witnessed the rapid
flowering of a popular version of American exceptionalism,
a view which crystallized around the belief that America,
in contradistinction to Europe and the rest of the world,
was magically endowed by the singular accomplishment of experiencing all at once and continually, progress, freedom,
equality, and democracy. Even when this collective value
complex failed to square with reality, the ordinary American, far from being discouraged and resentful, knew that
he was better off than anyone else anywhere else, and the
future looked bright indeed.[12] While the conservative outlook still sought inspiration and guidance from European
cultural achievements, the predominant view was suffused
with nativism and the spirit of adventure. No wonder, then,
that Andrew Jackson exercised such a strong attraction to
common folk when he broke the hold of the Virginia "aristocracy" and took over the reins of power in the nation's
capitol. He was an appropriate cultural hero to those
countless faceless Americans who sought their place in
the sun—who, in fact, claimed such recognition as a birthright. The democratization of the system, however superficial in some respects, was nevertheless a powerful expression of egalitarian aspiration that conservative forces could not dispel. Even as the secession issue over
slavery drew more to the fore, conservatism lacked a national base. The Federalist party waned and died; the
Southern Confederacy siphoned off what was most vital in
the conservative tradition, and in the process transformed
a cultural ideal into a vested interest, pure and simple.[13]

As previously stated, conservatism reached its pinnacle
of influence during the early nation-building period: con-
stitution-making and constitutional interpretation were the
indisputable achievements of the conservative strand in the
creation of American democracy, even though it was a conservatism that had its roots in Lockean liberalism. Realism and restraint combined to help lay the foundations of
republican institutions. In a world that had only recently
emerged from royal absolutism and feudalism, the real meaning of democracy was dimly perceived and largely misunderstood. Whatever dangers flowed from arbitrary despotism,
the greater danger still reposed in dispossessed masses who
were readily controllable but potentially volatile. Democracy was at best a two-edged sword: it could lead to greater
prosperity or to anarchy. The conservative did not want to
take too many chances: good ends did not justify any means.
His own stake in society loomed largest. Whether or not
democracy was the wave of the future, as Tocqueville maintained, it was a wave that all conservatives agreed had to
be contained. The masses were not ready to take command of
their destiny. That was a prescription for chaos.

But in the second quarter of the nineteenth century,
the period dubbed by many historians as the era of "Jacksonian democracy," the rise of equalitarianism seemed all but

irresistible. In America, the popular imagination easily confused substance and shadow, preferring appearances to reality. Jacksonian democratic rhetoric carried the day; actuality was something else again. Economic and political policy helped to make America stronger while exacerbating the socio-economic cleavages between the few and the many; tolerance of slavery was widespread; Jackson waged punitive and partially successful campaigns to exterminate native-stock Indian tribes.[14] But there was the vast territorial frontier west of the Mississippi to be conquered and set-tled, a "safety-valve" for the land-hungry poor and get-rich-quick speculators. Democracy neither flowered nor flourished during these years, but it did extend its reach, and it created a myth disguised as ideology that obscured the relationship of democratic egalitarian ideals with the pursuit of self-interest, an approach that a later age con-veniently rationalized as the survival of the fittest.[15]

The obvious discrepancy between promise and fulfill-ment, which poorer Americans could accept by placing their faith in "opportunity" and "striving," the ideology that placed the common man on a pedestal even as conditions fre-quently pointed in an opposite direction, was not so easily wished away by more thoughtful critics. What was being sac-rificed in this mindless embrace of materialistic values un-der the illicit notion of human progress struck conservative thinkers as self-deception. Democracy contained the seeds of its own eventual destruction. The liberated masses were ill-equipped to handle the reins of self-government in a judicious and enlightened manner; uncurbed political corrup-tion and the decline of civility were the twin evils of too much democracy. Too much equality spelled the death of lib-erty. Quality should not be sacrificed to quantity. All human beings were morally equal, surely: not all were ca-pable of responsible conduct. Education, wealth, and sta-tus still counted. Standards were always upheld by the few and debased by the many. Conservatives had no trouble con-sulting history to verify this point.[16]

Yet the tide was coming in and conservative thinkers were now swimming against it. In the earlier period, the views and policies of an Adams, Hamilton or Marshall were not always popular, but they were respected and had a close relationship to necessity even when they may have departed from emerging democratic values. As the nineteenth century progressed, this was no longer true. Ideas solidified into ideology, as liberalism and democracy united in expressing the questionable assumption that only the achievement of po-litical democracy would insure a more equalitarian and pros-perous society for all. Conservative thinkers were alert to the fallacy of this proposition long before twentieth cen-tury liberals began to have serious doubts about it.

Alexis de Tocqueville was perhaps the first to make a distinction between liberty and equality and to argue that the achievement of either could be at the expense of the

other. Orestes Brownson worried about the relationship between liberty and authority, and wondered whether a genuine
political democracy could afford to sacrifice one to the
other. John C. Calhoun saw majority power as a threat to
minority rights and sought to change the system so that
this might not happen. George Fitzhugh, that other staunch
defender of the slave culture, saw in Lockean individualism
and the exploitation of the industrial worker in the North
a sure sign that dry rot was setting in; he knew that the
liberal tradition was not all it pretended to be. But it
was Abraham Lincoln, the statesman-orator who rose above the
tragedy of civil war to cast a clear-eyed look at the nation's failures and accomplishments, and with memorable el-
oquence, explained how liberty, equality, and justice were
intertwined; democracy itself depended on all three equally,
not any one primarily.[17]

In the last quarter of the nineteenth century, something happened to the conservative impulse; it turned sour
and betrayed its communitarian ideal to the materialistic
pursuit of self-interest.[18] In William Graham Sumner and
Social Darwinism, conservative thought enjoyed a brief ascendancy, but the price was high: laissez-faire economics,
survival-of-the-fittest sociology, and the politics of expediency all combined around a conservative-liberal ideology that substituted property rights for the traditional
liberal commitment to broad-based human welfare.[19] Henry
Adams, the last and best of the late nineteenth century
thinkers, wrote an obiturary to the death of idealism and
civility in his classic work, The Education of Henry Adams,
just before liberalism received a new lease on life as the
Populist-Progressive ferment swept away the excesses of an
anti-democratic Social Darwinism.[20]

This all-to-brief summary of some leading figures in
nineteenth century political and social thought only hints
at the possibility that a conservative tradition did emerge,
distinct from mainstream liberalism (except for the Social
Darwinist phase), and that this tradition deserves to be
recognized. If "tradition" is too strong a term, and if
such a handful of thinkers does not have enough in common
to constitute a "conservative tradition," this is less important than the fact that democracy meant quite different
things to liberals and conservatives in the nineteenth century, and this difference became even more pronounced in
the twentieth century. Although both liberals and conservatives prized the expansion and deepening of political democracy in the United States throughout this period, the e-
galitarian ideal which liberals assumed to be implicit in
the pursuit of liberty was questioned, if not denied, by
conservatives. In their view, meaningful liberty was
threatened by equality. These divergent, and perhaps incompatible, conceptions of democracy have continued to
plague American thought to this day; and the widening gulf
between these two value-orientations lies at the center of
many policy differences, and affects the ability of the

American system to more effectively reconcile beliefs and practices.[21]

Historically, the one authentically creative phase of conservative political theory in America occurred during the creation of the Constitution in 1787; in a certain sense, conservatism never again proved so influential. Except for the Bill of Rights Amendments, such leading constitutional principles as the rule of law and judicial review and balanced government are the chief legacy of the conservative tradition at its most creative moment. Having done so much so early to shape American political institutions, it is a curious anomaly that conservative political theory never again shined so brightly or encountered such success, with the possible exception of the present moment.[22] This has been a paradoxical development, if only because the American public seems to prefer the conservative's choice of stability over change and individual self-reliance over government controls to the liberal's reliance upon governmental power to remedy political and social inequities. But in actuality, liberalism, as defined by the evocative phraseology of the Declaration of Independence, which identifies both liberty _and_ equality as the cornerstones of a democratic philosophy, has provided the operating guidelines for both institutional change and moderate reform throughout much of American history.[23]

The implications of this strange inconsistency for both American thought and behavior are not easily evaluated. For one thing, it is obvious that Americans have elevated ambiguity to a first principle; they take pride in the fact that their democratic philosophy and institutional arrangements can assimilate contradictory values, and that, in the long run, both stability _and_ change, liberty _and_ equality, minority rights _and_ majority rule are reconcilable. Liberal-conservatism, or conservative-liberalism, from this perspective, is better than either unadulterated liberalism, or conservatism.[24] But is this true? Is it possible that the inability to make a clear choice between contrary political values is a weakness rather than a strength of the American system? This is not an easy question to answer, and any conclusion can be only tentative and suggestive. The fate of conservative political thought offers some insight here. Even as its appeal diminished, except for a small band of ideological purists, its practical importance has increased. As a result, ambiguity has been converted into a dubious principle for political behavior; and the ethical content of both liberalism and conservatism has degenerated into the politics of what's-in-it-for-me expediency, in which power is an end, not an instrument of the public good. The fear of ideological extremism is legitimate, but the price of ambiguity can be high. Coherence, consistency, and application are the hallmarks of good political theory. There is a great need for Americans to gain a better appreciation of the efficacy of ideas in determining the quality of problem-solving and policy decisions. Good thinking is based upon

47

good conceptualization. A clearer view of conservative political philosophy should assist in this endeavor.[25]

In an attempt to clarify the criteria which underlie the selection of thinkers and the decision as to what constitutes the "conservative tradition" in recent American political thought, I would like to suggest three basic assumptions which might characterize a conservative stance in American political thought. Although this approach may miss the greater degree of refinement which most scholars bring to the task,[26] I would prefer instead to let individual thinkers reveal their own interpretation of conservative values. A person's thought patterns, ideological orientation, and mode of thinking are largely conditioned by, and reflective of, either a conscious or less conscious commitment to certain major premises concerning the nature of man, society, and the state. A conservative, by definition, whatever else he or she believes, accepts the following three basic assumptions regarding the nature of man, society, and the state, but accept them with qualifications that will be stated later in the analysis:

(1) **Man's Nature**—A conservative view of man emphasizes the non-rational, non-altruistic, non-hopeful side of human behavior. Restraint and self-discipline are considered to be rare traits of character and are more likely to govern the actions of the cultivated few than of the masses. This general pessimism regarding man's capacity for rationality and social progress makes a conservative think twice before supporting institutional reform, for any such change is likely to have adverse effects upon the equilibrium of society. In short, a conservative view of basic human nature strongly emphasizes the imperfectible and selfish side of common human behavior and rejects the liberal's more optimistic belief that improving conditions will improve behavior generally.

(2) **Man and Society**—A conservative view of society is oriented to the past. It is deeply respectful of the continuities which circumscribe social change, and conscious of the network of reciprocal rights, duties, and obligations which define social roles. The conservative is strongly attached to family and communal ties. He can be just as individualistic as a liberal, but his individualism is tempered by an enduring sense of social affiliation and self-society interdependence. Whereas liberalism, especially in its 18th century origins, places the individual above society and postulates an antagonistic relationship between self and society,[27] conservatism views the self-society relationship as being more fused and interrelated. To some extent, the conservative feels that man's social existence takes precedence over his individual being. The past guides and restrains any desire or need for innovation or change. In addition, many conservatives tend to be anti-pragmatic and anti-secularist. Principles matter. Religion matters. Morality is not relative. There are certain moral absolutes that should guide behavior and circumscribe political action.

48

(3) <u>Man and Government</u>—According to the conservative, human beings are too selfish and egoistic to permit a permissive institutional structure to govern their activities. Nevertheless, true freedom depends upon good order; respect for authority is a necessary attribute of stable government and an ordered society. In contrast to the liberal's commitment to egalitarianism and popular democracy, a conservative view of the state has both elitist and authoritarian overtones. Those who qualify on the basis of merit and achievement deserve to rule; the rest owe obedience. An upper-class meritocracy should control the levers of power within a system of checks and balances. To a considerable degree, the chief end of government is to maintain order and the supremacy of a privileged class.

There are some difficulties, however, with the above portrayal of basic conservative assumptions. Circumstances have greatly affected these attitudes and values over the course of American history, and, in some instances, have caused a shift of emphasis, and even a transformation, in the basic value orientation.[28] The conservative view of human nature compels an awareness of complexity and a realistic emphasis upon man's limitations. The American mind has not been comfortable with this conservative view; for the historic American attitude toward human nature has been characterized by an optimistic faith in social progress and the benefits of an unfettered individualism. In this respect, conservatism is un-American; and conservative thinkers have generally had a hard time applying their assumptions to the conditions of American life. Americans view society more often as an enemy than as a friend; they feel that it interferes with individual rights and desires. And they believe that present and future are much more important than the past. So the conservative is bound to be out of kilter with the prevailing view of the self-society relationship. The conservative view of the state is also quite unappealing to the average citizen, since even a hint of adherence to elitist, aristocratic, or authoritarian ideas is deemed contrary to democratic norms and values.

While these characteristics have been true historically, the ground under both liberalism and conservatism has shifted appreciably in this century. More often than not, it is the liberal who now accepts a more realistic view of man's rationality, emphasizes the interdependence, rather than the separation, of the self-society relationship, and is willing to endow government with power commensurate with its increased responsibilities for social welfare. The conservative now places greater stress on human rationality, individual freedom divorced from social considerations, and a deepening distrust of state power. As the ground shifts underneath, basic premises erode and internal contradictions become a major problem for relating throught to action.

In present circumstances, a contemporary liberal must give precedence to equality over liberty; a contemporary conservative can be consistent in his long-standing preference

49

for liberty over equality. But a conservative is faced with the inconsistency of other values: he must relate the requirements of personal freedom to an increasingly dehumanizing social order, and must reconcile respect for authority with governments that are becoming increasingly bureaucratized monstrosities.[29] It is these internal strains and stresses that conservatives must explore and disentangle; the task is difficult in a time of transition and ideological impurity.

The Achilles heel of conservatism is its uncritical pro-big business bias—a bias which seems to characterize almost all conservative thought other than the philosophical variety; that is, pragmatic and ideological conservatism.[30] What is missed completely in this frequently uncritical defense of the business ethic—that the pursuit of private profit is the chief strength of the American system—is the fact that it contravenes more worthy conservative ideals—such as respect for traditionalism translated into what is best, rather than what is worst, in moral striving. What is best in conservatism is what is best in the American democratic tradition: the emphasis upon maximizing individual freedom, no matter how difficult it may be to define the concept. Less commendable is the tendency of conservatives to sacrifice the ought to the is—and to make pure selfishness the chief end of social and political activity.[31]

This confusion of values robs conservative thought of much of its potential attractiveness. The independence that conservatives cherish is frequently compromised on the altar of valueless work and an empty prosperity. It is rare indeed to find conservatives—or anyone, for that matter—willing to sacrifice momentary self-interest for an ideal. At its best, conservatism is a subversive doctrine, since it will choose quality over quantity, obligations over rights, and the individual over the state. But there is little evidence that conservatives really would honor an ethical end over a dubious means. Conservatives are preservationists by choice; what divides conservatives is disagreement over what is worth preserving.

Although few individuals actually think or act ideologically, it would be a mistake to conclude that everyone's basic assumptions do not have ideological attributes.[32] People act on what they believe, and whether rational or non-rational in source and execution, a conservative outlook is a distinctive quality of human thought and behavior. In political terms, one's ideological proclivity goes a long way toward determining both policy and value choices.

DILEMMAS OF CONSERVATISM-LIBERALISM

Conservatism, like its opposite ideological outlook, liberalism, can be characterized in two ways: as a fairly consistent set of assumptions regarding the nature of man, society, and government, and as a response to social, economic, and political changes that take place in a particular society and polity as a result of historical developments. In actuality, these are interacting forces. Historical changes in the form of technological advances, population growth, and the means of allocating benefits within society provoke different responses from individuals, depending on whether the change itself is beneficial to the individual on a personal level. There is usually a close correlation between an individual's assessment of self-interest and his or her ideological leaning. Which comes first, however, is not readily determined.

Individuals go through an early socialization process, involving the family, culture, and personality that establishes patterned responses. These responses express, when applied to political and social matters, values that tend to favor a conservative, or liberal, or even a radical stance. In the course of anyone's life, this constant interaction of new experiences and more or less patterned responses to outward circumstances can be mutually reinforcing, strengthening one's ideological predisposition; alternatively, it can serve to weaken this ideological predisposition, inducing a confused uncertainty over what one thinks and believes. In some instances, the process may lead to a shift in ideological allegiance. So the intensity of belief, the consistency of belief over a lifetime, and the likelihood of ideological change of view will vary from person to person. All of these possibilities complicate any attempt either to define or to answer satisfactorily the question: what does it mean to be either conservative or liberal in one's ideological outlook?[1]

Therefore, it may be appropriate to distinguish pragmatic, ideological, and philosophical responses to external reality. A pragmatic conservative or liberal, for instance, eschews consistency and adjusts his values to circumstances; a shrewd appraisal of self-interest usually dictates behavior. An ideological conservative or liberal is likely to be strongly committed to certain "principles" or "values" which he is unwilling to compromise if it can be avoided. A philosophical conservative or liberal differs from an ideological conservative or liberal to the extent that he needs to keep means and ends in closer harmony with one another, and seeks to avoid both the pragmatist's tendency to make expediency an end in itself and the ideologue's tendency to justify almost any means in order to achieve certain preferred ends. It is necessary to distinguish these three types within both liberalism and conservatism, even though the distinctions cannot be clear-cut.

To the degree that there is a certain regularity or persistence in ideological outlook, one finds certain values or assumptions influencing policy-choices. One cannot really be liberal—or change-oriented—without entertaining a rather optimistic view of man's ability to shape ends to human purposes, to view the self/society relationship as two somewhat separate entities, and to regard government as an instrument of redistributive justice—that is, as responsible for looking after the interests of the many, and not just of the few. Similarly, one cannot be conservative—or change-resistant—unless one also adopts a rather pessimistic view of man's capacity to impose his will on events, emphasizes the social dimension of individual behavior, and defends a limited role for government in the area of expanded welfarism. To the conservative, the individual rights and freedom he prizes are endangered by any form of governmental paternalism. To the liberal, the individual rights and freedom he cherishes are endangered by any failure of government to intervene on behalf of the less-privileged many against the interests of the more-privileged few.

In a sense, each is accusing the other of violating basic democratic principles. The liberal is charged with authoritarian paternalism; the conservative with authoritarian elitism. In other words, the liberal denounces the conservative for wanting to substitute authoritarian elitism for democratic consensus. The conservative unmasks the liberal's self-deception in thinking he is any less authoritarian when he converts government into a vast paternalistic bureaucracy which itself becomes the main threat to libertarian democracy. The problem is that both may be right, yet neither can reconcile means and ends in a way that would safeguard both democratic values and their ideal social order. In this respect, the dilemma of the conservative/liberal is the need to close, not widen the gap, between theory and practice.

Ordinarily, a conservative favors the status quo and the liberal supports reform of existing practices in the expectation of some sort of human betterment. In the contemporary historical context, conservatives are defenders of individualism against most forms of collectivism, while liberals are critical of public policies which, in their view, seem likely to perpetuate existing socio-economic inequities and to favor the wealthier few at the expense of the less privileged masses. Yet the contemporary liberal has become less enamored of collectivist solutions to severe socio-economic problems, such as welfarism and unemployment, as government has become increasingly more bureaucratic and incapable of operating in a fiscally responsible manner. And the contemporary conservative has become more aware of the ever-growing interdependence of the socio-economic system as institutional and moral restraints on individual selfishness have eroded to such a degree that a negative attitude toward change appears to be no solution at all. The traditional liberal faith in rationality, science, and progress has been severely tested by the evidence of human irrationality and impotency that is manifest in the history of this century, even though human technology has presumably improved the chances of achieving greater direction and control over human destiny.[2] The traditional conservative faith in free competition, individual incentive, and private enterprise capitalism seems increasingly divorced from the realities of highly concentrated political and economic power and the threat this power poses to individual freedom.[3]

The cornerstone of democracy is the belief in self-government as a realizable goal.[4] Today, liberals vie with conservatives in expressing their loss of confidence in man's capacity to govern himself in accordance with democratic norms and procedures. Disillusionment is pervasive in both camps, and the assumptions that once clearly distinguished liberals from conservatives no longer hold firm.[5] It is for this reason that one should expect to see the shifting grounds of conservative/liberal value orientations mirrored in the thought of key thinkers. Two individuals stand out in this regard. Reinhold Niebuhr and Sidney Hook are probably the most representative examples of what can be called the dilemmas of conservatism-liberalism, marking the transition from 19th to 20th century thought in the United States. They are also the two thinkers who have most effectively bridged the gulf between the narrower world of abstract intellectualism and the broader world of popular understanding.

If the 19th century was preeminently the age of individualism and of the consolidation of political democracy in the United States, the 20th century has been an age of expanding collectivism and of the emergence of socio-economic democracy as the culminating ideal of a democratic polity.[6] The transition from one democratic model to another has been accompanied by a good deal of confusion, debate, and disagreement as to whether this change should be encouraged or resisted; and has been referred to by at least one historian, Edward A. Purcell, Jr., as "the crisis of democratic theory."[7] If it is true that the rationale for the American experiment in democracy relied upon certain universal values incorporating the underlying assumptions of the American Revolution and Declaration of Independence--principles of a priori individual rights, an appeal to natural law as the basis of positive law, and a rationalistic conceptualization of contract theory as the basis of popular government-- then the reaffirmation of empirico-scientific, relativistic, and historically conditioned values by a legion of social scientists in the early years of this century has shattered this rationale. By the third decade of the 20th century, as Professor Purcell has indicated, "Naturalistic attitudes had spread into law, philosophy, and the social sciences... and their implications raised fundamental questions about

the validity of traditional democratic theory."[8] The rise
of fascist totalitarianism in Europe, the economic decline
of capitalism during the Depression-ridden thirties, and
the increasing impotence of democratic states in dealing
with historical change further challenged the viability of
traditional democratic theory. Either a major transplant
operation had to be instituted to repair defects in both
democratic theory and practice, or else the patient had to
be left to its own recuperative resources, such as they
were. Survival seemed problematic in either case.[9]

The liberal response to this situation was to embrace
the new insights which underscored man's potential to master both nature and himself, by applying scientific knowledge to socio-economic problems.[10] If this meant re-exam-
ining, rejecting, and replacing older assumptions with a
newer version of democratic governance, so be it. The sooner it could be effectuated, the better. The conservative
response was less cohesive; and ultimately it fragmented.[11]
For some thinkers, the chief task was to expose the inadequacies and excesses of an exclusive reliance upon a relativistic, secularistic, and scientific value orientation
as the underpinning of democratic theory. Others sought
to revivify an absolutist appeal to natural law and objective values as a means of reconciling the competing demands
of power and ethics. And still others found in the various
manifestations of Marxism-Communism the deadly enemy that
had to be defeated at any cost, even if it meant employing
undemocratic means to achieve the desired end.

The dilemma of conservatism-liberalism that developed
in the 20th century involved primarily a gradual breakdown
in the traditional Lockean-Jeffersonian liberal tradition.
A democratic system designed in the 18th century to curb
monopoly political power seemed unable to deal with an increasing concentration of economic power. Political democracy was one thing; socio-economic democracy another—and
public policies which were most likely to advance the latter
might endanger the former, and vice versa. It was the old
Tocquevillian dilemma of doing justice to both liberty and
equality. The dilemma was less troublesome in the 19th century thanks to the national preoccupation with settling a
continent, expanding opportunities, and steady progress toward the ideal of political democracy. An individualistic
ideology seemed quite appropriate to progress, prosperity,
and reconciling liberty with equality. But all this changed
when it became evident that expanding political democracy
did not necessarily produce greater socio-economic democracy;
in fact, the opposite might occur—a society of growing middle-class affluence amidst gross inequities, racial injustice, and an inadequate social welfare system. A liberal
solution to the growing cleavage between political and socio-economic democracy required a turning away from the traditional liberal reliance upon private sector individualism
to a greater reliance upon governmentalism as the means of
rectifying socio-economic injustices in behalf of the egal-

itarian ideal. And although conservatives early recognized the fact that individual freedom would be seriously endangered by this development, the quasi-welfare system that accompanied the transformation of 20th century liberalism from an individualistic to a collectivistic ethos, gained widespread public endorsement. Meanwhile, conservatism, by retaining its faith in private-sector capitalistic solutions against public-sector governmentalism, seemed, to much of the voting electorate, to be upholding privileged-class interests at the expense of the larger public interest. The conservative-liberal dilemma, therefore, involved the need of reconciling both liberty and equality, political and socio-economic democracy, in the 20th century.

Confronted by such intense and contradictory forces, the tendency among most thinkers was to choose one or the other horn of the dilemma. A liberal/conservative dichotomy survived, however battered and unsatisfactory these ideological designations appeared to be. One thinker, however, sought to resolve the situation by combining the strengths of each ideological tradition while avoiding their respective weaknesses. This is why Reinhold Niebuhr occupies such a pivotal role in the transformation of American thought from 19th century individualism toward 20th century collectivism. It is not entirely possible to disentangle the liberal and conservative strands in his complex thought processes. In some respects, he is the only thinker who straddles these ideological positions; he is the most instructive thinker from the standpoint of both success and failure in resolving the conservative-liberal dilemma.

Reinhold Niebuhr

Reinhold Niebuhr defies precise ideological classification. He certainly cannot be called a conservative thinker in any obvious sense, since he is a major spokesman for social, political, and economic reforms. At the same time, he is a leading critic of liberalism—or at least those elements of the liberal creed which he feels are non-viable, if not actually pernicious.[12] Although he continued to find value in the Marxist critique of bourgeois civilization, he found the Marxist view of human nature and history to be grievously deficient. Because he is a theologian, the label "neo-orthodoxy" is applied to his religious writings, which draw heavily upon such disparate sources of Biblical revelation and interpretation as St. Paul, St. Augustine, and Martin Luther, and which aim at a renewal of Protestant Christianity that would have meaning for modern man. There is no doubt that Reinhold Niebuhr can be considered one of the most respected and influential thinkers in American religious, social, and political thought in this century; yet there are conservative, liberal, and radical strands to his thought which make it difficult to determine his proper place in the ideological spectrum. This lack of ideological consistency proved to be the source of both strength and weakness in his thought.

Niebuhr launched his career as the pastor of a small Lutheran church in the heart of industrial Detroit, an experience which deeply influenced his thought. His congregation, although it contained a millionaire or two, consisted of mostly lower and working class people. Thirteen years of intimate daily exposure to the harsh realities of their lives convinced Niebuhr that the highly moralistic and falsely optimistic liberalism he had been exposed to in college was far removed from the needs and prospects of so many poor Americans.[13] The central core of his thought— that man's tragic, inescapable involvement in sin and death defines the boundaries of human existence—took root at this time. As he began to write the books and articles that flowed in a continuous stream until his death in 1971, Reinhold Niebuhr established himself as "a shaping influence in theology, social ethics and public policy,"[14] but filled the role more as a critic than as a systematic thinker. Ultimately, the integration he sought finally eluded him, and he can be seen in a conservative, liberal, or radical light depending upon one's own presuppositions.

If it is generally the case that liberals tend to adopt a more optimistic view of human nature and a more hopeful attitude toward man's capacity for rationality than do conservatives, Niebuhr qualifies as a charter member of the conservative club. In the early 1940's he published a major two-volume study, The Nature and Destiny of Man, which compares "the Christian view of man" to the "classical view" that originated in Greek metaphysical philosophy and which now, according to Niebuhr, dominates modern culture.[15] For Niebuhr, the superiority of the Hebraic-Christian conception of man resides in the unitary role performed by "faith in God as Creator of the world (which) transcends the canons and antinomies of rationality, particularly the antinomy between mind and matter, between consciousness and extension."[16] Because all metaphysical dualisms invariably fail to do justice to the good/evil, rational/irrational, free will/determinism antinomies of human existence, Niebuhr rejects both idealist and naturalist views of man in favor of the Christian view, which he feels does achieve this unitary goal. Man's essentially sinful nature, especially the sins of pride and a love for power, can be fully understood and dealt with only from such a perspective:

> Only in a religion of revelation, whose God reveals
> Himself to man from beyond himself and from beyond
> the contrast of vitality and form, can man discover
> the root of sin to be within himself. The essence
> of man is his freedom. Sin is committed in that
> freedom. Sin can therefore not be attributed to
> a defect in his essence. It can only be under-
> stood as a self-contradiction, made possible by
> the fact of his freedom but not following necess-
> arily from it.[17]

As the above passage clearly shows, Niebuhr is a dialectical thinker—irreconcilable opposites frame all aspects of human life and thought, yet at some point the tension has to be relieved by an accommodation of opposite values, in order to give a meaning to human existence. But unlike the Hegelian search for an illusory absolute as the culminating synthesis, or the Marxist vision of a final elimination of class warfare via communism, or the liberal faith in the superiority of mind over matter, Niebuhr's solution to the dialectical conundrum is found in a Christian tradition that unites the finite and the infinite in an act of faith and serves as a guideline for ethical behavior.[18] Despite the eloquent and logical persuasiveness of his analysis, however, Reinhold Niebuhr does no better than his antagonists in giving a universally valid reason for choosing his path rather than another.

The sins committed in the name of Christianity are probably as numerous as the benefits that have ensued from Christian belief. Niebuhr would no doubt agree to this. There is a curious ambivalence in the pragmatic-relativistic appreciation of human contingency and the universalistic-absolutist assertion of human sinfulness that splits Niebuhr's thought into two halves that do not finally come together, despite his attempts at unity. The history of Christianity in the world reflects the unresolved tension of a _dualistic_ metaphysics that has all too often meant that one vital aspect must be sacrificed to the other. Niebuhr's search for both a relative and absolute basis to morality caught him in a spider's web of contradictory values and uncertainty. Making a virtue out of necessity, he resolved the problem as best he could by refusing to make a final choice, so that the inner tension of his thought reflects this unresolved dualism. The meaning of good and evil is a determination that has unavoidable consequences but no objective basis that might bestow a quality of needed legitimacy and universality to the quest. Niebuhr's dialectic is a worthy effort, but it will hardly satisfy anyone who cannot accept the religious premises upon which it rests.

In 1932 Niebuhr published Moral Man and Immoral Society, the book which overnight placed him in the front rank of contemporary social critics and is one of the seminal works of our time. If it is true that collectivism, defined as the individual's increasing dependence upon society, has become the outstanding characteristic of the present age, then Niebuhr was the first major thinker to come to grips with the implications of this development. As group behavior rapidly became a central feature of contemporary life while individual behavior became a more dependent, less self-reliant factor, Niebuhr saw a moral problem that would grow in seriousness and might conceivably destroy democracy itself, if it could not be successfully combatted. In essence, Niebuhr noted the tendency of human beings to act more selfishly, impulsively, and exploitatively in their relations with one another when part of a social group than as single individ-

57

uals acting separately. By extension, this would be even more true of individuals in the largest of all social entities, the national state. The usual appeals to morality and rationality are less binding, and less in evidence, in group behavior.[19] In fact, power relationships rather than ethical considerations quickly become the determining factor in behavior.[20] Simultaneously, a cultural lag ensues, for conditions change faster than human value perceptions, and illusions take the place of reality.[21] Instead of alleviating social injustice, technology then serves a different purpose: those who have power use it to increase their power at the expense of those most in need.[22] Here is an excellent example of Niebuhr's acute analysis of what happens to the ethics/power equilibrium when modern society shifts to collectivist patterns of organization and conduct:

> The fact that the hypocrisy of man's group behavior...expresses itself not only in terms of self-justification but in terms of moral justification of human behavior in general, symbolizes one of the tragedies of the human spirit; its inability to conform its collective life to its individual ideals. As individuals, men believe that they ought to love and serve each other and establish justice between each other. As racial, economic and national groups they take for themselves, whatever their power can command.[23]

The question therefore presents itself: how can individuals be expected to maintain a respect for civility and a consideration for others under circumstances which neither encourage nor reward such conduct? Forty years after Niebuhr recognized the early stages of this central human dilemma, the problem has assumed crisis proportions.[24] Does he offer any solutions? Unlike many conservatives, Niebuhr does not see any hope in restoring a sense of community-mindedness within the larger collectivity because in his view the will-to-power is ineradicable and not subject to social control even under the best of conditions.[25] What is possible, in Niebuhr's judgment, is yoking the religious impulse to the cause of social justice as a means of transforming methods based strictly on power means into ethical ends.[26] Since self-interest is related to one's class status, social justice depends ultimately upon the uses and abuses of power. Niebuhr does not shrink from using coercive power for what he would consider to be worthy ends.[27] And in 1932 he was at least a step ahead of most liberals, and perhaps leaning toward radicalism, when he designated equality as "the ultimate social ideal."[28]

But Niebuhr also recognizes the dangers to a democratic society implicit in any effort to alleviate social injustice by using the coercive power of government—and he insists that the means count as much as the end.[29] On the other hand, Niebuhr does not feel that violence or revolution are necessarily immoral acts, for "a political policy cannot be intrinsically evil if it can be proved to be an efficacious

instrument for the achievement of a morally approved end."30
He would permit a pragmatic test for determining when and
under what circumstances the risk of violence might be tol-
erated.31 To put it bluntly, Niebuhr sanctions the use of
coercion against those individuals and groups who would
stand in the way of achieving a more equitable society.
Here is the key passage in his analysis:

> A rational society will probably place a
> greater emphasis upon the ends and purposes for
> which coercion is used than upon the elimination
> of coercion and conflict. It will justify coer-
> cion if it is obviously in the service of a ra-
> tionally acceptable social end, and condemn its
> use when it is in the service of momentary pass-
> ions. The conclusion which has been forced upon
> us again and again in these pages is that equal-
> ity, or to be a little more qualified, that equal
> justice is the most rational ultimate objective
> for society. If this conclusion is correct, a
> social conflict which aims at greater equality
> has a moral justification which must be denied
> to efforts which aim at the perpetuation of
> privilege.32

Actually, Niebuhr is very enamored of Gandhian techniques
of non-violent civil disobedience, and applauds the religious impulses behind such political activism.33

Niebuhr sees the relationship between self and society
as fraught with ambiguity, social instability, and incipient corruption. The best that men can hope for is a more
realistic attitude toward what is possible and an uneasy
compromise between individual responsibility and social im-
morality.34 In this regard, despite all its failures and
lost allure, the Christian faith still can fill the void
in the twilight zone between power and ethics. At the
heart of Niebuhr's social analysis there is this paradox:
he desires the kind of change that would bring about a de-
cidedly more equitable society than present power arrangements would countenance, yet holds out little hope that it
is in man's capacity to advance very far along this road
without paying the sort of price which a democratic society
cannot afford; that is, the erosion of individual freedom.
His conservative realism works against his radical vision
of what ought to be, and his liberal concern for means over
ends robs his social justice ideal of potency. It is a
very real dilemma that he—and we—are caught in.

In one of his most important books, The Irony of American History, Niebuhr surveys the state of American democracy and finds wide discrepancies between professed norms
and operating realities. Written in the early 50's, at a
time when the Cold War struggle between Soviet Communism
and the Western democracies was much to the fore, Niebuhr's
book is concerned with assessing the strengths and weaknesses, both internal and external, of America's coming of

age as a major world power. He chooses the term "irony" to describe the situation in which so many contemporary issues requiring decision arise from good intentions and worthy ends, but depend on means that are either inadequate or morally questionable; thus ideology takes the place of wisdom, and power itself becomes an end intead of a means.[35] Niebuhr believes that individualism has been the main component of the American creed, but that, ironically, collectivism has been the main basis of practical success, such as the institutionalization of welfare capitalism.[36] Fortunately, as American power has expanded, the pluralist nature of American politics and institutions has served to check excessive abuses of power.[37] Niebuhr knows that the inequities of American society are unconscionable; but in relative terms, he feels that the record is better than might be expected, thanks to the pragmatic underpining of the ideological illusions that are implicit in liberal utopianism.[38] The main illusion is the liberal belief that man is more rational than he is. Niebuhr warns his countrymen that strength breeds arrogance and a denial of human fallibility.[39] Unfortunately, the succeeding two decades of American foreign policy confirmed his deepest forebodings, as the "arrogance of power" syndrome permeated the decision-making process in the post World War II period.[40] The inability to keep means and ends in a reasonable balance has led to some tragic consequences for America and for the world.

Reinhold Niebuhr sees the same great flaw in Marxist states that he finds in liberal ones—the rationalistic illusion that man can impose his own terms on history. Man, as both creature and creator of history, needs to accept the irremediability of sin and to pay more attention to limits, resisting the temptation to don the mantle of omnipotence.[41] Niebuhr's conservatism is again in evidence as he elevates "balance of power" to a leading principle for insuring a more stable and just order.[42] All forms of moralistic idealism receive his strongest criticism:

> The inhumanities of our day, which modern tyrannies exhibit to the nth degree, are due to an idealism in which reason is turned into unreason because it is not conscious of the contingent character of the presuppositions with which the reasoning process begins, and in which idealism is transmuted into inhumanity because the idealist seeks to comprehend the whole realm of ends from his standpoint.[43]

One wonders whether he is fully conscious of the irony of his own position as a political thinker: as a persistent fighter against all forms of injustice, Niebuhr inhibits prospects for substantive change by embracing a self-limiting concept of human selfishness, egoism, and sin.

Perhaps the most attractive quality of Niebuhr's thought is his deep-seated appreciation of the complexity, ambiguity, and irony of human aspiration in the face of impossible odds, a viewpoint summed up by his famous aphorism from The Children of Light and the Children of Darkness: "Man's capacity for justice makes democracy possible; but man's inclination to injustice makes democracy necessary."[44] And yet there were serious fissures in this socio-political philosophy; his pragmatic resiliency and his capacity to reconsider his stance as circumstances changed existed in an uneasy tension with basic assumptions about man's nature and history, and the bedrock necessity of a Christian faith that could be asserted, but not proved or objectified. This dilemma led Niebuhr to promote a vaguely defined socialism in the 1930's and to reject New Deal experimentalism, substituting an either/or solution for a more realistic critique of the failures of capitalistic democracy. By the 1950's, Niebuhr had made his peace with the system he had once condemned so sharply; and, as Edward A. Purcell has indicated, the conservative underside of the relativist theory of democracy promulgated by Niebhur, Dewey, Beard, and others began to surface.[46] Although it is certainly not true that Niebuhr became a thoroughgoing conservative in his later years, his earlier radicalism was very much muted, and even his biting rejection of classical liberal doctrine seemed less tenable. Here is his own evaluation of this change of mind:

> American conservatism, which is nothing more than a decadent liberalism, would be doubly unacceptable. My conservatism relates to an increasing appreciation of the organic factors in social life in contrast to the tendencies stemming from the Enlightenment which blind modern men to the significance of these organic factors, and treat the human community and its instruments of order and justice as if they were purely artifacts.[47]

Niebuhr's harshest critics have been Charles Frankel, Morton White, and Wilson Carey McWilliams. Frankel's chapter on Niebuhr in his The Case for Modern Man accuses Niebuhr of adopting an absolutist standard—his metaphysical concept of original sin—in attacking the failures of liberalism and in the process ascribing to liberalism "a perfectionist theory of human nature (which) is in fact a parody of liberal theory."[48] There is much more to Frankel's critique, but its main charge stems from Frankel's defense of the secularist, relativist, and rationalist features of liberal theory against attempts like Niebuhr's to substitute a religious metaphysics for an empirico-naturalist theory of democracy.

Morton White is a positivist (i.e., empirico-scientific methodology is the only proper basis for value judgments) who accuses Niebuhr of adopting a priori presuppositions without recourse to empirical testing, and of promoting a determinist theory of history which unjustifiably reduces man's freedom to act.[49] According to White, if one discards Niebuhr's theological faith and doctrine of original sin, then nothing is left, for the latter depends upon the former.[50]

Wilson Carey McWilliams claims that Niebuhr shared much the same value attitudes he condemned in his critique of liberalism. The generation of intellectuals who came of age at the time of World War I all experienced the disillusionment of Wilsonianism in one way or another, and they sought a more realistic basis for evaluating American democracy. Niebuhr's inability to offer an alternate conception of liberalism to replace that which he so persistently scorned spells "the very brankruptcy of Niebuhr's ideas," according to McWilliams.[51]

As a rejoinder to these rather harsh critics, one could do no better than read through the volume of essays compiled by Charles W. Kegley and Robert W. Bretall, covering the entire gamut of Niebuhr's theological, social, and political thought; taken together, these essayists represent a tribute by twenty notable writers to a man they esteem as a truly seminal figure in 20th century thought.[52] They regard Niebuhr as a great thinker, in spite of his ideological uncertainties and the elusiveness of so many of his key concepts. What stands out, finally, is the record of a man who used his Union Theological Seminary sermons, and his numerous scholarly and topical writings as a sounding board for the perplexities of a troubled time. From this perspective, Reinhold Niebuhr can be studied with continuing profit.

In the final analysis, Niebuhr's very strengths and weaknesses mirror one of the conservative-liberal dilemmas which continues to plague American thought. The assumptions of an optimistic, progressive-looking liberal faith undergird democratic theory. Conservative pessimism and conservative values have been a vital corrective ingredient in this same developing democratic creed. For example, the concept of popular participation is a necessary, but not sufficient, basis for democratic governance. Elitism, however defined, will continue to be a dominant factor in any system where power resources are inequitably distributed within the larger population. Distrust of power, and its inevitable potential for corruption and abuse, was unquestionably the centerpiece of Reinhold Niebuhr's socio-political philosophy. The need for accountability, as well as the need to effectively serve the public good, remains the main problem for any viable democracy. As is the case with all scholar-critics, Niebuhr was better at diagnosis than he was at offering solutions to the problems he regarded as central to the democratic process. And when the greatest problem of all is an insoluble dilemma, the contributions of thought can only be measured in driblets, not in large chunks.

Sidney Hook

When a notable thinker, in the course of a long and productive scholarly career, shifts ideologically from radicalism to conservative-liberalism, does this mean that he has changed or that the times have changed? Is it a case of inconsistency or consistency? Is it a tribute to the thinker's capacity for personal growth and flexibility of mind, or a serious weakness in the basic assumptions which have governed his thinking all along? These questions are important when considering someone like Sidney Hook, who, for over half a century, has been an opinion-molder, a highly regarded teacher and philosopher, and one of the most widely read intellectual critics of the age. A defender of democratic socialism and a radical critic of capitalism in his earlier career, toward mid-career Professor Hook held high the banner of liberalism in its more progressive coloration; but finally, in recent years, a decided conservative tone has erupted in his writings; his earlier radical-liberalism has evaporated, and a conservative-liberalism has taken hold.[53] Such labeling, needless to add, is imprecise; what is noteworthy about Sidney Hook's intellectual pilgrimage concerns the relationship between ideology and history. This provides a clue to how one might proceed in searching to understand the above statements.

The two shaping influences upon Sidney Hook's intellectual life have been Marxism and Pragmatism.[54] In the 1930's, he was a leading contributor to the pro-Marxist Modern Quarterly, edited by V.F. Calverton. As the economic crisis deepened and the presidential election of 1932 approached, he joined with fifty-one other intellectuals in supporting the candidacy of the Communist candidates for President and Vice President, because he believed that capitalism was obviously the cause of this crisis and that the moderate changes espoused by Democratic, Republican, and Socialist party candidates were simply unacceptable; for Hook, this was an either/or situation, and the Communists, he believed, were at least on the side of total change in behalf of the underclass, which at this time probably constituted a majority of the population. As a disciple of John Dewey, Hook sought to wed pragmatic-scientific humanism to the Marxist insight that economics and power were at the root of all social injustice and economic inequality.

But disillusionment rapidly set in, for the prime historical example of applied Marxism, Stalin's Russia, quickly revealed itself as a gross betrayal of humanistic and democratic values. Hook rejected Communism, as did so many other leading "radicals" of the time, but clung to his belief in the socialist vision of a better world. Stalinism split the left in America and destroyed any prospect that radicalism could achieve a cohesive intellectual unity.[55] At the same time, Hook criticized liberalism for its tendency to sacrifice the good of society to a self-centered individualism, harking back to the Lockean strand in American liberal thought and its increasingly obvious deficiencies. In the Marxist dialectic, he saw an effective method for uniting the antinomies of human existence in a way that would not be a surrender to the status quo. Like so many radicalized liberals of the 30's, Hook accepted collectivism as the necessary antidote to an exploitative capitalism; true freedom and equality could only be realized, he believed, through transforming man into a more socially responsible being. In this regard, Marxism was the acceptable guide, the means whereby liberalism could be transformed into democratic socialism. It was only after it became clearer to him that a true balance between individualism and collectivism was an unlikely development from Marxism, that Hook began to question his earlier allegiance and to regain his faith in pragmatism as the basis for criticizing and repudiating Marxism.[56] In books and essays, Hook became one of the leading American authorities on the history of Marxist ideas and the inadequacies of Marxist theory. He also changed from being a severe critic to a moderate defender of American institutions, if not actual practices.[57]

The one thing that has not changed is Hook's faith in the scientific method applied to human affairs.[58] If man has the courage to rely upon his natural intelligence, to gather the necessary facts, and to abide by those decisions which have the greatest benefits for the greatest number, much of human tragedy, Hook believes, can be substantially reduced, if not eliminated. All forms of absolutism, including moralistic assertions of either/orism and fanatical idealism, receive Hook's scorn. Here is the measure of his pragmatic faith in particularity, as opposed to all forms of universalism:

> In its broadest sense as a philosophy of life, it (pragmatism) holds that the logic and ethics of scientific method can and should be applied to human affairs. This implies that one can make warranted assertions about values as well as facts... Most daring and controversial of all, pragmatism holds that it is possible to gain objective knowledge not only about the best means available to achieve given ends—something freely granted—but also about the best ends in the problematic situation in which the ends are disputed or become objects of conflict.[59]

But critics have pointed out how pragmatism, which purportedly represents the philosophical rationale of liberalism, actually serves conservative interests, and instead of scientific objectivity, the real implications of pragmatic truth-testing is an either/orism that leads to the suspension of critical judgment when other than pragmatic values are being weighed.[60]

In recent years, Sidney Hook has re-discovered Thomas Jefferson and a classical liberalism that some would call conservatism today. But instead of the eighteenth-century rationalist who saw universality in certain "inalienable natural rights," Hook sees a different Jefferson—one who had a keen sense of the relativistic interaction of rights, interests, and conditions, so that means ultimately shape ends, not vice-versa.[61] There are two types of liberal—

the "ritualistic" and "realistic" liberal.[62] The former prefers moralistic rhetoric and slogans to the expression of good logic and analysis of concrete issues.[63] The latter is "the genuine liberal who faces problems as they arise, instructed by experience but without recipes, is a lone thinker usually uncomfortable even in an organization of liberals."[64]

In an earlier, more radical frame of mind, Hook had felt that political and economic democracy were mutually supportive, and that either without the other, substantially weakened the democratic cause.[65] In other words, liberty depended upon equality for its meaning. Now, this no longer seems true to Hook. Instead of having its foundation in equity and equality, freedom depends upon national security and domestic peace; stability takes precedence over change, if change itself threatens individual rights and freedom.[66] In the late 60's, Hook became one of the sharpest critics of the "new radicalism" on campus, finding nothing good and much that was evil in the student rebellion. Here is a sampling of his subsequent disenchantment with radical politics:

> I do not recall any other period in the last fifty years when intellectuals themselves have been so intolerant of each other, when differences over complex issues have been the occasion for denunciation rather than debate and analysis...In the long run, the preservation of democracy depends upon a passion for freedom, for the logic and ethics of free discussion and inquiry, upon refusal to countenance the measures of violence that cut short the process of intelligence upon which the possibility of shared values depends.[67]

The three values he presently equates with democracy are individual liberty, pluralist society, and pragmatic-scientific methodology in the pursuit of truth and as the regulative principle of democratic politics. The three values that he feels offer the main threat to this conception of democracy are imposed egalitarianism, big government, and moralistic assertions of absolute rights. His anti-Communism has been unwavering, despite détente and the abatement of Cold War conflicts. At a time when many scholar-critics and revisionist historians find little difference between communism and capitalism as repressive systems, Hook insists upon their irremediable divergence in ideological and power aims, and deplores the tendency of so many intellectuals and self-professed radicals to find so much to criticize in the American system while conveniently closing their eyes to the continuing inhumanity of communist systems.[68] Hook is a critic of détente, because such a policy mistakenly denigrates the importance of ideology as a hidden and potent weapon threatening the cause of freedom in the world. Hook has moved so far away from his earlier love-affair with Marxism that he now sees politics, not economics, as the real issue. The preservation of political democracy takes precedence over the expansion of economic democracy. Sidney Hook has been a passionate, fearless, and eloquent advocate for those ideas and values he deems important for the preservation of a free society. This preservation must now take precedence over any political effort to expand democratic ideals, such as economic equality or greater social justice, if these ideals pose any risk to the most crucial value, liberty. In today's climate of opinion, this makes him at least a moderately conservative thinker.

There is other evidence that marks the conversion of the former radical critic into a conservative apologist for institutional stability over substantive reform. Hook is now critical of many past efforts at institutional reform precisely because these efforts created greater evil than the evils they attacked.[69] He is presumably referring to the rise of an unmanageable government bureaucracy which has become the main threat to individual freedom. Although there is no evidence that he is a staunch defender of the status quo or that he has lost any of his confidence in the pragmatic-scientific approach to problem-solving, there is a definite softening of critical judgment. Even more alarming is his disconcerting tendency to adopt an unpragmatic and moralistic either/orism toward dissenters who reject Hook's personal value preferences. Somehow or another, the pragmatic spirit of tolerance of ambiguity, respect for complexity, and appreciation of compromise gets short shrift in Sidney Hook's later writings.[70] It is easier to detect what he is against than what he is for. For this reason, his liberalism seems curiously reactionary, and his conservatism lacks substance.

But it would be wrong to dismiss Sidney Hook's later phase as a decline in what is otherwise a meritorious achievement. From first to last he has been an independent thinker, a courageous defender of his convictions regardless of what passed for conventional wisdom, and a libertarain of the first order.[71] In fact, despite all his ideological shifting of gears, this remains the centerline of his thought. A fierce dedication to freedom, symbolized by the autonomous individual capable of transcending his subjectivity and selfishness by a commitment to scientific objectivity and methodology, has always been Sidney Hook's personal ideal. Unfortunately, Hook's personal example does not altogether conform to the ideal, and it may well be that the ideal itself is deficient. All too often these days, a value-commitment to scientific methodology and objectivity masks ideological commitments that are still the main roadblocks to the professed goal—the pursuit of objective truth.

The conservative-liberal dilemma that both Reinhold Niebuhr and Sidney Hook were anxious to clarify, if not resolve, finally comes down to the meaning of equality. The traditional meaning of equality poses no problem: equality under the law and equal opportunity in education and economic endeavor. There has always been a liberal-conservative consensus regarding this meaning of equality. The problem arises when the question is asked: is this enough? If political democracy and socio-economic democracy can be equated, and if one believes that the achievement of the former is tantamount to substantial progress in the latter sphere, then there is no problem, and no dilemma either. It is simply a matter of protecting the libertarian tradition against those who would seek to capture the government in behalf of values which a substantial majority of citizens would never accept—values that would relate to either radical authoritarianism or ultra-conservative authoritarianism. There is a problem, however, if one concludes that political democracy can advance, while socio-economic democracy lags so far behind, that the discrepancy between liberty and equality requires remedial action. Those who see the matter from this perspective define equality as involving a moral commitment to equality of condition, or result; in other words, it is the responsibility of government to devise programs—such as a guaranteed incomes policy, national health care, or major tax reform whereby the rich pay more and the poor get more—to create a more equitable society.

This is not to say, however, that total equality is contemplated by those who define equality in these terms. This would require a radical prescription for change. It is possible to advocate systemic reforms that are meant to make socio-economic democracy a more substantive reality in America without being in favor of radical structural change. But there is an aspect to this definition of equality that does pose a serious problem for democracy. It would require a greater concentration of political power, bureaucratization, and possibly endanger individual freedom.[73] So the dilemma is real. And it is the meaning of equality that places everyone—liberal and conservative and radical alike—at a crossroads. A decision either way can have fateful consequences—that is, whether equality should retain its older meaning or should be given a new meaning that would endow government with the authority to push for remedial equality. Ultimately, the road one choses reflects one's understanding of democratic values, and does require a choice that may indeed favor one value over the other—more or less liberty versus more or less equality.

Reinhold Niebuhr, who shared with Sidney Hook an early exposure to Marxism and a concomitant revulsion against the failures of liberal-capitalism, differed from him in finding a metaphysical faith to give substance to his ethical realism; Hook never doubted the efficacy of a naturalistic faith in a secularist anti-absolutism. In Hook's view, man needed only himself to give life purpose and meaning. For Niebuhr, this was never enough. Therefore, the quality of their conservatism has differed markedly. Niebuhr's conservatism was anchored in his profound sense of man's tragic destiny: there was never any question in his mind that man was a social being, that faith and history, self and society, the relative and the absolute, were two sides of the same reality.

Hook's growing conservatism was the product of disillusionment and historical conditions which endangered the ideal he most cherished: individual autonomy.[74] When it no longer seemed possible that collectivism itself could be the main guarantee of expanded freedom, Hook launched a systematic attack upon the Marxist ideas he had once embraced.[75] But he made the mistake of ignoring the one insight which Marx, more than anyone else, established as the most significant aspect of the self-society relationship: man is a social being; self and society are not separate entities. This is why one of the strongest fighters against social injustice among contemporary thinkers could finally pull his punches and settle for a draw. For the later Hook, individual welfare no longer depended upon what happened in the social sphere; it was enough that the state protected those who defended its momentary interests and punished those who, for whatever reasons, felt alienated and oppressed.[76]

The times indeed did change for the worse, and Hook had good reason to be alarmed at the inroads that were being made against the individual freedom he valued so highly; Niebuhr, however, retained a greater appreciation of the interdependence of self and society than did Hook. Hook's conservatism was a retreat to an individualism without much social support; it was a disservice to the scientific-pragmatic assumptions he so wholeheartedly believed in; what had been questions of more or less now became matters of either/ or, at least in those areas where attacks on the existing order struck Hook as being mindless and irresponsible. The only trouble with Sidney Hook's criticism is that it often crossed the borderline into territory that sometimes made dissent itself objectionable if it strayed beyond the pale of consensus democracy. For Niebuhr, conservatism strengthened his liberalism, and although it led to unresolved contradictions in the body of his thought that weakened its potential as guidance for others, it fortified his personal example as a thinker who never flinched from the need to equate freedom and equality. Unlike Sidney Hook, Reinhold Niebuhr could not bring himself to favor either at the expense of the other.

Not least of the conservative-liberal dilemmas in the history of American political thought has been the strange reversal of roles in respect to underlying assumptions. A contemporary liberal is less optimistic, has less faith in man's rationality, and reveals greater distrust of the power of government to remedy injustice than his liberal forefather. A contemporary conservative is more optimstic, more ready to appeal to man's better nature, and more trustful of the need for government to regulate human affairs, provided that it does not expand its responsibilities in the realm of welfare and economic controls.[77] There is still much uncertainty about what government can and should endeavor to do in both camps; conservatives and liberals would both like to see a contraction of the powers of government generally; both traditions seek to safeguard the area of individual liberty against the arbitrary power of government. But the liberal continues to be committed to the ideal of equality, especially when equality is defined as a commitment to expanded equality rather than simply equal justice and equal opportunity; whereas the conservative sees imposed equality as a threat to the rights of property and to those who have already achieved wealth and status within the existing power structure. To the liberal, government policy must help the little guy, even if it is at the expense of the big guy, because in his view, effective freedom depends upon a more equitable economic order. To the conservative, government policy must favor the big guy so that the little guy may receive a fair share of the fruits of a healthy Gross National Product; and real freedom depends upon a minimum of governmental interference in the private economic sector. At a time when government has reached a nadir of impotency in solving pressing problems and advancing the public good, both conservatives and liberals are disenchanted with government as it exists.[78]

Although the above comparative analysis relates primarily to policy choices, there is a deeper matter which confronts the political philosopher who is less concerned with public policy than with the nature of democracy itself: that is, the relationship between ideals and practices, and the reconciliation of ethical and power factors. There have been a number of twentieth-century thinkers who have, in different ways, adopted a conservative perspective in confronting these difficult but significant aspects of democratic theory. The thinkers dealt with in the following chapter have each sought to examine the relationship of democratic theory to changing historical reality. As a group, they have little in common, except for the high quality of their theoretical and analytical pursuits.

CONSERVATIVE POLITICAL PHILOSOPHY

In the twentieth century, philosophical conservatism has run a wavering course in respect to both the basic assumptions that have characterized the conservative mind and the pursuit of a commonly understood conservative theory of politics. Those thinkers who might be singled out for their notable contributions as intellectual historians, philosophers, and political analysts to a conservative tradition in American thought display greater differences than similarities; no twentieth century conservative thinker can be considered either truly representative of the genre, or even "conservative" in any definitive meaning of the term. A perfect illustration of this muddled situation can be found in the short-essay responses of fifty-six leading intellectuals of varied ideological persuasions in the September, 1976 issue of _Commentary_ magazine. The following is a sampling of representative views:

"...certain positions once associated mainly with conservatives have lately found favor among liberals, and vice versa."[1]

"Conservatives have done a far better job of containing their extremists than the liberals have in containing theirs...If one has to be something today, the term conservative is nothing to fear."[2]

"...the 19th century liberal—out of John Stuart Mill, perhaps—would today be called a true conservative."[3]

"Conservatism and liberalism no longer, if they ever did, represent ideological polarities."[4]

"Socialism, after all, has drawn upon large components of the conservative tradition—above all, the conviction that society consists of something else than an aggregation of autonomous individuals."[5]

"Conservative theory is intent on balancing two contradictory values: social continuity and individual liberty. In the domain of social continuity, the conservative is not a defender of liberty..."[6]

"...the American people continue to vote for liberals while increasingly identifying themselves as conservatives."[7]

"Yet in the tumultuous 60's, numbers of liberals came to appreciate the conservative strengths—a connection with the past, a recognition of the fallibility of humankind, a respect for the processes of government and, yes, even for the much maligned system."[8]

"Actually the differences between liberals and conserv-

5551.3

atives have always been more a matter of temperament and style, background and position, than of ideology."[9]

"American conservatism is merely a series of rationalizations for holding onto what one has."[10]

"Conservative is almost by definition a concept virtually devoid of specific content."[11]

"American conservatives have always found it difficult to uphold American tradition, for the main American tradition is change, the non-conservative belief that the new is better, that science can ultimately solve all problems."[12]

"Modern 'liberalism' is emphatically conservative, being committed to an intensely pragmatic approach in all matters and choosing to stigmatize as 'extremist' all radical forms of political advocacy."[13]

"Conservatism in America today is a reaction to the 'revolutionary' reforms of the New Deal."[14]

Part of the problem is the diffuseness of twentieth century conservatism, the fact that a mixed conservative-liberal institutional and ideological tradition has left no room for a philosophically coherent and agreeable conservatism. Part of the problem is the continuing American distaste for any idea that seems to promote some form of elitism in the face of an apparently democratic polity which still cherishes the equalitarian ideal.[15] Whether or not one believes elitism and democracy are compatible, it is the hallmark of conservative political philosophy to defend meritocracy as a necessary attribute of a good democratic society and state. From this standpoint, the danger of instability that inheres in greater "participatory democracy" needs to be curbed, and, as much as possible, the power of the masses needs to be defused. Conservative thinkers differ in their ideas on how this might be accomplished without sacrificing democratic structure and principles; but they agree in blaming the weaknesses and ineffectuality of democratic government on the unlikelihood that a better caliber leadership will emerge, or a better integration of responsibility and power will be achieved, unless merit can be substituted for the popular lottery system that now prevails. The popular will, for its own ultimate good, requires containment, if government is to improve on the performance scale. The conservative solution to the perennial problem of democracy may not be generally acceptable, but the willingness to probe for an answer in spite of considerable opposition, and perhaps even complacency, deserves to be taken seriously.

The seven names selected for treatment in this chapter neither exhaust the possibilities nor necessarily represent a one through seven ranking of outstanding examples of philosophical conservatism. And in two cases, those of Santayana and Hayek, there might be some question whether they can be called authentic American thinkers, given their predominantly European backgrounds. However, each of these individuals has

72

had appreciable influence upon the thinking of others, and each has made a valuable contribution to an ongoing examination of the meaning of democracy in America.

George Santayana, for example, challenged many of the central tenets of the dominant American philosophy of pragmatism and questioned the legitimacy of any democracy which failed to measure up to a qualitative elitism. Walter Lippmann, a widely read and respected journalist-scholar, could be considered more liberal than conservative if one merely noted his critiques of public policy, but in The Public Philosophy he presented an important statement consonant with a conservative political philosophy. As a political economist, Friedrich von Hayek has raised issues that go to the very heart of the relationship between capitalism and democracy, and has posed a need for a revitalized conservatism that is close to the traditional meaning of liberalism. For this reason, I believe, he shares better the designation of philosophical conservative rather than the libertarian label that he usually receives. Leo Strauss, a long-time political philosopher at the University of Chicago, enjoyed a reputation among many of his former students and professional colleagues as the preeminent contemporary scholar in conservative thought. Willmoore Kendall never achieved the wide readership or eminence of the other thinkers treated in this chapter, but he probably had a greater impact on those who seek to anchor a conservative political philosophy in democratic soil than any other thinker of his time. Hannah Arendt's thought has been wide-ranging and perceptive, and has focused upon the complex means-ends relationship that has been a persistent concern of philosophical conservatives. Hans Morgenthau, although most of his writings are topical and concerned with foreign policy, has written copiously on the American value system with the object of trying to join theory and practice in behalf of a realistic fusion of liberal and conservative values. Taken individually, these disparate thinkers are notable for the distinctiveness and unrepresentativeness of their writings; but taken as a whole, they show the strengths and weaknesses of the conservative dilemma: a defense of elitism that would make democracy stronger and not simply destroy it. In giving more power to the few and less power to the many, the philosophical conservative is also seeking to ground government in ethical principles, and to show how politics and morality need not be incompatible.

George Santayana

If temperament and family background offer vital clues to the formation of personality, then George Santayana could be looked upon as a product of mixed Spanish-American ancestry, marked by a cosmopolitan detachement and a misplaced puritanism. There is a close parallel between Santayana's autobiographical quest for self-discovery and his mature philosophical writings: he was introspective and spiritually obsessed in the Puritan mold, yet capable of transcend-

73

ing the narrow confines of his withdrawn temperament and reaching out to experience the world in all its shades of darkness and light. The only son of a Spanish father, and a Spanish-born mother who had been married previously to a Boston-bred American, George Santayana spent part of his boyhood in Spain with his father and part of it with his mother, who had chosen to reside more or less permanently in the homeland of her deceased former husband and her three daughters. He later attended Harvard University; but in 1912, when he "retired" from teaching in his late forties, he left America, never to return, and lived off and on in England, Spain, France, and in Italy, where he died in 1952. At the time of his death at the age of 89, he had achieved a world-wide reputation as an important twentieth century philosopher.

Although numerous labels have been applied to Santayana—such as philosophical dualist, idealist, pro-Monarchist—he defies easy classification. As a philosopher, he wrote two major works, the multi-volume Life of Reason, and Realms of Being. In addition he published numerous other philosophical books and essays, none of which fits readily into a particular philosophical tradition, and all of which reflect a highly individualistic approach to philosophy, in their disregard of systematic analysis in favor of distilled wisdom.[16] Yet his essential vision was metaphysical, and his writings display a need to reconcile the real and the ideal, matter and spirit, existence and essence.

Santayana is one of those thinkers whose philosophical ideas are likely to be overshadowed by the lyrical beauty of his writing and the mesmerizing effect of a poet-philosopher. He wrote one novel, The Last Puritan, which is considered by literary critics to be a minor classic: its portrait of two generations, a turn-of-the-century father and his son, who struggle against and achieve a kind of liberation from, their Puritan ancestry, is a deeply felt and faithfully rendered exercise in socio-psychological criticism. Then, in a three volume memoir, Santayana provided a blend of subjective-objective reminiscences that are equally fascinating as autobiography and as social observation. Although a certain amount of political analysis crops up regularly in most of his writings, a substantial volume entitled Dominations and Powers, which he wrote late in life, represents his most sustained effort in dealing with political theory.

In short, Santayana cannot be considered either a major political theorist or a good example of conservatism, but he merits attention because of his attempt to reconcile power and ethics. In all of his writings, his primary interest is directed toward making the real ideal. There is much that is paradoxical in his thought. He distrusted science and religion, but called his philosophy naturalism and died after having been a long-time guest in a Catholic convent. He elevated the life of the mind over the life of action, but lived very much within the world and was a capable social critic. For Santayana, there was no certainty, no absolute, yet he could not really accept the pragmatist's claim to approximate truth; he believed instead, that there was a realm of essence which superseded the realm of existence. Above all, he was a man who sought the path of wisdom, and made the quest for wisdom the foundation of his life and philosophy.

Santayana views man as a spiritual being grounded in materiality. But he is most skeptical of the claim that Reason, Will, and Spirit can be reconciled in human history. Spirituality is more a matter of human aspiration and perfection than of religious affiliation. Since all aspects of human behavior have a moral dimension, spirit and matter interpenetrate at all levels of existence. Power as an end is evil; consequently, politics needs a religious or spiritual underpinning if morality is to prevail, just as the real needs the ideal if there is to be any meaning in life.[17] The spiritual element may be neglected, but it cannot be exorcised; even politicians have a choice between merely selfish and less selfish political actions.[18]

Santayana divides his book, Dominations and Powers, into three main parts which conform to the main elements of society—the generative order, the military order, and the rational order—depending upon whether economic, military, or philosophical problems are uppermost for insuring man's well-being. Anything that releases the moral will to fulfill itself is good, but the obstacles to this idealization of human existence are difficult and many. Santayana's deep-seated conservatism comes through when he declares: "...it's not worthwhile to insist on wanting what you can't have. The best way to make things come about as you wish is to learn to like the way they have of coming about of their own accord when you give them a gentle push."[19] True liberty is not doing as one desires but as responsibility dictates.[20] Inequality is the price of individuality and mindless social conformity is the death of moral excellence. Santayana is an aristocrat at heart; genuine morality is a hard road to negotiate, and in the end, only a few can be expected to make it finally to a worthy destination.

As for government, Santayana favors "ideal monarchy." He acknowledges that such a government does not appear to be possible any longer in the modern world, but believes, nevertheless, that it is the only type of government which permits a maximum of central direction with a minimum of interference in social and individual behavior.[21] Unfortunately, Santayana champions this preferred system while failing completely to analyze either the historical or problematic aspects of the case for such an "ideal monarchy." Evidently, monarchy is the best example Santayana can find of a form of government which avoids both irresponsible democracy and extreme authoritarianism, or totalitarianism. In his earlier work, Reason in Society, he advocates a Platonic Timocracy, in which the rulers have been exposed to the highest attainments of civilized humanism and are thus capable of ruling

75

for the public good.[22] There is no doubt that Santayana
welcomes a strong hand at the helm and a considerable governmental authority—at least in the three areas of population control, national security, and general prosperity,
the areas he deems most central for good government. He
tends to denigrate constitutional democracy, and neatly
sidesteps the issue of what might prevent even an enlightened ruler from abusing power.[23] Reason can redeem human
nature; the virtuous, cultivated, moral leader may be rare,
but not unknown, for "all integrated psyches are virtuous
and their natural masks are masks of virtue..."[24]

In Santayana's view, progress does not always bring
improvement; in fact, established authority, whether in
church, state, or society, is bound to set standards that
are worthy of emulation.[25] Behind the concept of "we the
people" lies a concept of "fundamental needs and capacities,
not...casual desires or conventional judgments."[26] And this
is the moral dimension that must be actualized. It represents Santayana's ideal of rational government, a government
"which speaks to its people in the name of the nature of
things and acts by that authority."[27] A government "for the
people," in Santayana's view, cannot be chosen by popular
majority vote, but should be drawn from those few who have
been "educated and trained in the science and art of government: persons able to discern the possibility or impossibility of human ambitions."[28] Since man is basically weak and
selfish, a benevolent dictatorship is both necessary and
desirable.

As can be seen, Santayana has either a naive concept of
power or a misplaced faith in the self-restraint and moral
superiority of a selective meritocracy. His personal and intellectual preference for the life of the mind over the messy
unpredictability of the real world spills over into his political theory; there is too much utopianism and not enough realism in his analysis of the political world. As a humanist,
Santayana is unequaled among contemporary thinkers; and there
is genuine merit in the way he is able to universalize the
ethics-power dilemma; but his political theorizing reveals
its deficiencies whenever he might be expected to give concrete backing for analysis that too often approximates vague-
ness and excessive abstraction. He is at his best when he is
simply reflecting on his own life, recounting his recollec-
tions of such teacher-colleagues as William James and Josiah
Royce, or concocting shrewd comparisons between American and
English traits of character as he did so charmingly in Character and Opinion in the United States.[29] He is too much
the poet and not sufficiently the political scientist in his
major attempt at political philosophy.

Santayana dedicated his life to the search for a realm
of meaning that could aid man in applying reason and morality
to the treacherous terrain that dominates the human landscape,
but his solution was simply too rarified, too delicate, for
the rough and tumble of ordinary life. Democracy cannot afford to rest its case on such flimsy and circumstantial evi-

dence. If liberty is indeed the prerogative of the few,
and equality a sham, then democracy is doomed. Santayana,
like most conservative thinkers, had too little faith in
men and too much faith in man. The contradiction escaped
him, as it has so many conservatives. Man is an abstraction: the concept means everything and nothing. Moral man,
economic man, political man, social man—all are abstractions that some thinkers like to cite as ultimate authority
for this or that quality of human existence. Concrete existence, however, defies such analysis; the road of good intentions is sometimes paved with evil deeds. Idealism frequently degenerates into ideology and destroys the basis of
democratic politics. Authority is either conditional or unconditional. Constitutionalism and the rule of law are the
conditional constraints on authority in a viable democracy.
There is no substance to a morality that is dependent upon
a ruler who is above the law. Santayana failed to appreciate this fact, and this failure overshadows whatever value
there may be to his political philosophy. The pursuit of
excellence has always been a legitimate human aspiration,
and it has certainly been a common theme for all conservative thinkers, but excellence can be defined in many ways,
not merely as moral superiority. It is the common failing,
or arrogance, of conservative thinkers like George Santayana to ascribe this quality to the few and deny it to the
many. It is doubtful whether reality or history can support
such a narrow view of the human condition.

Walter Lippmann

There are few contemporary political thinkers who can
be considered outstanding because of the range and depth of
their work; Walter Lippmann, who died in 1974, unquestionably qualifies for this honor. Of course, it is necessary
to state at the outset that he can not be considered "conservative" in the usual sense of the word, since he has never been a defender of the status quo and his liberal credentials are quite in order. On the other hand, it is also
true that his special brand of "liberalism" does not meet
contemporary liberal criteria, in that he was, for over half
a century, a consistent critic of New Deal style liberalism
for its surrender to "socialistic" or "collectivist" tendencies expanding both the authority and power of the central
government at the expense of individual liberty. As an unrelenting opponent of both laissez-faire liberalism-capitalism and welfare-statism, Walter Lippmann has been censured
by ultra-conservatives and mainstream liberals, but he has
remained his own man throughout, cleaving to his own special
vision of the liberal promise, while advocating conservative
solutions to the present malaise of the times.

So Lippmann's inclusion in a conservative tradition
needs to be qualified. He draws his liberal values from
the American founders, but realizes that constitutional
structures do not guarantee democracy. He believes that
the people themselves have to imbibe these charished ideals

continuously, so that these values will remain part of an ongoing consciousness; only then will the people insist that government acts with a respect for the spirit, as well as the letter, of democratic institutional practices, and with a readiness to apply these principles to the moral as well as practical aspects of democracy-in-action. Because he believes Americans are permitting themselves to forget this vital part of their legacy, he grew increasingly pessimistic and even despairing of America's ability to preserve this precious democratic franchise. And because he clings to the belief that it is not too late to reverse this decline and recapture the true liberal ideal, he urges this process of reexamination and reclamation upon his countrymen. At the same time, Lippmann believes liberalism itself has to be transformed, and that America must back-track to the crossroads where the wrong turn was made earlier in this century. In this respect he is a conservative thinker; he holds up a picture of liberalism that no longer seems to be the picture many contemporary liberals like.

Perhaps the two main intellectual influences on Lippmann's thought were William James and George Santayana, both of whom were his teachers at Harvard University, and whose philosophical positions were poles apart. Much of his mature thought is a recognition of the complementariness of James's respect for particularity and Santayana's belief in a universal moral order. The synthesis Lippmann sought may finally have eluded him, but then who else has succeeded in this worthy endeavor?

The only child of German-Jewish parents from a moderately wealthy upper-middle-class New York City background, Lippmann had advantages which were open only to the few in the early part of this century—travel abroad, the best schools, early exposure to the cultural arts, and the right social contacts. Despite a brief affair with moderate radicalism at Harvard as president of the Socialist Club, a period spent as an apprentice to the famous "muckraker," Lincoln Steffens, and as an assistant to the Socialist mayor of Schenectady, New York, Lippmann's early liberalism was rather conventional, even after he became one of the founding editors of The New Republic. One of his early heroes was Theodore Roosevelt.[30] His later career included an acquaintance with Colonel House, Woodrow Wilson's able first deputy in foreign affairs, and Newton D. Baker, Wilson's Secretary of War. The latter contact resulted in Lippmann's taking a position as an assistant in charge of labor relations that affected our war production efforts. The former contact led to his becoming a member of Colonel House's staff in the later stages of World War I; in this position he contributed to the formulation of the famous Fourteen Points that were supposed to become the basis of an enduring world peace.

But government service proved disillusioning to the young man, and in the post-war period he became a journalist-scholar, writing editorials for the old New York World, articles for The New Republic, a regular column of opinion and an-

78

alysis for the New York Herald Tribune, as well as a half-dozen important books of political analysis. He married twice, became a widely read and well-regarded political observer, and lost faith in Franklin Roosevelt and the New Deal because of its collectivist tendencies and its willingness to sacrifice personal liberty on the altar of Big Government.

As a political economist, Lippmann argued a heretical thesis that has stood the test of time: "The concentration of control in modern industry is not caused by technological change but is a creation of the state through its laws."[31] According to Lippmann, the privileges and monopolistic practices of the corporate structure are the result of political favoritism and legal advantages that can be reversed without any threat to the democratic system or a prosperous economy. It is only the will to do this that has been lacking. Here is Lippmann's argument, stated with clarity and prescience in The Good Society, published originally in 1936:

> Because of the limitations of our understanding and of our power, the dynamics of human capacity follow the rule that the more complex the interests which have to be regulated, the less possible is it to direct them by the coercion of superior authority. This is not the current view. It is generally supposed that the increasing complexity of the social order requires an increasing direction from officials. My own view is, rather, that as affairs become more intricate, more extended in time and space, more involved and interrelated, overhead direction by the officials of the state has to become simpler, less intensive, less direct, more general. It has to give way, as we shall see later, to social control by the method of a common law.[32]

This is not the sort of thing one might expect from a liberal thinker; in fact, it is what Lippmann would call a return to the true liberal faith.

According to Lippmann, the reason for the perilous state of democratic governments is too much democracy! Long a critic of majority opinion and of the capability of the average person to choose good leaders and support good policy changes, Lippmann feels strongly that the American system has tilted dangerously toward irresponsible popular democracy at the expense of responsible elitism:

> If I am right in what I have been saying, there has developed in this century a functional derangement between the mass of the people and the government. The people have acquired power which they are incapable of exercising, and the governments they elect have lost powers which they must recover if they are to govern...A mass cannot govern...Where mass opinion dominates the government, there is a morbid derangement of the true functions

of power...The derangement brings about the en-
feeblement, verging on paralysis, of the capacity to govern. This breakdown in the constitutional order is the cause of the precipitate and
catastrophic decline of Western society. It may,
if it cannot be arrested and reversed, bring about
the fall of the West.[33]

The weaknesses and decline of democracy in the West
throughout the twentieth century can be attributed to poor
leadership, which has been caused by an ill-informed and
self-centered public.[34] The general public can be united
in behalf of idealistic and public-spirited goals only in
wartime; as soon as peace returns, the old patterns of
thought and behavior also return. Knowledge, intelligence
and wisdom are at a premium at any time and place; but they
are even more needed when popular opinion seeks to dominate
the decision-making process.[35] Democracy tends to produce
too few Churchills and too many Neville Chamberlains for
its own good.

While the Founding Fathers envisioned a national legislature that would initiate policy and an executive branch
responsible for implementing that policy, Lippmann would reverse the order. The executive should be freer to initiate
policy based upon his popular electoral mandate, and should
receive an increase in power commensurate with augmented
responsibilities; the legislative branch should maintain
close surveillance and should impose accountability on the
administrative side of government, but allow "the executive
(to be) the active power, the petitioning, the approving
and the refusing power."[36] Lippmann desires stricter separation of authority and power between the two branches, rather than the increased blurring, overlapping, and plain confusion that is now occurring, hastened by the newer concept
of shared functions and powers. The collective judgment of
the public as voters is not to be trusted; no electoral majority can adequately express the views and desires of "the
people;" therefore, the public interest should be left to
the executive to define, not for popular sentiment to determine.[37] Unlike most contemporary liberals, Lippmann is
not willing to shunt aside this concept of a public interest as being meaningless, or ascertainable only through the
political process of negotiation, bargaining, interest-group
competition and compromise. This concept necessitates and
defines responsible leadership, for "the public interest may
be presumed to be what men would choose if they saw clearly,
thought rationally, acted disinterestedly and benevolently."[38]

In essence, Lippmann would distinguish sharply between
the representative function of government, which is best
served by the national legislature, and the actual governing function, which is best expressed through executive power. Even when this distinction is incorporated into the
structure of government, as in parliamentary-type democracies, Lippmann sees little evidence of separation in practice, for popular opinion plays too strong a role and con-

tributes to a "derangement of powers" and an enfeebled executive leadership.[39] Totalitarianism would have been much
less of a threat to democratic government in this century if
the internal weaknesses of liberal democracies had not been
so great.[40] The expansion of mass education has not had the
positive effect it was supposed to have in developing an "enlightened citizenry," for the "post-revolutionary man, en-
franchised and emancipated, has not turned out to be the New
Man. He is the old Adam. Yet the future of democratic society has been staked on the premises and the predictions of
the Jacoban gospel."[41] Lippmann seems to feel that public
opinion must count for less than it does, and that political
leadership should be released from its over-dependence upon
the popular mind, if democracy is to survive in the world.

The heart of Lippmann's political philosophy is contained in the latter part of The Public Philosophy, his only
major effort to prescribe a political theory that might preserve and strengthen democracy. He believes the moral foundations of Western democracies are being eroded by a widespread failure to respect the "traditions of civility" that
once reinforced the "public philosophy" and kept the irresponsible propensities of democracy in check.[42] What is this
public philosophy which Lippmann deems so crucial for the
well-being of democracy? It is "a body of positive principles and precepts which a good citizen cannot deny or ignore."[43]
Whether or not this concept can be empirically demonstrated,
it is nevertheless at the heart of a viable democratic polity. It also has a long, respectable, and much-maligned historical tradition behind it—the natural law tradition. This
appeal to the moral principles of liberty, equality, and justice significantly influenced the architects of democratic
government and helped to make their efforts seaworthy, for
"in our time the institutions built upon the foundations of
the public philosophy still stand."[44] But unfortunately,
"they are used by a public who are not being taught, and no
longer adhere to, the philosophy."[45]

If one grants Lippmann's diagnosis of the increasing
failure of democratic governments to realize their earlier
promise—and this point has been made with virtual unanimity
by contemporary radicals, conservatives, and liberals who
still cherish the ends of democratic government—then it is
easy to conclude something is needed that is not now being
done to make such systems work as they were designed to work.
Here, however, is where controversy and disagreement reign
supreme: hardly anyone agrees on what should and can be done
to improve, let alone save, democratic government in the modern world. Walter Lippmann is one of the few thinkers to
come to grips with the problem in a way that does not alienate democratic means and ends. The answer lies in a "renewal" of the once efficacious "public philosophy." Rationality, morality, and civility are the key terms in Lippmann's
lexicon of prescriptive change. Everything has a price—including unrestrictive liberty, ideal equality, and absolute
justice. The price is a certain amount of self-restraint,
self-discipline, and self-sacrifice. The problem is where

to draw the line; how can the proper balance of liberty and authority be restored—the perennial question in political philosophy. One way of achieving this noble end is to think of liberty, equality, and justice as privileges, rather than rights; as responsibilities, not desiradata.[46] Individualism, without a sense of limits imposed by obligation, may infringe on someone else's rights and desires; obligation, without due respect for democratic rights and priorities, destroys everyone's real freedom.

The means of reconciling these essentially divergent tendencies is the public philosophy, according to Lippmann: a higher standard by which conduct can be measured and sanctioned. Rationality requires that limits to personal freedom be set; these limits, however, need to be stretched to accommodate both the larger public good and individual rights.[47] Everything is not relative—as the conventional wisdom seems to acclaim. There is good and evil in the world—as well as right and wrong behavior, truth and falsity.[48] The past should be the proper guide to present and future conduct; the "tradition of civility," which sets standards and distinguishes better from worse, relates the private to a public world, and creates the sense of community which is the proper antidote to unrestrained individualism.[49] But it has to originate from within men, not from without—by voluntary compliance, not by coercion. A more civilized life is possible if the wisdom of the past and the acceptance of unspecified but nevertheless real "rules of conduct" can be acquired by the masses of men and women. Man is a dual creature—both material and spiritual—and only when the latter qualities are nurtured can man hope to realize his better nature.[50] Neither separation nor fusion is the answer: the two equally vital realms have to achieve a meaningful and realistic balance.[51] This ideal but necessary balance requires the subjugation of popular impulses to public principles—and this can happen only when the "public philosophy" is recognized and accepted as the guiding light.[52]

In summary, there appear to be three crucial assumptions which encapsulate Lippmann's critique of existing democratic practices and his proposal for democratic renewal:

(1) The tradition of natural law and rational order in the universe has been the dominant Western tradition for values and moral guidance. It is still valid.

(2) Liberal democracy, as it has evolved in recent decades, has tended to forget, when it has not actually renounced, this tradition. This forgetfulness is the main cause of present weakness in the liberal democratic tradition.

(3) Only a renewal of belief and commitment to the "public philosophy" embodied in this tradition can save the Western world.

Even liberal commentators have been rather harsh in dismissing Walter Lippmann's proposal as less than satisfactory. In a study of Progressive Era thinkers, Charles Forcey deplores Lippmann's drift toward conservatism after his earlier flirtation with socialist ideas and a middle-period when he was still a certified liberal attached to the progressive wing of the movement; he accuses Lippmann of advocating "ideas both destructive of middle-class values and of democracy itself."[53]

Morton White has taken issue with recent attempts to revivify the hoary natural law doctrine, charging that it postulates self-evident moral principles that are impossible to clarify or define, but are nevertheless employed with the authoritative backing of religious and other parochial institutions concerned about protecting their vested interests. White admits that Lippmann provides a secularized version of natural law doctrine, whose interpreter would be the "wise statesman" unconstrained by the popular will; but he condemns all such attempts for being "obscure...and incapable of the philosophical load which has been put upon them."[54] Lippmann's public philosophy, in White's judgment, is another such futile attempt to discover universality in the particular—an undertaking that is both questionable and philosophically disingenuous. Since Platonic "essences" are empirically suspect, Lippmann's public philosophy is no less wrong-headed, according to White.

The only trouble with this criticism is that it stems from another kind of either/orism: only empiricist assumptions are valid; metaphysical ones are invalid. This is a rather narrow and biased view of philosophy. For whether one agrees or not with Lippmann's approach, it is not so easily dismissed; values and moral choices may be undemonstrable, objectively speaking, but are not less vital, even when taken on faith. Failure to pursue the ethical norms of democratic governance is what has caused the crisis of legitimacy which now appears so widespread. On this point, Lippmann surely deserves any benefit of the doubt. At least he recognizes the dilemmas of liberalism in an age of disintegrating hope.

Perhaps the harshest judgment of Lippmann's stature as a political thinker can be found in Benjamin F. Wright's 5 Public Philosophies of Walter Lippmann. In an analysis of his writings, Wright accuses Lippmann of weathervane gyrations across the ideological spectrum; this situation is understandable in a writer who was as much a journalist as he was a scholar, but it casts doubt upon the theoretical value of his contribution to political thought.[55] Yet it is widely acknowledged that for over half a century Walter Lippmann was probably the most respected and influential political commentator of his generation; it was the basic unity of the vision behind his probing intelligence that characterized his political writings and made him an opinion-molder, not just an academic philosopher.[56]

There are, however, critical questions that need to be raised concerning Lippmann's latter-day conservatism. First, in an era which has witnessed such systematic abuses of power by both totalitarian and democratic leaders as have

83

appeared in this century, it is hard to understand Lippmann's confidence in allowing even greater power to accrue in the executive department of government. This is especially true in a period when legislative impotence and executive supremacy are becoming increasingly common and when constitutional accountability is becoming more difficult to sustain even in the healthiest democracies. The "public philosophy" would seem to be a rather weak vessel for the rough seas ahead. Such blind faith in the capacity of the few, even if bolstered by a hefty conversion among the many, to attain the degree of rationality and moral excellence that the "public philosophy" demands, on the face of it, borders on naïveté. The evidence to support such a faith in human rationality is surely meager.

Second, Lippmann's repeated strictures against what he calls "majority rule democracy" misrepresent the nature of the American political system. It is doubtful that American democracy has ever functioned according to the dictates of the majority rule principle. The actual power Lippmann keeps ascribing to the popular will is questionable and misleading. The pluralist model—or consensus democracy—has long been acknowledged to be a more accurate rendition of how the American political system works and is supposed to work.[57] Even defenders of this model concede that minority (elite) power interests are more significant than any popular majority, whether expressed through Congress or through the top elected executive officer, in determining who gets how much of the Gross National Product pie.[58] Radical critics of the pluralist model are even less convinced that the majority has much real effect upon public policy.[59] So Lippmann's analysis of this important matter finds little support, and conservatives are even farther removed from delegating any substantial power or influence to the masses.

Despite significant changes in his thinking over the years, Lippmann has held to one constant throughout his writings: democracy must flourish independent of, not dependent upon, the role of the masses and general public opinion. A deep distrust of popular government and the idea of consent, or popular sovereignty, is a dominant theme in his political thought. His hope has always been that a responsible elite might be encouraged to develop and then given power commensurate with its leadership responsibilities. In the final analysis, this elite is neither political nor economic, but cultural: Lippmann's single greatest trust is in a highly educated, selectively chosen, and independently empowered meritocracy. The case for Lippmann's political philosophy stands or falls on this issue.[60]

And third, there is a question whether the idea of popular sovereignty, the principle of government by consent of the governed, can tolerate this kind of elitism, for it denigrates the role of politics as the ultimate equalizer of power and interest conflicts in the name of compromise. That ethical considerations are frequently the first and most serious casualty of this approach to democratic government may be as obvious as Lippmann says it is. But the alternative may be more dangerous than Lippmann can bring himself to admit. Even a benevolent elitism is no substitute for the messy give-and-take of majority rule/minority rights confrontations, the outcome of which, in any given case, is bound to be some form of consensus rule or minority veto power in temporary control of things.

The main weakness of Walter Lippmann's political philosophy is an unresolved internal contradiction between the highly rational, autonomous individual capable of willing his own values and goodness, and the collectivist nature of contemporary life, wherein the individual is more and more dependent upon society for his well-being. Lippmann underestimates the non-rational side of human nature, and here his liberal and conservative assumptions are reversed, for his optimistic faith in the ability of the few to overcome selfishness and to operationalize the public philosophy is contradicted by his pessimistic lack of confidence in the rational and moral capacity of most human beings. There is a broken connection in this aspect of Lippmann's thought process; he fails to show how so much irrationality can produce the needed rationality at the top. And he over-estimates the capacity of rational men for social responsibility. He is willing to trust governmental rule to an intellectual elite—a dubious idea, since intellectuals are notorious for both their lack of good political sense and for their excessive self-centeredness. As though intellectuals are any more immune from stereotyped thinking than the masses—one of Lippmann's more original concepts was to show how man's thinking is filtered through the lens of emotional wish-fulfillment rather than rational open-mindedness.[61] To be perfectly blunt: is there any such thing as a disinterested man or woman? Are rationality and selflessness qualities of the few, or are they just as rare among the scientifically trained experts with any more confidence that democracy will be well-served than is presently the case under political leaders selected on the basis of popularity or propelled into office by political machines and special interest groups? At best such a leader is subject to democratic politics— which is more than can be said of most experts, who are not likely to appreciate, either by training or inclination, the extrovert skills of wheeling and dealing, giving and taking, and always settling for less than is desired. The elitist expert is the wrong horse to back if democracy is to reconcile means and ends. Lippmann's understandable preoccupation with moral ends keeps him from dealing adequately with immoral means. One can applaud the intention, but the results are still unsatisfactory.

Walter Lippmann's strength as a political philosopher is in his willingness to grapple with the need to fuse ethical and power factors in the search for a viable democracy. His weakness is equally evident: the many have to be trusted and given more power if the few are to remain accountable to the democratic principles which everyone admires and then proceeds, frequently, to betray.

Friedrich A. Hayek

The gods must have smiled ironically when two world-renowned economists, Gunnar Mrydal and Friedrich A. von Hayek, were simultaneously honored with the 1974 Nobel Memorial Prize in Economic Science, since no two thinkers could be farther apart. Mrydal has long been a leading advocate of governmental intervention in the interests of promoting both greater economic stability and social justice; Hayek has been an equally notable exponent of a "hands-off" policy for government, and a return to a truly "free" market economy. Although both scholars received the prestigious award "for their pioneering work in the theory of money and economic fluctuations and for their pioneering analysis of the interdependence of economic, social and institutional phenomena," their reputations rest as much upon numerous forays into intellectual history and socio-economic-political analysis as on their specialized economic theories.[62] Hayek's 1944 book, The Road to Serfdom, was a rarity for the time, a scholarly best-seller, attracting a wide audience as well as generating intense controversy. Except for a twelve-year period as a Chicago University Professor, Hayek has lived and taught in Europe, and he is not, strictly speaking, an American thinker. Nor does he call himself a "conservative," preferring instead the label "liberal;" but it is obvious that his brand of liberalism is similar to "classical liberalism" of the Old Whig variety, and is therefore opposed to some forms of contemporary conservatism as well as to New Deal liberalism. However difficult he may be to classify, and however dubious his American credentials, there is one very good reason for including him in this survey: Hayek's The Constitution of Liberty is the single most impressive contribution to conservative political philosophy that has yet appeared. This 1960 publication combines rich historical analysis with a searching examination of how "true liberal and/or conservative" values can be applied to contemporary political science. His intellectual heroes include James Madison, Lord Macaulay, Tocqueville, Lord Acton, and Edmund Burke.[63] He favors democracy, but opposes unlimited government, especially of the majority-rule variety; he parts company with many conservatives in rejecting their authoritarian and elitist proclivities, and concludes: "It is not who governs but what government is entitled to do that seems to me to be the essential problem."[64]

Is human rationality man's greatest asset, or is it a liability? The question appears almost absurd on the face of it, since who would deny that man's mind is what most distinguishes him from the animal species? There is another way of looking at the matter, however: to the degree that man tries to impose a predetermined scheme on the natural order of events, he is asking for trouble; for any direct human intervention in the socio-economic-political order is contrary to man's best interests. This viewpoint has always been a major issue among right-wing conservative thinkers, who contend that this unwarranted and wrong-headed transgression of the limits of human rationality poses the most serious threat to a more stable and more desirable social order. This split between right- and left-wing conservatism has to do with whether one views power as a negative or positive factor in governing human affairs. Left-wing conservatives, such as Walter Lippmann or George Santayana, are not adverse to using the power of government to implement values they uphold; right-wing conservatives, such as Ayn Rand or Milton Friedman, would reduce the power of government over all aspects of human life to a minimum, and resist any effort to increase the power of government, whatever the purpose. Hayek would be somewhere in the middle of this division. He is against both privilege and indiscriminate elitism, and yet, unlike right-wing conservatives, he would endow government with responsibilities in some areas of public policy despite his strong antipathy toward government interventionism.[65] For left-wing conservatives, freedom ultimately depends upon necessity—that is, obligation and social responsibility are an important part of both self-realization and advancement of the public good; for right-wing conservatives, individual freedom is an absolute good, and a palpable wall exists between what is best for the individual and what society may deem best for the individual.

This split in conservative thought has significant consequences. It means there is little agreement among contemporary conservatives regarding the traditional assumptions about man, society, and the state, and there is considerable disagreement on the effects of conservative values on the employment of political power.[66] For some contemporary conservatives, like Rand and Friedman, tradition, authority, and order no longer represent the bedrock values of socially responsible conservatism; to others, like Strauss and Morgenthau, these values still matter very much, and the kind of conservatism which seeks to disconnect the individual from his social and/or political base elicits their disapproval. Hayek has tried to moderate these two positions. However, despite the good intentions and noteworthy efforts of Hayek and Frank Meyer, the gulf between these two divergent conservative outlooks is likely to widen and eventually to destroy whatever coherence the conservative tradition has managed to establish.[67]

Friedrich Hayek deplores the illusion of omnipotence and omniscience that has been the chief result of the tremendous prestige of modern science, for the so-called "knowledge explosion" is less than it appears to be, and there is no obvious connection between needed understanding and applied knowledge: "While the growth of our knowledge of nature constantly discloses new realms of ignorance, the increasing complexity of the civilization which this knowledge enables us to build presents new obstacles to the intellectual comprehension of the world around us."[68] Those rules and procedures which have evolved over time are what have made human freedom possible; the notion that freedom permits a person to actualize personal desires is essentially self-defeating, for freedom is only for those who can deal with it properly, not for everyone equally.[69] Freedom does not in any sense depend upon equality—it is exclusive, not inclusive, and is only open to the few who can really appreciate it: "The significant point is that the importance of freedom to do a particular thing has nothing to do with the number of people who want to do it: it might almost be in inverse proportion."[70] Paradoxically, freedom depends upon conformity to the "spontaneous forces of growth" in history, and not on technological advances or on the uses of political power.[71] In fact, according to Hayek's argument, these latter forces represent the chief threat to the realization of a truly libertarian social order. True progress comes through the unfettered achievements of a creative few, not the impersonal activities of government.

The greatest enemy of a free society is the planned society. All forms of socialism are abhorrent to Hayek and lead down "the road to serfdom," to recall the title of an earlier work.[72] Inequality and diversity can be equated; equality and uniformity go together; therefore the less egalitarian a society is, the more likely its development will be broadly beneficial to all the people, provided real merit can rise to the top and a privileged minority is prevented from merely perpetuating its privileged status.[73] Hayek believes in a kind of "survival of the fittest" form of institutional development, and he condemns any effort to impose change by "contrivance or design."[74] Believing that "we must always work inside a framework of both values and institutions which is not of our own making," he applauds the English libertarian tradition and condemns the French revolutionary tradition which mistakenly substituted the equalitarian ideal for a soundly based ideal of freedom.[75]

Morality is a means, not an end. Liberty and responsibility are indivisible. Hayek makes no allowance for social or economic handicaps that limit the individual's opportunity to make the most of his freedom. He makes no concession to conditions of inequality. On the other hand, he places no limitation on the right of the individual to be himself, regardless of the social situation; and he advocates absolute tolerance for any and all forms of individual expression, as long as they do not infringe upon others' coequal rights. He distinguishes individual from social responsibility, accepting the former and rejecting the latter.[76] Moral and legal equality are justified; social and material equality are not. The Good Society rewards merit, not social justice as a matter of individual right. Whether being poor is due to the accident of upbringing or to unfulfilled opportunity, the "have nots" have no claims upon the "haves," since human progress depends upon the incentive motive that enables the few to set the standards by which civilization improves itself.[77] Democracy depends not on any principle of majority rule but "on the belief that the view which will direct government emerges from an independent and spontaneous process. It requires, therefore, the existence of a large sphere independent of majority control. Advance consists in the few convincing the many."[78] Therefore, the single greatest threat

88

to democratic government is irresponsible majority power.[79]
A responsible elitism is the main hope for broad-based human betterment.

Freedom under law is the central concept of Hayek's political philosophy. But he also makes it clear that man-made positive law is not enough to insure freedom. In tracing the evolution of the concept of the rule of law from earliest times to the present, Hayek shows how general moral principles and constitutional limits on power provide a large framework for prescribing "the Constitution of liberty," yet "the rule of law...is also more than constitutionalism: it requires that all laws conform to certain principles."[80] This means that there are certain moral guidelines and established principles which constrain the exercise of power by legislative and executive officials over and beyond institutional mechanisms. These "rules" may not be altogether explicit, and the judicial system may have to exercise some discretion in interpreting them, but such general principles nevertheless exist as part of a democratic-libertarian tradition.[81] The point is that such general principles should guide and determine the outcome of policy-making. One cannot but wonder whether Hayek's argument here contradicts his otherwise strong commitment to a laissez-faire role for government.

Hayek does not close his eyes to the dangers of unrestrained growth in monopolistic economic power, but insists that the legal system can and should be adjusted to take care of gross inequities. What concerns him most, however, is that the present demand for "distributive justice" will weaken or destroy the "rules of law." This must not be permitted: "Within the limits set by the rule of law, a great deal can be done to make the market work more effectively and smoothly; but, within these limits, what people now regard as distributive justice can never be achieved."[82] It is not surprising, therefore, that Hayek reserves his strongest invectives for the recent inroads of "socialism," which he also associates with the "welfare state," since he sees this as the main threat to freedom everywhere. Government paternalism is neither helpful nor innocuous; by its dependence upon the efficiency expert, administrative-bureaucratic over-load, and the myth of democratic control, it is bound to lead to the loss of real freedom and responsibility.[83] The impersonal operation of a free market economy, according to Hayek, is the best guarantee of social progress and the safeguarding of individual liberty.[84]

Anything that denies individual free choice is bad—this applies to programs ranging from health insurance to social security plans. The idea is good, and should be supported, but the means should not rest upon a government monopoly in this vital area of human concern. Neither publicly-financed free medical services nor involuntary social security plans are the best way of solving these problems; the private sector should be given the responsibility in these endeavors.[85] Hayek believes that the attempts of modern governments to deal with social evils by collectivist methods present a greater problem than the social evils themselves. In other words, a mistaken remedy can do more harm than the acknowledged disease itself.[86] Even progressive taxation policies, especially when they escalate percentages on upper levels of income, are mistaken; although the intent may be to reduce inequality, the result is to undermine incentive, which is the main instrument of social progress.[87] The majority which determines the tax rates must also assume the greatest share of the tax burden.[88] Inflationary and deflationary conditions are caused by wrong political decisions and government policies; thus, the remedy lies in choosing the proper policies.[89] "Most competent students agree that the difficulty of preventing inflation is only political and not economic."[90] In effect, Hayek is saying that political interference in the private economic sector is the main cause of economic instability, and that a laissez-faire approach is the only guaranteed remedy for continued economic stability and progress.

Part of the reason why Hayek can be considered a strong candidate for the position of "premier conservative thinker of the twentieth century" is his scholarly productivity. In the eighth decade of his life, the books and the articles keep coming at an astonishing rate. For many years he has been engaged in a three-volume study entitled Law, Legislation and Liberty, which is to be a culminating analytical-philosophical treatise on the virtues, as well as necessity, of a libertarian ethic, the evils of all forms of collectivism-socialism, and some practical suggestions as to how the rule of just law can be linked to a concept of the public good in place of the present hegemony of interest-group liberalism, which Hayek believes to be a most dangerous tendency in democratic governments today.[91] Although he admits to its possible utopian elements, he feels that a dual legislative system whereby one branch would be immune from popular control and charged with special responsibility for maintaining the supremacy of an individualist-property dominant-free market system would go a long way toward improving present governmental performance. Here is a key passage setting forth this interesting proposal:

> We should want an assembly not concerned with the particular needs of particular groups but rather with the general permanent principles on which the activities of the community were to be ordered. Its members and its resolutions should represent not specific groups and their particular desires but the prevailing opinion on what kind of conduct was just and what kind was not. In laying down rules to be valid for long periods ahead this assembly should be 'representative of' or reproduce a sort of cross-section of, the prevailing opinions on right and wrong; its members should not be the spokesmen of particular interests, or express the 'will' of any particular section of the population on any specific measure of government.

They should be men and women trusted and respected for the traits of character they had shown in the ordinary business of life, and not dependent on the approval of particular groups of electors. And they should be wholly exempt from the party discipline necessary to keep a governing team together, but evidently undesirable in the body which lays down the rules that limit the powers of government.[92]

There is little doubt that if one accepts Hayek's basic premises, the logic of his analysis is persuasive and clear. What one has to do, therefore, is subject his premises to careful examination. They might be stated as follows:

(1) Human rationality is incapable of controlling events or designating what constitutes the good society. The scientific reliance upon "laws and regularities" is less than helpful and somewhat misdirected when applied to society. Hayek's conservative view of change is neatly expressed in this aphorism: "The world is fairly predictable only so long as one adheres to the established procedures, but it becomes frightening when one deviates from them."[93]

(2) The law, not political action, is the great strength of democratic systems of government. Law is grounded in tradition and custom, and "the only manner in which we can in fact give our lives some order is to adopt certain abstract rules or principles for guidance, and then strictly adhere to the rules we have adopted in our dealing with the new situations as they arise."[94]

(3) The political system should not encourage, defend, or perpetuate privilege. Because he believes this, Hayek refuses to consider himself a conservative and refers to himself as a true liberal, for the "essence of the liberal position...is the denial of all privilege, if privilege is understood in its proper and original meaning of the state granting and protecting rights to some which are not available on equal terms to others."[95]

(4) Politics and economics should be distinct and separate spheres of activity; anything that interferes with this situation endangers democracy. In fact, political freedom depends upon maximum economic freedom, or insulation of the private enterprise sector from political control and interference.[96] All the troubles of the post-World War II era can be traced to having abandoned this principle of sanctified individualism for the mirage of collectivism in its various manifestations, from welfare statism to fascist and communist totalitarianism. A minimum of regulated competition and total abnegation of planning controls is the only way true liberty can be restored. "When it becomes dominated by a collectivist creed, democracy will inevitably destroy itself."[97]

A point by point refutation of these assumptions would probably include the following criticism:

91

(1) Man's need to do everything in his power to exercise some control over events and the course of history is neither an exercise in futility nor a hopeless undertaking. Even if it is true that rationality conceals considerable ambivalence and can, on occasion, lead to greater harm than good, there is no reason to conclude this is always the case. Man's failure to at least try to control events may well be tantamount to an abdication of genuine human responsibility. Although the means will always be in dispute, the end need not be an either/or proposition, as Hayek seems to suggest is the case. The insoluble philosophical and practical dilemma of free will versus determinism is not resolved by putting all one's eggs in the basket of either impersonal determinism (i.e., Marxism) or personal indeterminism (i.e., Hayekism). Both views are polar extremes which may help in correcting the excesses of differing philosophical assumptions, but are not helpful when it involves choosing the best road to follow. Liberty and security are equally cherished common values, and if it is true that they are frequently in conflict with one another, it is also true that any social philosophy which would sacrifice one to the other is inherently unsatisfactory. Hayek would sacrifice needed social security for the many to achieve maximum liberty for the few. This is no more defensible than the Marxian willingness to sacrifice liberty for greater mass social security.

(2) A democratic legal system does not and cannot rely solely upon the law to maintain confidence in, and retain the legitimacy of, the system. The voluntary nature of compliance to law in a democratic polity rests upon a reasonable harmony between changing community attitudes and established legal principles. At no point does Hayek appear to recognize the significance of this third level of community opinion mediating between the law and its enforcement procedures. The law and its correlative principles, have to be adjusted to the changing needs of people from time to time, if they are to command voluntary acceptance and if the requirements of coercive implementation are to be reduced. Hayek would have it the other way; the law comes first and foremost, while the changing needs of people hardly count at all. Granted that good law is necessarily rooted in slowly evolving custom, tradition, and morality, this is not to say that bad, unjust, or unrealistic legal sanctions should not be protested, questioned, and even under certain circumstances, defied! At the very least, some such adjustment is both desirable and propitious if stability and change are to be reconciled in the interests of broad-based community support and voluntary compliance with the law. Hayek's position on this issue is both one-sided and unqualified: the principles of law are ascertainable and immutable, not adjustable. In the absence of consent, coercion is in order. Hayek fails to appreciate that coercion can take more than one form; structured roadblocks to change can be just as coercive as unstructured governmental power.

(3) It is hard to fault Hayek for the clear and forthright way in which he renounces any use of political power to

perpetuate unfair, undeserved privilege. However, throughout his analysis, he is guilty of the intellectual sins of calculated omission and biased selectivity, for he completely ignores the fact that reducing political control will not prevent, and in fact is likely to expedite, unequal proliferation of concentrated economic power. This, in turn, cannot help but affect the exercise of political power along undemocratic lines. In a thinker as sophisticated and acute as Hayek, this failure, or unwillingness, to deal with the tendency of economic privilege to become self-reinforcing and self-perpetuating at the expense of the democratic process and the public good, is perplexing. In this respect, his political philosophy degenerates into insubstantial assertion rather than cogent analysis.

(4) The straw man that Hayek has created, and which he calls "collectivism," is easy to attack and repeatedly knock down, but is devoid of substantive reality. With a minimum of historical analysis and differentiation, Socialism, Communism, Welfare Statism, New Deal type liberalism, are all lumped together, and conveniently, if inaccurately, labeled "the road to serfdom." He rejects outright any in-between development, such as a "mixed capitalistic economy," or a "mixed socialist economy." The situation is either/or. There are only two roads—one leading toward collectivist totalitarianism and the other toward laissez-faire capitalism. The choice is stark and the inevitable results uncompromising. There can be no compromise with liberty. Any weakening of individual liberty in the quest for a more equitable society will spell the end of democracy. If Hayek's conclusion is correct, then his premises are perfectly acceptable.

There is, however, another aspect of Hayek's thought which dilutes the strength of his analysis. His desire to reduce the role of government in the economic sphere while enhancing it in the social sphere is something of a contradiction. The great emphasis he places upon the regulative value of law does not mesh with his laissez-faire politics. He is not quite so willing to abandon the interconnectedness of self and society as are the libertarian-individualists who are featured in the next chapter; neither is he quite so willing to enshrine morality as a religious principle as the traditionalist-conservatives are anxious to do.

Hayek's desire to reconcile these two disparate tendencies in contemporary conservatism places him in Frank Meyer's "fusionist" classification, but he encounters the same difficulties that Meyer was never really able to resolve.[98] One of the main differences between liberals and conservatives is their contrasting views of the meaning of freedom: that is, whether freedom is viewed primarily as a means to other ends or as an end in itself. The liberal is on the side of positive freedom, and the conservative on the side of negative freedom. But since both ideologies tend to exhibit the defects of their virtues when stated in an extreme form (Rousseau versus Locke, for example), a conservative like Hayek obviously wishes to moderate these two extreme tendencies.

Difficulties with his theory arise whenever he attempts to clarify this worthy objective, for his main concepts, like "law," "serfdom," and "liberty" cannot sustain the weight of his analysis without fuzziness and contradiction. As is so often the case, he falters when he tries to eat his cake and have it too.

Whatever fault one may find with Hayek's premises, arguments, or conclusions, there is good reason to recommend The Constitution of Liberty as one of the best sources for a conservative political philosophy that attempts to relate the older liberal tradition to the social-political-economic problems of the contemporary world. However one may finally judge Hayek's success or failure in this regard, one can pay tribute to a mind that exhibits outstanding qualities of thoughtfulness, clarity, and scholarship. Whether or not one agrees with Hayek's basic position, it will be clear that one has engaged in dialogue with a probing intelligence and with a man whose defense of the libertarian ideal one cannot help but admire, even if his political philosophy also raises questions about misplaced priorities. Contrary to Hayek's major postulate, it may still be more accurate to conclude that equal priority must be given to both liberty and equality, rather than one at the expense of the other. Somehow, a viable democracy must find the means of reconciling liberty and equality. Is it possible that this is exactly what the 1974 Nobel Prize committee was trying to say when it bestowed recognition upon two thinkers who represented so well both horns of the dilemma?

Leo Strauss

Perhaps the only truly consistent thread that has connected conservative thinkers throughghought history has been a deeply felt concern to relate moral means to the exercise of power in politics and government. Whereas liberals tend to stress the ends of protective liberty and increased social justice, conservatives tend to emphasize the ends of objective morality and principled behavior.[99] Liberals have generally embraced the rise of modern positivism and relativism as standards for determining preferred values and the founding of a morality grounded in contingency. For the contemporary liberal, there is no longer any justification for dogmatically asserting any particular expression of human conduct as being clearly and unalterably right or wrong, permissible or sinful, good or evil. The circumstances and consequences of an action largely determine its appropriateness; and morality is relative, in that what may be good and advantageous in one situation may be the exact opposite in another, depending upon either extenuating factors or the way in which individuals are being affected. A liberal philosophy of man respects the problematic and quixotic elements of human action and looks for relative criteria for judging anything. Nothing is either/or. Everything is shades of greyness. The scientific method, the rigorous claims of empirical validation, and the close interrelatedness of cultural-social-economic factors reveal to the liberal both a world of unprecedented complexity and contingency, and the means by which man can exercise some control over his destiny. For the liberal, power and ethics are intertwined and often conflicting factors in determining what is desirable and proper behavior. Morality is what does the most good for the greatest number of people. It is essentially pragmatic and utilitarian.

Conservatives reject this approach to morality, considering it to be destructive of civilized standards, sure to undermine the pursuit of excellence, and absolutely pernicious in its appeal to the worst, rather than the best, aspects of human nature. A conservative thinker clings to the belief that there is an objective, universal, and unconditional side of morality, rooted in Christianity and Western humanism. In this tradition it is possible to discover what is right and wrong conduct, to relate ethics to clearly defined principles of individual rights and social responsibility, and to maintain standards in spite of the incursions of mass culture. It may be that only the few are truly capable of benefiting from, and exercising leadership in, this endeavor; but the conservative welcomes everyone to try and hopes there will be sufficient response to improve the quality of democratic society and polity. And as for modern science, the conservative has reservations as to whether it can be trusted to enable man to find the right path, or whether it is more susceptible to the dubious arts of manipulation, propaganda, and undemocratic social engineering; and he resists the widespread tendency to substitute a false god— science—for the true God of established religion.

Conservatives are moralists in the old-fashioned sense: they seek moral certitude in an increasingly secularized and immoral world, and they assert principles above pragmatic expediency in the interests of standards they acknowledge require the sort of self-discipline and commitment that most human beings are incapable of accepting. Democracy, to the conservative, is qualitative, not quantitative—it is the Good Society, not the Great Society. And because they realize their minority status, they try all the harder to shore up the dike as the waters of secularism and relativism and technocratism threaten to destroy the precarious fabric of civilization.[100] This may explain why a conservative political thinker like Leo Strauss attracts a small but dedicated band of followers: he stands firm on the battlements awaiting the inevitable onslaught of superior numbers, convinced of the rightness of his cause, and willing to die fighting but unwilling to consider any compromise with the enemy. One can respect such principled honesty even as one may question the persuasiveness of the message.[101]

Leo Strauss, who died in 1973, was a long-time professor at the University of Chicago, a highly respected teacher of political philosophy, and the author of numerous books, most of which dealt with a close textual analysis of classical and modern political theorists, such as Xenophon, Plato,

Aristotle, Machiavelli, Hobbes, Locke, and Rousseau. He was German by birth and came to the United States shortly before World War II. It is doubtful whether any contemporary scholar-teacher surpassed Leo Strauss in his knowledge and learned excavation of the classical period of Western philosophy. While there might be disagreement over the interpretation of Strauss's thought, it is easy to respect the intellectual originality and brilliance of his scholarly production. While he lived, Strauss was also a storm-center of academic controversy; there is no indication that it has subsided since his death at the age of 73. He has long been a pivotal figure in the endless conflict between the more or less dominant "behavioralist" movement in the political science discipline and the "traditionalists" in political theory.[102] As an outstanding exponent of classical political philosophy in a period when this approach had fallen out of favor among political scientists, and as an unbending critic of the newer developments in his field, Strauss both symbolized and actualized the tremendous internal struggle that has divided many contemporary political scientists into two camps, those who embrace and those who reject the empirico-scientific approach to a study of politics and government.[103]

It might prove convenient to consider Leo Strauss's political philosophy under three topics, coinciding with his major concerns. These could be stated as: (1) the nature and role of political philosophy; (2) a defense of objective morality; (3) an attack upon the main thrust of a scientific approach to the study of political behavior. Although all three points are highly integrated elements of his writings, reinforcing one another, it is possible to illustrate each major area of concern by focusing attention on a number of his works. For example, What is Political Philosophy? clearly addresses itself to the first area of concern, and provides a succinct introduction to the Straussian approach to political study. He announces flatly that there can be no harmony of interest between scientific and philosophical approaches to the study of political phenomena. The two approaches are incompatible.[104] Political philosophy obtains its validity as a mode of inquiry because it is preeminently normative; that is, it seeks to know truth, not use it; to achieve knowledge of the good life and the good society, rather than to offer prescriptions for them.[105] Since Strauss sees little evidence that his view is in the ascendancy, the conclusion that follows brings forth a strong indictment of what passes for contemporary political philosophy:

> Today, political philosophy is in a state of decay and perhaps of putrefaction, if it has not vanished altogether. Not only is there complete disagreement regarding its subject matter, its methods, and its functions; its very possibility in any form has become questionable.[106]

Strauss feels that political philosophy, even when it has not been displaced by "scientific empiricism," has become so fragmented that it lacks any substance or coherence.

The key question is being neglected for a lesser question;
not "how," but "why," should be the beginning and end of
philosophical analysis.[107] The heart of the matter is the
nearly universal tendency to separate fact and value in the
quest for neutral, value-free, and verifiable political knowledge. Such an approach is non-productive of real knowledge,
which in Strauss's view partakes of <u>both</u> subjective and objective characteristics, not one at the expense of the other.[108]
"The scientific approach tends to lead to a neglect of the
primary or fundamental questions and therewith to thought-
less acceptance of received opinion."[109]

Until some attention is given to the nature of the best
political order, irrespective of historical flux, opinion is
all that political inquiry can adumbrate. History is no real
guide for understanding political needs.[110] Principles, not
practices, are what count. It is not possible to make value
choices without an objective basis for distinguishing right
from wrong, better from worse. In <u>The City and Man</u> Strauss
continues to define this central theme of his political philosophy. The choice is between a reactivated study of classical political philosophy and a surrender to ideology.[111]
Studying the history of political philosophy, however, offers
no substitute; in fact, it compounds the distortion.[112] Only
a thorough, careful, and systematic study of "the teachings
of the political philosopher as they themselves meant them"
can begin to restore political philosophy to its rightful
and needed place as queen of the sciences.[113] The modern
preoccupation with scientific methodology can only arrest,
if it does not deny forever, the hoped for change and improvement. Aristotle's <u>Politics</u>, properly studied and understood, still contains more wisdom and truth than all the
efforts of latter-day positivism combined.[114] Implicit in
this approach is the suggestion that Strauss is promoting
his own method of textual analysis of the classical philosophers as the way to the promised land.

Leo Strauss uses the term "natural right" to designate
his conception of a pre-existing tradition of objective moral standards and principles. In fact, the Straussian position stands or falls on this issue. The fundamental assumption of his political philosophy is essentially Platonic <u>and</u>
Aristotelian: a dualistic metaphysics in which man transcends his corporeality by postulating an ideal realm of "natural right" as the repository of truth, knowledge, and wisdom; Strauss would say that this "natural right" tradition
exists, can be known and revealed.[115] Furthermore, "the contemporary rejection of natural right leads to nihilism..."[116]
Because modern science rejects outright a teleological cosmology, in which "all natural beings have a natural end, a
natural destiny, which determines what kind of operation is
good for them," modern man is being led astray.[117] Morality
depends upon certain universally valid principles which transcend history and are revealed only to those who are willing to
abide by their dictates; this means "oughtness" supersedes
"isness."[118]

Strauss agrees with Max Weber's distinction between facts and values, but disagrees with Weber's conclusion that there "cannot be any genuine knowledge of the Ought."[119] One cannot shirk the responsibility of making distinctions between better and worse, good and evil. True objectivity requires the ability to make value judgments.[120] But like all philosophers who have adopted a dualistic metaphysics and epistemology, Strauss has difficulty demonstrating how to get from "A" to "B"—that is, how to understand the proper meaning of, and relationship between, the general and the particular. Why should the general take precedence over the particular? Do individuals exist for morality or does morality exist for individuals? This crucial question has serious implications for Strauss's position. The Straussian answer, of course, is that morality cannot be relativized— it can only be obeyed. The prevailing contemporary view, however, is that morality cannot be known either absolutely or definitively, and for this reason, it is an individual and/or socio-cultural matter within the context of historical change. For Strauss, on the other hand, morality must be tied to a conception of the Good—and the Good has but one meaning, identifiable by the meaning attached to "natural freedom and natural equality," found in the classical origins of political philosophy.[121]

Through the medieval period, this concept was generally understood and accepted; but a watershed occurred in the seventeenth and eighteenth centuries with the advant of modern science and the "wrong-headed" interpretations of Machiavelli, Hobbes, Locke, and Rousseau by most modern scholars. This individualistic tradition in political philosophy paved the way for both liberalism and collectivism, ideologies which subvert the classic "natural right" tradition in political philosophy.[122] Liberalism damaged this tradition by shifting emphasis from duties to rights, thus substituting a doctrine of man's infinite perfectibility for man's imperfect nature.[123] The displacement of classical political philosophy by modern political philosophy has broken the connection between the "is" and the "ought," or power and ethics:

> This break with rationalism is, therefore, the fundamental presupposition of modern political philosophy in general. The acutest expression of this break which can be found in Hobbes' writings is that he conceives sovereign power not as reason but as will.[122]

In a brief essay, entitled "An Epilogue," which was included in Essays on the Scientific Study of Politics, a compendium of anti-behavioralist studies by four former Strauss students and colleagues, Leo Strauss listed his main objections to the empiricist coloration of so much contemporary political science. Besides reiterating his detestation of "historicism" and "positivism" as the twin evils of contemporary political analysis, Strauss went on to enumerate specific reasons for his rejection of "the new science of politics":

(1) Political science derives its authority and value from political philosophy, not vice versa. The divorce between politics and ethics ensued when the formerly intimate relationship between political philosophy and political science dissolved.[125]

(2) Natural and human sciences do not conform to the same principles. "The principles of action are the natural ends of man toward which man is by nature inclined and of which he has by nature some awareness. This awareness is the necessary condition for his seeking and finding appropriate means for his ends, or for his becoming practically wise and prudent."[126] Theory and practice, according to Strauss, do not inhabit the same worlds empirically, and only a rationalistic philosophy can unite these two realms.[127]

(3) The citizen is the center of political activity for the classical theorist; but in the new political science, he is displaced by the demand for neutrality created by the fact/value split. The new political science is, therefore, incapable of regarding the individual in his particularity as a moral end, and instead, looks upon him as an object of political manipulation for the purpose of social engineering.[128]

(4) The goal of the new political science is to predict behavior rather than to provide wisdom and guidance.[129]

(5) Politics, ethics, and rationality are intertwined in the classic view of philosophy, while the new political science sees no necessary connection between moral and practical concerns.[130]

There is much more to Strauss's critique of "the new science of politics," but his essential argument is that factual and value judgments, empiricism and rationalism, the "is" and the "ought" should not be separated in the pursuit of an illusory scientism that ignores the distinction between objectivity and subjectivity and places human and moral factors within the context of a one-dimensional cosmology.[131] "The new science rests on dogmatic atheism which presents itself as merely methodological or hypothetical."[132] Because it depreciates the ideal of a common good and the possibility of attaining the good society, the new empiricism is incapable of giving to democracy what is most needed: a basis for reconciling the ideal and the real.[133] This failure of the new political science is complete and irremediable. According to Strauss, "...the ultimate aim of political life cannot be reached by political life, but only by life devoted to contemplation, to philosophy."[134] As with Plato, Strauss looks toward the possibility that leaders might become philosophers and philosophers might become leaders: only thus can man, through culture, realize fully his better rather than his lesser nature and his purpose in life.

If the pursuit of excellence is a worthy endeavor, and if this pursuit requires standards that were established once and forever in a past golden age of philosophical inquiry, then Leo Strauss may be the best guide for navigating the treacherous waters toward a safe haven, avoiding being pounded to pieces by the Scylla of positivism and the Charybdis of Machiavellianism. On the other hand, if Strauss is less in tune with the infinite than he is mired in quicksand, it is likely to be a lonely voyage with only a handful of loyalists aboard. Critics have pointed out that "Strauss's method is subject to abuse," and the teacher himself was not immune from such a charge.[135] In spite of the commendable aim of studying the great thinkers of the past by putting on their own shoes, so-to-speak, and understanding their ideas as they presented them and without resort to spurious claims of relevance, Strauss's interpretations do not escape a high degree of arbitrary and subjectively imposed value judgments. His study of Machiavelli, for example, is studded with such questionable and even distorted comments as the following: "Machiavelli's teaching is immoral and irreligious...If it is true that only man will stoop to teach maxims of public and private gangsterism, we are forced to say that Machiavelli was an evil man."[136] The fact is, Machiavelli was a much more complex thinker than this Straussian evaluation suggests.

There is more than a hint of moral self-righteousness and intellectual arrogance in much of Strauss's writings. At the same time, he is seldom dull and consistently brilliant as he peels away the outer layers of a text in quest of the inner meaning—which may or may not be exactly what the author had in mind. The main problem, however, is his basic premise: he asserts a dualistic mind/matter metaphysics and does little to prove its efficacy. He rightfully dismisses the validity of such a proof, but since he is so antipathetic toward any substantive role for an empirical science of politics, much of his anti-positivism degenerates into polemics. To some degree, he misrepresents the "behavioralist" approach to a study of politics and squeezes his interpretations of the great thinkers into a procrustean bed of his own devising. It is noteworthy that he largely ignores the body of scholarly interpretation surrounding the thinkers he deals with, and makes something of a fetish of the Straussian encounter with the great thinkers of the past. In a way, Strauss is to political philosophy what the gourmet is to food: he exalts his superior knowledge while admitting the fact that only a few are capable of appreciating the bill-of-fare. This point is illustrative of an elitist bias which permeates all aspects of Strauss's thought, for good or ill. He said it best in this passage from "An Epilogue": "That which at least everyone who counts politically is supposed to look up to, that which is politically the highest, gives a society its character; it constitutes and justifies the regime of the society in question."[137]

As a conservative political philosopher, Leo Strauss is atypical, in that he preferred the contemplative over the activist stance, and found his inspiration in a Platonic realm of higher morality rather than Burkean realm of prescriptive rights and traditions. There is an esoteric quality to his writings that encourages would-be disciples but discourages the seeker of relevance, however defined. In other respects, however, he is a typical conservative think-er. He would like to save democracy from degenerating into mass mediocrity and a glorification of atomized, anti-social individualism. He seeks to recreate an aristocracy of mer-it within the democratic society by revitalizing liberal ed-ucation for the qualified few, rather than emphasizing mass education for all. Religious instruction would be an impor-tant part of this program.[138] He has no doubt that there are philosophical principles and moral standards that can be applied, under the guidance of the enlightened few, to achieve a better life for human beings in general. His scholarly ca-reer was devoted to the effort of excavating the buried parts of a rich and promising city of man that had once existed, and that might again be resurrected, in order to arrest the process of decay that had set in with various forms of mod-ernism. His anti-modernism made him a conservative polit-ical thinker; the quality of his thinking makes him a worthy guide to conservative political philosophy. If there is any validity in thinking of political philosophy as an end in it-self, intellectually stimulating but of limited practical val-ue, then the writings of Leo Strauss are among the most potent stimulants there are.

Willmoore Kendall

Three recent estimates of this political scientist who died in 1967, would place him high in any hierarchical rank-ing of contemporary political theorists. For Jeffrey Hart, "Willmoore Kendall remains, beyond any possibility of chall-enge, the most important political theorist to have emerged in the twenty-odd years since the end of World War II."[139] George H. Nash credits Kendall with "the most comprehensive and daring reinterpretation of America's political heritage developed by anyone on the Right since World War II."[140] John P. East, in an essay review of Kendall's major writings which appeared in the Fall, 1973 issue of the Political Sci-ence Reviewer, declared: "...as regards the American polit-ical tradition, it is easily argued that Kendall is the most original, innovative, and challenging interpreter of any per-iod."[141]

Yet, there is also evidence that he was considered a pariah by many of his academic colleagues, exhibited an oc-casionally unstable personality, had the unprecedented dis-tinction of having Yale University "buy up" his tenured con-tract in order to get rid of him, and enjoyed an up and down career at a succession of university posts. Having earned an Oxford B.A. and M.A. in the late 30's, he wrote what some consider to be a "classic in the field of political theory" for his Ph.D. dissertation at the University of Illinois, John Locke and Majority Rule.[142] Politically, he seems to have flirted with "the Trotskyist Left" while at Oxford and later as a United Press correspondent in Spain shortly be-fore the Civil War erupted in 1936; but the apparent take-over of the Republican government by Communists disillusioned him, paving the way to a deeply-felt anti-Communism and mark-

ing his swing to the Right. In later years, he was quite
willing to refer to himself as "an extreme Conservative."[143]

The two most notable intellectual debts he acknowledged
were to R.G. Collingwood, his Oxford mentor, and to Leo
Strauss, whose close textual analysis of the Great Tradition of Political Philosophy he sought to emulate, especially in his studies of John Locke and The Federalist Papers, and of whom he wrote: "The Strauss revolution in the
interpretation of modern political philosophy is the most
decisive development in modern philosophy since Machiavelli
himself."[144] In his last years, he was one of the editors
of National Review, the fount of contemporary ideological
conservatism, but there is ample evidence that he was more
critical of, than compatible with, his fellow conservatives,
and that he adhered to an original version of the conservative tradition that defies neat classification, but commands
respect. As a political theorist, Kendall wrote no major
treatise beyond his published doctoral dissertation on Locke,
and many of his later books were either collaborations or
simply compilations of his shorter pieces. He evidently had
difficulty finishing planned projects. However, the posthu-
mously-published Contra Mundum probably contains all that is
most relevant and potentially lasting in his contribution to
political theory. And at least one essay, "The 'Intensity'
Problem and Democratic Theory," which may be the last thing
he wrote, can be considered a major writing from any standpoint.[145]

Although most conservatives tend to favor some form of
elitist rule—fearing the effects that a thoroughgoing populist democracy might have on cherished conservative values,
the prospect that any such accretion of minority power might
also threaten the pluralist nature of American democracy has
been of concern to other conservatives. Willmoore Kendall
has never lost faith in the ultimate ability of "the people"
to express their interests while still honoring the vision
of the Founders, which, in Kendall's view, eschews both numerical majority rule and elitist minority rule in favor of
consensus rule. Surprisingly, this position would appear to
correspond with the contemporary liberal defense of consensus pluralism, yet Kendall is a severe critic of two leading
pro-pluralist liberals, Robert A. Dahl and James MacGregor
Burns.[146] He accuses these thinkers of betraying the unex-
celled vision of the Founders. By advocating a strengthened
Executive, a weakening of institutionalized separation of
powers, and a reformed Congress, they would destroy real consensus in behalf of an unfettered numerical majority will.

So the meaning of consensus democracy is very much at
issue in distinguishing Kendall's theory of American democracy from that of liberals such as Dahl and Burns. While
Dahl argues forcefully that the dangers of "majority tyranny"
are a myth, but the reality of "minority tyranny" is a continuing threat to the effectiveness of American government
because of the "undemocratic" nature of the legislative power structure, and while Burns talks about the four-party sys-

102

tem" of presidential versus congressional politics that invites deadlock and paralysis in the system, Kendall takes both these thinkers to task for their distorted understanding of what consensus democracy really represents in the American constitutional system.[147] Above all, it means there is no easy, quick, or sure way to get the popular support necessary to implement the major policy or structural changes (i.e., liberal reforms) that liberals desire, without tearing the social fabric apart and undermining democratic values. It means that the executive, legislative, and judicial branches of government should not be permitted to "make policy" on their own, heedless of "the deliberate sense of the American community": all three major organs of government must reflect a popular consensus behind proposed change before such changes can be instituted.[148] Otherwise, important minority interests will be ignored, and the "tyranny of the numerical majority" will prevail at the expense of the vital popular support that democracy requires for any substantive change.

It is ironical that, at a time when many pro-pluralist liberals find the political elite more democratically responsible than the masses, a conservative theorist like Kendall reaffirms his trust in the people. At the same time, he wishes to revitalize the concept of consensus in order to slow down the forces of change and make it difficult for any particular organ of government to act in the name of the people in the absence of a true political consensus.[149] Kendall would no doubt have been pleased if he had lived long enough to witness the disarray in the liberal camp as the emergence of the "imperial presidency" and the decisions of the Warren Court revealed the dangers that lurked behind a broken consensus.

Kendall maintains that the chief defect in the liberal's desire to make the system more responsive to a numerical majority and less dependent upon a difficult-to-achieve consensus relates to the "problem of intensity," which, in Kendall's opinion, is the major problem of democratic political theory today.[150] Democracy may be a form of government highly dependent upon popular support for policy changes, but the intensity factor can hardly be overlooked, given the widely-accepted view that the "majority" is usually ill-informed, apathetic, and weakly predisposed toward rationality, while minority opinion is likely to be extremely intense on both sides of a controversial issue. How these interests may be accommodated is a thorny problem for any viable democracy: the reconciliation of majority and minority interests must not do violence to the underlying democratic consensus. The problem is such that merely "counting heads" cannot suffice; democratic theory must find a way to make allowance for the intensity of individual preferences.[151] The capacity for self-government is at stake in this matter, which even transcends the issue of individual or minority rights. This is why the one-man-one-vote principle is a misnomer. Preferences are weighed as well as counted, and "the heavier ones tip the scale more than the lighter ones."[152] So some technique of weighing is inevitable; since the distribution of power is unequal, the integrity of a democratic system requires a means of achieving consensus decision-making on all important policy matters.

Kendall next concludes that the criterion for weighing is a crucial concern for a theory of democracy. If policy change is weighted on the side of a powerful minority interest, the result is bound to weaken legitimacy; if policy change is weighted on the side of an equally powerful majority that transgresses the legitimate concerns of powerful minorities, this poses a serious danger to political stability.[153] Either way, democracy is bound to be the loser. In effect, Kendall rejects both the Adams-Hamilton minority rule model and his version of the Dahl-Burns majority rule model because neither can effectively safeguard against serious abuses of power.

The solution is a consensus model wherein the "whole people" have the real power of decision, for "what makes a democracy workable, and hence viable, is precisely the apparently impossible combination of these two principles (majority rule, minority rights) in a 'system' whose characteristic feature is this: it gets its decisions made by the majority, but in such a fashion that those decisions elicit what amounts to unanimous, or virtually unanimous, support or acquiesence."[154] Kendall seems to feel that it is possible to take into account "correct reciprocal anticipations," whereby the intensity of opposition to policy change can be gauged in advance, and if sufficiently strong, can act as a signal to policy-makers to cease and desist. For instance, if the judiciary should attempt to impose equalitarian standards for revamping educational procedures upon a community where popular resistance is notable, then the status quo should be maintained. Any appeal to "democratic ideals" or "equal rights," even when upheld by a judicial interpretation of the law, is indefensible under such circumstances.[155] "A democratic system which fails to provide adequate reciprocal anticipation among the participants does so at its peril."[156]

Finally, Kendall gets back to home base. In place of the populist, or majority rule model, which he attributes to a misguided liberalism, he offers the _Federalist_ mode, or the liberal's much maligned Madisonian model. According to Kendall, this model emphasizes the need for consensus "if the people as a whole" manifests itself, rather than the "will of the people" expressed through just one branch of the government at a time.[157] And in the absence of a clear mandate for change, expressed through popular elections reflecting a genuine rapprochement between majority and minority interests, the status quo deserves to be maintained.[158] Only thus can the democratic character of the system be preserved.

Needless to say, the liberal response to this analysis would be to show how the very opposite of Kendall's intention would no doubt result from a system where consensus

104

had to be achieved before any change could take place. Discontent is not likely to be contained in a situation where inequities are allowed to fester and vested interests cannot be brought under some degree of accountability to the majority interest. Can stability be maintained if it means that the strong and powerful can have their way while the weak and powerless are resigned to their lowly fate? What about the politics of paralysis and deadlock that would so often follow in the absence of consensus rule? There are two sides to consensus: change and stability. A political theory that sacrifices either to the other is bound to reveal its inadequacy. It may well be that Kendall is correct in showing the dangerous implications of a democratic theory which would seek to by-pass consensus politics in favor of some form of numerical majority rule, but his own version of consensus politics has one notable drawback: in a democracy, those who would benefit most will be the few, not the many.

To challenge an orthodox view of a major development in political science takes either courage or arrogance, for it is rare that such a challenge stands up under the barrage of criticism that can be anticipated from the scholarly fraternity. To do so as a neophyte in the profession is virtually unprecedented: but this is what Willmoore Kendall chose to do in his Ph.D. dissertation, in which he interpreted John Locke as the philosopher of an undemocratic collectivism rather than of democratic individualism. To succeed—at least to the extent that his version of Lockeanism, although not irrefutable, nevertheless continues to remain influential—is nothing short of amazing. His success was aided by the soundness of, and the relevance of, his interpretation of a key problem of democratic theory: the means by which majority and minority interests should be accommodated. It must also be added that the bite of originality and a powerful mind were also very much in evidence.

Put briefly, Kendall argued that Locke was not the great defender of individual natural rights and limited governmental power that he has been considered to be; but he was, instead, "an extreme majority rule democrat."[159] Locke's tendency to equate individual self-interest with commonality of interest, if applied systematically, easily becomes an authoritarian prescription for subjecting individual interests to that of the sovereign power—which in Locke's scheme of things would be a popularly elected representative assembly functioning in accordance to the majority rule principle.[160] According to Kendall, Locke erroneously assumes that public opinion embodied in a legislature will be responsible and responsive to the broader public interest.[161] At the same time, Locke endows the commonwealth with power commensurate with the need to prevent unregulated individualism from deteriorating into anarchy; in the process, obligation begins to take precedence over rights.[162] Sovereignty and individualism merge; rights and duties now bear the stamp of community power rather than individual protection.[163] The shift is all in one direction, however: the majority's right to rule as it sees fit and the citizen's duty to obey the majority becomes irrevocable; and

105

"the proper interest of the individual becomes merely un-
questioning obedience to the will of the many."[164] In conclusion, Kendall finds in Locke a potentially dangerous,
anti-democratic doctrine: the numerical majority rule advocated by Locke may readily become authoritative edict, and
even the rule of law or constitutional limitations cannot
save a political system which makes majority rule the locus
of sovereignty. It is a warning to all liberals who would
trade institutional checks and balances for the majority
rule principle in the interests of "better government." The
real Lockean lesson has been concealed by a good deal of
wishful thinking. Kendall's reinterpretation of Locke pur-
ports to uncover a majoritarian-authoritarian collectivist
in place of a natural rights democrat.

As a conservative political philosopher, Willmoore Kendall was opposed not so much to change, as to the direction
it might take. If it meant "the development and perfection
of our heritage," then change was good, but if it was "calculated to transform that heritage," it must be resisted at
all cost.[165] His scholarly labors were dedicated to extract-
ing from a careful reading of the works of the Founding Fathers, especially The Federalist Papers, a true understanding
of the nature of the American democratic tradition. Kendall's
conservatism is simply stated: "fidelity to the principles of
the founders."[166] Beyond this, there is need to recognize a
fact that is too often ignored: "The American political tradition itself is a Conservative tradition with a Conservative
content..."[167] Liberals have conspired to obscure this basic
fact about America by (1) reinterpreting the First Amendment
in behalf of individual rights, at the expense of a homogen-
eous moral-religious consensus that presumably should hold
the society together; (2) using every opportunity to convert
American government into an absolute majority rule (i.e.,
plebiscitary) system; (3) equating justice with equality,
and being "friendly toward the kind of leveling whose predictable result would be world-wide uniformity."[168] An "o-
pen society" is a pernicious ideal, since "any viable society has an orthodoxy—a set of fundamental beliefs, implicit
in its way of life, that it cannot and should not and, in
any case, will not submit to the vicissitudes of the market
place."[169]

Kendall emphatically opposes liberalism by rejecting
equality as a legitimate democratic ideal. He accepts legal
and moral equality; but insists upon a restrictive interpretation of the meaning attached to this famous phraseology of
the Declaration of Independence.[170] He categorically opposes
any public or governmental commitment to "assure to all of
our citizens genuine equality of opportunity; to remove from
our national life...all identifiable barriers to equality of
opportunity; to leave nothing undone that could contribute
to equality of opportunity..."[171] Such a policy would penal-
ize those responsible citizens whose unqualified commitment
to individual initiative has been the mainstay of the American way of life, and would produce a weakening of society's

moral fabric.[172] Once again, it is characteristic of Kendall that he calls 'em as he sees them, even when his conceptualization of the American tradition conflicts with a more popular version:

> The Conservatives could argue, again with considerable show of reason, that the Open Society is on the face of it unworkable, because its very idea presupposes a demonstrably false view of human nature since human beings as we know them, and particularly as we see them in America, cannot be prevailed upon to behave as the Open Society expects them to behave (i.e., to tolerate the dissemination of opinions that they deem outrageous). They could demonstrate and back up the demonstration with overwhelming evidence that the open-society conception of America is, on the record to date, unacceptable to vast numbers of Americans, and that this is a fact that the Liberals, however right they may be in theory, ignore at their peril.[173]

Moderation was evidently not a virtue to Willmoore Kendall; one gets the feeling such a stance would be deemed, purely and simply, a cop-out. His world-outlook incorporated neither shades of grey nor technicolor, but rather sharp contrasts of black and white. He defended Senator Joe McCarthy, long after many other loyalists had defected in disgust at the man's tactics. He could have been called a militant anti-Communist. He was attracted to moral absolutes—a man of ends whose own authoritarian propensities were barely concealed. Moderate liberals and conservatives elicited his scorn, since the America he loved was in peril, and the tradition he worshipped was vulnerable to its myriad enemies, mainly on the Left. He was wary of not only the danger of Communist espionage and subversion, but also "the liberal philosophy of natural rights and civil liberties," which weakened the ability of the state to protect itself against its enemies.[174] He seemed to relish the controversy he created and relished espousing unpopular causes. Reading Kendall is like a ride on a Coney Island roller-coaster: lots of abrupt ups and downs, twists and turns; and seldom a dull moment. Even when one disagrees with him, as frequently one must, there is probably more excitement and intellectual pleasure engaging in a dialogue with Willmoore Kendall than with just about any other thinker one can name. His extremism was real enough, but so was his scholarly originality and analytical brilliance. As a conservative political philosopher, he is less than trustworthy; but he is also deeper than most. Unfortunately, he was probably his own worst enemy.

Hannah Arendt

No aspect of conservative political philosophy has been more misunderstood than the appeal to authority—or rather, to the authoritative affirmation of standards that establish guidelines for right and wrong behavior, regulate civic morality, and limit individual self-expression for the good of the social order. The American political and social experience has been inimical to this outlook since the predominant secularism of the Founding Fathers fostered the principle of religious pluralism, and a "Protestant ethic" blurred the line between the pursuit of material acquisitiveness and the virtuous life. As a result, Americans have largely succeeded in segmenting the moral and secular demands of life; in the process, an appeal to individual rights has inevitably tended to take precedence over the appeal to social duty. Any manifestation of authority appears to threaten democratic values, and a convenient but dangerous split occurs between man's individual rights and his social responsibilities.

An extreme individualism that eventually takes on ideological content can mask the dichotomy between self and society, making it difficult to bridge the chasm between individual desire and social necessity. A relativistic secularism, which emphasizes such values as "freedom of choice" and "do your own thing," further sanctifies individualism, and, at the same time, helps to undermine the equally important need to contain the anarchic, anti-social excesses of unrestrained individualism. Authority, because it challenges the major tenet of democracy, individual natural rights, is seen in a strictly negative context. So a conservative thinker is not only challenging prevailing orthodoxy, embodied in institutional and ideological power structures, but is bound to be accused of either misunderstanding or attacking democratic norms.

Yet, there is good reason to wonder whether a conservative political and social philosophy does not offer a needed corrective to a dominant liberalism that is sometimes blind to the schizoid tendencies inherent in a liberal tradition which contains the seeds of its own extremism—that is, a commitment to relativistic and secular values which denies the need for an integrated self/society, authoritative/individualist, political/social structure. Among contemporary thinkers of note, Hannah Arendt, who was born and received her early education in her native Germany, but was forced to flee Hitlerism in the 30's to save her life, has addressed herself to this problem in a succession of incisive studies that blend historical scholarship, philosophical analysis, and a sharp awareness of what is relevant for a better understanding of the contemporary socio-political world. When she died at the age of 69 in December, 1975, Hannah Arendt was widely acclaimed as one of the handful of truly original and first rate political philosophers of the period.

There is an astonishing quality of breadth and depth in her writings. The Origins of Totalitarianism, which traces the strain of anti-Semitism in modern history, and links it to the psycho-social background of mass movements during the rise and fall of Hitlerism, is now considered a classic study. The Human Condition is regarded by many as an analytical masterpiece, as it explores philosophical aspects of the impact

108

of industrialism on the modern social fabric. There is also her more controversial profile of Adolf Eichmann, Hitler's chief instrument for implementing his genocide policy against European Jews during World War II, whom she describes as the bureaucratic personification of "the banality of evil." Then seizing on one of the more significant political phenomena of the times, she wrote a book-length essay, On Revolution, an insightful comparative analysis of the American, French, and Russian Revolutions which offers a rich tapestry of historical and political analysis. A collection of essays, Between Past and Future probably comes closest to revealing her basic values and expresses a philosophical conservatism that avoids the twin pitfalls of ideological one-dimensionality and pragmatic superficiality—characteristics so prevalent in much of what now passes for conservative political thought.[175]

Another collection of essays, Crisis of the Republic, continues her concern with showing how weaknesses in democratic political systems, if not corrected, invite a more serious breakdown in the institutional structure. In Men in Dark Times and Rachel Varnhagen: The Life of a Jewish Woman, Miss Arendt turns her attention to biographical themes, but retains her firm grasp of the interactions between the person and the times. At the time of her death, she had completed two of a three volume philosophical treatise, entitled The Life of the Mind, published posthumously, containing the sections on Thinking and Willing, but without the concluding section on Judging.[176] What is most striking about these various works is the masterful integration of historical, political, and philosophical analysis.

According to Arendt, the modern mind is a divided phenomenon; political action lacks philosophical direction; and philosophy lacks practical relevance. This "opposition of thinking and acting...depriving thought of reality and action of sense, makes both meaningless."[177] The recovery of a more coherent and integrated tradition of thought wedded to action constitutes the major task confronting modern man. Contemporary man's disdain of the past, which has made the wisdom of the past embodied in tradition virtually inaccessible, came about when the French Revolution unleashed mass demands for a better life, demands which could not be accommodated within existing institutional structures. The industrial revolution made mass misery remediable, but at the price of civic morality; and the rise of totalitarianism in both its bureaucratic and political guises left the individual impotent against the conformitarian pressures of modern life.[178] The accompanying loss of faith in the possibilities of redemption through reason and community has sparked the decline in the belief that man can exercise any control over his tragic destiny.[179] In this respect, Kierkegaard, Marx, and Nietzsche are the true apostles of the emergent modern consciousness, since they are "guideposts to a past which has lost its authority."[180] The intimate and invaluable connection between being and doing has been broken,[181] and the vi-

tal distinction between the sacred and the profane dissolved.[182] The politicization of man, another name for "the
world alienation of man," followed.[183] The ensuing split between thought and action is the hallmark of the contemporary
value crisis.[184]

The objective world of process and the subjective realm
of meaning are united through history.[185] Contemplative
thought and political action were once mutually reinforcing
historical realities; but with the widespread acceptance of
Cartesian doubt, and the subsequent decline of Christian
faith, discontinuity has triumphed. Meaning has been reduced to the level of human activity and has been robbed of
its transcendent character; expedient means are confused
with ethical ends;[186] and individual self-worth becomes the
casualty of a dehumanizing mass society.[187] Arendt deplores
the egalitarian, leveling trend that undercuts authority and
hierarchical order,[188] for it is the latter which gives freedom its substance,[189] and legitimizes the exercise of power.[190]
Even the highly regarded democratic ideal of Church/State separation elicits Arendt's disapproval, for this, too, has contributed to the slippage of authority; and Arendt regards
authority as "the miracle of permanence" that once had "endowed political structures with durability, continuity, and
permanence."[191] The triadic interrelatedness of religion,
authority, and tradition represents the ideal good that no
longer exists, as it did briefly in Greek and Roman times.[192]
Arendt concludes:

> For to live in a political realm with neither au-
> thority nor the concomitant awareness that the
> source of authority transcends power and those who
> are in power, means to be confronted anew, without
> the religious trust in a sacred beginning and with-
> out the protection of traditional and therefore self-
> evident standards of behavior, by the elementary
> problems of human living together.[193]

If the rule of law is the bedrock requirement of a
healthy democracy, then any form of "disobedience to the law,
civil and criminal" poses a threat to democratic legitimacy
and opens the way for eventual revolutionary changes that are
bound to be disastrous.[194] "The simple and rather frightening truth is that under circumstances of legal and social
permissiveness people will engage in the most outrageous criminal behavior who under normal circumstances perhaps dreamed
of such crimes, but never considered actually committing
them."[195] It would appear, therefore, that Hannah Arendt is
quite concerned about any resort to "civil disobedience," on
the grounds that it would merely serve to weaken institutional processes and would invite greater disorder than even a
stable political system can accommodate. At the same time,
she recognizes that a government based upon popular consent
also needs to acknowledge the right to dissent.[196] As a form
of "voluntary association," civil disobedience is in accord
with the American tradition.[197] Organized minority protest
against majority power could be legitimized by taking it out

of the context of law-breaking, and by accommodating such activity within the political structure itself, much as special interest groups are permitted to use lobbying tactics on government officials in order to exert influence on the decision-making process. It is an interesting proposal, but it is doubtful whether the potential efficacy of "civil disobedience" could be sustained in a "politics as usual" environment.

Hannah Arendt is at her best as an historian of ideas, and despite occasional lapses into obfuscation, her analysis is consistently stimulating and frequently profound. Her concerns are exemplary: she seeks for man's better nature to manifest itself in a modern political culture that offers very little nourishment for that better self. That the humanistic tradition can be utilized more effectively to obtain solutions for contemporary human problems, and that freedom itself derives its real strength from legitimized authority, cannot be denied. But there is a dilemma at the heart of Arendt's political philosophy, and it cannot be satisfactorily resolved if the need for a better life for the many is to be taken into account. For the elitist overtones of Arendt's political philosophy are evident; and the restoration of civic morality, which Arendt considers essential in combatting the present value crisis, cannot possibly be effectuated without involving the very masses she holds in such unrelieved contempt.[198] Any solution that sanctions a permanent rift between the few and the many, with all the benefits flowing to the top and only meager leavings for the bottom, is bound to be self-defeating in a world of growing socio-economic interdependence and egalitarian aspiration. Once this alternative is ruled out, ipso-facto, one is left with no solid ground on which to build a better structure of values. There will simply not be enough people around to really enjoy the good life. As Hannah Arendt knows, violence is the handmaid of unfulfilled expectations. Hanna Fenichel Pitkin has drawn the appropriate lesson from this outlook:

> This is a distressing doctrine, for on the one hand it means that the great values offered by political life are by their nature confined to a wealthy elite, so that the great majority of mankind is condemned to exclusion from self-government and full human development. On the other hand, it is difficult to believe in the great value that theorists like Aristotle, Tocqueville, and Arendt attach to political life, if, by definition, it is impotent to deal with the real needs of most people. One wants to object: no wonder the political debates of those aristocrats were above mere economics and devoted to 'higher things'; they helped themselves to what they needed economically outside of politics, by forcibly excluding from the political realm those who needed to raise economic questions. What is so noble about that picture?[199]

Critics of mass society, like Hannah Arendt, are standing on one leg—a tiring and immobilizing stance. They see only the bad and none of the good in a multi-faceted reality—as Daniel Bell has persuasively argued:

> If it is granted that mass society is compartmentalized, superficial in personal relations, anonymous, transitory, specialized, utilitarian, competitive, mobile, and status-hungry, the obverse side of the coin must be shown, too—the right to privacy, to free choice of friends and occupation, status on the basis of achievement rather than of ascription, a plurality of norms and standards, rather than the exclusive and monopolistic social controls of a single dominant group.[200]

True enough, anything that enhances genuine individual freedom is good and anything that denies meaningful individual autonomy is bad; but concepts like mass society, anomie, and alienation, are usually so indiscriminately applied by social scientists of all stripes that they become merely convenient whipping posts serving ideological needs and purposes. Although Miss Arendt is too subtle a thinker to deserve this criticism in any definitive sense, it is still a fact that she does not entirely escape the charge of intellectual myopia: the values she champions are special, suitable for a rather exclusive club composed of those who have already made it, and have acquired the cultural veneer that insulates them from the day-to-day struggles for survival. Conservatives can afford to uphold a standard of excellence as long as they don't have to punch a time-clock or face economic uncertainty. This is not the fate of the masses, even in a relatively affluent society. They can't enjoy the luxury of being free in that sense, and, needless to add, in a democracy, they count too.

In conclusion, Hannah Arendt's recent writings are too critical of American society and institutions to permit labeling her a conservative thinker. In fact, Nathan Glazer, who has been drifting steadily rightward in recent years, chastized Arendt harshly for being unfairly critical of American developments and "soft on Communism" in a recent essay in _Commentary_ magazine:

> If Dr. Arendt's naked facts are so faulty when she deals with topics that touch on totalitarianism, a subject on which she has given us so much wisdom, it is not surprising that her facts seem even odder when she comes to areas in which she is less at home, and in particular the problems of the American economy.[201]

On the other hand, the numerous tributes to her intellectual achievement which have appeared since her recent death single out her stance as a defender of individual freedom against all forms of authoritarianism as the basis of her true importance.[202] However one regards her repeated admonitions against the extension of "participatory democracy" and mass culture—and in this area she does stand for a con-

servative defense of established values—there is no justification for slighting the liberal, even radical, thrust
of her vision of a more qualitative democratic ethos.[203]
As Margaret Canovan has pointed out in a study of Hannah
Arendt's thought: "The central point of her thinking is her
insistence that men are unique individuals capable of original action."[204]

Although her thinking about politics occasionally becomes overly abstract and unrealistic, Arendt achieves a
deeper level of philosophical acuity that makes her an enduring critic of those elements in the democratic experience
that need to be fought and eliminated. Among these elements
are the mindless emotionalism of public opinion, and the
American tendency to reject the wisdom of the past out of
hand in favor of a preoccupation with nowness. In this
respect, Hannah Arendt was more often on target than Nathan
Glazer and other critics recognize. She is a political philosopher who will probably still be read after many better
acclaimed thinkers recede into the mists of time.

Hans J. Morgenthau

If one were to judge a political thinker on the basis
of the accuracy of his critical analysis and the subsequent
correctness of his policy stances, then this German-born,
former Chicago University professor must be ranked high indeed. Not only was Hans J. Morgenthau one of the very few
voices to proclaim the utter folly and moral bankruptcy of
America's military intervention in Southeast Asia long before the tide of popular support began to recede in the late
sixties; if his advice had been followed, it is quite likely
that recent American history would have been different and
probably better. As a long-time student of foreign relations
and power politics, Morgenthau recognized the changes that
were occurring in the world power structure long before either the American leadership or the public could bring itself
to lift the veil of illusion that increasingly characterized
cold war decision making. He advocated a "new realism" that
would transcend the ideological fixations which distorted
and ultimately proved disastrous for American foreign policy
and internal stability. In retrospect, he was on the right
track when so many others were on the wrong track; and if in
no other respect, Morgenthau deserves credit for being a
thinker of uncommon perspicuity and wisdom.

Most of his writings over a quarter of a century have
been critical commentaries on current events and have focused upon personalities, events, and historical currents.
They appeared in such periodicals as The New Republic and
Commentary, and were later collected in a succession of volumes. A strong theoretical substructure has always infused
his writings with a distinctive political philosophy that
the late George Lichtheim quite aptly referred to as "the
politics of conservative realism."[205] Pinning a label on
the protean theorizing of a Hans Morgenthau is probably an

exercise in futility.[206] At the same time, there is good
reason to single him out as both symbol and actualizer of
this strand of philosophical conservatism, which has represented a notable contribution to the response of political
theory to the conditions of the twentieth century.

Despite their many differences, Santayana, Lippmann,
Hayek, Strauss, Kendall, Arendt, and Morgenthau are similar
in their searching, insightful, and intellectually powerful
understanding of the interrelatedness of morality and politics. Together, they represent a rich legacy of critical analysis that seeks to discover both the discrepancies and the
integrative possibilities of democratic promises and practices, as well as an earnest effort to uncover principles
that might enable modern man to do a better job in guiding
his human destiny.

Most contemporary political thinkers can be placed in
one of two separate camps, depending upon whether they accept
or reject the hegemony of empirical methodology and the goal
of a science of man. The question is: Should the social sciences embrace a positivistic or a philosophical mode of inquiry? In other words, should the social sciences emulate
the tremendous strides of the natural sciences in providing
man with descriptive and predictive knowledge based upon a
rigorous application of the scientific approach to a study of
man, society, and the state; or is this an impossible, if not
self-defeating endeavor, given the greater complexity, unpredictability, and multi-purpose quality of human behavior in
comparison to that of the physical world? The stakes are
high, the controversy rages. Even when one recognizes the
overriding need to reconcile these two seemingly incompatible
approaches to the study of man, it is difficult to do so, or
even to remain neutral, since circumstances, as well as a
basic disjunction of interests, compels one to choose between
the two camps.

To a considerable degree, liberal political thinkers
tend to grasp that horn of the dilemma which opts for a science of man, society, and political processes, while conservative political thinkers tend to reject this approach for a
more historical and philosophically grounded approach to the
study of man, society, and government. The liberal desires
knowledge that can be applied to problem-solving and to the
enhancement of man's potential control over his destiny. The
conservative desires knowledge that can be applied to a better understanding of man's limitations in an irrational universe, and to an enhancement of man's moral capacity to do
what is right rather than what is merely useful. These are
fundamentally opposed world-views, based upon contradictory
ends and contradictory value preferences. However desirable
it may be to somehow achieve the best of these two equally
valid outlooks, it must be obvious that such a solution is
illusory. Americans have probably come closer to reconciling
the irreconcilable in practical terms than any other people
in history, but the evidence is accumulating that contemporary conditions no longer permit such an accommodation, and

114

that the need to make hard choices will become more insistent over time. As this unenviable and unprecedented situation looms on the horizon, the liberal-conservative split will take on crucial significance. Hans Morganthau recognized this dilemma earlier than most, and deserves to be listened to with respect.

Is science the enemy of morality? A superficial answer to this question is that they are separate and distinct realms which should not be confused, that science aspires to value-free objectivity, descriptive accuracy, and predictive power, whereas morality is mired in subjectivity, imprecision, and normative ambiguity. To adopt this position, usually referred to as "philosophical positivism," means divorcing fact and value, means and ends, object and subject, in the quest for knowledge. In this view, science and morality perform different functions: science seeks knowledge and morality seeks meaning, and in essence these represent different kinds of truth. Scientific truth can be confirmed through cause-effect regularities and sufficient empirical data; morality requires a transcendent order of meaning which may or may not be earth-bound, but still leaves the question of truth unverified. Scientific and philosophical modes of truth-seeking collide only when traffic signals that are designed to regulate their activities are not obeyed. The findings of each will be contaminated if either should invade the other's realm and challenge the integrity of two entirely distinct modes of inquiry and truth-seeking.

Hans Morgenthau rejects this widespread point of view regarding the proper relationship between science and morality. In one of his earliest works, Scientific Man Versus Power Politics, he launches a vigorous critique of this tendency to "reduce" the study of man to "scientism," and to substitute a misguided quest for objectivity for a truly philosophical approach that would seek to unify ethical-scientific modes of inquiry. In a later book, Science: Servant or Master?, he picks up the same theme and talks about the "moral crisis of science," which has coincided with a general disintegration of human values in the world.[207] In Morgenthau's view, preoccupation with a narrowly conceptualized scientific approach to politics has deprived political science of its major mission: helping man to achieve wisdom concomitant with the increased severity of contemporary problems.[208] It has also generated illusions as to the degree of rationality and control that is possible, given the irrational basis of human striving,[209] and has broken the circuit which connects practical life with man's transcendental value aspirations.[210] Thus, "the moral disintegration of science through the loss of its transcendental meaning leads in the end to the destruction of science itself as a system of theoretical knowledge."[211] Yet, having stated lucidly and effectively his opposition to a narrowly scientific approach to the study of man, Morgenthau offers only vague allusions to a "divine order" and an equally dubious glorification of the "scholar-philosopher" as more reliable guides to the sort of wisdom which he prefers as an antidote to a debased scientific util-

115

itarianism.[212] He provides little in the way of practical wisdom when it comes to answering the key question of political science: who should rule, and according to what procedure? He is most concerned about the bureaucratic rigor-mortis that characterizes government today; but except to point out the danger of a democratically unaccountable "technological ethos" taking power away from the elected political elites, through increased dependence upon their "expertise," he develops no theoretical model that might show how "the science of power" can be brought under democratic control and oriented to the needs of people.[213] Social critics are not obligated to provide solutions to the ills they identify, but a good political philosopher must assume responsibility for converting criticism into theoretical prophylactics. Morgenthau is an excellent diagnostician, but a poor dispenser of remedial measures, for a patient that is in dire need of them.

Hans Morgenthau is best known for his monitoring of international politics since the end of World War II; and for the many articles he has written, which criticize the assumptions and the perceptions of changing historical conditions that have influenced a succession of American leaders. He is also the author of a highly respected and widely used textbook for students of international relations, Politics Among Nations, now in its fifth revised edition. So his writings have had a wide audience, and must have influenced the thinking of many individuals. As a charter member of the "realist" school of power theorists, Morgenthau has been associated with Walter Lippmann, George F. Kennan, and Reinhold Niebuhr as a leading spokesman for an anti-Wilsonian critique based upon a long-standing American tendency to equate the national interest with America's moral mission to convert the world to democracy.[214] Instead, these men have insisted upon a more limited role for American power, wherein traditional American ideals are better integrated with America's newly-enhanced power responsibilities, and are not considered as a means of imposing a misplaced "moralism" on a world which is neither ready for, nor would necessarily benefit from, the American version of the good life. In effect, Morgenthau classifies modern thinkers into two diametrically antagonistic schools of thought, depending upon whether they are "moralistic-idealists" or "realistic ethicists."[215] The former category contains those who believe human nature is essentially plastic, that institutions can be readily improved, and that rationality is a resource that should be more widely employed in the interests of human betterment. The latter category comprises those who see human nature as essentially Hobbesian (i.e., egoistic, amoral, aggressive), conflicts of interest and value irremediably embedded in the human condition, and morality as a thin veneer masking a good bit of rotting wood. Those whose assumptions are oriented to the former position are likely to become neither reliable nor prudent policy-makers; those who are oriented more to the latter set of assumptions qualify for Morgenthau's honor roll.

116

The main source of trouble in democracies, Morgenthau believes, is that mass public opinion exerts an inordinate influence upon foreign policy, "for it is the very nature of the conduct of foreign policy in a democracy that what theoreticians regard to be the sound principles of foreign policy must be adapted to the preferences of public opinion and to the pressures of domestic politics, and thereby corrupted and distorted."[216] Consequently, the failures of American foreign policy in the post-war period, especially the Vietnam debacle, have been more reflective of "the blindness of power" than of the "arrogance of power," as critics like former Senator William Fullbright have long argued.[217] Too often in the administrations of Kennedy, Johnson, and Nixon, rhetoric has betrayed truth, and the vital sense of trust that underlies the moral consensus uniting "citizen to citizen and the citizens to the government" has eroded to a dangerous degree.[218] Morgenthau finds an alarming continuity in the general practice among twentieth century American presidents, reinforced by public opinion, to employ different standards when judging other nations from those used when judging ourselves:

> Thus, the American political mind has been engaged in a three-cornered war. It has been at war with the political realities, which do not yield to the invocation of moral principles. It has been at war with its moral principles, since it must condone implicitly what it condemns explicitly and is powerless to change. And it has been at war again with its moral principles, since it practices with a good conscience what it condemns in others. It bridges the gap between its moral principles and its political practices by juxtaposing its selfless intentions—most eloquently propounded, for instance, by Wilson in justification of the intervention in Mexico—with the evil purposes of other nations.[219]

What Morgenthau seems to be asking for is a more discriminating foreign policy, which is geared to a more honest and realistic estimate of the national interest, and capable of dealing with human weakness and complex power factors. Most importantly, it must eschew extreme swings of the pendulum from isolationism to globalism and back again to neo-isolationism, an all-or-nothing approach, that in Morgenthau's view has dominated American policy-making in this century, mostly to bad effect.[220]

Modern government has been overtaken by events. The age of the super-powers is over. The nation state is obsolete. National security is less vulnerable to ideological differences among powerful nations than it is to relatively weak nations which happen to exercise economic control over vital resources, such as oil, and which are, therefore, immune from the traditional subservience to greater military power. With nuclear power largely neutralized, "a nation or group of nations, completely devoid of a modern industrial and technol-

117

ogical capacity and military potential, is able to wield political power over nations far superior to them in that capacity and potential."221 Such far-reaching and profound
changes in the world cannot help shake presuppositions about
power relationships.

But there is an additional problem of even greater seriousness: the apparent decline of democratic government everywhere. It is Morgenthau's contention that the forces of
a modern technological-communications-transporation revolution are making it increasingly difficult for democracies to
maintain even minimal standards of electoral competition,
and government accountability and responsiveness to the public interest. The responsibility for safeguarding the lives
of its citizens, preserving a tradition of individual liberty, and promoting a better life for its citizenry have become
less dependent on the behavior of public officials and more
affected by private economic interests that are trans-nation-
al in their mode of operations. "Thus governments, regardless
of their individual peculiarities, are helpless in the face
of inflation; for the relevant substantive decisions are not
made by them but by private governments whom the official governments are unwilling or unable to control."222

The direct consequence is that the impotence of government invites mistrust and instability. The void is soon
filled by a technostructure which eschews democratic politics for the arts of manipulation and bureaucratic control.
The inevitable by-product is erosion of democratic accountability. "For it is the great political paradox of our time
that a government, too weak to control the concentrations of
private power that have usurped much of the substance of its
power, has grown so powerful as to reduce the citizens to impotence."223 Once again, there is evidence that an incisive
intelligence informs Morgenthau's dissection of the body politic, but little evidence that he is prepared to offer any
possible solution to the dilemma he so deftly identifies.

In common with the more perceptive conservative political philosophers, Hans Morgenthau believes there is an objective moral order which can be applied to practical judgments,
so that distinctions of right and wrong conduct can be ascertained, and hopefully, wise choices can be made. Morgenthau's
deep-seated pessimism regarding the intractable irrationality
and selfishness of human nature permeates all aspects of his
thought. He is not exactly sure how this moral dimension can
be tapped, except that it is "the recognition of wisdom as a
distinct quality of the mind," and a prerogative of the few
rather than the many.224 Paradoxically, a thinker who emphasizes man's innate sinfulness, selfishness, and irrationality,
and who sees the lust for power as the greatest of all evils
from which no one is immune if the opportunity should present
itself, would also elevate reason to a high ideal and practical necessity. In effect, Morgenthau desires to heal the
split between the philosopher and the practitioner, a rift
that he attributes partly to "the decline of the political
philosophy of liberalism,"225 caused by the demands of the

welfare state, and partly to the inability of contemporary man to retain faith in "the teachings of tradition."[226] Above all, the growing estrangement of power and ethics has contributed greatly to the widespread failures of government in the contemporary world:

> The relationship between morality, on the one hand, power and interest, on the other, is three-fold. First, morality limits the interests that power seeks and the means that power employs to that end. Certain ends cannot be pursued and certain means cannot be employed in a given society within a certain period of history by virtue of the moral opprobrium that attaches to them. Second, morality puts the stamp of its approval upon certain ends and means which thereby not only become politically feasible but also acquire a positive moral value. These moral values, then, become an intrinsic element of the very interests that power seeks. Third, morality serves interests and power as their ideological justification.[227]

Granting the justification of Hans Morgenthau's analysis, how then can this situation be corrected? In The Purpose of American Politics, he uses the term "equality in freedom" to characterize his conception of a morally-based American democracy.[228] Behind the multi-purpose, pluralistic nature of American civilization lies a transcendental moral law which gives meaning to human existence and sets standards of ethical striving. This moral law is both universal and absolute. The enemy is reason of state, on the one hand, popular expediency on the other. Only when the American people are willing and able to reclaim their heritage "of certain self-evident truths which men do not create but find in the nature of things," can one anticipate a restoration of genuine democracy.[229] Morgenthau, however, is typically vague when it comes to defining either the moral law or the certain self-evident truths. He knows it when he sees it being violated, as he did in the celebrated Charles Van Doran quiz show scandal, but he cannot precisely characterize it.

Ultimately, Morgenthau cannot escape the contradiction that lurks at the center of his political philosophy. He is a thoroughgoing realist-pessimist about man's capacity for goodness and rationality; yet he proclaims the existence of objective moral principles and "accessibility of objective, general truth."[230] As George Lichtheim has shown, there is a curious inconsistency between a Hobbesian view of human nature and a belief in moral transcendence, especially when the social and altruistic side of human experience is so completely eradicated. But as Rene Dubos has reminded us: "Since earliest recorded history altruism has become one of the absolute values by which humanity transcends animality."[231]

Hans Morgenthau views conservatism through a split

screen. On one hand, he has a high regard for the contributions that the conservative philosophy has made to the
early development of American institutions, especially in
that finest of all political documents, <u>The Federalist</u>.
Above all, he applauds the realism of the Founders for their
acceptance of human imperfection, a position that contrasts
with the dubious rationalism of 18th century Enlightenment
thought.[232] On the other hand, he acknowledges that, on a
practical level, conservatism has been inappropriate to the
American way of doing things; because unlike Europe, America
never acquired an aristocratic tradition to set a standard
for the preservation of conservative values. Since the status quo, for most Americans, has never held much charm, "the
very dynamics of American society are incompatible with a
conservative position regarding the purpose of politics."[233]
Americans, by virtue of necessity, have been oriented toward
the future. Therefore, the paradox of conservatism in the
American experience can be stated as follows: "While in philosophy and method, conservatism is the most potent single
influence in American politics, the purposes of our politics
from the very beginning have been unique and revolutionary,
not only within narrowly political terms, but also in the
more general sense of being oblivious to tradition."[234] In
other words, the weakness of conservatism in American thought
is its lack of content; yet its importance is not negligible,
since the nation's constitutional system and political tradition reflect essentially conservative values, especially those
that place a premium upon stability, checks and balances, and
pluralism. If Morgenthau is correct, then the most valuable
role conservatism can play in the contemporary world is to
eschew ideology and to defend the basic structure of the governmental system.

A pervasive either/orism characterizes Morgenthau's
thought processes: man is this and not that, power is always
harmful and never beneficial. In addition, he couples a profound sense of man's fallibility with dogmatically asserted
assumptions about the nature of man, society, and the state.
It is hard to escape the conclusion that such a view requires
value preferences which are bound to subvert a democratic.
ethos. Tradition, order, equilibrium, and the need for strong
authority at the top—these represent his hierarchy of values,
and reveals a contempt toward the many in favor of the meritorious few. A morality that does not respect the common man
and his capacity for self-improvement under favorable circumstances is tantamount to abnegating the possibilities of democracy. The irreconcilable contradiction which has doomed
conservative political philosophy in the United States to
relative impotence, despite the sustained acuity of much of
its critical analysis, is that it does not speak to the mass
of human beings. For the average person, it offers nothing
except authoritarian paternalism and a recognition of ethical
principles that are valid only for those who have already
achieved the good life, in usually a life associated with the
scholarly and cultural milieu of an intellectual aristocracy.
In the final analysis, there is no way that a truly conserva-

tive philosophy of man can have much appeal or efficacy for the ordinary citizen struggling just to make ends meet and hoping tomorrow will bring just a little improvement in his socio-economic status. If democracy is still a way of organizing society and government so that the many, not just the few, may hope to enjoy the opportunity for meaningful participation in decisions that affect their lives, then the ordinary citizen will have to look beyond conservatism for a socio-economic-political outlook that will serve his interests.

Still, whatever one's criteria, the political philosophers examined in this chapter set a high standard of intellectual performance. It is becoming increasingly evident that the quality of conservative/liberal theorizing that was achieved by the thinkers discussed in this chapter has not been matched by the spokesmen of the newer varieties of conservatism, which came to occupy the foreground of intellectual debate in the United States at mid-century. It is only in relatively recent years that this has begun to change again, as conservatism experienced something of a renaissance in the 1970's.

CONSERVATISM AND THE IDEAL OF UNFETTERED INDIVIDUALISM

It is generally agreed that a major split occurred in conservative thought at around the time of World War II. Two strands of conservatism emerged in the post-war period, each claiming adherents, and each disagreeing as much with the opposing camp about the true meaning of conservatism as they disagreed with the liberal camp over basic political values. Although given various labels, these two develop-ments within conservative thought can be referred to as traditionalist versus libertarian-individualist versions of the conservative creed.[1] By and large, those thinkers fea-tured in the preceding chapter can be classified as tradi-tionalist conservatives, since they believed that the self/society relationship was one of interdependence, and that the organic interrelatedness of past and present determined the nature of conservative values. However, a group of think-ers who professed allegiance to conservative values, but re-jected this basic assumption of self/society interdependence, began to attract a following, and sought to push conserva-tism in a different direction from that envisioned by the traditionalists.

Taking economics, rather than politics, as the area of central concern, these libertarian-individualist conserva-tives harked back to the classical liberal separation of self and society, emphasized the independence of these two dimen-sions of reality, and viewed contemporary tendencies toward collectivism as a grave threat to individual freedom. In effect, conservative thinkers began to diverge in their bas-ic assumptions regarding the nature of man, society, and the state. This division has not only hindered conservatism from achieving coherence in its constant struggle with liber-alism, but it has also raised questions as to whether there really is any common ground on which all strands of conserv-ative thought may unite.

The four thinkers who have been most directly identified with this challenge to conservative orthodoxy are Ayn Rand, Milton Friedman, Frank Meyer, and Robert Nozick. However, there are important qualifications to be made in the case of the late Frank Meyer, since he eventually dedicated himself to finding a basis of accommodation between these divergent developments in contemporary conservative thought and sought to repair the damage that was being done to the movement.[2]

Still, there is a marked divergence, if not an unbridge-able chasm, between those who can be classified as tradition-alist, or organic conservatives, and those who could be called libertarian, or individualist conservatives. Given the nature of political, social, and economic conditions in America to-day, one would have to conclude that the fundamental differ-ence between these two conceptions of conservatism is that one is moderate and the other radical in its attitude toward change. Traditionalists, while remaining severe critics of the existing state of affairs, nevertheless favor incremental change in behalf of their professed values. Libertarian-individualists, on the other hand, wish to safeguard and maximize personal freedom above all else; to achieve this end, they require a substantial dismantling of the welfare state and the restoration of an earlier form of laissez-faire, free-market capitalism. Under present circumstances, such changes would indeed necessitate a radical reorganization of the socioeconomc system. So there is a question whether the libertarian-individualist strand in conservative thought crosses the boundaries of conservatism into some form of radicalism.

Does real freedom depend upon an unfettered, pristine, free-market capitalism? Are the rights of property ownership and control the cornerstone of a truly democratic system? Does government pose the primary threat to maximum freedom of individual choice? Is self-interest, properly understood and unregulated, far superior to all forms of social dependence and altruism in achieving a true harmony of interests for the long-term betterment of society? Is equality of opportunity desirable, and equality of condition undesirable, for effective progress? Does freedom rest entirely upon the absence of coercion, or is freedom possible only through the willingness of the individual to accept some forms of social control? Although libertarian-individualist and traditionalist conservatives can not be quite so neatly divided as these questions suggest, it is a fact that libertarian conservatives would be uncompromising in their defense of the former assertions, while the traditionalist conservatives might be inclined to make concessions to changing circumstances regarding various of the latter assertions, and even welcome some as compatible with a conservative outlook.

Perhaps the major difference, however, between libertarian and traditionalist conservatives is that the traditionalist seeks objective moral standards implicit in tradition and history as a way of integrating power means and ethical ends. The libertarian sees even this as a threat to individual autonomy, and rejects authority in all its possible manifestations, including its religious or moralistic guise. Given these pronounced differences and contradictory premises, it is no wonder that these two strands within conservative thought have driven a wedge between those thinkers who have taken these divergent roads. Interestingly, Frank S. Meyer, who certainly could be classified as a libertarian conservative, refused to accept such a verdict: in books and articles he tried to show that the areas of agreement between the two camps were far more significant than their differences. However, there is little evidence that his "fusionist" efforts had more than a paper-thin success, since the schism continues to hamper efforts toward a unified conservative movement.

It is clear that these two strands of thought view the nature of man, society, and the state from contrasting perspectives. Whereas the libertarian emphasizes the autonomy of the individual, the traditionalist emphasizes the dependence of the individual upon certain forms of social order.

Whereas the libertarian looks to economics as the source of human well-being, the traditionalist looks to culture as a means by which human excellence can prevail over selfishness. Whereas the libertarian is close to anarchism in seeking the smallest possible role for state power, the traditionalist favors a strong state, and leans toward both authoritarianism and elitism, provided, of course, that those who govern are qualified by virtue of their non-dependence upon politics as usual. At the same time, these two varieties of conservatism are united in their opposition to a liberal political orientation and in their commitment to the maintenance of the established distribution of power and wealth in society. Neither would like to see government play a positive role in behalf of distributive justice or imposed equalitarianism.

Libertarian and traditionalist conservatives begin to travel even farther apart when it comes to a question of what should be done to ensure personal freedom of choice. The libertarian conservative becomes almost radical in his insistence upon removing the bonds that circumscribe individual autonomy; whereas the traditionalist conservative seeks to balance the equally necessary attributes of freedom and authority. The traditionalist, in other words, is more moderate in his attitude toward change, taking into account not only what is desirable, but also what is realistic. But as Kenneth and Patricia Dolbeare have pointed out in their book, American Ideologies: The Competing Political Beliefs of the 1970s, both forms of conservatism are caught in logical and tactical dilemmas, because a democratic polity, requiring majority popular support for change, does not respond well to the elitist nature of both these forms of conservatism.[3]

Ironically, the libertarian conservative is close to being a classical liberal of the Lockean-Jeffersonian-Adam Smith pedigree; for a laissez-faire, least government the best, free-market approach characterizes both ideological movements. The explanation, of course, is related to changes in society, and to the substantial merging of the private and public, and economic and political, spheres. The libertarian conservative would strive to separate the two spheres by every means possible, and to restore both integrity and autonomy to the private sphere; but there is serious doubt whether this is either desirable or possible, given the increasing interdependence of economic and political power. Although both types of conservatism deplore this situation, and reject the liberal propensity to extend public controls over private activities, they are at odds when it comes to the question of the relationship between private and public morality. The libertarian sees public morality being taken care of simply by allowing self-interest to find its own level of ultimate mutual benefit. The traditionalist, needless to say, has no confidence that this will happen, discounts the prospects of even minimal rationality in human affairs, and seeks to ground private morality in an authoritative network of superimposed public morality—however difficult and vague this may turn out to be in practice.

A closer look at views of some leading representatives of the libertarian school of conservative thought is in order. Despite marked diversity even among libertarian conservatives, there is evidence that there is a common bond uniting these thinkers. Furthermore, their position on the ideological-philosophical spectrum has attracted considerable interest, and exercises a wider influence over the general populace than the more erudite traditionalists, since both Ayn Rand and Milton Friedman have managed to attract a large readership by virtue of Rand's best-selling novels and Friedman's _Newsweek_ magazine columns. For this reason alone, attention needs to be paid to this school of thought.

Ayn Rand

Should Ayn Rand be taken seriously as a thinker? It is not an easy question to answer. For over thirty years, since the publication of her popular novel, _The Fountainhead_, Ayn Rand has had an army of readers, many of whom respond to her writings as a disciple does to a guru—and she is quite capable of cultivating, perhaps even exploiting, this phenomenon; recent paperback editions of her books have included a special tear-out postcard, inviting readers to receive a "charter subscription" to the fortnightly _Ayn Rand Letter_, a supplement to _The Objectivist_, a monthly magazine she has edited and for which she has written much of the material since the early 60's, "if the philosophical ideas expressed in this book interest you..." Despite this substantial popular following and the incalculable influence her ideas obviously exercise over the minds of many individuals, she is generally ignored by scholars and other intellectual commentators, except for an occasional aspersion directed at her "fascist" mentality. And yet, no contemporary conservative thinker can rival the coherence, consistency, and range of her thinking or can match her popular appeal. From this standpoint, if from no other, Ayn Rand must be taken seriously as a writer and thinker in the conservative mold.

Who is Ayn Rand? The question echoes the theme of her massive novel, _Atlas Shrugged_, in which, for two-thirds of the thousand-plus pages, John Galt is a character who remains _in absentia_, but whose spiritual presence is manifest from the beginning—and who brings the story to its climax as a voice on the radio, addressing a disoriented, almost paralyzed nation, attacking the old morality and proposing a new morality that the author believes is the only hope of salvation. There are two Ayn Rand's. One was born in Tsarist Russia, was twelve years old at the time of the Soviet seizure of power in 1917, and shortly thereafter emigrated to America, where she wrote successful novels, essays, enjoyed a long and apparently happy marriage to the late writer, Frank O'Connor, and became the leader of an intellectual cult centering around her Objectivist philosophy. The other Ayn Rand is the liberal's ogre: a writer who is looked upon as a pseudo-thinker and a pernicious fanatic whose simple-minded love affair with capitalism partakes more of neurotic obsessiveness rather than a penetrating intelligence. Which Ayn Rand is the real one? The question has no objective answer; she is one of those writers for whom there can be no in-between: one either accepts or rejects her, and she would be the first to acknowledge that these are the two usual reactions to her philosophical position. This revealing passage, a 1968 introduction to a reprinted edition of her most popular work, The Fountainhead, says it all:

> It does not matter that only a few in each generation will grasp and achieve the full reality of man's proper stature—and that the rest will betray it. It is those few that I have always sought to address. The rest are no concern of mine; it is not me or The Fountainhead that they will betray: it is their own souls.[4]

One can admire the honesty, intelligence, and passion that permeates Rand's writings, take pleasure in the narrative power of her fiction, and respect the logical clarity of her thinking in the numerous essays that she has written over the years on both topical and philosophical subjects; but her ideas must be examined and evaluated before a verdict can be rendered. The task is made somewhat easier because Ayn Rand does not obfuscate, and there are several ideas or themes that are repeatedly emphasized in all her work. First of all, America in particular, and the world in general, is undergoing a "moral crisis" in which man's reason has been pushed aside and the irrational aspects of human nature are glorified. She equates reason with individualism, capitalism, and a self-interest morality; irrationalism she equates with mysticism, altruism, and collectivism.[5] Moral bankruptcy, cultural disintegration, intellectual myopia, and spiritual abnegation are characteristics which apply to the present state of civilization.[6] The cause of this deepening catastrophe is self-evident: the capitalistic system of free enterprise, the free-market economy, and freedom from all governmental interference is being regularly betrayed by friends and supporters as well as destroyed piece by piece by liberal and leftist enemies.

Capitalism "is the only system geared to the life of a rational being...No politico-economic system in history has ever proved its value so eloquently or has benefited mankind so greatly."[7] The two chief threats to ideal capitalism are the "morality of altruism," which Rand explains as any action which places the interests of society against the rights of the individual, and "political statism," which in "fact and principle...is nothing more than gang rule,"[8] a denial of individual rights. "Those who advocate laissez-faire capitalism are the only advocates of man's rights."[9] Man has two choices: he can assert his will, dominate those forces that would seek to deny his real humanity, and employ his reasoning faculties to make the most of his individuality, or he can meekly surrender to a pragmatic, anti-philosophical, anti-individualist ethic.[10] The consequences of this choice are nothing less than man's decline or resurrection.[11]

Ayn Rand makes a virtue of selfishness; the core of her "Objectivist" philosophy is the right of each person to live his own life without assuming either responsibility for, or being dependent upon, anyone else's equal right to individual happiness:

> The basic _social_ principle of the Objectivist ethics is that just as life is an end in itself, so every living human being is an end in himself, not the means to the ends or the welfare of others—and, therefore, that man must live for his own sake, neither sacrificing himself to others nor sacrificing others to himself. To live for his own sake means that _the achievement of his own happiness is man's highest moral purpose._[12]

This typical passage from her writings again underscores the essentially anti-social and self-centered quality of her thinking, which, on the face of it, appears to be not only a direct attack upon Christian values but also an unequivocal rejection of democracy. Rand would probably agree to this interpretation, except that she would no doubt also argue that it is the debased versions that presently pass for Christianity and democracy which she is attacking, not the humanitarian aspirations of those historical forces. In her view, these movements deny the real life-giving elements of human existence, while proclaiming the opposite, because they practice a false morality.[13] Salvation lies in adopting a new morality—a self-created, self-directed, and self-interested morality based upon enlightened reason and philosophical principles that unite mind, will, and personal freedom in opposition to social conformity, political control, and economic collectivism. Morality and rationality are one and indivisible.[14] "Thinking is man's only basic virtue, from which all the others proceed. And his basic vice, the source of all his evils, is the nameless act...the act of blanking out, the willful suspension of one's consciousness, the refusal to think..."[15] There is no dark undercurrent of sub-conscious psychological complexity or non-rational obstacle courses to maneuver around and defeat in achieving this goal of ultimate rationality in Ayn Rand's philosophy—for her, Freudianism does not seem to exist—and the only real obstacle is a blind and shallow dedication to conventional ideas and thinking.

Kira, the heroine who is eventually murdered by the border patrol guard as she attempts to flee Soviet tyranny, makes this eloquent plea for personal autonomy in an earlier discussion with a Party official, in this passage from an early novel, _We The Living_, which goes to the very heart of Ayn Rand's philosophy:

> "Don't you know," her voice trembled suddenly in a passionate plea she could not hide, "don't you know that there are things, in the best of us, which no outside hand should dare to touch? Things sacred

128

because, and only because, one can say: 'This is _mine_'? Don't you know that we live only for ourselves, the best of us do, those who are worthy of it? Don't you know that there is something in us which must not be touched by any state, by any collective, by any number of millions?"[16]

It may be worth noting that in expressing this philosophy, Ayn Rand was probably three decades ahead of her time. The 1970's has witnessed a growing desire among many people for personal liberation from dull marriages, dull jobs, dull life-styles, and dull routines. Whether fad or something more permanent, this new "liberated outlook" is affecting a large number of middle-class Americans who normally would not go beyond occasional fantasy to act on such concerns. This new "cult of the individual," if it can be called that, may never become more than a sub-cultural phenomenon, but it is quite likely that Rand's books will become even more popular if this trend continues.[17] She was there before just about anyone else.

Ayn Rand's political ideas are scattered throughout her writings, but a consistent pattern emerges: the New Left movement of the 1960's was a simple-minded, media exploited, irrational product of a pluralist socio-economic-political system that had lost its bearings, since "rule by pressure groups is merely the prelude, the social conditioning for mob rule."[18] Because civil disobedience invariably infringes upon the rights of others, it is an unacceptable form of protest.[19] In fact, the premier right, and the basis of all individual rights, is the right to accumulate, own, and control property:

> It is only on the basis of property rights that the sphere and application of individual rights can be defined in any given social situation. Without property rights, there is no way to avoid a hopeless chaos of clashing views, interests, demands, desires, and whims.[20]

The legacy of American New Deal type liberalism has been the gradual, but insidious and inevitable trend toward the triumph of the world's single greatest evil: collectivism, or statism, which Rand defines as governmental control over all aspects of human life. Totalitarianism is just as real a probability in so-called democratic societies as in the more obvious cases of the Communist countries. The result is the same, even if the time-span is longer in one instance than in the other. Only radical surgery can arrest this development, and only a broadened intellectual elite which accepts the Randian philosophy can save us.

It is of some importance that former President Richard Nixon's appointment of Alan Greenspan as Chairman of the prestigious Council of Economic Advisors, one of the key advisory positions for economic affairs in the government, meant that Ayn Rand's economic principles were likely to influence government policy-making during a time of severe national economic crisis. Mr. Greenspan is an admitted disciple of Ayn Rand's philosophy, has written articles for her publications, has known her for over twenty years, and on the record thinks very much along her lines.[21] At a time when very few public officials of either major political party have advocated classical laissez-faire capitalism, the Greenspan appointment in the waning days of Mr. Nixon's discredited presidency caused more than a few raised eyebrows. The point to be made here is simply that Rand's influence, however evaluated, has a practical, as well as theoretical, dimension.

It is hard to quarrel with one aspect of Rand's economic analysis: free competition is a vital element in advancing democratic capitalism. Quite correctly, she deplores the substantial undermining of competition that has accompanied the increasing concentration of economic power in the United States. She agrees totally with the Adam Smith concept of an "invisible hand" behind the sacred principle of supply and demand: if left alone, a free-market economy will always achieve an equilibrium of profit, prices, and wages to the mutual benefit of all segments of the society. However, when it comes to identifying the source of this threat to free enterprise capitalism, Rand makes a questionable assumption based upon unempirical, narrowly ideological, and grossly superficial analysis of the relationship between politics and economics. In all her work, never once does she even hint at the possibility that political power may be not the independent and dominant factor she claims it is, but rather a servant of ecomomic resources and power inequities.

The fact is, there is only one culprit and one threat to economic well-being, according to Rand: governmental interference in the private economy. The source of all monopoly control, non-competitive business practices, and abuses of power can be attributed to the rise of Big Government and the insidious inroads of Socialism on the free-market system. Rand has absolute faith in the honesty and responsibility of the business-corporate structure, reinforced by "natural economic laws" properly understood and applied. Government has corrupted and misled those businessmen and industrialists who have looked to government for aid and special favors; it is the self-reliant, self-confident, independent-minded individualist who remains the exception, suffers for his strength and autonomy because of the prevalent mass mentality, and is the hope for change and social improvement.

Except for Randian converts, such a vision is fantasy. Economic problems are multi-causal, a mixture of controllable and uncontrollable factors, and economic power may dominate political power certainly as often as the opposite occurs, although this is disputed by those who define democracy exclusively in respect to the ideal of liberty, without any regard for the ideal of equality. Human greed is not an exclusive property of statist-minded politicians. This unwillingness, or failure, to appreciate the complexity and interdependence of political-economic-power factors is an unrelieved

130

defect in her analysis; the analysis becomes arrogant in its pretension to omniscience. Her mind and values are one: to respect the one is to accept the other.

There is no way Ayn Rand can be eased into the conservative tradition without considerable qualification. As she has stated with characteristic forcefulness: "Objectivists are not 'Conservatives'! We are radicals for capitalism: we are fighting for the philosophical base which capitalism did not have and without which it was doomed to perish."[22] She despises the words "moderation" and "compromise"; there is no conservative political figure in recent public life who gets her support or respect, and this includes former Presidents Eisenhower and Nixon.[23] Her main intellectual mentor is Ludwig von Mises, an earlier critic of liberalism and the planned economy. John Dewey, the so-called Progressive Education Movement, government anti-trust policies, the progressive income tax, all welfare programs, American pragmatism, Keynesian economic theory, the organized labor movement, and anything that even remotely results in socialist-collectivist ideas come under the relentless fire of her pen. At the same time, she glorifies technology, laissez-faire capitalism, and a certain type of businessman who exemplifies the ideal of independent-mindedness, such as the Randian supermen and superwomen Howard Roark, Dominique Francon, Kira Argounova, Dagney Taggart, Hank Reardon, and John Galt, the heroes and heroines of her fictional writings.

The problem of assessing Ayn Rand as a socio-economic-political thinker appears easy on the surface: either one is attracted to a thinker who relishes either/orism, sees everything in stark black-white terms with absolutely no concession to shades of greyness or ambiguity, or one does not. It is that simple. And yet, the task of evaluation is not quite so easy or simple in the case of Ayn Rand. For one thing, she is a widely read and very popular author, whether or not one counts avowed disciples of her Objectivist philosophy; and her influence is immeasurable, for good or ill. There is another reason why she cannot be so readily dismissed: her conservatism may be more radical-activist than status-quo passive, but it nevertheless echoes and links up with ideas that have long been an integral aspect of the conservative tradition in American thought, as well as of earlier liberalism. The cornerstones of her political philosophy are individual rights, laissez-faire capitalism, the sacredness of property, and moral absolutism. These are all important ingredients of the conservative-liberal tradition, however modified by individual thinkers. The main exception is her unique brand of conservatism which postulates a complete and unbridgeable separation between self and society, repudiates the importance of the social dimension of human existence, and substitutes a willed activism for the usual conservative tendency to trust tradition and institutional authority as the main source of behavioral guidelines. Ayn Rand takes conservatism around full circle: the situation, as diagnosed, is truly desparate for contemporary man, and nothing less than a radical change in morality and behavior can cure it. Failure

131

to achieve this end is tantamount to self-destruction.

Even if one pre-supposes that a fair-minded appraisal of Ayn Rand's political philosophy is possible, despite considerable knowledge and understanding of political economy, her writings are completely devoid of a realistic conception of political power. There is an utter emptiness at the center of her analyses: she is shrewdly selective when it comes to the corruptions of power, and all her important fictional characters are either good guys or bad guys, individually responsible or irresponsible, one-hundred percent honest or totally corrupt. To fully document this charge would take more space than one cares to give to the enterprise; a brief summary of the leading characters in her novels will suffice. There is the inevitable conflict and contrast between the incorruptible Howard Roark and weak-minded, corruptible Peter Keating in The Fountainhead; the self-destruct realism of Kira's communist lover, Andrei, matched against the self-destruct idealism of her beloved husband, Leo, in We the Living; the exalted individualism of Hank Reardon and the debased conformitarianism of James Taggart in Atlas Shrugged.

Even when allowance is made for symbolic expression in imaginative literature, there is a disconcerting unreality that permeates Ayn Rand's fiction and detracts from its value as both philosophy and literature. The allurements of power and its tendency to corrupt idealists and realists alike, the selfish and the unselfish, the child and the parent, in fact, all aspects of human intercourse, must be dealt with in all its complexity and unpredictability. A philosophical metaphysics or political theory that fails to appreciate this basic fact of life is courting impotence—and this is exactly where Ayn Rand goes off the track. It is not altogether a question of ideological affinity or antagonism that is at issue in evaluating Randian conservatism: there is an apparent inability to adequately analyze power relations, and a calculated avoidance of these relations except insofar as her purposes may be completely didactic, setting up her characters and situations in order to facilitate communication of her pet ideas and themes in a context that undermines their validity. In this respect, Ayn Rand is occasionally provocative and entertaining, but she remains a one-dimensional thinker, more interesting from a psychological standpoint than as an important figure, however ideosyncratic, in the conservative tradition in American political thought.

There is good reason to conclude that Ayn Rand's essential appeal is to the disconnected individual. She is a magician who can transform weakness into strength, a sense of loss into a new sense of identity, and can open up a path of personal redemption for the elect who follow her prescription. She is a faith-healer who exalts the mind and denigrates the emotions, while at the same time showing how one can become worthy of salvation by abdicating one's critical faculties and surrendering completely to the soothing nostrums of a simplistic world-view that identifies selfishness with strength and altruism with weakness and that advocates a

132

morality of superman and superwoman superiority. To qualify
for this exalted status, one need only reject the soft-minded
and weak-hearted claims of the liberal outlook. In short,
there is a therapeutic quality in Ayn Rand's work which touches
the psychological needs of certain individuals; and in this
respect her ideas may or may not be harmful—no one is sufficient authority on the mind to make this determination. On the
other hand, taken as a whole, her philosophy cannot score high
on any substantive criterion for evaluation. Her lack of interest in analyzing real power structures and interrelation-
ships or in formulating a theory of power must weaken, if it
does not ultimately destroy, the value of her political ideas.
Her ability to sugar-coat the raw unsightliness of her extremist socio-economic-political philosophy in imaginative literature has helped to widen her influence, and may give her the
largest readership audience any conservative thinker has ever
enjoyed, with the possible exception of William F. Buckley Jr.
At the same time this wide popular appeal does not reflect the
value of Rand's philosophy of man, society, and the state. In
this respect, there will undoubtedly continue to be much disagreement; however, as a self-proclaimed radical-conservative,
the contradiction between these two terms—radical and conservative—is as wide and unbridgeable as the Atlantic Ocean.

Milton Friedman

If one were to judge a thinker on clarity of thought, the
ability to present complex problems in understandable terms,
and a high score for predicting what would happen if such and
such economic policies were pursued, then Milton Friedman,
Chicago University economist, would surely deserve high praise.
Whether or not one agrees with his basic premises, one must
recognize that no one has done more to raise doubts about the
wisdom of Keynesianism, the main guideline for American economic policy in the post World War II period, or has commanded
more respect as an economist of brilliance. His book, Capitalism and Freedom, is one of the few important works in recent
conservative thought. As a frequent lecturer, a part-time
journalist, a teacher, and an advisor to presidents, Milton
Friedman's influence has been extensive both in and out of
government. Along with F.A. Hayek, Milton Friedman gives contemporary conservatism stature and substance. He does this,
let it be known, at a time when his ideas are contrary to much
of what passes for conventional wisdom in economic and political matters.[24] To liberals, he is the "enemy." To many fellow conservatives, especially of the traditionalist persuasion,
he is heretical. Yet his following from top to bottom of the
educated stratum is unmatched, for as William Breit and Roger
L. Ransom have commented: "...most of all, it is the force of
his personality which has allowed his heretical and radical
ideas in defense of market capitalism to capture the imagination of scores of economists and legislators."[25]

Milton Friedman, the son of Eastern European immigrants,
was born in Brooklyn, New York, in 1912 and grew up in Rahway,
New Jersey, in near-poverty circumstances. But his intellect-

133

ual precocity and hard work enabled him to attend Rutgers University. Thanks to a scholarship, he attended the Chicago University graduate school, where he majored in economics. There he came into contact with scholars like Arthur Burns, Frank Knight, Henry Simons and Jacob Viner, all of whom were right of center, and it was then that his neo-classical economic views took shape. Most importantly, however, he gained a life-long appreciation of the mathematical and empirical sciences, so that the later clarity of his writing style and thought draws heavily upon his respect for scientific objectivity; although critics would accuse him of being a prime example of ideological purity. His subsequent career has involved mostly teaching, research, lecturing, and writing; in the process, he has become one of the leaders of the "Chicago school" of neo-classical economics.[26]

The attack against teleology, the religious belief in divine purpose governing the operations of the universe, and the rejection of secularized, discoverable, economically-rooted "natural laws" that had been so central to the thought of both the classical economists of the Manchester school and Marx-Engles, was masterfully presented in a 1949 publication, Human Action, by Ludwig von Mises, an Austrian economist who spent many years teaching at American universities.[27] This is probably rarely read; but nevertheless it has the capacity of profoundly affecting the thinking of a thoughtful reader predisposed to accept its basic premises. Whether this happened to Milton Friedman is unclear; but there is no doubt that von Mises can be considered the "father" of neo-classicism and the libertarian-individualist strand in contemporary conservative thought.

For von Mises, social man displaces economic man. There is no economic need or desire that does not have a wider importance for the society, as well as the individual, and it is the choices made in this broader context of human behavior which determine's man's welfare.[28] Government—or the state— is the one overwhelming threat to individual and social well-being.[29] Laissez-faire has had no more steadfast defender than Ludwig von Mises, who believed that capitalism, in its reliance upon a genuinely free-market, anti-monopolistic, competitive, profit-oriented political economy, represented the sole protector of personal well-being and freedom. Freedom of choice, regardless of consequences, is the bedrock of human action. George H. Nash is no doubt correct when he states: "...it would be difficult to exaggerate the contributions of Friedrich Hayek and Ludwig von Mises to the intellectual rehabilitation of individualism in America at the close of World War II."[30] Milton Friedman continues this tradition.

The meaning of freedom is crucial to conservative thought. This leads to a key question: What is the main obstacle to the maximization of individual freedom? Contemporary conservatives of all stripes are in agreement that the excessive political power of the government is the culprit. Whether economic power, even in the private sector, is equally at fault, is an area of disagreement among conservatives. Some would decry capitalism, or at least they find as much to condemn in the economic as in the political spheres of power; however, it is doubtful whether any conservative envisions any alternative to a private-enterprise based capitalism. Liberals, on the other hand, have become increasingly defensive and skeptical about Big Government; but at the same time, they conclude that the real problem is the increasing dominance of economic power and privilege in the private corporate sector at the expense of political democracy, coupled with excessive inequity of power and influence throughout the system. Thus, they reason, it is only through government, and the willingness to use political power in behalf of "social justice," that economic selfishness and greed can be tamed. Far from representing the main threat to individual freedom, government can and should be the means of enhancing equality, upon which the freedom of the many depends. The gap between these two value-orientations is wide indeed, and it is the line which divides contemporary conservatives and liberals.

Milton Friedman, therefore, throws down the gauntlet to those who mistakenly think that government can play a beneficial role, even under the best of conditions:

> ...the scope of government must be limited. Its major function must be to protect our freedom both from the enemies outside our gates and from our fellow-citizens: to preserve law and order, to enforce private contracts, to foster competitive markets. Beyond this major function, government may enable us at times to accomplish jointly what we would find it more difficult or expensive to accomplish severally. However, any such use of government is fraught with danger. We should not and cannot avoid using government in this way. But there should be a clear and large balance of advantages before we do. By relying primarily on voluntary cooperation and private enterprise, in both economic and other activities, we can insure that the private sector is a check on the powers of the governmental sector and an effective protection of freedom of speech, of religion, and of thought.[31]

The way to reduce the power and authority of government is to disperse power broadly throughout the system, especially by devolving more responsibility and initiative to state and local communities, rather than permitting and encouraging an ever greater concentration of power at the national level. This reverse development, according to Friedman, would be salutary for one reason alone: it would enhance individual freedom of choice. If one did not like what government was doing in one place, one could readily move elsewhere in the country. This is not the case, however, when the government which monopolizes all the power resides in Washington, D.C.[32] Human diversity, which is the linchpin of personal freedom, cannot flourish under the coercive authority of centralization.[33]

Since 1933, and the onset of the New Deal tradition, liberalism in the United States has betrayed its inheritance. It traded a long-standing commitment to personal liberty, political and economic laissez-faire, and free-trade policies for statism, collectivism, and welfarism—policies that have severely weakened the traditional foundation of individual liberty.[34] Political freedom, in Friedman's view, requires a healthy system which maximizes economic freedom, for only in this way can political and economic power be kept separate as a check on each other, curbing the inevitable dangers to individual freedom that each poses.[35] Left to itself, the interplay of market forces will eventually insure economic and political progress without any sacrifice of individual freedom.[36]

Economists and political scientists have drawn the wrong conclusions from the failures of capitalism in the Great Depression; this is one of Friedman's most startling and controversial departures from consensus historiography. He claims that the failure was not caused by defects inherent in the economic system, but rather by misguided political and economic policies—in other words, the wrong kind of interventionism.[37] It was created by top banking interests, inept presidents and their advisors (notably Hoover and FDR), and bad economic analysis, and not, as has generally been accepted, by structural defects of market capitalism. The economic crisis of the 1930's was a man-made phenomenon that could have been avoided. The criticism of President Hoover's policies, which in Friedman's view were simply an early phase of the same mistaken approach which Roosevelt later adopted, could not have been more misplaced, since both embodied unwarranted state intervention in economic affairs. Both Hoover's efforts to provide public subsidies for failing businesses and Roosevelt's various experiments in public-private sector collaboration, were policies which were certain to exacerbate, rather than reduce, the economic dislocations that characterized this period. Friedman believes that the real strength and beauty of market capitalism is that it is self-corrective over time, and requires only minimal amounts of the right kind of political interventionism for growth and stability. It is easy to see why his views have become so controversial, and have had such wide appeal, given the rather sorry performance record of both the economy and polity in the years since the Depression.

Milton Friedman is best known for his adament belief that monetary policy, not fiscal policy, is the preeminent way to maintain economic progress and stability. Judicious manipulation of the money supply, rather than tax reform, direct tampering with the discount rates, or other "fine-tuning" political measures, would be Friedman's solution for combatting economic declines. Perhaps this has been the area of clearest difference between Friedman and liberal economists like Paul Samuelson or Walter Heller; the latter are much stronger believers in the efficacy of government intervention in behalf of fiscal management, especially in respect to reducing levels of unemployment as well as inflation rates, if such is possible.[38] At any event, in public debates, articles, and books, Friedman has shown an avid willingness to confront his critics out in the open, no holds barred; and the general consensus is that Friedman frequently comes off better than his critics. However, the interpretations of the empirical-statistical evidence which should decide the outcome of the debate, is still in dispute, since assumptions invariably affect conclusions and policy options; therefore, government policy-making tends to fluctuate between inadequate representations of both liberal and conservative assumptions, largely depending upon whether a Democratic or Republican president occupies the White House.

The governmental institution that regularly receives Friedman's strongest criticism is the Federal Reserve Board. Although an independent agency of government, the Federal Reserve system, established under Woodrow Wilson in 1913 as a major reform of the national banking system, has a major responsibility for both fiscal and monetary policy. It is mainly against policies in the latter area that Friedman has conducted an unremitting campaign over the years; in addition, he has charged that the Federal Reserve Board had a major responsibility for the 30's Depression.[39] Professor Friedman's own summary view of the situation deserves to be quoted:

> The Great Depression in the United States, far from being a sign of the inherent instability of the private enterprise system, is a testament to how much harm can be done by mistakes on the part of a few men when they wield vast power over the monetary system of the country.[40]

Surprisingly, Friedman's criticism has not abated during the many years that his old mentor and ideological compatriot, Arthur Burns, has been Chairman of the Board.

Perhaps Friedman's greatest economic triumph was his long, and finally, successful advocacy of a major change in international currency policies: a free-floating exchange rate and elimination of government controls in this area. It was a long time coming, but by the 1970's, the change did occur, and dire consequences have not followed, although it is still hard to measure and evaluate the consequences of the situation.[41] He still deplores the numerous departures from a free-trade policy and the various attempts to impose wage and price controls.[42] For a conservative, to use one of his own favorite terms, he has been one of the most persistent opponents of "the tyranny of the status quo."[43] Indeed, for his views to become translated into policies would necessitate radical changes in the political economies of many democratic systems, including that of the United States.

Milton Friedman is particularly incensed about the preoccupation of liberals with government-directed policies to alleviate unemployment by government intervention as well as various forms of public subsidies or make-work projects. Such policies raise taxes, threaten individual liberty, and inevitably fail to accomplish their main purpose of drastically curtailing unemployment.[44]

In the face of so much uncertainty and lack of knowledge of what will work best, Friedman is quick to counsel doing nothing, since whatever government does try to do will surely make things worse rather than better.[45] Although this may appear to contradict what has just been said concerning the radical implications of his ideas, it is still the case that Friedman would have government do little or nothing unless it is prepared to follow his own precepts.

Two of Milton Friedman's most innovative proposals have been the voucher system that would enable parents to send their children at public expense to "approved" private schools in lieu of public educational facilities; and the "negative income tax," or "guaranteed income" from the government for every citizen who falls below a certain "poverty" level.[46] In the case of educational vouchers, it would serve the purpose of widening freedom of choice and would also give public education some much-needed competition. A negative income tax would eliminate a good percentage of existing welfarism, introduce greater fairness and uniformity into what is presently a chaotic and grossly inequitable situation, and reduce dependency upon government by virtue of minimal entitlement rights.

Although there has been very limited experimentation with the voucher plan, it has not drawn much attention. The negative income tax proposal, however, continues to generate interest across the ideological spectrum, and came close to enactment via former President Nixon's Family Assistance Plan. At the very least, a pervasive disenchantment with this country's existing welfare system, and increased talk about the need for some kind of publically-subsidized income policy in one of the world's most affluent countries, creates a large audience of potential supporters for Friedman's proposals. Once again, it seems like a strange thing for an anti-government conservative to advocate. Friedman would probably answer: direct money assistance to the needy would not require a huge bureaucratic delivery system, and would not be seriously detrimental to the incentive principle, as long as payments were kept at a relatively modest level.

The great strength of the free-market economy, according to Friedman, is that it functions impersonally, and thus fairly, and works to the mutual advantage of everyone eventually.[47] He is just as tough on business monopolies as on other forms of monopoly and claims that the absence of regulation will itself insure competition and economic stability in the long-run. Friedman would like to see the "graduated income tax" eliminated and corporate taxes abolished.[48] But the most astonishing aspect of Friedman's proposals is the fact that he is convinced that a proper regulation of the money supply will bring about greater equity _and_ stability. His assurance on this point is breathtaking:

> History offers ample evidence that what determines
> the average level of prices and wages is the amount
> of money in the economy and not the greediness of
> businessmen or of workers. Governments ask for the

138

self-restraint of business and labor because of
their inability to manage their own affairs—which
includes the control of money—and the natural human tendency to pass the buck.[49]

Capitalism is good because in the long-run, if not always in the short-run, it provides the greatest extent of
opportunities for personal satisfaction and self-fulfillment.[50]
When capitalism fails to deliver on its promises, it is almost
invariably because of some form of misguided governmental interference, not because of any defect in capitalism itself.[51]
Public housing did poorly when private housing would have
done better.[52] Minimum wage laws hurt the poor because they
eliminate jobs that would otherwise be available and "make
unemployment higher than it otherwise would be."[53] Price
support programs for farmers, which are now in their fifth
decade, have done infinitely more harm than good, despite
occasional reduction in subsidy payments.[54] All forms of
paternalism are a threat to genuine individual autonomy.[55]
Finally, Friedman points to the dismal record of government
interventionism since the early 1930's, and concludes as
follows:

> If a balance is struck, there can be little
> doubt that the record is dismal. The great part
> of the new ventures undertaken by government in
> the past few decades have failed to achieve their
> objectives. The United States has continued to
> progress; its citizens have become better fed, bet-
> ter clothed, better housed, and better transported;
> class and social distinctions have narrowed; popu-
> lar culture has advanced by leaps and bounds. All
> this has been the product of the initiative and
> drive of individuals co-operating through the free
> market. Government measures have hampered not
> helped this development. We have been able to
> afford and surmount these measures only because
> of the extraordinary fecundity of the market. The
> invisible hand has been more potent for progress
> than the visible hand for retrogression.[56]

The case Milton Friedman has made for his libertarian-
individualist brand of radical conservatism commands respect,
if for no other reason than the fact that he has more often
been right than wrong in predicting the consequences of particular economic and political policies. At a time when
there is nearly universal agreement that government is flab-
by rather than firm, good at overpromising but abysmal in
delivering the goods, and so wasteful of the taxpayer's money
that it is a wonder it hasn't provoked a major revolt by now,
Friedman's analysis looks remarkably sound. In fact, the be-
ginnings of a major "taxpayers revolt," originating in California, did develop in 1978, using the ballot box of electoral politics rather than "the politics of extremism," further underscoring Milton Friedman's prescience. After so
long being a voice "crying in the wilderness," he is edging
closer to the mainstream, or perhaps the mainstream is mov-

ing closer to Friedman.

What is troublesome, however, is his questionable tendency to undercut complex problems and to see a panacea for all the nation's economic ills in a better regulated money supply.[57] Beyond this, Friedman's analysis contains an even more disturbing element that relates directly to libertarian conservatism. There is an unrealistic, and historically unproven belief, or assertion, that man is more responsive to rationality than non-rationality, and can be trusted to restrain himself from indulging in survival-of-the-fittest kind of behavior, if only he is allowed to do his own thing unhampered by political activism and governmental interventionism. Friedman is a utopian rationalist who gives no quarter to Marxian socialists on this score; and it puts him at odds with most of the conservative thinkers dealt with in this book.[58]

The flaw in Friedman's political-social-economic philosophy is the same as that which underlay William Graham Sumner's brand of Social Darwinism earlier in the century: self-restraint cannot be counted upon where human wants are demonstrably unlimited. Unrestrained capitalism is likely to cater to this human failing more than it is likely to counteract it. On the face of it, one could argue that it is the latter that we need more of: that is, a way of putting something of a damper on human selfishness, not unleash it, letting the chips fall as they may. Despite all of its performance failures, the political sector may well be more trustworthy than the economic sector in maintaining and strengthening democracy.[59]

Frank S. Meyer

Why is it that so many of the intellectuals who became associated with the conservative journal of opinion, National Review, in the 1950's and 1960's, had once been securely on the radical side of the political spectrum? As John P. Diggins has demonstrated in his highly interesting analysis, Up From Communism, such latter-day spokesmen of conservatism as James Burnham, John Dos Passos, Will Herberg, Max Eastman, and Willmoore Kendall, not to mention the ex-communists, Wittaker Chambers and Frank S. Meyer, were radical socialist activists in their youth. The one thing they all had in common was an abhorrence of liberalism, for "liberalism was still held responsible for all that had gone wrong in the modern world."[60] In their judgment, liberalism was "soft on communism"; and since communism was "the enemy" dedicated to the destruction of democratic capitalism everywhere, the liberal was wrong-headed, and frequently in the enemy camp, on this vital issue. Professor Diggins raises the intriguing question: Why did these individuals make "the peculiar odyssey from the revolutionary Left to the militant Right, without so much as pausing in the 'Vital Center?'"[61] It was the Cold War, and "the apparent failure of the Left to meet the challenge of communist totalitarianism which discredited lib-

140

eralism and helped shape the mood of disillusionment from which the intellectual Right drew its appeal."62

Yet the fact that liberalism itself was so often caricatured and misrepresented by these conservative ex-radicals raises the question of whether deeper personality, temperamental, or psychological forces were more decisive than conscious rationality in this development. Diggins hints at this possibility, but leaves it as suggestive rather than provable. Some people evidently need certainty in their lives. Strangely enough, Marxism, Catholicism, and Communism have this much in common: they each, in different but complementary ways, offer definitive answers to the meaning and purpose of life in a way that a more agnostic and relativistic liberalism eschews. A surprising number of these men became Catholic converts later in life. Frank Meyer did so a few hours before he died.

Frank S. Meyer was a regular columnist for, and on the editorial board of, National Review, when he died in 1972. Born in Newark, New Jersey, he was a graduate of Princeton and Oxford Universities. While in England, he was an active member of the Communist Party. Upon returning to the United States in 1934, he continued his communist activities. In 1945, and possibly influenced by Friedrich Hayek's The Road to Serfdom and Richard Weaver's Ideas Have Consequences, he renounced his previous affiliations, and started on the road that led him to become a major contributor to such rightist publications as the American Mercury, The Freeman, and National Review. Meanwhile, his books, such as The Moulding of Communists, an insiders view of communist organizational techniques that make mandatory the justification of ends by any means, In Defense of Freedom, and The Conservative Mainstream, as well as numerous articles, marked him as one of the leading conservative theorists. In these endeavors, he carved a place for himself as both a major figure in the libertarian-individualist wing of conservative thought and a unifier of all strands of conservatism under the rubric of "fusionism."63

Meyer took issue with traditionalist conservatives for seeking continuity with the past instead of realizing that "the very circumstances that call conscious conservatism into being create an irrevocable break with the past."64 In its opposition to what it deems destructive tendencies in the modern world, conservatism cannot afford to be merely reactive; it must be active—even militant—in behalf of its preferred values.65 Edmund Burke, as good a conservative as he was, should not be regarded as the repository of all that is best in conservatism. What Meyer is really getting at, of course, is that the individual, not society, should be the main concern of contemporary conservatives. Communism, Marxism, Nazism, Liberalism, and Socialism have this in common: they all would give the state unlimited coercive power over the individual.66 The historical destiny of conservatism is to resist such a reversal of the democratic creed. Despite disagreement among conservatives on which values should be considered uppermost—tradition, order, virtue, authority, reason, freedom—what unites conservatives is more important

141

than what divides them. According to Meyer, an emerging conservative consensus can rally around the following seven propositions:

(1) "Conservatism assumes the existence of an objective moral order based upon ontological foundations."[67]

(2) "Within the limits of an objective moral order, the primary reference of conservative political and social thought and action is to the individual person."[68]

(3) "The cast of American conservative thought is profoundly antiutopian."[69]

(4) "Conservatives may vary on the degree to which the power of the state should be limited, but they are agreed upon the principle of limitation and upon the firmest opposition to the Liberal concept of the state as the engine for the fixing of ideological blueprints upon the citizenry."[70]

(5) "American conservatives are opposed to state control over the economy..."[71]

(6) "Against the Liberal endeavor to establish sovereignty, nominally in the democratic majority, actually in the executive branch of government, they strive to re-establish a federal system of strictly divided powers..."[72]

(7) "Conservatives see Communism as an armed and messianic threat to the very existence of Western civilization and the United States...they see the defense of the West and the United States as the overriding imperative of public policy."[73]

After the original liberal-conservative consensus that had helped to shape the constitutional-institutional system broke apart, "nineteenth century conservatism was all too willing to substitute for the authority of the good the authoritarianism of human rulers, and to support an authoritarian political and social structure."[74] At the same time, liberalism, which had been identified with individual liberty and laissez-faire, betrayed its moral purpose by embracing utilitarianism.[75] Now that conservatism has an opportunity to recoup on its past failures and reclaim its rightful heritage, the desired unity is threatened by the traditionalist—libertarian cleavage. Meyer assumes the task of showing how these two schools of thought can be reconciled in a way that promotes the eventual triumph of conservatism as the dominant American ideology.

The solution to the problem involves mutual recognition by adherents of both camps that the moral order which traditionalists wish to activate and the individual freedom that libertarians wish to safeguard are equally necessary attributes of "a good political order."[76] Both camps are opposed to an overly materialistic-relativistic value system and to state interventionism. There is no reason why this "double allegiance to virtue and freedom" cannot be integrated.[77] Both sides need to be less doctrinaire about their order of priorities and more aware of the basic complementariness, rather than conflict, of these conservative values. By directing their energies against the common enemies—statist liberalism and totalitarian communism—rather than inflexibly advocating their own preferred values, traditionalists and libertarians might easily reach an accord.[78]

George H. Nash finds that the conservative movement made substantial progress toward this goal during the late 60's and early 70's; he feels that Frank Meyer deserves much of the credit for this development. However, Nash acknowledges that "nagging internal tension remained," and attributes this to the fact that "much of the new conservatism of the 1950s and beyond sought to articulate a 'public philosophy' and the wish to be let alone."[79] Professor Nash does feel that considerable cooperation within the divergent conservative groupings was achieved on a practical level, even as the differences remained important and unresolved on a philosophical level. Others may be less convinced that such was the case. The point is, however, that Frank S. Meyer devoted his considerable talents to showing how, at a time when its prospects were getting brighter than ever before in recent American history, the conservative movement in contemporary America could unite around certain principles, rather than continue to weaken and fragment because of unresolved internal contradictions.

A close look at Meyer's writings, especially _In Defense of Freedom: A Conservative Credo_, will reveal how much more sympathetic he is to the libertarian-individualist, rather than traditionalist, view of conservatism. In fact, he must be considered one of the pillars of the libertarian wing of conservatism. He cannot see any way that the individual might benefit from being subordinated to society. He rejects the organic view of the self/society relationship. For Meyer, self and society are two distinct and separate entities; he is very much in the classical liberal mold in this regard.[80] Man is a social being, true enough, but not in a way that would endow society "with moral duties and rights of its own."[81] In Meyer's view, any political or social philosophy which looks upon society as greater than the sum of its individual parts is not just deficient, but pernicious. He criticizes many of his fellow "New Conservatives" for elevating tradition over the power of reason, but he commends them for their strong commitment to established moral principles.[82] Freedom is the absence of coercion.[84] A good society, and a good political order, are those which best provide for the conditions that maximize individual freedom.[85]

The traditionalist conservative does not view the state as inherently evil. The libertarian conservative does. Any concession that is made to enhancing the power of the state will inevitably be at the cost of individual freedom of choice. The trouble with politics as it is generally practiced today is that there is too much resort to political expediency and not enough attention is paid to political principles.[86] The liberal is almost as bad as the Marxist or fascist, since he is so willing to confuse what is best for the people and what is right for the individual.[87] Duty is an illusion when it it is at the expense of individual rights.[88]

In Meyer's opinion, traditionalist conservatives are wrong in thinking that virtue can be fostered by the state under the right sort of circumstances. For Frank Meyer, there are no "right circumstances": any concession to social coercion, even for a good cause, simply invites political coercion.[89] Virtue is best insured by maintaining economic freedom, rewarding initiative, and keeping the government out of the private sector.[90] Anything that is likely to bring about individual dependence upon public authorities is bound to result in harm to the cause of individual freedom.[91] The Constitution itself needs to be restored and interpreted in the light of what the Founders knew and understood, rather than, as is so often the case now, through various ideological blinders. And on the question of liberty versus equality, Meyer is quite clear about his feelings:

> The freedom of the individual person from government, not the equality of individual persons, is the central theme of our constitutional arrangements. Nor is this merely a matter of two different emphases. Freedom and equality are opposites; the freer men are the freer they are to demonstrate their inequality, and any political or social attempt— like those so frequent in the 20th century— to enforce equality leads inevitably to the restrictions and the eventual destruction of freedom.[92]

Although Frank Meyer truly believed that it is possible to reconcile the question of whether the individual achieves his well-being mainly by enhancing individual autonomy or through his community associations, it is doubtful whether the discrepancy can be successfully resolved either on a practical or a philosophical level.[93] It is simply another version of the relationship between duties and rights. Any resort to communal norms invariably emphasizes duty over rights, and any commitment to an absolute individualism is bound to sacrifice duty to rights. One can postulate a condition of voluntarism in either case, but the results will always differ. Although the proper notion of the self/society relationship may be one of interdependence, the fact remains that the underlying assumptions of the traditionalist conservative veers toward a belief in a dependency relationship, while those of the libertarian conservative favors a belief in extreme independence. Neither does well in dealing with self-society interdependence, since this requires non-conservative assumptions.

If conservatism by definition looks to slow down change, a degree of flexibility may be needed in an interdependent self-society situation so that either accelerated or decelerated change would be permitted. This is putting it abstractly; but one can appreciate the fact that the conservative is on weaker ground in this regard than the liberal; for to preclude the possibility for needed change because of the restrictive nature of one's world-view and preferred values is itself a surrender to necessity. The conservative is much more a prisoner of his initial preconceptions than is the liberal, although the liberal is hardly immune from this failing. The only difference is that the conservative position, especially as presented by Frank Meyer, contains within itself the seeds of its own extremism, and it is only a short step from a means-oriented to an ends-oriented conservatism, wherein authoritarianism displaces democracy. When ends count more than means, authoritarianism is sure to follow. It is a longer step for liberalism, if only because this ideological-orientation is more attuned to relativism than absolutism.

Robert Nozick

Robert Nozick, a philosophy professor at Harvard University, has written a major philosophical treatise which does for libertarian-individualist conservatism what John Rawls's A Theory of Justice does for egalitarian liberalism: that is, each sets forth the main outline for a theoretical defense of its ideological predispositions.[94] Both books have received a good deal of attention; in fact, they each represent a high point in philosophical analysis. Nozick's Anarchy, State, and Utopia won the National Book award of 1975 in Religion and Philosophy, wherein it was cited as "an enduring contribution to American political philosophy."[95] It would seem that at long last conservatism had found its true philosopher. Or is this really the case? One critic, Brian Berry, calls Nozick "the thinking man's Gerald Ford"—and claims the book is nothing more nor less than a high-powered rationale for ultra-conservative politics.[96] So, with an apology to the reader for dealing with a difficult, superbly argued, and generally well-regarded philosophical treatise in so summary a fashion, it will serve the present purpose to sketch the main thrust of the argument that Nozick presents in behalf of his minimal state theory.

The problem with any government is that it enjoys a monopoly of coercive power that infringes upon individual rights. In order to minimize the impact of such coercive power on individual well-being, it is necessary to limit the scope of government. Obviously, the very least one can expect of government is to maintain order, uphold the law, and safeguard contractual, or property, rights. Beyond this government should not go, according to Nozick. When government does transgress this limited role, it is already violating individual rights.[97]

Nozick rejects the anarchist non-governmental view of political power. "The moral prohibitions it is permissible to endorse are the source of whatever legitimacy the states' fundamental coercive power has."[98] He seems to favor private "protective associations" as intermediaries between state and individual.[99] In this way, man's dependence upon the state is minimized.[100] Protection becomes the one and only function of the state.[101] Rights are residual—meaning that they adhere to the individual, not society.[102] Nozick rejects the doctrine of fairness—that benefits should be dis-

tributed according to need.[103] The state has no rights that
are not also individual rights.[104] The state can intervene
to prevent individuals from violating the rights of others—
but nothing more.[105] "The minimal state is the most extensive state that can be justified. Any state more extensive
violates peoples rights."[106]

Nozick devotes considerable space to a re-evaluation of
Locke's theory of limited government and although he is deeply respectful of Rawls's A Theory of Justice, he finds its basic principle of distributive justice faulty.[107] It reduces
the individual to the level of group behavior and robs him of
his self-determination.[108] It places too much of a burden
upon social cooperation at the expense of self-determination.[109]
And what is worse, it maximizes the state's coercive power
over individual well-being.[110] Rawls's "difference principle," which asserts that no one should receive more until the
least advantaged receive a fair share of what there already
is, introduces a note of moral arbitrariness that Nozick
feels is contrary to the very principle it upholds.[111]

In Nozick's view, equality is a pernicious value; it creates a situation of unfairness in direct opposition to what it
professes to accomplish, since it would enable the worst off
to take advantage of the best off at the expense of both
groups ultimately.[112] The concluding passage of this stimulating book shows how a utopian and minimal state can be
equated:

> The minimal state treats us as inviolate indi-
> viduals, who may not be used in certain ways by oth-
> ers as means or tools or instruments or resources; it
> treats us as persons having individual rights with
> the dignity this constitutes. Treating us with res-
> pect by respecting our rights, it allows us, individ-
> ually or with whom we choose, to choose our life and
> to realize our ends and our conception of ourselves,
> insofar as we can, aided by the voluntary cooperation
> of other individuals possessing the same dignity.
> How dare any state or group of individuals do more.
> Or less.[113]

This bare-bones analysis does not begin to do justice to
the virtuosity of Nozick's dialectical skills and the intri-
cacy of his argumentation. It is a work that requires many
readings, and even then, one cannot be sure that one has truly grasped its brilliance. On the other hand, it will leave
many readers cold. There is little historical, sociological,
or any other kind of analysis to enrich his philosophical arguments. Although his argumentation matches his premise, the
premise itself still leaves much to be desired. Society and/
or the state is more than the sum of its individual parts.
This assumption, too, has a rich intellectual legacy behind
it, and has most often been associated with conservative
thought. To treat the individual person as an absolute and
society or the state as merely the repository of coercive
power seems rather odd, if not mistaken. Simply stated, Nozick presents an extreme view of the self/society relation-

ship. His political philosophy has reactionary overtones: it harks back to Social Darwinism and seems to be a reincarnation of Herbert Spencer's survival of the fittest, individualistic ethic.[114] Even contemporary conservatives should have second thoughts in following Robert Nozick's lead here.

To some extent, conservatism has reversed itself. In a previous age—back around the eighteenth century—conservative thinkers were the main adherents to a communitarian ethic which tied the individual tightly to the social and political experiences of his time; society and self were thought to be part of the same continuum. Government existed to serve man, and the corruptions of power were but one side of the coin; on the other side was the need to use government to advance social, as well as individual, purposes. Now all this has changed. Contemporary conservatives differ a good deal among themselves regarding both ends and means; but one thing they seem to have in common is an increasingly negative attitude towards both society and government—and a fierce commitment to liberty, as opposed to equality. In an age when the common man is finally coming into his own everywhere, this harsh preference for an individualistic ethic that undercuts communitarian aspirations leaves a conservative philosophy without a broad-based constituency. This is another way of saying it lacks democratic integrity.

Whether or not one can be sure about an "entitlement" revolution in the making, the fact remains, American society generally seems much more attuned to opening up opportunities for greater individual life-style choices, along with the traditional desire for maximizing political and economic freedom. On the surface, this would appear to coincide with the values long espoused by libertarian conservatives.[115] On the other hand, other conservatives, particularly those featured in the preceding chapter, see a greater need to apply the brakes to this across-the-board concept of "entitlement" in order to strengthen the social bonds of community, family, and religious authority as the only alternative to the social anarchy and moral nihilism that in their view an entitlement revolution will invariably foster. While libertarian conservatives seem quite willing to support anything that will 'liberate' the individual from all forms of coercive power and control, the traditionalist conservative sees grave dangers to individual well-being and social stability in such a development. The divergence between libertarian and traditionalist conservatives on this central issue is fundamental and irreconcilable.

PART II CONTEMPORARY CRITIQUES OF LIBERALISM

"The cost of deep commitment is a
certain measure, more or less, of
intolerance, and the cost of tolerance is a certain measure, more or
less, of moral apathy."

—David M. Potter

"Men who become convinced their
cause is just resort to means to
attain it that they otherwise would
not consider."

—James Neal

"Ten years ago, government was widely viewed as an instrument to solve
problems; today, government is the
problem."

—Charles Schultze

"Most reforms in every democracy
have been carried out in the teeth
of the popular fear of and resistance to change."

—Henry Fairlie

CHAPTER 6

ULTRA-CONSERVATISM: THE RADICAL RIGHT

The dynamic of change has been the most characteristic feature of the American experience. And never was this more true than during the first two decades following the end of World War II when a three-pronged revolution swept America and the world. One aspect of revolutionary change was the "population explosion," especially in the United States, which led to an unprecedented expansion in educational facilities and those cultural artifacts catering to a "youth culture." Some have argued that the youth radicalism of the late 60's was a direct result of this unprecedented bulge in the generational life cycle that created strains and tensions that could not be contained within normal bounds.[1] The other main aspects of revolutionary change were tied to a simultaneous communications-transportation revolution, highlighted by television, relatively cheap automobilies, coupled with easy credit policies, and the jet airplane. Almost two decades of economic stability in the United States also fostered the suburbanization of America—changing the iconology of urban, rural, and suburban America, bringing reality to the dream of owning one's own home to vast numbers of Americans, while black Americans in the millions exchanged Southern rural poverty for Northern urban poverty, but not without precipitating a "consciousness revolution" that brought the egalitarian ideal embedded in the Declaration of Independence to center-stage. Such rapid and profound social change was indeed the major fact of life for a whole generation of Americans.

As might be expected, change on this unprecedented scale, affecting the mobility, values, and life-style of so many Americans, was not without its psychic costs.[2] One's sense of identity, closely related to the continuities of family and community life, became harder to achieve. Status anxiety and loss, as well as the fall-out from insatiable consumeritis, affected everyone to some degree, and in political terms, traditional ideological patterns disintegrated as private pursuits and public actions drew ever farther apart. Ideology, for increasing numbers of Americans, became less a matter of personal choice than a reflection of media reporting, image-making, and mass manipulation.[3] In an area where most Americans had little direct knowledge and experience—foreign policy—they were increasingly dependent upon government or media experts to tell them what to think and how to behave.[4] As America acquired "super-power" status, and accepted the responsibility as chief defender of the "free world" against the imminent threat of communist aggression emanating from Russia, China, or Cuba, the general public lacked conceptual understanding of what it all meant, while their own confusion was only a little greater than that exhibited by their leaders in Washington. The result was a national tragedy: involvement in a series of Southeast Asian wars. It would appear that Americans had a much better grasp of the uses and abuses of power when the nation was weak than when it was strong.[5]

One important assumption underlying this study is the belief that there has been an authentic, substantial, and consequential alternative to mainstream liberalism throughout the history of American thought and institutional development, sometimes fusing with prevailing liberal doctrine, but mainly offering an alternative view of American politics and society that has had influence but little broad-based acceptance. But there has existed another side to conservative political and social thought that is far removed from this responsible conservative tradition—a strand that may indeed draw nourishment from both the liberal and conservative traditions—but which cannot be defended from a substantive philosophical perspective or as a beneficial influence on American politics.

Although many terms have been applied to this persistent current in American life and thought, its contemporary designations refer to a "politics of unreason," "the paranoid style," "the radical right," "the politics of hysteria," "the politics of extremism," and so on.[6] Ultra-conservatism is another such term, which will be used here to designate a phenomenon of contemporary American politics which includes the rise and fall of "McCarthyism," the unsuccessful bid of Senator Barry Goldwater to capture the presidency for the Republican Party in 1964, and the various radical right movements of the post-war period, with special focus upon the John Birch Society as perhaps the most politically active, if not necessarily the most typical, of these movements.

It is unfortunate that the prominence of these developments over recent years has tended to distort the image of conservatism in the public mind. Even if there is legitimate debate over whether ultra-conservatism links up with other aspects of conservative thought, there is valid reason to view these developments as a tributary to the mainstream of conservative thought in America, and therefore important in their own right but reflective of historical forces that helped divert attention away from traditional conservative political thought toward a more ideological offshoot of same.[7] At any event, this will be the approach taken here to these various developments.

Defining "extremism" in the American political context is tricky business. To label anyone an "extremist" in America is tantamount to branding that person a deviant, or what is perhaps worse—un-American.[8] "Extremists" are absolutists—in refusing to accept things as they are, especially some form of social injustice, they believe that it is important to risk personal approbation or injury in expressing some form of moral protest, such as civil disobedience.[9] Such individuals are sometimes dismissed as fanatics or psychological misfits, and when they advocate revolution and violence in behalf of their cause, they are automatically branded with the epithet "radical" and looked upon as criminals, whether they have actually done anything in this respect or not. There is also that form of "extremism" which usually fares better, and in fact comes disguised as authentic American-ism, so that unlike the left-radical, the right-radical can often find a comfortable lodging place in the American polit-ical environment during times of stress in American national society, such as was the case during the late 40's and the decade of the 50's at the height of cold war anti-Communism.[10]

To further complicate the problem of definition, it is also necessary to go beyond historical and political analy-sis into what many students of the subject feel are the socio-psychological roots of the "extremist" syndrome.[11] It is quite obvious that "extremists" in one context may be regard-ed as anti-democratic, and in another context, pro-democratic. The Abolitionists who spoke up against slavery in the pre-Civil War period were considered fanatics by many people at the time and accused by some later historians of major res-ponsibility for precipitating the Civil War on the grounds that their agitation prevented a peaceful solution to the sla-very issue. Yet it is also possible to honor the Abolition-ists in historical retrospect for striking a needed blow in behalf of a dormant American conscience.

The essence of extremist politics is the willingness to employ extra-legal means to achieve one's ends and defeat one's enemies. As Henry David Thoreau knew, "extremism" in the guise of moral protest is a necessary attribute of any healthy democratic society. And as the Weatherman faction of the Students for a Democratic Society demonstrated, "extrem-ism" that accepts violence as a necessary means for achieving social change must be contained and resisted. The problem is that it is not always easy in practice to separate legitimate dissent and moral protest in defiance of law and the kind that poses an illegitimate threat to a democratic society, especially when segments of the institutional structure en-courage that form of "extremism" which wraps itself in the cloak of super-Americanism when in reality it does indeed threaten the very foundations of a democratic polity. In this respect, ultra-conservatism qualifies because it is ess-entially anti-pluralist, contemptuous of the compromise na-ture of American politics, and capable of using undemocratic methods to achieve a different American society and polity purged of those who do not support their way of thinking.[12]

An ever growing volume of literature has grown up around the McCarthy era. Just about all of it is censorious of not only the role played by the Wisconsin Senator in exploiting latent popular fears of communist influence within the Amer-ican government in flagrant disregard of democratic norms, but also critical of an atmosphere of repression which was encouraged by seemingly responsible political leaders for partisan advantage, and disturbed by what appeared to be a deep reservoir of fascist-type thinking exercising a much

more pervasive influence upon the popular mind than reasonable expectation would have countenanced.[13] While a decreasing number of "far right" or "ultra-conservative" holdouts
still see heroic qualities in the late Senator's historical
performance, the general consensus has concluded otherwise.

In fact, the McCarthy era still presents itself as a
perplexing episode in American history precisely because the
nation itself had reached an apex of international power and
internal prosperity, despite serious dislocations accompanying the reconversion from wartime austerity to peacetime affluence. There was the political turmoil created by "hungry"
Republicans anxious to reassert congressional authority vis
à vis a swollen executive power and a feisty Harry Truman,
whose liberalism was well ahead of what most of the country
was willing to accept. In spite of all this, the period was
marked by considerable national self-confidence and stability. Yet the events of the fifties, dominated by this most
improbable combination of political irresponsibility and social malaise, also brought to the White House for eight years
one of the most personally popular presidents in American history—Dwight D. Eisenhower—and a resurgent conservatism. It
is hard to resolve these contradictions in retrospect. It is
even harder to understand how so much divisiveness could have
existed at a deeper level of national consciousness while the
surface waters remained relatively calm.

Of course, this was also the period that saw the "cold
war" heat up in Korea, a near confrontation between the U.S.
and Communist China over off-shore islands between Formosa
(Taiwan) and mainland China, the Middle East Suez Crisis of
1956, and the abortive Hungarian uprising against Soviet control in Eastern Europe. Stalin died in 1953, but his legacy
lingered on in the foreign policy sphere, while the threat
of communist aggression and the new protective attitude of
the United States "super-power" toward all arbitrarily designated "free world" countries irregardless of size, importance,
and internal stability became the uppermost concern of the
American people and its policy-makers. Some historians would
later conclude that the sudden change from "isolationism" and
semi-isolationism to "internationalism" and the assumption of
major responsibility for the fate of the rest of the world
all happened too fast and without real preparation, so the
necessary re-thinking and need to educate public opinion to
such a dramatically new role was bound to create a situation
where experience was lacking and over-reaction was unavoidable.[14] But a deeper question still challenges the search for
truth: why did it happen as it did; does McCarthyism reveal
a major defect in the American mind or was it a freak occurrence that is non-repeatable?

McCarthyism

Joseph R. McCarthy grew up in rather humble circumstances on a farm in Wisconsin. He was a pilot in World War II

and spent time in a South Pacific combat zone, although contrary to his own version of events, experienced no military action. Before the war, he worked his way through law school, became a circuit court judge in 1939, and after leaving the service, took on the long-shot chore of defeating Senator Robert M. LaFollette, Jr., who was up for reelection, and pulled it off.[15] Then for four years he was a nondescript senator with an undistinguished record. It was on February 9, 1950, that his name first attracted national attention with a speech before a Wheeling West Virginia Republican Women's Club where he proclaimed that he possessed the names of Communist Party members presently employed in the State Department and with the knowledge of State Department officials. Here is an excerpt from this historic speech:

> While I cannot take the time to name all of the men in the State Department who have been named as members of the Communist Party and members of a spy ring, I have here in my hand a list of two hundred and five that were known to the Secretary of State as being members of the Communist Party and who nevertheless are still working and shaping the policy of the State Department.[16]

The results of this minor political talk were electrifying. The Associated Press picked up a local reporter's coverage of this casual event and gave it national circulation, featuring McCarthy's charges against the State Department harboring Communists. A "rough draft" of the speech was given to reporters beforehand but the transcription was unfortunately erased the next day by the radio station as a matter of course, and to this day there is some uncertainty as to whether Senator McCarthy actually said what he was reported to have said, since he extemporized from the prepared text a good deal. Subsequently, he backed down on the original number of 205 and changed it to 57 "card carrying members loyal to the Communist Party," which casts some doubt on McCarthy's veracity.[17] He followed this up with charges in the Senate during the next few months.

A Senate sub-committee under the chairmanship of Senator Millard E. Tydings of Maryland was designated to hear McCarthy's charges. The committee was stacked against McCarthy and began with only Senator Hickenlooper sympathizing with McCarthy.[18] Instead of an objective inquiry with follow up investigation of McCarthy's "cases," the committee majority virtually prejudged the "uselessness" of McCarthy's accusations, was convinced of his "irresponsibility," and made it as difficult as possible for McCarthy to present his case. McCarthy, of course, did nothing to help his own side, since he was frequently abrasive toward colleagues and indulged in a good deal of rhetorical over-kill.

Membership in a number of "Communist Front" organizations was all he could do with his first case, that of New

York City judge, Dorothy Kenyon, and as one author has suggested, "in most instances, Miss Kenyon's connection with those groups had been fleeting or non existent."19 Then there was the fact that her name was not among those he alluded to in the Wheeling speech nor had she anything to do with the State Department. Meanwhile, McCarthy launched a counterattack to discredit the committee and had help from top Republicans who were anxious to reap a political harvest from the "sell out of China." The final report of the committee was a complete rejection of McCarthy's charges and the "evidence" he had presented against nine cases of State Department employees who were "known Communists," and the committee went on to accuse McCarthy of a "fraud and a hoax" perpetrated against the Senate and the American people. Republican Senator Henry Cabot Lodge was the main dissenter from the majority report, charging the committee with conducting a "superficial" and "inconclusive" investigation.20

In September, 1949, Congress passed the McCarran Internal Security Act, calling for the registration of Communist front groups, the emergency detention of persons believed likely to commit espionage and sabotage, and the tightening of laws against sedition and espionage. Liberals were generally opposed to the bill as passed as an infringement of civil liberties. One can see how an atmosphere was developing which greatly helped McCarthy attract support which might not have been forthcoming under more "normal" conditions.

The remarkable thing about McCarthy is that the more his "recklessness" was exposed and the questionable nature of his substantive charges against individuals was revealed, the more attention he received from the press generally, and the stronger he appeared among certain segments of the population.21 The Senator suddenly found himself with more speaking engagements than he could handle and he was credited with behind-the-scenes activities that helped defeat Senator Tydings for reelection in 1950. His influence began to be felt everywhere, both in and outside the legislature. He took on the Truman administration full force, seeking to discredit many present and past administrative-appointees, such as United States Minister to Switzerland John Carter Vincent and Owen Lattimore, a frequent consultant to the State Department on Far Eastern affairs, whom McCarthy accused of being Communists or "fellow travelers."

Whatever justification there might be for concern over some obvious incidents of "disloyalty" among important government officials going back to the 1930's, and the fact that Soviet espionage did infiltrate some aspects of policy-making both before and after World War II, such as in the case of the Assistant Treasury Secretary, Harry Dexter White, there was enough ambiguity in a situation where policy-making advocacy and outright disloyalty were hard to disentangle at best, to cry aloud for a "proceed with caution" approach to government anti-subversion actions.22 This was especially true when such accusations were directed against individuals who could not defend themselves quite so easily when a U.S. senator like McCarthy ran rough-shod over civil liberties and received accolades for it from influential segments of the political system. Earl Latham, in <u>The Communist Controversy in Washington</u>, has provided this fair-minded summary of the problem:

> The temper of the time was suspicious, excited, emotional, pathetic, and hard. There was rage and outrage, accusation and defiance, a Babel of shouting anger in these tense years. At the center of the storm of recrimination which flew so violently for so long there was a Communist problem, and there was a Communist issue. The <u>problem</u> was a matter of fact and law, and was dealt with (not inadequately) by the official agencies of the government—the removal of security and loyalty risks (however painfully and awkwardly accomplished) from employment, the prosecution of leaders of the Communist Party by the Department of Justice under the Smith Act of 1940, the prosecution and conviction of defendants charged with espionage activity, the discipline of recusant witnesses in the courts, and the conviction of defendants accused of perjury. These were, to repeat, matters of fact and law. The Communist <u>issue</u>, however, was a complex clash of attitudes and predilections, of dispositions and predispositions, of views about what should be and what should not be. It was a disagreement about the basic values of the American political system, in the course of which disclosures concerning Communists were used by partisans of various fealties to serve sectarian ends—Republicans against Democrats (or rather, most Republicans against most Democrats); conservatives against liberals; and Congress against the Executive. The Communist controversy in Washington bore with heavy stress upon the effective conduct of office and laid a costly tax upon that charity which assumes the good faith of decent men in government.[23]

Finally, when McCarthy's unprincipled behavior could no longer be ignored, he was forced to defend himself before his Senate peers in the famous "Army-McCarthy Hearings." It was a drama of an unprecedented nature viewed by millions on television. As Robert Griffith said, "never before had an audience of eighty million been made privy to the inner secrets of government."[24] When McCarthy started to "investigate" the army and humiliated the Secretary of the Army, Robert T. Stevens, the army retaliated by accusing "favoritism" in McCarthy's efforts to get a commission for his "chief consultant," G. David Shine, when the latter was about to be drafted. Then the "Paress case" erupted. Paress was an army dentist who was discharged because he refused to answer questions concerning his political affiliation with a possible Communist front organization. McCarthy demanded a court-martial

of the dentist and accused top army officers of a "cover up."
As Chairman of the Permanent Sub-Committee on Investigations,
McCarthy was a power in the Senate; yet the Executive branch
had to respond to McCarthy's attacks on the army and Defense
Department. Thus hearings were called and an investigation
of McCarthy's charges was authorized to be conducted by Mc-
Carthy's own committee. Since Roy Cohn was one of the key
figures in the charges of "favoritism" concerning G. David
Shine, a new counsel was appointed, Roy Jenkins from Tennes-
see. South Dakota's Senator Karl Mundt took over as chairman
of the committee.

Two months of hearings ensued. Public opinion, when able
to view directly McCarthy's conduct and tactics, turned against
him. McCarthy destroyed himself. The hearings ended incon-
clusively. But a Select Committee under Senator Arthur Wat-
kins was authorized to hear the charges brought against Mc-
Carthy of desecrating the "high traditions and dignity" of the
Senate. On conclusion of the hearings, the committee recommended that McCarthy be censured for his refusal to appear before the Sub-committee on Privileges and Elections in 1952 and
for his repeated abuse of senate colleagues. The Senate voted
67-22 to "censure" McCarthy. This ended his "power" and his
"career" despite the fact that he remained a senator. He died
a few years later of "liver disease" possibly caused by "acute
alcoholism." However, if the decline and fall of Joseph Mc-
Carthy came swiftly, it did not necessarily mean the end of
McCarthyism, for as one writer has suggested: "...though the
hearings marked the decline of McCarthy's personal power, his
followers remained potent. The House Un-American Activities
Committee was still asking McCarthy's questions, impugning the
loyalty of hundreds of Americans. Powerful legislative com-
mittees at the state level were destroying reputations with
emulative abandon."[25]

The term McCarthyism has gained dictionary status—referring to "smear tactics," "guilt by association," and a calculated violation of civil liberties. But the historical meaning of McCarthyism is still unsettled. Perhaps the most impressive defense of Joe McCarthy was a collaboration of two
avowed right-wing conservatives, William F. Buckley, Jr., and
L. Brent Bozell, McCarthy and His Enemies, who argued that Mc-
Carthy was as much victim as victimizer. They contend he performed a heroic role in alerting the nation to the very serious
problem of Communists in government. He was vilified by the
liberal press for his efforts, and despite certain personal
weaknesses and excesses, he was more right than wrong, and suffered from a malicious campaign of "McCarthyism in reverse,"
which was more a "cover-up" for liberalism's faults than justified criticism of McCarthy. Despite McCarthy's erratic and
sometimes questionable behavior, he was correct in charging the
government with "excessive laxity" in its security practices
and his single-minded dramatization of the "disloyalty" and
"communist subversion" issues was long overdue. And despite
his generally poor presentation of the "facts" behind his "case
histories," a more careful investigation by "fair-minded" of-

ficials and subsequent disclosures largely vindicates Mc-
Carthy's more serious charges. Finally, a "liberal conspiracy" launched such a successful attack to discredit McCarthy
that a smokescreen was thrown around the real issue of Communists in government so that most of those who were undoubtedly guilty got away with their communist shenanigans and the
people never did get a real opportunity to learn the truth and
the extent of the "Communist problem" in American government.
American policy in significant respects, especially regarding
Chiang Kai-shek and the China situation, was adversely affected because of "disloyal" government officials like John Stew-
art Service, John Carter Vincent, John Patton Davies, and
Owen Lattimore.[26]

The anti-McCarthy position can be summarized as follows.
As a result of McCarthy's scare tactics, civil liberties were
abrogated, many innocent people had their reputations seriously
damaged and in some cases their careers wrecked; instead of
"innocent until proven guilty," those charged as "disloyal"
or "security risks" were exposed to a dubious "reasonable
doubt" criterion which has a questionable constitutional basis. Even if there were a number of Communists and "fellow
travelers" in government during the 1930's and 1940's, there
were extremely circumstantial and even extenuating motivation-
al factors at issue, and little harm was actually done, regardless of the numbers involved. At any event, by the 1950's, at
the height of the anti-Communist mania, the movement was in decline in the United States, and even Old Left radicals had become disillusioned with a Communist movement which so obviously took its orders from Moscow. The affect on policy was minimal, if not non-existent. Partisan politics exaggerated the
policy consequences of Communist influence in American government. China, for example, was not "lost" because of the anti-
Chiang bias of certain key officials of the State Department,
but because of Chiang's own weakness and failures. Furthermore, two American presidents—Truman and Eisenhower—were in-
timidated by McCarthy's antics, and the main result of Mc-
Carthyism was to diminish America's standing in the world and
temporarily weaken those democratic safeguards that Americans
cherish as being the cornerstone of the American system. The
essence of democracy is that the means count more than the
ends; in no sense should the end justify the means. This
principle was bent out of shape during the McCarthy era.[27]

Two influential studies, Seymour Martin Lipset's and Earl
Raab's The Politics of Unreason and Richard Hofstadter's The
Paranoid Style in American Politics, develop the theory of status displacement to account for McCarthy's substantial mass
following.[28] People who experience rather sudden wealth or
are anxious about competition from other individuals and
groups that threaten to displace them in the economic order
are inclined to project their anxieties and insecurities on
those who appear to threaten their position in the social order. It is a form of status anxiety translated into status
politics. McCarthy's pronounced anti-elitism and attacks on
liberalism fit in nicely with such people's concerns, and they

became his most ardent supporters. Although small in over-
all numbers, they nevertheless insured his early success.
The notions of a "Communist conspiracy" to subvert American
government and the excessive power of an elitist "American
establishment" appealed immensely to this group. Although
many were working-class Catholics, others were middle-class
and even wealthy representatives of small-town and self-em-
ployed socio-economic categories.[29]

Michael Paul Rogin, in The Intellectuals and McCarthy,
takes issue with this thesis. According to Rogin, McCarthy
was no more and no less than an extreme version of conservatism in American life and thought, and the fact that he found
considerable support from the Taft wing of the Republican
Party confirms this. He was first and foremost a single issue man—anti-Communism—and thus had little to offer beyond
that, and no real political movement formed around him:

> The danger of McCarthyism, on the other hand,
> while real, was not the danger of a mass movement.
> McCarthy had powerful group and elite support. He
> did not mobilize the masses at the polls or break
> through existing group cleavages. McCarthy's power
> was sustained only in part by the vague discontents
> of frustrated groups. Communism and the Korean War
> played crucial roles. The real danger posed by Mc-
> Carthy should not distort our understanding of a-
> grarian radical movements in America, nor should
> the pluralist criticisms of mass movements blind
> us to the real nature of McCarthyism.[30]

McCarthy was a divisive influence in American politics
in the 1950's and his importance was primarily political.
His successes were largely accidental: "McCarthy acquired
his vogue and most of his meaning from immediate political
circumstances which begot him, and for which he was the temporary instrument."[31] Earl Latham also believes those aspects of American life McCarthy fed on and exploited for his
own ends are a permanent feature of the American scene—a
kind of "fundamentalist conservatism." And Robert Griffith
cautions against any simplistic single-cause explanation of
McCarthyism:

> Behind the rise of Joe McCarthy to national power
> lay at least five interrelated and interracting
> lines of causation: a fear of radicalism which some-
> times bordered on the pathological; the course of
> America's cold war with the Soviet Union and its
> not-so-cold war with North Korea and China; the
> singular character and abilities of Joseph McCar-
> thy; the structure of power both within the Senate
> and between the Senate and the Executive; and the
> routine operation of American party politics.[32]

In contrast to this tendency to emphasize the special
circumstances and uniqueness of Joe McCarthy's successes and
failures are a group of political scientists who see McCarthy

as an inevitable by-product of a serious flaw in American
pluralist society: its innate conservatism and indiscriminate anti-radicalism.[33] A recent volume of essays, The Spec-
tor, provides a representative sampling of the "revisionist"
view of McCarthyism.[34] Not only do the writers reject the
notion that McCarthyism was a mass movement of sorts revolv-
ing around "the politics of status anxiety," but emphasize
the fact that "...it was a conventional politics rooted in
the actions and inactions of conservative and liberal elites."[35]
In other words, McCarthyism was all-too-typical, and not at
all a-typical, of a socio-economic-political system that is
democratic in name, but not in fact, where elitism rules virtually unchallenged and equity gets short shrift. Robert
Griffith, who seems to have adopted somewhat stronger views
on the subject since his earlier book, sets the tone in his
introductory essay:

> By 1950...political leaders had succeeded, through
> the manipulation of popular myths and stereotypes,
> in creating a mood conducive to demogogues such as
> Joseph McCarthy. The Wisconsin senators' crude at-
> tacks on American policy and policymakers resonated
> through the political system not because of their
> uniqueness, but because of their typicality.[36]

What others call pseudo-conservatism these writers would
point to as the real nature of conservatism in American life
and thought. Opposition to change; upholders of wealth, privilege, and all forms of vested interest; defender of states'
rights, police power, and ultra-nationalism; instigator of
repression under the guise of social order and harmony—these
are the obvious attributes of a conservative value orientation that would destroy democracy while professing to preserve it:

> Throughout most of American history conserva-
> tives have labored more strenuously to preserve so-
> cial harmony than to liberate the individual. Un-
> sympathetic to the notion of a managed society,
> which they have variously called the 'welfare state,'
> the 'planned society,' or 'socialism,' modern Ameri-
> can conservatives have sought instead to build a har-
> monious society by creating a deep-rooted moral and
> intellectual consensus. In their view, deviant be-
> havior and ideas were heretical and ought to be
> suppressed, because they posed a threat to social
> cohesiveness. It was this theoretical postulate,
> together with the belief in human fallibility, that
> moved postwar conservatives quickly toward repress-
> ion of internal dissent.[37]

There is no obvious answer to the question as to whether
McCarthyism represented an all-too-typical manifestation of
traditional American conservatism helped by an elitist acquiesence and "the paranoid sense of the enemy, the conspiracy,
and the apocalyptic confrontation which have been central to
our history,"[38] or simply an historical aberration that tem-

porarily deranged the more normal functioning of American democracy. The answer one chooses, however, will affect both one's view of conservatism and the democratic viability of the American political system. Since shades of McCarthyism have cropped up all too regularly throughout American history, often clothed in nativist, racist, or religious bigotry, as well as various forms of political repression, it would seem to be anything but a sometime occurrence. Whether it represents authentic or pseudo-conservatism is a bit harder to resolve. The fact is, conservative politics in America has drawn heavily upon this underground river of incipient repression and paranoia. McCarthyism was just one of its many manifestations.

Barry Goldwater

In the mid-1960's, conservatism found a spokesman who could command a national audience when Arizona Senator Barry Goldwater won the Republican Party nomination in 1964 and the right to run against incumbent President Lyndon B. Johnson. The political debacle which ensued not only temporarily deciminated Republican Party representation in Congress, but seemed to prove again how unresponsive the American political system is to presidential candidates who are perceived to be too "radical" (either on the Right or Left of the ideological spectrum). Just as happened in 1972 when the "radical" George McGovern was soundly defeated by the "centrist" Richard Nixon, Senator Goldwater encountered bitter division within his own thinning party ranks and scared off a good many would-be supporters because he was regarded by too many voters, whether correctly or not, as a man who would institute radical changes of a reactionary nature, or act irresponsibly in the conduct of foreign relations, if he were to become President of the United States.

So two factors were operating to doom Goldwater's candidacy from the start: his nomination by a major party occurred only because the San Francisco Convention was dominated by an unrepresentative majority of "hard-core" ultra-conservatives, while the electorate-at-large remained essentially middle-of-the-road and politically moderate in ideological outlook; and during the campaign itself, the Johnson forces were successful in exploiting this inherent weakness of the Goldwater situation to further alienate the public against Goldwater's ascribed "radicalism."[39] In the end, Goldwater's massive political defeat was in the cards from the moment he was nominated. In the aftermath, ultra-conservatives consoled themselves with the heady experience of actually having had a candidate of their own ideological preference running for the presidency on a major party ticket, while the majority of disaffected conservatives surely learned this lesson for the future: given the nature of American coalition party politics, only "mainstream" moderates have any chance of electoral success. Less accountably, the Democratic Party repeated the same mistake in '72.

162

The operating word in all this is "perceived radicalism." There is a good deal of evidence that the defeated
major party candidates of both 1964 and 1972 were actually
less "radical," and posed less of a threat to the "politics
of moderation" than they were "perceived" to be by the general public. Although some allowance does need to be made
for each candidate's individual failings and for marked ineptness in campaign strategies, the evidence clearly shows
that both Goldwater and McGovern were vulnerable to widespread distortion regarding the extent of their "radicalism";
and in both cases, the "politics of fear" overcame the "politics of moderation," to the serious detriment of both their
candidacies. One of the mysteries of American politics is
the contradiction within a public which appears to desire,
for a change, an "honest politician" who "addresses the issues," states what he "stands for," and disdains the mealy-
mouthed, hypocritical, "all things to all people" equivoca-
tions that seem to be the obvious road to success in American politics; but at the same time, if given a rare opportunity to vote for such a candidate, the public perceives
him as too "radical" and "deviant" to cope with the demands
of "consensus politics" and act as a responsible "moderate."
Of course, all of these terms are subject to varied interpretation, but the point is still valid: an honest politician is likely to seem too radical to most voters, given the
peculiar nature of the American political process. Naturally, there is no way of knowing whether Barry Goldwater or
George McGovern would have made "good" Presidents. It is
worth noting, however, that in the light of what is now
known about their luckless antagonists in '64 and '72, it
is unlikely that they could have been worse. But the contradiction that both candidates tested and failed to surmount
probably represents a significant weakness in American society and politics.[40]

Yet what some would perceive as weakness others might
see as strength. It is quite possible the Goldwater and Mc-
Govern candidacies were political aberrations that did not
reflect the realities of American politics and represented
gross misjudgments of what most people desire from their
presidential candidates.[41] If it is true, as many empirical
studies have indicated, that a substantial majority of Americans are non-ideological and do not respond positively to
either pronouncedly liberal or conservative political philosophies, then it follows that other factors, such as personality, sectionalism, incumbency, socio-economic, religious, cultural, and even momentary perceptions, are likely to become
much more significant in determining patterns of voting behavior. From this standpoint, one could conclude that neither Goldwater in '64 nor McGovern in '72 qualified as a strong
candidate because they purposefully elevated ideology over
these other bases of voter interest and thus defied the traditional character of the political system. This does not
entirely resolve the contradiction of an electorate which
shies away from issues-oriented politics while pretending to
be receptive to it; but it does explain the self-delusion of

those who would persist in expecting a more coherent ideological response than is ever forthcoming. At the very least,
it also accounts for the fact that the American public is
either politically apathetic or pragmatically neutral, and
therefore predisposed against any sort of ideological politics.[42]

A slim volume that may have been ghost-written, The
Conscience of a Conservative, by Barry Goldwater, appeared
in 1960.[43] It enjoyed a phenomenal success, going through
more than twenty printings. In little more than a hundred
printed pages, Senator Goldwater called for a new conservative politics based upon "the wisdom and experience and the
revealed truths of the past (applied) to the problems of today."[44] Claiming that "the radical ideas that were promoted
by the New and Fair Deals under the guise of Liberalism still
dominate the councils of our national government," he raises
the question of why the American people overwhelmingly pro-
fess conservative principles while opting for non-conservative solutions to current political and social problems. He
is perplexed that "conservatism" seemed to be almost a "dirty
word" among leading intellectual circles, while at the same
time there is increasing evidence that vast numbers of Americans believe wholeheartedly in conservative values. Whereas liberals are preoccupied with man's economic wants, conservatives "take account of the whole man," especially the
spiritual side of human nature.[45] Above all, conservatives
are the true defenders of personal freedom in an age where
concentrated economic and political power poses a major
threat to the precious heritage of individual rights and liberties.[46]

In Goldwater's view, the liberal wings of both major
political parties have been in the ascendancy since the days
of Franklin Roosevelt, and the result has been the creation
of a bureaucratic leviathan—"big government"—as well as a
serious weakening of the federal principle of government.[47]
According to Goldwater, the Constitution has been systematically violated; this is especially true of the Tenth Amendment, which sanctifies states' rights and restricts the authority of the central government over many areas of public
policy, such as public education and civil rights. The contemporary Supreme Court has been especially derelict in this
respect.[48] Social and political change must not be imposed
by government fiat; the admittedly slow, but constitutionally
sound, process of persausion and education is the only justi-
fiable route when seeking democratic change.[49]

As for policy, Goldwater would remove all government
controls on agricultural production, which have been in effect since New Deal days, and would let the farmer take his
chances on a "completely free market."[50] Although he is not
opposed to unionization per se, he does feel that labor unions have become too powerful by virtue of their exclusion
from the anti-trust laws, the legally sanctioned closed-shop
in many states and involuntary use of union dues in the cam-

164

paigns of favored politicians; he is in favor of "right to work" legislation that would make joining unions an optional rather than compulsory matter. He believes "freedom of association" in all respects should be under "legal protection."[51] Property rights are an important attribute of human freedom.[52] The progressive income tax is a fraud, for "government has a right to claim an equal percentage of each man's wealth, and no more."[53] Here is the heart of Goldwater's political philosophy:

> The government must begin to <u>withdraw</u> from a whole series of programs that are outside its constitutional mandate—from social welfare programs, education, public power, agriculture, public housing, urban renewal and all the other activities that can be better performed by lower levels of government or by private institutions or by individuals... The need for 'economic growth' that we hear so much about these days will be achieved, not by the government harnessing the nation's economic forces, but by emancipating them. By reducing taxes and spending we will not only return to the individual the means with which he can assert his freedom and dignity, but also guarantee to the nation the economic strength that will always be its ultimate defense against foreign foes.[55]

The welfare state weakens individual character and the nation's moral fiber, and it is also a major cause of escalating taxation.[56] The expansion of the federal government into areas like education, which were previously forbidden to it, has resulted in greater controls on individuals and in a widespread, but misplaced, egalitarianism.[57] Finally, in foreign policy, there is no substitute for victory—and this means a heightened offensive capability, military supremacy, economic strength, the assertion of American power wherever there is a challenge to American interests, a foreign aid program which wins friends and strengthens them against would-be Communist enemies, and most of all, a strong containment policiy against Communist expansion everywhere.[58] As he later said of America's Vietnam involvement, it was a blunder to have "stumbled into the Vietnam war," but even a greater mistake going to war "without an attendant commitment to see it through to victory."[59]

In his post-election collection of short essays, <u>The Conscience of a Majority</u>, Goldwater continues to hammer at "the failure of liberalism" and the need for a revitalized conservatism to help restore "the national conscience." He also has some sharp things to say about the communications media, especially the TV networks, for deliberately distorting his "image" in the 1964 presidential campaign. He feels that the average American, "the silent majority," is fed up with an omnipresent Big Government and ready to move in a different direction, away from the permissiveness and the disrespect to all forms of authority that liberalism sanctions and toward a real

individualism. He cites numerous incidents from the 1964
election campaign in which his statements were reported out
of context, in order to create the impression that Goldwater
advocated indiscriminate use of nuclear weaponry and the abolition of the social security system, and that he was an example of the fascistic mentality.[60] He blames the Eastern
Liberal Establishment, and the Republican Party luminaries
led by Governors Nelson Rockefeller and William Scranton for
"creating a caricature of Goldwater that was so grotesque
that, had I personally believed all the allegations, I would
have voted against my own candidacy."[61] Paradoxically, "public opinion polls, which showed me running a very bad second
in the presidential race, consistently showed a majority of
Americans supporting the conservative concepts and principles
which I had always advocated."[62] If true, how can this discrepancy be accounted for? The answer: middle America, repository of the majority conscience, was presented with a false
"image" of the Republican Party presidential candidate and
was thereby denied an opportunity to vote their true interests.[63] As long as liberalism maintained its control over
the media and intellectual establishment, conservative principles and values would be unable to get a fair hearing.

How much objective truth is there in Goldwater's analysis? Was he a victim of news media exploitation and distortion, or a freakish and unrepresentative choice of a minority
political party whose defeat was inevitable, given the strong
ideological cast of his thinking and policy positions? Did
a reigning liberal orthodoxy deny breathing space to a broad-
based conservative revival?[64] Was Goldwater a man behind the
times or ahead of the times? Was he too much an ideologue,
and not enough a political leader who instilled confidence
in his ability? In the view of Theodore H. White, Goldwater
was never able to compensate for the fact that he "was running not so much against Johnson as against himself—or the
Barry Goldwater the image-makers had created."[65]

Although there can be no definitive answers to such questions, a few points might be emphasized. First, a combination
of unusual circumstances, including the recent tragic assassination of President John Kennedy, combined to make 1964 a
rather special year in American presidential politics. Rockefeller's vacillation, Scranton's lack of personal charisma,
and Nixon's disastrous political set-back in seeking the California gubernatorial election of 1962 weakened each of these
potentially stronger rivals and made it possible for Goldwater to seem more politically appealing to Convention dele-
gates than he was to the public. And with the Southeast Asia
matter still in the future, Johnson was in a strong position
to retain the office, regardless of whom the Republicans ran
against him.

Second, there is no doubt that Goldwater and his supporters overestimated the desire of Republicans for a truly strong
conservative candidate. They also miscalculated the speed at
which political re-alignment was proceeding across the nation

in the wake of Democratic Party losses in the South over the civil rights issue, and deterioration of the old New Deal coalition; as Hubert Humphrey's campaign in 1968 showed, there was still life in the Democratic Party majority coalition. Political support on the scale needed for a Goldwater victory was simply not there: his strong ideological stance divided his party and alienated large numbers of potential voters.

Third, there was a large hole in Goldwater's critique of liberalism and in his contention that the public was ready for his version of "the proven and lasting values of the past" translated into public policy.[66] In a post-mortum article, "Electoral Myth and Reality: the 1964 Election," three political scientists found the empirical data weighted heavily against Goldwater on this crucial question:

> In general, the mass of public opinion has been quite unsympathetic to traditional Republican thinking in areas of social welfare and other domestic problems for several decades. A major Goldwater theme involved attacks against the increasingly heavy hand of 'big government,' yet this struck little in the way of a responsive chord. Most Americans in the more numerous occupational strata do not appear to feel the governmental presence (save for local civil rights situations) in any oppressive or day-to-day manner, and as a consequence simply have no reactions to the area which have any motivational significance. Among those more aware of the practices and potentials of federal government, a slight majority feels that if anything, governmental services and protections are inadequate rather than over-done. Thus for better or for worse, such contentions on Goldwater's part had little popular resonance.[67]

Goldwater was not the best medium to test the hypothesis of the latent mass appeal of conservative political philosophy. As many others have pointed out, there was nothing new and much that was old in Goldwater's political views; simplistic diatribes against big government, the welfare state, weakened federalism, and equalitarianism provide no basis for responsible political leadership at a time when world power requirements, population growth, and modern technology have given the federal government increased responsibilities. A Jeffersonian liberal solution to contemporary problems is a utopian fantasy. If this is the best a conservative political philosophy can offer, then it is an exercise in futility.

There is an amazing paucity of concrete analysis, realistic policy alternatives, and substantive ideas in Barry Goldwater's speeches and writings. At best, he displayed personal courage and selflessness in his efforts to fill the vacuum that existed in the conservative camp. He recognized the need for a rallying point around which a conservative political movement might coalesce, but he failed to elevate the tone of dialogue between the two camps, and only succeeded in substituting a pseudo-conservatism for the much needed voice of authentic conservative thought and practice. Philosophical and pragmatic conservatism could not join hands in the wake of Goldwater's failure; they were wider apart than ever.

The John Birch Society

Since World War II, one of the more striking aspects of the American political scene has been the attacks upon mainstream consensus politics implicit in the rise to prominence of ideological politics on both the Right and Left of the political spectrum. Even before the New Left of the late 60's came to the fore, disrupting college campuses across the country and exposing the so-called military-industrial complex as the chief danger to a democratic society, the Far Right was active on a number of fronts, stirring things up, drawing support to its varied banners for a militant anti-Communist crusade. Rightist rhetoric found most of America's political and economic leadership derelict for being "soft on Communism," the nation in dire peril of Communist subversion and take-over, and a liberal conspiracy aiding and abetting the Communist forces, seeking to destroy the American Constitution and the country's Christian inheritance. The 1950's was a spawning ground for Far Right groups, since the "Communist menace" provided a convenient catalyst for crystallizing certain endemic anxieties and fears. Among the more notable "charismatic" figures that achieved notoriety during these years, were Robert Welch, founder and chief organizer of the John Birch Society, Dr. Fred Schwarz, founder and director of the Christian Anti-Communist Crusade, and the Reverand Billy James Hargis, the guiding light of the Christian Crusade.

There is no way of accurately knowing just how substantial the following of Far Right organizations has been over the years, but it has been estimated that about twenty percent of the total population either overtly or tacitly agrees with their basic philosophy; and in some sections of the country, such as the South, Southwest, and Southern California, the Far Right has periodically exercised considerable influence upon local politics and social structures. Nationally, the impact of the Far Right has tended to dissipate, and the politics of consensus has held firm, with the possible exception of the '64 Goldwater candidacy and the various forays into national politics of George Wallace, long-time Governor of Alabama.

Social scientists have been hard at work analyzing empirical data and speculating about the overall significance of this phenemenon in American politics, but so far there has been little agreement, except to underscore the fact there do seem to be some common elements uniting various manifestations of the Far Right: these movements all demonstrate a politically and socially divisive, intolerant, dogmatically ideological, and largely negative response to certain historical trends in the contemporary world. The main area of disagreement among social scientists and historians is the question of whether such rightist groups indeed pose a serious threat to the underlying stability and structure of American society, or whether they merely express the union of elements of fundamentalist Christianity with "know-nothing" politics, a fusion that has surfaced all-too-regularly in American history. The John Birch Society is generally regarded as one of the more instructive contemporary versions of this historical tendency.

Robert Welch, a Massachusetts businessman whose family owned the Welch Candy Company, invited a group of eleven "influential and very busy men" from various parts of the country to meet with him at Indianapolis, Indiana, in February, 1959, for an exhausting two-day presentation of his plan to establish a national organization with chapters throughout the country dedicated to the "fight against Communism." An amplified version of the notes he used during this memorable two-day lecture was later published as The Blue Book of the John Birch Society; in this work, Robert Welch sets forth the hopes, plans, and reasons for his organization with considerable practical realism.[68] By 1961, he was able to report: "We now have a staff of twenty-eight people in the Home Office; about thirty Major Coordinators in the field, who are fully paid as to salary and expenses; and about one hundred Section Leaders, who work on a volunteer basis as to all or part of their salary, or expenses, or both."[69] Although admitting that the growth of membership did not quite live up to original expectations, the report was optimistic, since the organization had encountered intense criticism from the "liberal establishment" and was having a notable impact disseminating its literature, gathering converts, and helping to save the country from the evils of Communism.[70] Robert Welch subsequently retired from his business activities to devote all of his time to promoting the John Birch Society, publishing a monthly magazine, American Opinion, which he had started in 1956, and continuing anti-Communist agitation in every way possible.

Welch makes a number of points in his initial presentation to the founding meeting of the John Birch Society. "For years we have been taken steadily down the road to Communism by steps supposedly designed, and presented to the American people, as ways of fighting Communism."[71] He mentions the foreign aid program which began under Truman in cooperation with U.N. relief and rehabilitation efforts as an example. "This pouring of American billions into foreign countries to make things easier for the Communists and their socialist allies and agents, is exactly what the Communists wanted the American government to do."[72] Contrary to the popular view, the internal danger of Communist take-over is much greater than any external military threat, and American leaders from the President on down were nothing less than treasonous in deceiving the American people into thinking otherwise.[73] Welch then gave his reason for calling the meeting and asking for help in launching an anti-Communist crusade:

> The only thing which can possibly stop the
> Communists is for the American people to learn the
> truth in time. It is to contribute my small bit to
> such an awakening that I have given up most of my
> business responsibilities and most of my income, in
> order through my magazine and speeches to bring
> some inkling of the truth to as many people as I
> can reach. I do not expect nor deserve any slight-
> est applause or sympathy for this sacrifice. I
> mention it at all for just one reason only—which
> is to show how deadly serious the situation appears
> to me.[74]

According to Mr. Welch, the stakes are nothing less than
the survival of American civilization: "This is a world-wide
battle, the first in history, between light and darkness; between the spirit of Christianity and the spirit of anti-Christ
for the souls and bodies of men."[75] Collectivism is a cancer
that will spread and devour the body politic unless resisted
and defeated.[76] Communist world conquest is just a matter of
time because of the incredible ability of Communist leaders
to dupe people into believing it is a humanitarian movement
when it is really a conspiracy of a very small minority. Because of its duplicity and the blind support of world-Commun-
ism by the American government, Communism will succeed unless
it is truly exposed.[77] The public in general is much more a-
ware of this danger than are the leaders, but the people are
being rapidly brainwashed by the liberal, pro-Communist communications media. This situation can be corrected by the
establishment of local chapters of volunteer citizens throughout the country; these volunteers would teach under the guidance of a strong, highly centralized leadership, with the express purpose of fighting Communism in all its insidious
forms.[78] This counterattack should remain within the law,
but must be capable of employing "mean and dirty" tactics,
when necessary, because the "Communists we are after are mean-
er and dirtier," and more dangerous because they are such masters of deceit.[79]

Most Communists wear invisible disguises and look like
everybody else.[80] Robert Welch is quite straightforward a-
bout the necessity of adopting the methods of the enemy to defeat that same enemy: "We have to face squarely up to the solid truth—that unless we are willing to take drastic steps, a
lot of them, and very drastic indeed, we haven't a chance in
the world of saving our lives, our country, or our civilization."[81] This means political action, and exposure of those
who pretend to be good Americans while actually doing Communism's dirty work.[82] And if this effort is to be successful,
it requires "positive leadership," such as Robert Welch represents.[83]

Next to Communism, government is the greatest single enemy of personal freedom.[84] It always takes more from the individual than it gives back.[85] The least government the best.

170

Any interference by government in the workings of a free market system is bound to be bad.[86] It appears that Welch equates the dangers of Communism with the increase in government power throughout the world in the 20th century.[87] A dedicated band of citizens, willing to take personal risks and exhibiting absolute faith in its leadership, is necessary to defeat the enemy within and without.[88] Only such unified purpose and energetic efforts can save America. Thus, "the purpose of The John Birch Society...will be to promote less government, more responsibility, and a better world,"[89] and The John Birch Society will function almost entirely through small local chapters, usually from ten to twenty dedicated patriots."[90] The ultimate goal is an organization with at least a million members.[91] The chief end will be a total destruction of the "Communist conspiracy" directed against America and the world.[92]

In 1964, Robert Welch published The Politician, an effort to give scholarly support to his charge of Communist dominance of American government.[93] It is a hard book to review, for even a fair-minded appraisal cannot avoid the conclusion that there is little to praise, and much to condemn, in this mindless attempt at historical analysis. Whatever failings Dwight D. Eisenhower may have had as President of the United States from 1953 through 1960, there is no justification for this piece of polemical nonsense and intellectual shallowness. The impression Welch seems bent on conveying is that President Eisenhower was a "tool of Communism," an unprincipled opportunist, and a man who virtually single-handedly opened the gates to Communist control of the world. In three-hundred printed pages, mostly devoted to an examination of the Eisenhower record, Welch finds nothing to praise, and much that he considers to be pernicious, in Eisenhower's military and political career. This sweeping indictment also includes most of the top officials in American government throughout the post-war years. The late first Secretary of Defense, James Forrestal, "whom the Communists later, either directly or indirectly, murdered" is one of the few exceptions.[94]

Among the charges Welch brings against Eisenhower is that the repatriation deaths of "at least two million victims" of "Russian, Polish, and other nationals, who were volunteers in our armies," resulted from Soviet pressure and Eisenhower's connivance.[95] Welch continues: "He was such a lousy soldier that practically all authority except of a political nature had to be taken out of his hands in order to win the war."[96] In addition, "he is demonstrably one of the most insincere, vindictive, and hypocritical human beings that ever lived."[97] As President, he was responsible for a massive cover up of Communists in government, and "of course in both the strategy and the tactics of this operation he has been guided by, and taken orders from, the Communist bosses who count on him merely for the execution of their planning."[98] He was able to become President of the United States only because "he had been planted in that position, by Communists, for the purpose of throwing the game."[99] Thanks to Eisenhower, the foreign policy of the United States clearly reflects Communist interests

and the Communist line.[100] Secretary of State John Foster
Dulles was "a Communist agent who has had one clearly defined role to play; namely, always to say the right things
and always to do the wrong things."[101] Throughout the book,
Welch tries to "substantiate" his charges with "documentary"
evidence; but one finds that most of his citations draw upon
other rightist publications and various "right wing" authorities. The book is a kind of self-fulfilling prophecy: a
Communist is anyone who does not believe in what Robert Welch
believes in, and assertion is the same as proof. It is a book
that only a true believer might appreciate.

Any issue of Robert Welch's American Opinion will reflect
the undeviating obsessions of a right-wing mentality: opinion
articles by Medford Evans, Gary Allen, E. Merrill Root, and
Dan Smoot, the magazine's "regulars," as well as articles by
guest contributors, provide a repertory of John Birch causes.
Although the anti-Communist issue is still alive and kicking,
there is ample space given over to a defense of laissez-faire
economics, attacks on sex-education, public education, consumerism, the United Nations and world government, détente in foreign policy, organized labor, prison reform, liberal-tainted
textbooks, and so on. The central thread that weaves its way
throughout the articles is the allusion to a "conspiracy of
insiders," or a power elite, working against traditional American values and strengthening the Communist cause everywhere.[10]
There is still a lot to be against; there are still targets of
opportunity to be hit by denunciation; and there are still
fears to be inflamed. Interestingly enough, moderate conservatives, including pre-Watergate Nixon, receive as much deroga-
tion as do liberals. The only notable historical hero is the
late Senator Joe McCarthy, who fought the good fight and was
crucified for his noble efforts.[103] The only thing that is
self-evident in such writings is predictability—one knows in
advance who and what is likely to be savaged and one can predict the "party line" on all public issues. It is written by
and for like-minded people.

Richard Hofstadter has suggested the following: "...it
has become increasingly clear that people not only seek their
interests but also express and even in a measure define themselves in politics; that political life acts as a sounding
board for identities, values, fears, and aspirations."[104] If
the personal need is sufficiently intense, the result may be
a suspension of rational control for the sense of security
which an emotionalized politics can provide. This is why damaged self-esteem, status anxiety, and a deep sense of grievance rooted in a feeling of powerlessness and loss of control
can sometimes be transformed into what Hofstadter calls the
"paranoid style," especially when social change and conflict
is rife.[105] Hofstadter presents this admittedly tentative hypothesis: "Pseudo-conservatism is in good part a product of
the rootlessness and heterogeneity of American life and, a-
bove all, of its peculiar scramble for status and its peculiar search for secure identity."[106]

172

As Milton Rokeach has argued in his influential study, The Open and Closed Mind: "It is not so much what you believe that counts, but how you believe."[107] Since a person's beliefs and expectations are part of a definable personality structure, mind and emotions interact constantly, and psychic needs can, for certain individuals, become a battleground for self-justification expressing itself through various forms of dogmatism, intolerance, authoritarianism, and closed mindedness. There is the need to be right, a need to feel that good is on one's side; in a world divided down the middle between the forces of good against the forces of evil, compromise is unacceptable, moral ambiguity abhorrent, and total victory for oneself against one's enemies absolutely necessary.

The result is the "politics of alienation," or a forsaking of the usual competitive demands of democratic politics for the more solid footing of revealed truth.[108] Too much of what comes under the heading of "modernism" is threatening, especially the leveling effects of egalitarianism and the depersonalization that accompanies bureaucratization; this prompts a desire to return to the values of "old fashioned individualism," and to regain a lost autonomy.[109] On the other hand, instead of reacting to this sense of alienation by social retrenchment, Barbara S. Stone concludes: "It appears evident that the stresses of modern life are such that individuals who would ordinarily be 'loners' feel compelled to political activism. Alienation here leads to activity rather than withdrawal."[110] The political sociologist, Daniel Bell, reinforces this point: "Today the politics of the radical right is the politics of frustration—the sour impotence of those who find themselves unable to understand, let alone command, the complex mass society that is the polity today."[111]

Perhaps the most difficult problem is determining whether the so-called radical right is simply an extreme version of conservative political thought, or something entirely different; a rejection of politics as it normally functions in the American context, a sort of "anti-politics," as John H. Bunzel has argued:

> The political character of the right wing, if it is to be carefully delineated rather than conveniently labeled, should be viewed not as the inevitable extension of conservative thought but as a distinct core of ideas and attitudes whose central meaning and purpose is subversive of the major tenets of true conservatism. The extreme right wing is angry at almost everything that has happened to the United States in the last thirty-five years because it is violently at odds with the main drift of the world of the twentieth century.[112]

One's response to this question will probably depend upon whether one feels that the radical right is a completely valueless and even dangerous aspect of the American political scene,[113] or, that it is, if not altogether praiseworthy, at least an understandable phenomenon that is more irrelevant than actually harmful. George Thayer has put this latter possibility in good perspective:

> Some groups are a potential threat to the stability of our society; others have ideas that at least deserve a fair hearing. Whatever is the case, we must learn to differentiate between the good and the bad. Too often we forget that many of these groups spring up to fill voids in our life that other forces in our society choose to ignore, just as groups spring up within the consensus to fill voids there. Sometimes we also forget that political minorities are filled with human beings with the same essential characteristics as everyone else. They are not mad, nor are they a different breed of animal; they are like many others—simply people who are concerned about, or who unconsciously reflect, various problems, the articulation of which is often unfamiliar and unwelcome by others. We also often forget that in many ways we all are members of one minority or another with distinguishing characteristics that set us apart from other men— whether it be in bed, in church, in our ethnic origins, on the playing fields, in business, in our tastes, in our habits, in our goals, or, finally, in our politics.[114]

Barbara S. Stone conducted her own empirical survey and concluded: "Many Birch Society members do not fall into the category of 'extreme conservative' and do not necessarily constitute a majority of self-confessed Birchites."[115] Other studies have emphasized the fact that the John Birch Society attracts recruits from a wide spectrum of occupations and socio-economic status. Leon Zinkler, a sociologist, attended a series of orientation meetings of one chapter and noted the following:

> Among the members were several low level executives with leading industrial and utility corporations, salesmen, housewives, a teacher in a private school, a detective for the New York City Police Department, a top-level post office official, a nurse, and a student. For the most part these upper echelon white collar employees maintained an upper middle-class standard of living, slightly above the average of the community.[116]

Many observers have noted particularly the close connection between "radical rightism" and "religious fundamentalism." John H. Redekop underscores this point in a case study of Billy James Hargis:

> It is this 'religification' of many traditional ultra-conservative values, rather than any inherently new ideas, which characterizes Hargis and the rest of the contemporary Far Right and makes them the significant movement they are at present...The major new ingredient which the Far Right has injected into the Amer-

174

ican body politic is nothing less than a frontal assault, in the name of Christianity, on the democratic political perspective, on its intrinsic secularity, and on its legitimization of conflict.[117]

It is one of the ironies of The John Birch Society that its highly authoritarian organizational structure, its stress on indoctrination procedures, the central role played by the founder-leader, Robert Welch, and its advocacy of tactics that emphasize ends over means, replicates the Communist contribution to political science to a startling degree. The authoritarian character of The John Birch Society was anything but accidental, as Mr. Welch admitted in his initial pitch to potential converts at the Indianapolis meeting: it was necessary, he argued, if the movement was to be strong enough to effectively combat the evil it was bent on eradicating. The fact that such an ends-justifies-the-means approach obviously contradicts the basic teachings of a democratic society and corresponds to the basic teachings of totalitarianism does not seem to bother the Birchite; this reinforces the possibility that the real appeal of such an organization is to a limited audience. The John Birch Society, like other radical right groups, caters to those individuals who have a socio-psychological need to find succor in a form of political activism that, paradoxically, is a risky undertaking in a society generally contemptuous of such "extremism," and yet is strangely satisfying to those who are willing to go all the way. Whether or not Robert Welch is a good politician, there is no doubt about his understanding of certain facets of human personality needs.

Finally, this much can be said about the relation between "the politics of extremism" and "conservative politics." Policy-wise, the two groups are quite close, and to some extent the conservatism of the dominant wing of the Republican Party offers a convenient meeting place for both groups.[118] Lipset and Raab have stated this point quite persuasively:

...running through most right-wing extremist groups is a conservative set of economic and political beliefs. They tend to oppose the welfare state, to view the growth of state power as evil, to see socialism and Communism as underlying all the political and economic reforms which involve any type of collective action to improve the situation of the more deprived parts of the population.[119]

At the same time, a difference of kind as well as a difference of degree separates mainstream conservative political thought from the pseudo-conservatism of the "radical or far right." That difference is marked by the basic rationalism which conservatives and liberals share even as they disagree about the extent and limits of rationality in political action, and the total absence of this faith in rationality that permeates the pseudo or ultra-conservative world-view. This is not a minor difference. These are diametrically different approaches to an understanding of political resources and to

175

the use of these resources to achieve human purposes. Ultra-
conservatism may fill a need and offer a relatively innocuous
alternative to other forms of reality-testing, but it is not
the most constructive political path that could be chosen.
It is a form of conservatism turned inside out. It makes conservatism look more funny than good.[120]

CHAPTER 7

IDEOLOGICAL CONSERVATISM: NATIONAL REVIEW

In 1975, the <u>National Review</u> celebrated its twentieth year of publication. It was founded by a group of intellectual conservatives as a sounding board for conservative opinion and values and, hopefully, as a vehicle to attract a wider national audience to a moderately conservative political stance. In both these respects, the magazine has been eminently successful. Under the aegis of that peripatetic national celebrity, William F. Buckley, Jr., the magazine's editor-in-chief, it has combined feature articles, editorial opinion, music, art, film and book reviews in a bimonthly news-magazine format, and has achieved a modest but influential circulation. Over the years, certain leading conservative figures, such as James Burnham, Russell Kirk, Erik Von Kuehnelt-Leddihn, Clare Boothe Luce, George F. Will, and William F. Buckley, Jr., reappear on a regular basis. Occasional defections from the ranks, such as the cases of Whittaker Chambers, Willmoore Kendall, and Max Eastman, have momentarily highlighted the difficulty of creating a viable consensus within mainstream conservative thought; but mostly internal dissension has been kept under control, and Mr. Buckley has wisely eschewed any catering to ultra-conservative "extremists" like Ayn Rand or Robert Welch, even at the cost of decreased readership support.[1] So under the conservative rubric, <u>National Review</u> continues to sponsor a diversity of views and even welcomes younger writers from time to time.

If there is one central theme which provides a certain unity of outlook it is a consistent attack upon all shades of liberalism. There is an obvious "enemies list" which receives special treatment, and although not systematically enumerated, it includes any and all public figures who are tainted by liberal doctrine. Beyond this, there are numerous attempts to defend conservative values in politics, literature, and aesthetics; but the magazine maintains a loose framework that permits a good deal of difference in emphasis and analysis among the stable of writers. Most of the magazine's content is more topical than philosophical, and more attuned to current politics than to either cultural or historical developments; but it does provide a meeting-ground for those conservatives who welcome an anti-liberal, pro-conservative journal of opinion which is intellectually respectable and not particularly reactionary.[2]

Writing in the mid-1960's, Jeffrey Hart issued the following pronouncement:

> Today there is something like a conservative intellectual Establishment. <u>National Review</u> has played a vital role in bringing about this transformation. There most certainly is an alternative to the revolutionary Left and a dissolving liberalism—an altern-

ative that is in harmony with our traditions and with the best that is in our actual civilization.[3]

One can agree with Hart's sympathetic appraisal without going overboard in thinking it also portends the impending early displacement of the dominant liberal ideological consensus. Conservative thought is no more unified than contemporary liberalism, and it is not alone a matter of ultra-conservative extremism versus moderate conservatism. As some conservatives have become more libertarian and less authoritarian in complexion, others have become more secularist and less religious in orientation; some conservatives accept some version of a mixed capitalist economy, while others reject this idea for a completely "free" and competitive private enterprise system.[4] It is not easy to devise a common strategy for policy objectives, to agree on fundamentals, or to join hands in a mutual endeavor under such circumstances.

The introduction to a collection of essays by thirteen leading conservative thinkers published in 1964, What is Conservatism?, offered this observation:

American conservatives are united in opposition to the growth of government power—of what is known as the welfare state—and to the centralization of that power in the Federal executive; they are opposed to the characteristic leveling egalitarianism of the time, an egalitarianism they see expressed on every level—political, social, economic, intellectual— of our national life; they reject what they consider the presently established national policy of appeasement and retreat before Communism, and they stand for firm resistance to its advance and for determined counterattack as the only guarantee of the survival of the American Republic and of our institutions generally.[5]

From a policy standpoint, this is probably close to the mark; but if one reads these essays in search of an answer to the key question, "What is Conservatism?", one is struck by the wide range of difference among the authors when it comes to defining such loaded terms as "freedom," "tradition," and "authority," and by the over-all difficulty in ascertaining the meaning of philosophical conservatism. In fact, it is the striving toward an ideological cohesiveness and an anti-liberal animus that marks such writers as less philosophical in orientation than driven by the need to define themselves by what they are against rather than what they are for. A closer look at some representative figures in the conservative movement will further illustrate this persistent difficulty.

James Burnham

In 1941 a book appeared which was destined to create a considerable stir in intellectual circles, and which has

178

since become something of a minor political science classic: The Managerial Revolution.[6] Noting that historical change was accelerating in the twentieth century and that established socio-economic-political structures in Western civilization were everywhere undergoing severe stress, James Burnham prophesied the onset of "a major social transformation that may be called 'the managerial revolution.'"[7] In Burnham's view, both capitalism and communism-socialism were doomed, and the present was a transition phase toward an entirely new kind of social organization which would be world-wide in scope: that is, the ascendancy of a ruling class made up entirely of technocrats in absolute control of the productive and governing apparatus of a highly centralized form of statism. Rivalry might continue to exist among nation-states, but a bureaucratic fusion of economic and political power would everywhere predominate. Democracy and totalitarianism would thus be superceded by a new type of society, characterized by a relatively small elite of manager-bureaucrats running things and by abject masses falling into line behind the goals and values of the rulers.[8]

Those who control the public sector will control the private sector, and neither property ownership nor capital resources will count nearly as much as technical knowledge and managerial expertise, which will be readily translated into political dominance.[9] "The basis of the economic structure of managerial society is governmental (state) ownership and control of the major instruments of production."[10] The Communist myth of a classless society and the democratic-capitalist myth of individualism are inevitable casualties of the managerial revolution.[11] Neither can provide satisfactory incentives for the needed economic growth.[12] "Managerial society is a class society, a society in which there are the powerful and the weak, the privileged and the oppressed, the rulers and the ruled."[13] There can be no separation of politics and economics: "In managerial society, the managers become the state."[14] Since there is little evidence that some form of collectivism, or statism, is not the wave of the future everywhere, "world society is now in the process of being transformed along managerial lines."[15] In the United States, the New Deal marked an early phase in this development, while Russia and Germany represent later stages of this ineluctable progression. World War II was a predictable result of a world socio-economic-political crisis. Burnham insists that he is presenting an objectively descriptive and not a subjectively biased account of social change. He claims that his moral values and personal interests conflict with the conclusion he has drawn from his analysis.[16] And although he acknowledges a growing awareness of the increased importance of the bureaucracy in modern forms of governance (without mentioning Max Weber's pioneer work along these lines), he believes that his theory of the "managerial revolution" is an original contribution, because he shows how the managers and the bureaucrats "fuse into a single class with a united interest."[17]

More than thirty years have elapsed since Burnham wrote this book, and it is now possible to view it in the perspective of the vast historical changes that have occurred in the world since then: he predicted some of these events, such as the rise of super-powers, and the decline of Western Europe; and he discounted many more, like the decolonization movement, the continuing vitality of both Communist and capitalistic economic systems throughout the world, and the independent role of charismatic political leadership in parts of the world. As might be expected in a book that relied heavily upon predictive trends and whose theoretical analysis was rather thin to begin with, Burnham was less prescient than he obviously hoped to be. If one makes allowance for the crudities of his general analysis, the tendentious theorizing, and his shallow prophesying, there is a residue of importance to this book. For one thing, Burnham captured the inner dynamic of a pervasive twentieth century phenomenon: a technostructure to some extent competes with and threatens to supercede established political and economic elites in advanced capitalistic and communist systems alike.[18] Also, he pinpointed the supremacy of economics over ideology, and especially the tendency of bureaucracies to control political structures. What he failed to do, however, is equally instructive, and reduces the value of the study: he cannot explain adequately why the "managerial elite" would necessarily be more successful than older elites in seizing and retaining power. The managerial revolution, to date, has been a partial revolution at best, and this is not what James Burnham had in mind when he wrote this ambitious book.

Despite the notoriety of his first published book, Burnham's most notable testimonial to conservative political thought is Congress and the American Tradition.[19] While all his other writings suffer greatly from polemical excesses and a pedestrian style, this 1959 publication still merits attention. As has been frequently noted, American conservative thinkers invariably defend the role of Congress in the American political system and, unlike many post-war liberals, decry any substantial increase in either executive or judicial power. Drawing upon historical documentation, particularly in reference to the Founding Fathers, and on a wealth of recent historical example, Burnham provides, in this book, a thoughtful critique of trends that he sees as a serious threat to the integrity of American democratic institutions, especially the decreased power of Congress over public policy. Congress, more than any other branch of American government, represents tradition, custom, and legitimacy; and the main consequence of an anti-legislative bias on the part of contemporary liberals have been a gross betrayal of the Founders' constitutional arrangements, a dangerous impetus given to increased bureaucratic power and control, and a severe distortion of the constitutional principle of balanced power.[20] Burnham is a strong critic of centralized power and plebiscitary democracy.[21] In contrast, "the diffusion and limiting of power have been of the essence, not a dispensable decoration, of the American system of government."22 He defends the Calhoun-Kendall concept of "concurrent majorities," which he feels Congress truly epitomizes.23 He blames the "advance of democratism" on the advent of a dominant liberalism which has, since the 1930's, pushed the American system toward "the general historical transformation of our era," a world-wide managerial revolution.24

James Burnham's least successful book is <u>Suicide of the West</u>, published in 1964.25 The grandiose title is meant to convey Burnham's conviction that all of Western civilization is in precipitious decline owing to the fact that "what Americans call 'liberalism' is the ideology of Western suicide."26 Citing names and publications, he lists thirty-nine statements, indicating value and policy preferences, which he believes a liberal would agree to and a conservative would dissent from. Two examples of these statements are: "everyone has a right to freedom of thought, conscience and expression," and "everyone has a right to form and to join trade unions."27 He then proceeds to criticize liberal assumptions regarding the nature of man, society, and the state, and concludes: "I rather think that the attitude toward tradition furnishes the most accurate single shibboleth for distinguishing liberals from conservatives."28

The book's analysis is too superficial to warrant extensive consideration, and too sweeping in its anti-liberal polemic to command much respect. Statements such as the following are all too typical of the quality of Burnham's analysis: "The average liberal is just not so concerned about, not so emotionally involved in nationhood, national patriotism, sovereignty and liberty as is a fellow citizen to his ideological Right."29 Ideological conservatives like James Burnham are so obsessed by the "liberal enemy" in their midst that they blame everything that goes wrong on a "liberal conspiracy" against American traditions and the American way of life. The evidence that they present to support this blanket indictment is strong on assertion or notably indiscriminate in tarring all designated "liberals" with the same brush, and replete with good-guy versus bad-guy overtones. Again, here is a typical example of Burnham's tendency to reduce complex historical developments to meaningless verbiage:

Liberalism cannot either see or deal with the domestic jungle and the backward regions—the two challenges are closely similar. Liberalism is unfitted by its rationalistic optimism, its permissiveness, its egalitarianism and democratism, and by its guilt. Consider once more the logic of liberalism in relation to the backward regions, bringing it to bear on the question of survival.30

When he gets away from denouncing liberals and deals with historical figures like Machiavelli, Mosca, Sorel, Michels, and Pareto, as he did in <u>The Machiavellians</u>, he can be a stimulating guide. However, even in this book, he has an axe to

181

grind; he makes no attempt to soften his contempt for the masses or his elitism, as this significant passage shows:

> The Machiavellian analysis, confirmed and re-
> confirmed by the evidence of history, shows that the
> masses simply do not think scientifically about po-
> litical and social aims; and that, even if they did,
> the technical and administrative means for implement-
> ing their scientific thought would necessarily be
> lacking. Beliefs, ideals, do sometimes influence
> the political actions of the masses; these are not,
> however, scientific beliefs and ideals, but myths
> or derivations.[31]

No one has offered a better critique of James Burnham than the one written in the mid-1940's by the great English essayist, George Orwell. Orwell not only questions the dub-ious predictive value of Burnham's "managerial revolution" thesis; he astutely dissects the distortions and contradic-tions in much of Burnham's analysis.[32] He notes that power has always been the central theme of Burnham's political out-look, and points out that Burnham frequently displays a se-cret admiration for strong power leaders, like Stalin, while seemingly warning against excessive concentrations of power in other contexts.[33] As a theorist of change, Burnham is a total failure, for "it will be seen that at each point Burn-ham is predicting a continuation of the thing that is happen-ing;" this, Orwell rightly points out, is an exercise in wish-ful thinking.[34] Because Burnham's view of the world is based on a simplistic Social Darwinist glorification of strength and abhorrence of weakness, there is no room for either ethi-cal constraints or humanistic respect for means over ends. The Nazi mentality, therefore, is an object of awe, as well as praise, in much of Burnham's early work.[35] Burnham is driven to activism by an apocalyptic vision of a world on the brink of imminent catastrophe; but the future never quite fulfils itself in conformance with the Burnhamian time-table.[36] Ultimately, according to George Orwell, James Burnham under-stands power no better than he understands history; the con-servative as ideologue is on an ego trip, not an intellectual odyssey.[37]

James Burnham exhibits both the strengths and weaknesses of an ideological conservatism. He is better at defending conservative values than exposing the inadequacies of liberal-ism. He is a traditionalist who earnestly wishes to under-stand the forces of change in the world; but he reveals his helplessness when faced by changes he does not like by failing to give either a persuasive description of alternate choices or an adequate explanation of why things are as they are. Un-fortunately, his critique of liberalism is more an exercise in personal therapy than substantive analysis.

Russell Kirk

Since the publication of <u>The Conservative Mind</u> in 1953, Russell Kirk has been a star in the conservative galaxy.[38] His analytical survey of conservative thinkers, from Burke to the present, displays scholarly erudition, provides a base-line for relating conservative principles to political and social thought, and is the first major attempt to define a conservative tradition within the welter of competing ideological positions. Although there is much one can quarrel with in the evaluative aspects of Kirk's study, one can appreciate the range and depth of his analysis. As an essayist and book reviewer whose writings have appeared mainly in the <u>National Review</u>, Russell Kirk has produced a considerable body of work over the years; but his crowning intellectual achievement has been a solid, insightful, and well-written book tracing the intellectual legacy which culminated in the American Declaration of Independence and the Constitution of 1787: <u>The Roots of American Order</u>.[39] Although fellow conservatives have not always agreed with Kirk's view of "principled conservatism," there is a large reservoir of respect for the contribution he is making toward a revival of conservative political and social ideas.

<u>A Program for Conservatives</u>, published in 1954, represents a sort of "conservative manifesto," pointing to the road which conservative thought should travel.[40] The most important characteristic of a conservative world-view, according to Kirk, is respect for the wisdom of the past, and acceptance of the past as a guide for present and future conduct.[41] Anyone who believes that man should intervene in human affairs, and should impose change in pursuit of an illusory concept of progress and social betterment, is violating the sacred well-springs of moral order and established authority.[42] Liberals and radicals are so enamored of Reason with a capital "R" and perfectability that they completely forget the tragic insight contained in the Christian doctrine of original sin. The average person is incapable of appreciating the fact that "society...is a delicate growth, kept in tolerable health only because some conscientious men, ordinarily few in number, devote their lives to conserving the complicated general ideas and political institutions and economic methods which we have inherited from our ancestors."[43] At the same time, Kirk refutes the class-bound implications of this assumption: conservatism, being a state of mind and not merely an expression of socio-economic standing, has just as much potential appeal to modest achievers as to high achievers.[44] In fact, conservative ideas and ideals have permeated American life and thought throughout the country's history.[45] Kirk argues thus: "What gives the true conservative his strength in our time of troubles is his belief in a moral order which joins all classes in a common purpose..."[46]

Conservatism respects individuality, not individualism per se.[47] The essence of conservatism is man's willingness to adapt to the eternal order of existence lodged in the changeless principles and patterns of the past.[48] Education should be intellectually demanding and should weed out those who cannot profit from an exacting standard of excellence.[49] For this reason, Kirk sees nothing good and much that is pernicious in John Dewey's celebrated influence upon American educational philosophy.[50] Secularist materialism and hedonistic pleasure-seeking are the twin evils of contemporary civilization; they create a massive social problem of chronic boredom and insatiable craving, as well as a mindless selfishness that destroys moral values.[51] The only antidote to this trend is a restoration of religious faith and piety.[52] Anything that contributes to greater leveling, equalitarianism, and utilitarianism meets with Kirk's unconditional disapproval.[53] Ability should be rewarded; inequality is a necessary attribute of a social order built upon hierarchy and authority.[54] "We are made for cooperation, not for strife; and order is not a corruption of the natural equality of man, but instead the realization of the providential design which made us one another's keepers."[55]

Reducing the power of government is the greatest challenge facing the world today; and it can be accomplished only through moral awareness and institutional-legal constraint.[56] Kirk is against any assumption by government of welfare responsibilities, because a centralized welfare system subverts individual initiative and rights and undermines localism, or "grass roots" democracy.[57] He sees no virtue in the ideal of a classless society; "privilege, in any society, is the reward of duties performed..."[58] Kirk does not believe that all change is bad; but he approves of only that change which respects traditions and social order.[59] Industrialization and urbanization have been the two main reasons for the "decay of the influence of tradition" in the modern world.[60] Rapid, untempered, excessive social change causes a repudiation of those "enduring values" which make life worth living.[61]

Russell Kirk takes pride in proclaiming the virtue of intellectual pursuits, and denouncing the dead-end character of materialistic striving.[62] The union of religion, tradition, and the wisdom of our ancestors should be man's chief goal: "We are free in proportion as we recognize our real duties and our real limitations."[63] The most important difference between liberal and conservative outlooks is the illusion, cherished by liberals, that man can transcend his essentially tragic destiny by an appeal to "Rationality with a capital R."[64] Atomistic individualism and the rejection of man's ultimate dependence upon a sense of community has been the main failure of liberalism, and the main reason why collectivist values have such a strong appeal to many people today.[65]

Unlike the liberal or radical, a conservative is non-ideological, because he believes solely in inward humanistic change, not outward impersonal change.[66] The right kind of paternalism is good; thus society has a perfect right to censor marked defiance of the public moral code.[67] Justice is based upon transcendental moral authority and is not a search for greater socio-economic equity, as the contemporary liberal might believe.[68] Kirk's conception of justice requires a dependence upon religious instruction and a firm rejection of relativistic values.[69] The lessons of the past point to one conclusion: "Every right is married to a duty; every freedom owns a corresponding responsibility; and there cannot be genuine freedom unless there is also genuine order in the moral realm and the social realm."[70] Values need to be anchored in permanence and hierarchical gradations of greater and lesser worth. Because most human beings prefer security over true independence of mind and action, only the few can benefit from freedom, "and in the long run, the security and contentment of the whole of humanity depend upon the survival of that freedom for the few."[71]

In The Roots of American Order, Russell Kirk discovers a tradition that goes back to early Christianity, Greek and Roman thought, and the medieval historical experience, and that unites faith, tradition, and morality in laying the foundations for the rule of law, republican government, and limitations on power—the three great principles of American republicanism. Borrowing heavily from the English libertarian tradition, Kirk shows how the colonial leaders were preservationists, rather than true rebels. They viewed George III, who was intent upon destroying self-government in the colonies, as the real revolutionary; and they declared independence, fought a war, and established a new system of government based upon principles that were not revolutionary, but were deeply rooted in Western history.[72] In fact, all that is best in the American political tradition derives from these roots:

> The written Constitution has survived and has retained authority because it is in harmony with laws, customs, habits, and popular beliefs that existed before the Constitutional Convention met at Philadelphia—and which still work among Americans today. The written Constitution produced by the delegates from the several states drew upon the political experience of the colonies, upon their legacy of English law and institutions, upon the lessons of America under the Articles of Confederation, upon popular consensus about certain moral and social questions. Thus the Constitution was no abstract or utopian document, but a reflection and embodiment of political reality in America. Once ratified, the Constitution could obtain the willing compliance of most Americans because it set down formally and in practical fashion much of the 'unwritten' constitution of American society.[73]

From a contemporary perspective, Kirk sees both gain and loss in the unredeemed promise of conservatism.[74] In the United States and Great Britain, he finds the political structure virtually intact, private property still "an institution of immense power," and conservative principles alive and well

185

among large segments of the population.[75] On the other hand, he sees grave danger in the trend toward mass society, the sovereignty of the lowest common denominator of popular taste and aspiration, and the mindless dependence upon government as a panacea for solving all the nation's ills. A further decline in the sense of community could conceivably destroy all that is best in Western civilization, because it would give collectivism its only real basis of mass appeal, with liberalism facilitating this gross miscarriage of justice.[76] Democracy is a false ideal: carried to an extreme, it stifles creativity and individuality, and sacrifices liberty on the altar of a misguided egalitarian ideal.[77] The restoration of a social and moral order that conforms to the traditions of the past is the greatest contribution conservatism can make to a strengthened republic.[78] The planned society, a lust for change, runaway secularism, loss of community, and discontinuity between past and present can be resisted, and these contemporary tendencies must be ultimately arrested. Only a revival of conservative principles and values can accomplish that end.

Two questions need to be asked concerning Russell Kirk's conservative vision. First, does his analysis correspond with objective reality? Second, are his professed values sufficiently all-inclusive that they offer a valid alternative to either liberalism or radicalism? In response to the first question, one can say that Kirk's analysis postulates the supremacy of ill-defined moral standards and practices, and denies the efficacy of economic and psychological motivations in human striving and behavior. Intellectually, this leads to a one-factor reductionism; practically, this position becomes an elitist definition of moral worth that excludes most of the human race. Even granting the impossibility of clearly explaining what objective reality is, it is obvious that Kirk's prescription for human society contains an exclusiveness that prevents the ordinary person from supporting it. As a political and social philosophy, Kirk's analysis is self-limiting. It is also unreal, for it elevates mind over matter in a way that does justice to neither. However, those who have the most to gain from a privileged status are in the strongest need of self-justification. Kirk's moral philosophy fills the bill quite well.

In regard to the second question, Kirk's conservative vision is unacceptable to many other conservatives; therefore, it is not a suitable foundation on which to build a cohesive, and widely accepted, conservative ideology. Kirk's thought is too narrowly elitist, too defensively authoritarian, too oriented toward the past to be a viable democratic conservatism. It is almost as though Kirk's real message is this: what is, is right. Even conservatism can, and should, be forward-looking. Not everything about the past should be glorified or preserved. Kirk would undoubtedly agree to this, but it is very difficult to determine what yardstick he would use to separate good from bad. It is perhaps instructive to note here that

186

Russell Kirk, on his own admission, was a last-ditch defender of the discredited presidency of Richard Nixon, in defiance of mounting evidence implicating Nixon in law-breaking and constitutional violations. In other words, established authority is its own justification. If Kirk cannot bring himself to correct or repudiate falsehood when it is clothed in the raiments of authority, tradition, or prescription, then there must be something lacking in his hierarchy of values.[79] Ethical standards that cannot be adjusted to changing circumstances foster rigidity, intolerance, and ideological dogmatism. Conservatives must be aware of this problem, and must search for a means of avoiding this pitfall without sacrificing their advocacy of certain traditional, preservative, and authoritative values. Russell Kirk does not avoid this conservative dilemma; in fact, he proceeds blindly into the pit.

The ideological conservative should be listened to with attention when expressing value preferences that are frequently ignored or denigrated by proponents of other ideologies. But any weakness in the liberal's addiction to moral relativism does not warrant choosing some form of moral absolutism in its stead, as Kirk would have it. It is a thin line separating democratic conservatism and non-democratic authoritarianism even in the guise of Kirkian benign paternalism.

William F. Buckley, Jr.

No individual has done more to spread the message of conservatism over the past two decades than this editor, lecturer, TV interviewer, columnist, and author. Although Mr. Buckley's caustic wit and skills as an entertainer frequently get in the way of his intellectualizing, there is no doubt that he is a serious defender of the faith. He constantly probes the outer edges of conservative doctrine in an effort to make his ideas more palatable to a wider audience and more forward-looking than is usual among conservative thinkers. Without being the most typical or original thinker among his colleagues, he is nevertheless capable of shifting from topicality to fundamental assessment smoothly and helpfully. Although much of his work suffers from the current events flavor of his primary preoccupations, it obviously attempts to link policy views to a more viable conservative philosophy. If he has been a good deal less successful in this endeavor than in developing ephemeral position papers, the reason is more a matter of choice than of inadequate ability. For he made a splash on the national scene with his first book, God and Man at Yale, written while he was still a student, and published in 1952, shortly after his graduation from that renowned instituion.[80] Since the book represented an uninhibited attack on a large number of faculty members and on what Buckley saw as a notable liberal-left bias within the social science and humanities departments of the university, it created something of a stir when it was published. And whatever limitatations the book contained, it served its purpose by pushing the young William

187

Buckley into the limelight.

God and Man at Yale is an impressionistic, subjective, non-empirical survey of the departments of Sociology, Religion, Psychology, and Political Science, drawing heavily on the courses Buckley took from leading professors and on his conversations with fellow students, as well as on the textbooks adopted as required readings for the various courses. With few exceptions, he finds the overwhelming majority of textbooks and teachers to be anti-conservative, pro-liberal, and in some instances, downright collectivist in orientation. He deplores the fact that Yale undergraduate students—who are the future leaders of the country's professional, business, and political elites—are being exposed to virtual indoctrination despite the lip-service paid to the concept of higher education as "the market place of ideas," a forum where diverse opinions, unpopular views, and ideological eclecticism should be respected and encouraged. Instead, he found that the academic environment was dominated by anti-religious agnosticism, Keynesian economic theory, and collectivist political and social ideas, systems of thought that complemented and reinforced each other. He quotes chapter and verse from textbooks, lectures, and student opinion to support his charges.

The main thrust of his attack upon this "reigning liberal orthodoxy" is to accuse the Board of Trustees, made up of influential former Yale alumni, of betraying their oath of allegiance to the institution and their responsibility to the students by permitting such a state of affairs to continue unhampered. Buckley questions the propriety and justification of appointing and maintaining so many instructors who "seek to subvert religion and individualism," while taking refuge under the misguided concept of "academic freedom."[81] Since he assumes that most Yale students and alumni are committed to Christianity and the Protestant Ethic, he is describing a situation in which the values of most Yale students, both present and former, are being systematically repudiated and subverted. Buckley also assumes, without any evidence to substantiate his position, that the average Yale student is highly susceptible to indoctrination and so impressed by the eminence of the Yale faculty that they offer little resistance to the liberal and radical ideas they are systematically exposed to. Even without evidence to the contrary, this remains a dubious assumption, and weakens his argument.

Although Buckley names names and provides a good deal of illustrative support for his thesis, the book is exceedingly superficial and rests upon weak foundations. Its notoriety stemmed from the audacity of the undertaking and to the unconventional circumstances: very few ex-students have ever been successful in publishing a book which expresses a personal grievance against the education they received, even when there may have been some truth to the allegations. In this instance, Buckley did pull it off; but his stark either/orism, which sees a threat to individualism in all forms of governmentalism, a threat to established religion in all forms of agnosticism, and a threat to elitism in all forms of collectivism, betrays his own narrow understanding of a democratic society. Buckley believes that the masses owe it to themselves to defer to the superior wisdom and ability of the elite, "for if we cannot rely on the elite among our citizenry—the beneficiaries of higher education—to accommodate newly perceived truth and to adjust their thinking and acts correspondingly, there is little to be said for conferring on the people at large the reins of our destiny."[82] The one area of weakness in all of Buckley's writings is this unwillingness, or inability, to show how elitism can be made accountable to democratic values and to prove that it is capable of assuming responsibility for the nation's destiny. If Buckley and other conservatives are correct, and the elites do govern America, then it is hard to understand why they should be so vulnerable to competing ideologies, especially when the masses have more or less assimilated an individualistic ideology that does not really conform to their true needs and interests.

As might be expected, Buckley's analytical faculties grew more refined and acute over the years, so that the crudities and shallowness of his first publication proved to be atypical of his thought processes. As time went on, his criticism of liberalism and his defense of conservative values made him a leading national spokesman for this ideological position.[83] The chief errors of liberalism, according to Buckley, are its reliance on government as a panacea for social ills, and its tendency to establish unrealizable goals that produce a backlash of mass frustration and unfilfillable expectations.[84] Only decentralized power and the economic initiative of the private sector can insure ordered progress and requisite stability. The great strength of conservatism is that it is "the politics of reality."[85] The constitutional Bill of Rights should not be regarded as an absolute; the social good requires some restriction on the abuse of freedom. Religion is a necessary attribute of civic morality. The relativism, agnosticism, and statism preached by today's liberals represent the greatest internal threat to American civilization; and Communism remains the greatest threat to national security, in spite of recent efforts toward co-existence and détente policy agreements. Even conservative presidents like Nixon and Ford have not fostered a rejuvenation of conservatism; political expediency has a way of undercutting the best intentions of those in power.

In accordance with good conservative doctrine, Buckley is opposed to popular democracy, since "instant guidance by the people of the government means instability, and instability is subversive of freedom."[86] The problem of poverty in the midst of relative plenty is irremediable, because at least a half of all poor people "are utterly lacking in self-discipline," and "cannot be persuaded even to flush their own toilets."[87] Although he has always entertained ambivalent feelings about Richard Nixon's qualification to be President of the United States, and has always distrusted the genuineness of Nixon's

conservatism, Buckley could never bring himself to condemn
Nixon for unconstitutional conduct and law-breaking; for "the
fact of the matter is that most Presidents are above many laws,
and if they weren't, they wouldn't be able to function in the
way we expect them to function."[88] Nixon is condemned for in-
eptitude and "incredible mismanagement of his case"—and that
is all!

Burkley is strongly antipathetic toward organized labor,
and feels that changing the laws which exempt some labor practices from anti-trust regulations is a reform that is long o-
ver-due. He has brought suit against the American Federation
of Television and Radio Artists for threatening to prevent him
from appearing on radio or television as a talk-show host if
he continued to refuse to join the union and pay its annual
dues. The Supreme Court initially refused to hear the case,
but it is still being appealed as this is written.

In his most interesting book, Four Reforms: A Program
for the 70's, William Buckley attempts to fill a glaring void
in conservative literature by carefully analyzing four areas
of continuing controversy dividing liberals and conservatives
on questions of public policy—welfarism, taxation, criminal
justice, and education—and making concrete recommendations
for needed reforms.[89] Since so much conservative thought has
been negative and anti-this or that, it is indeed refreshing
to encounter a positive program that a conservative might support, and that might also meet the test of political feasibil-
ity. The book offers an excellent combination of factualism,
problem-analysis, and policy prescription. It is obvious
that some change is needed in these areas, and Buckley asks
fellow conservatives to move away from status quoism and support improvements that would be "procedural rather than substantive."[90]

Taking issue with contemporary liberal thinking, Buckley
believes that a more egalitarian society depends upon expanding liberty rather than underwriting a public policy that
would expand equality at the expense of liberty. The trouble
with government-sponsored welfarism is that it is a bottomless
pit; the more money spent alleviating poverty, the more the
demand for assistance rises, so the welfare rolls in the 1960's
increased astronomically, even as unemployment remained relatively low.[91] In other words, liberal efforts to make welfare
a right, rather than a need, invited abuse of the system and
produced escalating costs that could not be justified econom-
ically.[92] States like New York and California, at the top of
per-capita income statistics, raised welfare benefits so high
that the remainder of the states suffered disproportionately.
Therefore, Buckley makes the following proposal:

> Congress shall appropriate funds for social wel-
> fare only for the benefit of those states whose per
> capita income is below the national average.[93]

Despite a wealth of statistical data, there is a question whether per-capita income is a reasonable yardstick for

measuring either need, or ability to pay the welfare costs. Reducing the general taxpaying burden for welfare does not solve the problem of widespread human misery rooted in the conditions of poverty, discrimination, inadequate education, and limited opportunity. Buckley believes "we have not very much time left in which to vindicate the democratic idea," and this means but one thing: reducing the burden of indebtedness that future generations will have to assume.[94] If this is more important than meeting immediate human needs more equitably, then William Buckley's proposal deserves to be given high priority.

As for the matter of taxation, Buckley advocates a flat percentage national income tax with few, if any, deductions. He joins hands with many liberals in rejecting higher percentage payments by the wealthier class. This is his proposed reform package:

> Congress should eliminate the progressive feature of the income tax.
> Congress should eliminate all deductions except those that relate directly to the cost of acquiring income.
> Congress should eliminate all exemptions.
> Congress should eliminate the corporation tax.
> Congress should reinburse taxpayers below the poverty line any federal taxes regressive in impact.
> Congress should levy a uniform tax of 15 percent on all income.
> Congress should assist people in the poorer states who live below the poverty level.
> Congress should collect income tax revenues in behalf of the individual states, at whatever rates are specified by the states.[95]

Buckley seems to think that a simplified procedure that eliminates the multitudinous "loop-holes" will insure greater equity and a truly "progressive" income tax system. It is a proven fact that the poor pay a proportionately greater percentage of earned income in various taxes than do the better off; but they also receive more in the way of transfer benefits, such as the costs of welfarism.[96] Everyone, regardless of income, should pay a fairer share of taxation. A more uniform tax system will dispense with the proportionality principle and will achieve greater equity with less bureaucratic waste and cost to the taxpayer. The American people, according to Mr. Buckley, have been sold a false bill of goods: the progressive income tax produces more inequity than justice.

Education has become one of the nation's biggest businesses, and total expenditures have risen from 2 to 8 percent of the GNP over the past quarter century. Buckley agrees with some recent studies, such as the Coleman Report and the Jensen-Herrnstein I.Q. findings, which tend to question the widespread assumption that formal education will, by itself, increase equality of opportunity; these studies have found that other factors, such as inherited intelligence and family background, count for so much more.[97] This implies the inutility of compensatory educational programs. What proponents of greater mass educational opportunity fail to recognize is that an appreciable segment of the population is incapable of benefiting from such programs. In response to a second educational issue, Buckley asserts that the First Amendment principle of church-state separation does not forbid public support of private religious institutions; the liberal tendency to claim that it does is discriminatory. Therefore, Buckley proposes the following amendment to the Constitution:

> No child shall be denied admission to a public
> school, by the United States or by any State, on account of race, creed, or color, or national origin,
> notwithstanding any provision in the Constitution of
> the United States or of any State. Nor shall any relief authorized by any legislature for children attending nonpublic schools be denied by virtue of any
> provision in the Constitution of the United States
> or of any State.[98]

According to Buckley, this change would resolve the present controversy over interpreting the First Amendment to prohibit government financial help to hard-pressed religiously-affiliated private schools, while preserving the principle of state-church separation. It would also be preeminently fairer than is the present situation. The question of busing should be left to the local community, and should not come under judicial edict, especially under the guise of judicial supremacy. Only in this way can the constitutional balance between local control and national need be restored.

Finally, he agrees with the charge brought by so many conservatives against recent Supreme Court rulings, that they "protect the rights of defendants" at the expense of the right of society to equal protection against criminal assault; these decisions have "caused the Bill of Rights to serve so perversely the interests of law-breakers."[99] The self-incriminating protection of the Fifth Amendment has weakened the adversary process and serves no legitimate end, according to Buckley. Therefore, he makes this proposal:

> The Fifth Amendment (as currently interpreted)
> should be repealed.
> Procedures should adapt to the criterion: Did he
> do it?
> Procedures should adapt to the goal of speedier
> justice.[100]

While criticizing such permissive rulings as the Miranda and Mapp decisions, Buckley ignores altogether he history of police intimidation and the lack of universal standards of justice among the states. Certainly, he is correct in deploring the failures of justice that have accompanied the plea-bargaining, prolonged trial delays, and evasive technicalities that have followed in the wake of Supreme Court decisions that tend to favor defendants rights. But it is doubtful whether the older habits were any fairer or constitutionally defensible. And there is a thin line separating procedural reform from substantive change—which can be a form of retrogression as well as progress. Here is a passage which gives a good indication of what seems to bother Buckley the most:

> We are encouraged to believe that the federal government breeds money, that rich people can support non-rich people, that over-secularized, racially integrated education can breed a harmonious and civilized citizenry, and that we move towards justice by forever elaborating the rights and privileges of the accused. These procedural superstitutions, sprinkled over our laws and our rhetoric, are the holy water of liberal ideology.[101]

At his best, William F. Buckley, Jr., is a thoughtful, concise, and lively commentator of the passing scene. He writes with verve, his logic is persuasive, and he is good at clearing away the underbrush so that one can gain a better view of the terrain. When not at his best, an anti-liberal tendentiousness covers over the weak spots in his analysis and reveals the elitist arrogance that underlies his outlook on life. As the one and only editor-in-chief of the National Review, he has created a forum where conservative ideas can be promulgated and measured against current policy debates. If ideological conservatism succeeds in developing a viable alternative to the intellectually dominant liberalism of the day, while expanding its clientele, then William F. Buckley, Jr., will deserve much of the credit. But the obstacle to this final achievement remains what it always has been, the discordant voices and uncertain loyalties within the conservative tradition itself. In a sense, much of ideological conservatism stands or falls on the personal efforts of William Buckley, rather than on its own merits. A case in point is represented by Peter Viereck, one of those many dissident voices within the conservative strand of American thought.

Peter Viereck

More than anyone else, Peter Viereck can be considered the intellectual founder of neo-conservatism, a term formerly applied to that resurgence of conservative thought that transpired in the 1940's and 1950's, and which is called here "ideological conservatism": By the 1950's, however, he was its leading critic.[102] In the late forties and early fifties, he spearheaded the call for a revival of conservative ideals and values, but disillusionment set in when the politics of the fifties brought out the worst, rather than the best, in conservative political thought and behavior, as the McCarthy movement held sway and right-wing extremism flourished. Without becoming any less conservative in his basic values, Viereck nevertheless found much to criticize in the Russell Kirk version of conservatism, and he seemed to lose interest in the

193

prospect of political activism with the debacle of Goldwater-
ism in the mid-sixties. Actually, Viereck has always been
more attuned to aesthetic and literary pursuits and his main
hope continues to be an eventual upgrading of the mass mind
and political leadership through a proper inculcation of conservative values via cultural, rather than political, reform.
His literary reputation rests more on his poetry than on his
prose writings, and it can hardly be said that he still holds
a central position in the conservative movement; still, he
retains importance because he has done so well at exposing
the weaknesses of conservatism, while also paying reverance
to its strengths, and this is something hostile critics on
the Left generally fail to do.

For over twenty years, Viereck's home base has been the
history department of Mount Holyoke College in Massachusetts,
where he has been a full-time history professor. His late father, George Sylvester Viereck, was also a writer; but his pro-
Nazi sympathies prior to World War II culminated in his arrest,
trial, and conviction for propaganda activities involving mail
fraud and the use of Congressional franking privileges. The
older Viereck served a prison sentence and was paroled in 1947.
When one of his brothers was killed in action at Anzio, Peter
Viereck turned against his father intellectually, if not emotionally, and after serving his war stint in North Africa in
the Psychological Warfare branch of the Army, he married the
daughter of Russian emigres, met philosopher George Santayana
and art critic Bernard Berenson, wrote and published poetry,
and began his teaching career at Holyoke in 1948, after earn-
ing a doctorate in history at Harvard.[103] Viereck's prose
works set forth his reflections on the need for a revivified
conservatism, as well as his growing anxiety that "new conservatism" was becoming "a facade for...thought control tyranny
in America"—exactly the opposite of what it set out to be initially.[104] Rather than holding high the banner of humane
ethical values, conservatism had degenerated into a defense
of economic privilege and political expediency.

Everyone an aristocrat! This is what Viereck would like
to see happen—conservatism for the many, not just the few.
It is the "aristocratic spirit" of noblesse oblige, duty to
public service, and dedication to ethical standards that characterizes the true conservative.[105] The great enemy of this
development is the pervasive onslaught of mass society and culture, where a mass-man mentality destroys individuality, reinforces conformitarianism, and elevates materialistic values
at the expense of man's true spirituality. In Viereck's view:

> The conservative principles par excellence are
> proportion and measure; self-expression through self-
> restraint; preservation through reform; humanism and
> classical balance; a fruitful nostalgia for the per-
> manent beneath the flux; and a fruitful obsession for
> unbroken historic continuity. These principles to-
> gether create freedom, a freedom built not on the
> quicksand of adolescent defiance but on the bedrock

of ethics and law.[106]

The rule of law is man's best hope for peace and order. All forms of political extremism spell insanity: "Today as in Metternich's day, the only sane asylum in a world of insane nationalism is an internationalism based on the middle way of balance and moderation."[107] And since the pressures of modern life conspire to create "over adjusted man," it is the "unadjusted man" who carries the burden of preserving and advancing humanistic values in the world. There is no room for either complacency or anarchic individualism in this situation; quality, not quantity, must be the guiding light.[108] The Christian-Judaic reverence for the moral law and the Anglo-American commitment to constitutionalism are the main sources of a valid ethics.[109]

Politically, the Far Right is just as dangerous to democratic values as the Far Left. Viereck has been a persistent critic of right-wing politics in America and he feels that both McCarthyism and the right-wing of the Republican Party have betrayed conservatism, and represent a counter-revolt against established liberal-conservative elites. Since 1955, when he first enunciated this theme in a remarkably prescient essay, some heavy scholarly artillery has substantiated the insight:

> But even more important than that old wound (the Rich Catholic role in McCarthyism being intolerantly overstressed by its liberal foes) is the McCarthy-Dirksen-Bricker coalition of nationalism, Asia Firstism and Europe-Last isolationism; and what is this coalition but a Midwest hick-Protestant revenge against the same 'fancy' and condescending east? That revenge is sufficiently emotional to unite a radical wing with a reactionary wing. The revenge-emotion of McCarthyism has united the old Midwest rich **Chicago Tribune** nationalists on the authoritarian Right. Both these Midwest groups are Protestant, not Catholic. Both are against an east viewed as Europe First and Asia Last— shorthand for an east viewed as aristocratic, internationalist, over-educated, and metaphorically (if rarely literally) Grotonian.[110]

Along with fellow historian-political scientists like Richard Hofstadter, Seymour Martin Lipset, and Daniel Bell, Viereck emphasizes the resentments of loss of status by the declining older middle-class as a prime source of populist support for rightist demagogues like Joseph McCarthy and George Wallace, who are shrewd enough to exploit this anti-establishment strain that has nowhere else to go politically. In another context, Viereck has acknowledged: "Appeals to status resentment are hard to prove because tacit and unconscious; they are the invisible writing in the white spaces of American politics."[111]

Peter Viereck does not go to the mat in defense of capi-

talism, especially laissez-faire economic conservatism, but
he does applaud the wisdom of the private enterprise system
in accepting some ethical restraints on the almighty profit
motive, although he does not substantiate his assertion.[112]
On the other hand, he does not rest his case for conservatism
on either economic or political grounds, but on a desire to
recover lost values inhering in tradition, culture, education,
and ethics.[113] "By being more contemplative than activist, by
asking all those basic questions the activists ignore rather
than by too glibly answering them, a conservative return to
values will transform politics and economics indirectly."[114]
More attention needs to be directed at nourishing the inner
man and there needs to be less dependence upon outer social
conformity. This is what the aristocratic spirit is all about.
"The inner aristocrat may be defined as the man who enforces
his civilized standards from within, by cultural and ethical
self-discipline."[115] Universal norms exist; the prevalent
willingness to sacrifice time-tested principles to pragmatic
expediency is the chief defect of the American way of life,
and only a transvaluation of values in the Nietzschean sense,
but purged of Nietzschean amoralism, can reverse this process. Viereck seems hopeful that it can be accomplished despite a good deal of evidence to the contrary.

Peter Viereck's conception of neo-conservatism offers a
synthesis of moderate social reform in the New Deal mold and
Burkean anti-egalitarian libertarianism.[116] He accuses fellow
neo-conservatives of a "rootless nostalgia for roots," an un-
historical reliance on tradition, and a wrong-headed authoritarianism.[117] Democratic pluralism and authoritarian elitism are incompatible. This is where so many conservatives go
off the track. Anti-statism unites contemporary conservatives;
a preference for elitism over pluralism divides them.[118] A
humanistic conservatism must eschew both political ultra-conservatism and cultural ethnocentrism; it also rejects the liberal's optimistic faith in human rationality, preferring the
tragic sense of human fallibility and innate sinfulness. Neo-
conservatism discredited itself in the eyes of genuine supporters and would-be supporters alike when it failed to repudiate
McCarthy in the early 50's, and played his game because of a
misplaced political expediency.[119]

Those conservative intellectuals later associated with
the National Review turned out to be the prime offenders, and
this is the main reason why Viereck now repudiates the movement he helped to launch in the late 40's. In other words,
conservatism failed the "integrity test," and must do penance
for that failure.[120] Adlai Stevenson, among post-war public
figures, both actualized and symbolized Viereck's ideal of a
liberal-conservative synthesis, and his political failure reveals in retrospect the poverty of public consciousess. Stevenson was that rare combination of integrity and wisdom—qualities in short supply at any time.

As a critic of ideological conservatism, Peter Viereck
became a man without a movement; he has had little impact on

recent developments in conservative thought. What is likely
to be the fate of ideological conservatism? Politically, it
is caught in a difficult, if not impossible, dilemma.[121] The
demands created by the continuing broad-based support of a
quasi-welfare state and the loss of political leverage in a
world of power politics reduce the mass appeal of conservatism; while conservative-minded Presidents like Richard Nixon
and Gerald Ford frequently act in ways that are contrary to
conservative ideals and principles. This poses harsh alternatives: conservatives can either withdraw from the prospect of
directly influencing policy-making or can adopt a strictly negative role as arm-chair critics. That such an organization as
the American Conservative Union would actually contemplate supporting a third-party movement against the ideologically ultra-
conservative Gerald Ford reveals the absurdity of the situation,
given the futility of third-parties in American politics. A
principled conservatism, however defined, has nowhere to go
politically. A mass popular base simply does not exist in the
present or forseeable future for principled conservatism.

Socio-culturally, the Russell Kirk-Peter Viereck brand of
"neo-conservatism" probably has more to offer than the National Review—William Buckley brand of ideological conservatism,
since it does respect the past in a society which embraces a
shallow nowness and cuts itself off from its rich heritage of
traditionalism and from the perennial search for enduring value within the flux of human existence. There will always be
a need for this approach to values. Even where it does not
dominate, it provides a needed corrective to cultural and moral relativism.

As Peter Viereck acknowledged, "neo-conservatism" was no
longer in good hands when it could offer only a mindless support of discredited political figures and an anti-populist
elitism that catered to socio-economic privilege. Anti-liber-
alism might sustain a journal of opinion like the National Review and keep the conservative legacy out of the hands of radical-right extremists, but it could not accommodate all shades
of responsible and/or principled conservatism. Recently, the
term "neo-conservatism" has been applied to an entirely different sort of conservatism that has achieved considerable intellectual respectability, even as other forms of political conservatism seem to be in decline.[123] Crystalizing around a
twenty-year old journal of opinion, The Public Interest, and
closely tied in with the monthly literary-political magazine,
Commentary, this so-called conservative-liberalism or liberal-
conservatism includes some of the most perceptive thinkers of
the day. It is now time to review this "neo-neo-conservatism,"
or whatever, in order to determine, if possible, how it fits
into the conservative tradition in American political thought.

197

CHAPTER 8

LIBERAL-CONSERVATISM: THE PUBLIC INTEREST

In the fall of 1965, the first issue of a new quarterly journal devoted to political and social analysis of current policy issues was launched. The editors were two political sociologists, Daniel Bell and Irving Kristol, and the authors of two articles in this first issue were Daniel P. Moynihan and Robert A. Nisbet, both of whom were to write frequently for the magazine during subsequent years.

In a brief statement of purpose, the editors offered this rationale for the new journal: "The aim of The Public Interest is at once modest and presumptuous. It is to help all of us, when we discuss issues of public policy, to know a little better what we are talking about—and preferably in time to make such knowledge effective."[1] The operating word here is effective. The editors believed there was a real need for a journal of opinion and analysis which purposefully eschewed ideological bias, paid scrupulous attention to empirical facts and data, and dealt with controversial policy issues in a hard-headed, realistic, and open-minded manner, letting the facts speak for themselves; hopefully, such a forum would point the way toward a better integration of social science research and political decision-making. And after more than a decade of publication, the journal has continued to offer a high quality of analysis in conformity with the original prospectus, with one exception. Despite a firm rejection of ideological intent, and the unequivocal assertion that "it is exactly such preconceptions that are the worst hindrances to knowing-what-one-is-talking about..(and) it is the essential peculiarity of ideologies that they do not simply prescribe ends but also insistently propose prefabricated interpretations of existing social realities,"[2]—there is marked evidence that a decided ideological slant has permeated every issue of the journal, influencing the type of articles that are accepted, and making the journal a prestigious disseminator of a revisionist liberalism which appears to be more comfortable with conservative political and social philosophy than are the dominant forms of contemporary liberalism.

For want of a better term, "liberal-conservatism" will be used here to designate these thinkers, although "conservative-liberalism" might serve just as appropriately, while a recent book of essays edited by Lewis A. Coser and Irving Howe, The New Conservatives: A View from the Left, applies the term neo-conservatism to these writers.[3] For reasons which will follow, it is probably more accurate to view The Public Interest as more a product of disillusioned liberalism than of outright conservatism. Beyond this, it is a fact that all the established writers associated with The Public Interest were once genuine liberals, and even radicals in some instances, but that they became more conservative as time went on, and for various reasons could not join hands with other elements of conservative thought in America.

A sampling of some recent articles in <u>The Public Interest</u> presents this interesting profile of a liberal-conservative ideology-in-the-making:

—Integration is not the answer to a better society.[4] In particular, busing "does not lead to significant measurable gains in student achievement or interracial harmony..."[5]

—Prison reform that looks primarily to rehabilitation efforts is of little use in reducing the rate of recidivism.[6]

—The Protestant Ethic, which emphasizes hard work, self-discipline, and achievement, is not moribund; in fact, it needs to be revived "if the so-called quality of life in our society is not to deteriorate from year to year."[7]

—More and better progress in the domestic policy area has been made by state and local governments in the United States over the past few decades than by the national government, contrary to liberal mythology.[8]

—Tax reform, which would require the wealthier segment of the population to pay a greater percentage of taxes on its income, and would eliminate tax "loop-holes," is not in the nation's best interest, nor would it lead to any appreciable redistribution of income in the United States.[9]

—The multi-billion dollar aid to education policies of the federal government have created a mammoth bureaucratic empire which has little to show for the enormous expenditures of public monies since the Johnson years.[10]

—Equality of opportunity is a legitimate democratic ideal. But equality of result is not, for "as the public sphere expands in the announced quest for greater equality, the almost certain outcome is greater inequality deriving from the transfer of income from lower to higher social levels."[11]

—Educational opportunity is not the royal road to greater socio-economic equality; reducing wage differentials, a notable adjunct of post-World War II employer-employee relationships, would be a more effective policy emphasis than government-sponsored compensatory education programs.[12]

—Low class status, not race discrimination, is the chief reason why such a large percentage of Black Americans score so high in unemployment, crime, poor housing, and poverty statistics. Real improvement will come faster and better with less government aid and more attention to the general economic health of the society as a whole.[13]

—The recent campaign reform bill which, among other things, will provide tax dollars for subsidizing presidential election, will create more problems than it will solve. A "full disclosure" law for receipts and expenditures would be sufficient to prevent a repetition of Watergate. Public financing is not the answer.[14]

—The chief defect of contemporary liberalism is that it is incapable of converting a basically utilitarian and individualistic ethic into a system which does justice to social obligation and responsibility. As a result, it has opened the way for New Left radicalism to fill the vacuum created by the failures of liberalism, to the detriment of both movements.[15]

In summary, liberal-conservatism appears to revolve around three main propositions:

(1) Increased public subsidies and ever greater government intervention does not truly solve problems; the Johnsonian-liberal "war on poverty" did little to improve the lot of the poor or to alleviate urban blight, although it did serve to line the pockets of the middle-class professional stratum.

(2) Cultural forces (i.e., the culture of poverty) are largely unresponsive to educational and governmental efforts to reform the system; a healthy and expanding economy in general will do more to reduce socio-economic inequalities than any amount of governmental intervention, such as compensatory educational policies, anti-poverty programs, etc. In effect, socio-economic inequalities are not really solvable through federal government political activism.

(3) Liberal intellectuals, rather than conservative and reactionary elements, have been the main culprits in the repeated failures of reform, for they tend to be collectively hypocritical, profoundly myopic, and generally unscientific in their approach to social problems. They prefer illusions to reality.

Needless to say, the liberal-conservative approach to policy matters has also had its critics. These are among the main charges brought against this school of thinking:

(1) Michael Harrington feels that the liberal-conservatives have falsely exaggerated the scope and achievements of liberal reform in the 1960's, as well as its failures. Not only did the federal government do too little rather than too much in tackling pressing socio-economic problems, but the wealthiest country in the world today "spends a smaller percentage of its GNP on social programs than any advanced nation, capitalist or Communist."[16] Liberal-conservatives, by accepting the dominance of powerful economic elites over the political structure, betray the real promise of democratic egalitarianism.

(2) Michael Walzer, David Spitz, and Mark Kelman question the liberal-conservative defense of inequality and the antipathy toward income redistribution policies. Talent is as much potential as actual; genetic endowment is only one aspect of achievement, not the all-important factor liberal-conservatives maintain it is. Inequality is self-perpetuating and monopolistic and at least partially undeserved.[17] Inequality generates greater inequality, and thus becomes more difficult to eradicate.[18] A democratic society that fails to sponsor policies that seek to alleviate inequality is weaken-

ing the foundations of liberty for the many, rather than just the few, and robs democracy of its real humanizing impulses. The unjust society that liberal-conservatives accept as the price of greater benefits for all, turns out, in reality, to be a myth, for "the trade-offs between growth and equality must be weighted more toward equality, for the welfare cost of growing inequality may well outweigh the gain of higher productivity."[19]

(3) David K. Cohen and John H. Goldthorpe dispute the claim of liberal-conservatives like Daniel Bell, who foresee a growing meritocracy in the United States in which education and knowledge are becoming the new arbiters of wealth, status, and power rather than either political or economic elites per se. The social structure, not individual ability, is the chief determiner of who gets how much of what there is to get.[20] In other words, an infatuation with the implications of post-industrial, technologically-based society which dominates the thinking of leading liberal-conservatives suffers from the same kind of evolutionary determinism that marked many earlier philosophies of history: predetermined values underlie their theory of historical change.[21]

It would thus appear that liberal-conservatives have been no more successful in overcoming their value preconceptions or in objectifying their interpretations of empirical data than have other thinkers of differing ideological complexions. Despite the aims and assertions of the editors of the journal, writers for The Public Interest have exhibited as much ideological purity, or impurity, as their fellow liberals or conservatives. There is a party line of sorts, and it is very much reflected in the essays that appear regularly in the journal. This is not to say, however, that the high quality of the analysis, the careful attention to empirical data, and the continuing preoccupation with the policy implications of socio-economic-political problems does not provide a valuable, informative, and provocative source of intellectual sustenance. A closer look at four leading figures in the liberal-conservative movement might help to clarify the relationship between the liberal and conservative aspects of their ideological orientation.

Robert A. Nisbet

For more than three decades, Robert A. Nisbet has been publishing books and articles that have dealt with the history of social thought and the applications of this history to current socio-political problems. He has gained a deserved reputation for sound scholarship and intellectual synthesis of a high order. He has also been an adept defender of conservative values, and an aware critic, capable of distinguishing authentic from inauthentic conservatism. Nisbet's intellectual labors have been directed at defining the conditions that would serve to reinforce community-relatedness and individual social responsibility. Since classical Lockean-Jeffersoan

202

liberalism tended to be both asocial and even anti-social, self-regarding rather than other-regarding, and more concerned about individual rights than about man's social duties, one looks to conservatism for the proper antidote to unrestrained individualism. In one of his earliest and most highly esteemed works, Community & Power (initially published as The Quest for Community), Nisbet equates the increasing corruptions of power in the modern world with a pervasive breakdown of institutionalized authority.[22] Family, church, and state are in decline, because personal alienation and cultural discontinuity have accompanied the displacement of the primacy of religion by secularized values.[23] Contrary to liberal doctrine, which equates individual good with society's good, Nisbet would reverse the emphasis, and would claim that what is best for society as a whole is also best for the individual.[24]

Democratic pluralism weakens and dies when the organized power of society and the state begins to operate directly upon individuals instead of through the intermediate realm of primary-group relationships. As the state absorbs more and more functions that were formerly the responsibility of the family, the community, and the church, a moral decline sets in and the individual becomes rootless.[25] Psychological well-being and social security depend upon a hierarchy of social relationships that thrive only in a decentralized power setting and are endangered by large organizational power structures.[26] Freedom and authority can exist only where individual and political power are subordinate to social legitimacy. Authority has to be plural in a democratic society. That is to say, authority is found in a network of intermediate structures connecting the individual to the state via society.[27] The condition of society is more important than the condition of either the individual or the state. And the good society depends upon the social bond, or the institutional patterns of norms and authority relationships mediating between self and society/state, nourishing love, friendship, mutual aid, and other forms of interdependence.[28] At the same time, Nisbet sees real danger lurking behind the erosion of authority and the breakdown in the collective conscience, such as Durkheim depicted in his concept of anomie. These are Nisbet's major assumptions:

(1) Freedom becomes meaningful and effective only in relation to the rules and norms which define it.

(2) Social morality is rooted in a sense of civility, whereby individuals relate positively to their social roles.

(3) The contemporary family is in transition from a tight-knit kinship-authority institution to one of limited involvement and increased divergence of interest among its members.[29]

Because the conditions of contemporary life no longer support a legitimate social structure, there has been increasing social dislocation, individual alienation, and a loss of functional significance within the established institutional structure. In his recent study, The Sociology of Emile Durkheim, Robert Nisbet shows his long-standing and profound respect for a thinker who combined liberal-humanitarian and conservative-traditionalist values, for the key to Durkheim's pioneer sociology is man-in-society.[30] And in <u>Social Change and History</u>, Nisbet traces the idea of progress from its origins in Greek and Christian sources, through medieval and pre-modern thought, to its culmination in the 18th-19th centuries as a secular faith that distorts reality because it confuses moral and material progress. Out of this analysis comes a conservative theory of historical change:

> In the realm of simple observation and common sense, nothing is more obvious than the <u>conservative</u> bent of human behavior, the manifest desire to preserve, hold, fix, and keep stable. Common sense tells us that, given the immense sway of habit in individual behavior and of custom, tradition, and the sacred in collective behavior, change could hardly be a constant, could hardly be ubiquitous. One need but look at the actual history of any given way of behavior in a group or society—the way of behavior we call the monogamous family in the West, for example, or the Christian religion, or the university—and while changes in these are indeed aspects of the historical record, such changes can only be understood against the background of persistence that must, if we are to understand change, be our point of departure.[31]

Like so many of his conservative contemporaries, Robert Nisbet was deeply disturbed by the revolt against the universities in the late 60's and wrote a book on the crisis, <u>The Degradation of the Academic Dogma</u>. Instead of blaming "radical or alienated youth" for the institutional disruptions and damage to property, but without condoning their behavior, he points the real finger of guilt at faculties and administrators at many of the country's most prestigious institutions of higher learning for being seduced in the 50's and early 60's by huge government grants for mostly Pentagon-related research; accepting such grants compromised the integrity of these institutions. In effect, the institutions were ripe for just such a challenge to their historic role in society, because of their failure to honor the traditional purpose of universities as enclaves of teaching, research, and knowledge as an end in itself. They ran blindly and willingly after Federal government money suddenly made available to individual professors and institutional research projects for purposes that violated the integrity of institutional life. Nisbet puts it this way:

> I firmly believe that direct grants from government and foundation to individual members of university faculties, or to small company-like groups of faculty members, for the purposes of creating institutes, centers, bureaus, and other essentially capitalistic enterprises within the academic community to be the single most powerful agent of change that we

can find in the university's long history. For the
first time in Western history, professors and scholars were thrust into the unwonted position of enter-
preneurs in incessant search for new sources of capital, of new revenue, and, taking the word in its larger sense, or profits.[32]

The consequences were predictable: as the university proceeded to sell its soul to Mammon, it undermined its ability
to deal constructively with the student rebellion of the late
60's.[33] Established patterns of authority were depleted and
corrupted by "the new men of power," so that "with the authority of the department, the faculty, the academic senate already diminished, there was really little to fear."[34] For
Robert Nisbet, the lesson of the 60's is quite clear: the university must stay out of politics, economic entrepreneurship,
and social problem solving.[35] The only valid purpose of the
university is to pursue knowledge for its own sake. The sole
function of the university is to "serve as a setting for the
scholarly and scientific imagination."[36]

Unlike conservative thinkers of the earlier nation-building period, Robert Nisbet cannot trust the constitutional structure of separated powers, checks and balances, federalism, and
judicial review to preserve democratic liberty. Instead, he
looks for a restoration of "traditional authorities"—church,
family, local community, school, and university—to keep power
in bounds, for "there can be no possible freedom in society a-
part from authority."[37] The boredom of affluence and a revolt
against reason characterized the rise of the New Left in the
1960's. Social change has been too swift and disrupting. What
is needed is a new "social contract" that distinguishes authority and power on one hand, and on the other gives moral direction to our lives.[38] But he does not explain how this can be
accomplished.

In an essay which serves as a critique of John Rawls's influential study, A Theory of Justice, Nisbet also takes aim at
popular reverence for equality, which he feels has become a
kind of new religion. Equality, not liberty, has become the
new theme song of a democratic society. Freedom defined as
free choice, opportunity, or autonomy, is giving way to freedom defined as absolute egalitarianism, or at least an ideal-
ized vision of this. In fact, no other concept serves so well
to differentiate liberal, radical, and conservative thought today. Whereas the conservative questions this new concern over
democratic equality, the liberal has simply adopted a long-standing radical preoccupation with socio-economic equality. Nisbet
doubts whether a majority of people would vote for greater equality as a supreme policy priority; but if the majority of intellectuals are for it, its claims may become all but irresistible,
even "if all evidence suggests that a very large number of Americans are indifferent, if not actually hostile, to any idea for
national social policy that has substantial equalitarianism behind it."[39]

Nisbet questions whether A Theory of Justice is a serious

work of social philosophy; in his view it is an exercise in
ideological or utopian thinking, similar to the 18th century
French philosophes. The trouble with Rawls's attempt to provide an irrefutable philosophical defense of equalitarianism
is that he assumes more than he can prove or reasonably demonstrate. It is just as wrong, according to Nisbet, to proclaim
a theory of justice that benefits the many at the expense of
the few, as it is to project one that would benefit the few at
the expense of the many. Any form of imposed justice defeats
the ends that it is meant to secure. Politics traditionally
is the arena where moral and political conflicts are resolved
in a democratic context through negotiation and compromise.
Nisbet feels that Rawls completely ignores this basic principle.[40] And the radical implications of Rawls's definition of
justice as "fairness," which would require a considerable redistribution of wealth and power within society, could hardly
be achieved short of a political revolution in which liberty
would be an obvious casualty. In Nisbet's view, John Rawls
has been no more successful than his predecessor, Rousseau, in
devising a formula that would advance equality while preserving liberty.[41]

Robert Nisbet sees a meaningful pluralism as the best
hope for a revitalized democratic society and polity. This
can happen only insofar as traditional institutional restraints are safeguarded, greater social cohesion is achieved,
and a sense of community is restored. This is the essence of
Nisbet's political and social philosophy:

> Living as we do in a world grown increasingly more
> centralized and collectivized, with the roots of
> localism and cultural diversity seemingly cut by
> the forces of modernity, it is possible to see in
> the plural community man's last best hope.[42]

The only difficulty with Nisbet's attractive analysis is
that he leaves out selfishness, a surprising omission in a
conservative thinker. If pluralism is defined as decentralization, diversity, and professionalism, the concrete values
he seems to applaud, then there is no assurance or any real
prospect that social responsibility will ensue on a sufficient scale to contain individual selfishness in behalf of
greater social cooperation and civic morality. Although he
devotes a stimulating chapter in The Sociological Tradition,
to a discussion of the contributions of such worthy thinkers
as Tocqueville, Simmel, Durkheim, and Weber to the problem of
the relationship of authority to power, the solutions are un-
unsatisfactory.[43]

If social institutions are to provide an adequate counterpoint to political institutions, then the economic structure has to be brought into the picture, too. Nisbet virtually ignores economic factors in his writings. There is a-
bundant social, political, and historical analysis, but little attention is paid to the discontinuities that mark the
interrelatedness of economic, political, and social variables.

Authority never exists in a vacuum, and an impression that it does creeps through much of Nisbet's analysis. The question, "Who shall rule?" is not readily answered by reference to political power; this is the earth-shaking insight we have all learned from Marx. Behind political power stands economic power. Before authority relationships can be purified of their dependence upon a configuration of wealth, status, and power, authority will have to be made more responsive to the collectivity. Nisbet certainly appreciates this point, but he is unable to give a satisfactory explanation of how it might be effectuated. Until this can be done, a conservative sociopolitical philosophy will suffer from a terminal case of anemia.

As an historian of ideas who blends sociological, aesthetic, and historical analysis in his assessments of "the great thinkers," Nisbet has few peers, especially in regard to 19th century social and political thought. One's knowledge and appreciation of such thinkers as Burke, Tocqueville, Marx, Simmel, Toennies, Weber, and Durkheim will be vastly enriched by reading Nisbet, whose writings seldom stray very far from the orbit of these particular intellectual stars of the modern age.[44] At the same time, his personal value preferences, strongly oriented toward stability, rather than change, suffuse his work and require more careful appraisal.

No one has surpassed Robert A. Nisbet in an understanding of the conservative perspective in the history of American political thought. He can be read with profit by liberal, conservative, and radical alike. But he he sees, what he wants, and what he can have are quite different propositions. He is not alone in being caught in the web of a liberal-conservative dilemma. It may well be a futile attempt to reconcile the irreconcilable.

Daniel Patrick Moynihan

Although still relatively young in years, Daniel Moynihan has had a remarkably rich background in government positions at the sub-cabinet and cabinet level under four presidents: Kennedy, Johnson, Nixon, and Ford. He has also spent two years as the American Ambassador to India; in 1975 he was appointed United States Ambassador to the United Nations by President Gerald Ford; most recently, he ran and was elected to a U.S. Senate seat from New York. Besides all this, he has been, off and on, a Professor of Government at Harvard University; and has published noteworthy books on the application of social science to public policy, in addition to countless articles. He has also co-authored a widely accepted contemporary classic in social science analysis, Beyond the Melting Pot. More than anything else, Moynihan represents that rare blend of thinker and practitioner; his scholarly work is suffused with a unique experiential perspective of intimate involvement with policy-making. He was captain and navigator of President Nixon's ill-fated efforts to push guaranteed income legislation through Congress in 1969; such legislation was, and is, considered by many, to be one of the most pressing needs of the nation. His minute recapitulation of that legislation's abortive life, The Politics of a Guaranteed Income, is an immensely valuable study of the policy-making process; and his earlier book, Maximum Feasible Misunderstanding, is an insightful footnote to President Johnson's "war on poverty." There is no question, regardless of one's ideological inclination, that Moynihan is a man who can be listened to and read with great reward. He is a self-proclaimed liberal Democrat who served with distinction as head of the cabinet-level Urban Affairs Council under President Richard Nixon. He is also one of the sharpest critics of what presently passes for liberalism; and he may be a conservative in wolf's clothing, if some of his critics are to be acknowledged. At any event, he may well be one of the most knowledgeable, able, and intellectually stimulating writers on the contemporary scene. He commands respect.

As a thinker, Moynihan prides himself on being a non-ideological pragmatist. The distilled wisdom of his intimate experience in government can be found in this statement from Maximum Feasible Misunderstanding: "The great questions of government have to do not with what will work but what does work."[45] Results are what matter. And the proper role of social science is not prediction, but accurate evaluation of what has already been attempted.[46] Moynihan feels that a great opportunity for effective social action was lost in the Johnson years, because the ideological fixation on "community participation and control" of anti-poverty programs unnecessarily stirred up a political reaction that blunted substantive policy goals and reduced poverty relief to a parody of what it was supposed to be. The chief target of blame is the liberal intellectual establishment, aided and abetted by an emergent new radicalism, which prefers symbolic victories to actual achievements. Instead of integrating needed innovative policy with the established power structure, the liberals responsible for the formulation and execution of anti-poverty programs overshot the mark, and almost unthinkingly, chose ideology over practicality by trying to impose community action on a system that was unready for such a radical change. Moynihan's stark conclusion: "The program was carried out in such a way as to produce a minimum of the social change its sponsors desired, and bring about a maximum increase in the opposition to such change, of the kind they feared."[47] Years afterward, Moynihan has the better of the argument; the Johnson war on poverty today seems to have few defenders.[48] The lesson is clear enough: in a democracy, how you do things is more important than what you want to do—and the latter depends upon the former for its effectiveness.

A study of the relationship between ethnicity and politics in New York City, which Moynihan co-authored with Nathan Glazer and published in 1963, investigated the way ethnic and racial attitudes of Negroes, Puerto Ricans, Jews, Italians, and

Irish influenced the political and social structure of the nation's largest city. Among other trends, the authors noted the alarming rise in female-headed families, especially among poorer-class Negroes, and the sharp rise in welfare dependency during a period of relative national affluence and economic growth. They attributed this lack of family stability to special characteristics of the black community, traits derived from the nefarious legacy of slavery and oppression, and in obvious contrast to the pattern of assimilation and stability of other immigrant groups. This accounts for the escalation of poverty relief and the heavy welfare dependency of this growing segment of the New York City population over the past few decades. Despite a steady rise in the number of New York Negroes who have achieved working-class and middle-class status, both militancy and dependency have increased at the same time. These groups of upward mobiles still far outnumber those who are unemployable, for whatever reason, but the "crisis of the city," including exorbitant welfare costs, high illegitimacy rates, and crime of every description, will continue to be exacerbated by "the disproportionate presence of Negroes and Puerto Ricans on welfare."[49] And while the conventional wisdom among social scientists today underscores the declining role of ethnicity in urban politics as assimilation proceeds along its rapid course, the authors argue otherwise. Their analysis is persuasive.[50]

The Politics of a Guaranteed Income is an impressive study that will long be consulted profitably by policy-oriented politicians and political scientists.[51] It is one of the ironies of recent American politics that a conservative-minded President, disliked by liberals throughout his political career, took the initiative in proposing a carefully sculptured welfare reform program that contained work incentive provisions, and a $1,600 base annual income supplement for all Americans who fell below the poverty line, and that was designed to include the working poor, as well as welfare poor, in its blanket coverage. Moynihan blames the program's ultimate demise on a pervasive liberal unwillingness to give Nixon credit for doing what they were unable to do alone, on Southern Democratic politicians insensitive to the real needs of a sizeable segment of their constituencies, and on the rhetorical overkill opposition by more militant black organizations which felt the initial money amounts were too low, and whose constituencies stood to gain much from such a program. After passing the House by an amazingly wide margin, it died in the Senate Finance Committee, defeated, according to Moynihan, by liberal votes, even though best estimates indicated it would have passed in the Senate if it could have reached the floor. In Moynihan's view, the predictable opposition from the ultra-conservative wing of the Republican Party would have been neutralized if any one of these other factors had not been activated against the proposal. Not all will accept the portrait Moynihan paints of a selfless President Nixon dedicated to revolutionary welfare reform in the best interests of the nation and taking political risks in the bargain; but there is no question Mr. Nixon endorsed the idea and understood that

209

it would mean a "guaranteed annual income," even as he kept emphasizing the "workfare" aspects of the program.

One can dispute the author's contention that passage of the Family Assistance Plan "would set a standard of social policy against which the rest of the world might measure itself,"[52] but still accept the fact that it turned out to be a near miss, legislatively speaking, and might well have accomplished its twin objectives of broadened welfare benefits and welfare reform, although even Moynihan admits that there is no way of being sure this would have happened even if it had been ratified and implemented. It is problematical whether real needs would have been met better than under existing welfare programs, and dependency reduced, if FAP had gone through, given the complexity, diverity, and history of inept administration of the welfare system. At the very least, it would have been an earnest effort to solve what the vast majority of Americans consider to be a virtual disaster—the present welfare system. It may have been a lost opportunity, because a conservative president like Nixon had advantages that more liberal presidents would have been denied: a chance to forge a consensus of support behind a policy that would have resulted in major social change. But even this was not enough to insure the bill's passage, for as Moynihan shrewdly observes:

> Family Assistance was neither a conservative nor a liberal measure in the meanings intended by those terms. It threatened 'conservative' interests and 'liberal' interests also, not least the liberal interest in appearing liberal. That there was a sizable liberal element in the Senate only meant that enemies towards the 'right' would be joined by not less determined enemies towards the 'left.'[53]

Surprisingly, Moynihan appears neither bitter nor dejected that a program that carried his authorship more than anyone else's was finally defeated. He is optimistic because a quantum change was almost successful, despite the prevailing liberal view that the American political system only functions incrementally.[54] He feels that this message was embedded in this eighteen month struggle for a guaranteed income policy, and could be beneficially applied to future efforts along these same lines.

A collection of previously published articles, entitled Coping: Essays on the Practice of Government, offers an excellent perspective on Daniel P. Moynihan's political philosophy. Liberalism is his preferred political stance; but it must be realistic, flexible, and pragmatically non-ideological rather than visionary, idealistic, and overly optimistic about what is possible in government. As he declares in the introduction: "After a period of chiliastic vision we have entered a time that requires a more sober assessment of our chances, and a more modest approach to events."[55] On this note of realistic disillusionment, Moynihan builds his case for social change that favors experiential guidance and eschews ideological rhetoric. It is Moynihan's firm conviction that conventional liberalism has failed because it has continually overshot its target, assuming mistakenly that everything should be poured into a liberal mold without regard for the hidden costs of unidirectional social change.[56] Ideological liberalism, when worn like a halo and wafted across the landscape like a smokescreen, hides reality, inhibits clear thinking, and converts dogma into necessity. Liberalism functions best in opposition; when it achieves ascendancy, as happened between the New Deal and Great Society periods, it becomes its own worst enemy, slipping into the easy uncritical complacency sometimes referred to as "the arrogance of power." Liberalism lost its viability when it failed to maintain a distance between its reform tradition and the mindless radicalism of 60's activism.[57] A self-righteous moralism is the true enemy of practical achievement. As liberalism lost its way in the 1960's, political disaster inevitably followed in its wake.[58]

After more than fifteen years in the forefront of governmental action, Moynihan renders this judgment: it is always better to acknowledge what you don't know than pretend to a knowledge that doesn't exist.[59] To over-promise, and not deliver, is worse than doing nothing.[60] Moynihan also feels that it is necessary to start early in trying to solve problems before they become too hard to deal with and ideological positions have hardened, which is the main reason American government functions so poorly much of the time.[61] "While the Federal government cannot always, or even frequently, control events, it can control the terms on which it negotiates."[62] As a liberal, he favors more selective government regulation of private industry in the public interest; as a conservative, he favors means over ends, and the possible over the desirable. Above all, "American liberalism needs to bring its commitments in balance with its resources—overseas and at home."[63]

High on the agenda of 20th century liberalism has been income redistribution. Narrowing the gap between "haves" and "have nots," alleviating the suffering of the under-class through expanded social security and welfare benefits, and greater educational opportunity for the children of the disadvantaged have figured prominently in liberal priorities and reform efforts. By and large, conservatives have questioned the wisdom of such an approach to the role of government on the grounds that the results would be opposite from what was intended: the undeserving poor would receive most of the benefits, the work ethic would be undermined, and a bloated bureaucracy would siphon off an unconscionable amount of the taxpayers hard-earned income. Whether the results of a moderate liberal-conservative dominance in the area of domestic policy substantiates either one of these alternative conceptions remains moot, since there is an insufficient empirical base either way and a good deal of conflicting opinion, much of it mired in ideological bias.

It is to Daniel Moynihan's great credit that he understands this dilemma for what it is: a no-man's land where the terrain is pitted with obstacles and all the helpful road-signs have been knocked down. Before one can decide in which direction to proceed, it is first desirable to estimate carefully the prospects for arriving at one's destination. Under such circumstances, a delayed decision may be wiser than a decision conceived too hastily.

The liberal-conservative supports the liberal agenda, but is afraid to expect too much or to aim too high given the complexity of the problems and man's inability to perform as well as he needs to. So the signals are neither red nor green, but amber: proceed with caution. Critics of this stance will charge that it is an abdication, pure and simple, and tantamount to doing less than needs to be done. It leads to conservatism by default, rather than to liberalism by choice. Even the Family Assistance Plan, which Moynihan considered replete with good things for just about everyone, was a good deal less than it appeared to be to some critics. As Gus Tyler observed: "In view of the way it was to be funded, FAP was far less a means of redistributing wealth than of reshuffling poverty."[64] There is no way the argument can be definitively settled. At the same time, both strategy and tactics rely heavily upon making just such a judgment. For this reason alone, Daniel Patrick Moynihan qualifies as one of the best guides there is around. He can speak as an outsider who is also an insider. Moynihan knows how to unify theory and practice.

Daniel Bell

Perhaps the one thing that all liberal-conservatives have in common is distrust of ideology. They reject both the neo-Marxist assumptions as to the irremediability of class conflict and the value of ideology in mobilizing mass support against various forms of social injustice. They view ideological thinking and commitment in strictly negative terms; inevitably, ideology weakens democratic pluralism and fosters a backlash response from the normally "silent majority," intensifying socio-political division and undermining the democratic value consensus. It was Daniel Bell's famous essay, "The End of Ideology," published in 1963, which sparked a raging controversy among social scientists regarding the proper role and function of ideology in a capitalistic system.[65]

According to Bell, ideological radicalism was both self-defeating and anachronistic; the attempt to yoke science and technology to promote economic development and improved living standards for the masses would only be hindered by ideological warfare. Defining ideology as a "secular religion," Bell argued for the dispassionate objectivity of the scientific approach to truth, unencumbered by the blinders of ideological distortion. Ends should no longer be at issue, just means. Whether it is a mixed economy, political pluralism, and greater decentralization, or the expansion of state welfarism, a consensus had been finally achieved and there was no longer any point to an appeal to ideology in behalf of fundamental change. Economic growth, not ideological conflict, would gradually forge a common purpose among antagonistic nations and groups; ideology simply gets in the way of this widely valued objective. The sooner this happens, the better for everybody.[66]

Needless to add, Bell's "end of ideology" concept was soon to be overtaken by events that were neither anticipated nor warranted by the foregoing analysis. Throughout the democratic West, the late sixties were marked by intensified ideological confrontations, especially among those who paraded under the banners of student-, youth-, black-, and people-power advocacy. Whether a temporary aberration, or a permanent challenge to Bell's thesis, these events raised questions about the viability of the "end of ideology" concept. Not only were the conservative implications of this critique of ideology open to question, but the definition of ideology which Bell advanced appeared both too narrow and biased. The fact that ideology can serve positive, as well as negative functions within society was completely ignored. As a counterweight to complacency and the power of vested interests, ideology can be seen as a necessary and desirable stimulus to change in democratic political systems. There is more to ideology than blind obedience to authority. So it all depends upon how one defines the function of ideology.

Daniel Bell's The Coming of Post-Industrial Society, published in 1973, and its sequel, The Cultural Contradictions of Capitalism, published in 1976, are impressive studies, which combine economic, sociological, and political analysis in an attempt at "social forecasting." Drawing more on Max Weber than on Karl Marx, Bell foresees a major historical shift in industrialized-capitalistic economies, from manufacturing-agricultural employment to service-technical occupations. In the process, theoretical knowledge and expertiese will become the main indices of policy-making.[67] And as the service sector expands, the goods-producing sector will contract. Presumably, this trend will eventually affect all advanced industrialized nations, pointing to a new era for socio-economic structures and human relationships—a "post-industrial era." Theoretical knowledge based upon technological mastery thus will become the decisive factor in shaping society. Management, not capitalistic entrepreneurship, will displace machine technology with a new form of intellectual technology.[68] Planning, coordination, and computerization will help to rationalize the system, while a highly educated, scientific-technical elite holds the real balance of power. Expertise, not ideology, will be the dynamic factor in social change.[69] Neither capitalism nor socialism in their traditional configurations will retain significance; both pose roadblocks to rationally-directed social change. Knowledge will displace property as the chief source of power in society.[70] Politics will no longer be an independent variable; the technostructure, to all intents and purposes, will carry the big stick, setting the tone of governance.[71]

The hallmark of post-industrial society, according to Bell, is the dominance of bureaucracy and the emergence of a new ruling class of professional technocrats, a managerial elite.[72]

But this can lead to either enhanced rationality, or its opposite, social order governed by "functional rationality and meritocracy" or "one becoming increasingly anti-institutional and antinomian."[73] This crucial development will hinge upon whether the growing split between culture and social structure will be repaired in time, and whether the new ethos will reinforce or undermine the need for greater rationality in human affairs. Here is how Bell explains the crisis:

> The essential division in modern society today is not between those who own the means of production and an undifferentiated 'proletariat' but the bureaucratic and authority relations between those who have powers of decision and those who have not, in all kinds of organizations, political, economic, and social. It becomes the task of the political system to manage these relations in response to the various pressures for distributive shares and social justice.
> What the concept of post-industrial society suggests is that there is a common core of problems, hinging largely on the relation of science to public policy, which will have to be solved by these societies; but these can be solved in different ways and for different purposes. The sociologist seeks those 'ordering devices' that allow one to see the way social change takes place in a society. The concept of the post-industrial society is one such 'ordering device' to make more intelligible the complex changes in Western social structure.[74]

The most intriguing aspect of Bell's analysis is his assertion that post-industrial society will favor communal values over strictly individual values.[75] A premium will be placed upon cooperation, not competition. White collar, professional, and technical employment constitute the expanding character of the labor force in America; this trend will escalate over time, and represents a sizeable growth in the non-profit public sector, especially government itself.[76] Thus, "a post-industrial society...is increasingly a communal society wherein public mechanisms rather than the market become the allocators of goods, and public choice, rather than individual demand, becomes the arbiter of services."[77] Government necessarily becomes the main instrument of meeting the rising expectations of a public oriented to a service economy. Human relations, not tending machines, will be the main occupational activity in the post-industrial society. As the national economy becomes increasingly more interdependent and geared to a mass culture, knowledge and technology will provide the means to a good life for the masses. A new age of advanced science will make all this possible. Knowledge itself, not productivity per se, will determine who gets how much of what there is to have.[78] The only fly in the ointment, from Bell's viewpoint, is that a split between social structure and culture may become aggravated if the literary intellectuals persist in promulgating a self-indulgent hedonism in opposition to "functional rationality and technocratic modes of operation."[79]

Here again, Bell betrays his liberal-conservative bias: anti-liberal, anti-intellectual, and enamored of the potential hegemony of a scientific meritocracy. However, he allows his acute descriptive analysis to mask dubious normative assumptions; this weakens what is otherwise a brilliant, incisive analysis of contemporary socio-political-economic tendencies. If it is true, as Bell insists, that "the major problem for post-industrial society will be adequate numbers of trained persons of professional and technical caliber," this represents a curious reductionism indeed, for it ignores completely the political dimension in favor of an economic determinism that harks back to the unscientific, ahistorical side of Marxism. At the same time, there seems little more than unfounded assertion in Bell's belief that "the university increasingly becomes the primary institution of the post-industrial society."[80] Because of the unprecedented reliance upon research and technical expertise, the university will be the indispensable partner of the administrative-scientific establishment in perpetuating economic growth.[81]

There is a contradiction within Bell's concept of post-industrial society that leaves the reader in a quandary. Having subordinated the political and economic sectors to the scientific-technocratic one, he then elevates the political: "the most important economic decisions will be made at the political level, in terms of consciously defined 'goals' and 'priorities.'"[82] And the decisive role played by government in the post-industrial society may reflect either a positive or a negative counterpoint to socio-economic change, depending upon whether a "communal ethic" replaces the traditional "individualistic ethic," and on whether capitalism can be molded to fit the new society.[83] In this respect, a "planned economy," created by a disinterested technocracy rather than by partisan ideological interests will be necessary.

Although everything will become more centralized from a policy-making standpoint, new technology will provide the means for maximizing the cooperative functioning of a complex society by developing a better minitoring system to measure performance and need.[84] Technocratic power is superior to the older forms of political and economic power because it optimizes rationality. In effect, the politician will have to re-tool, and become as well-versed in technological expertise as in dealing with people. This will be the measure of future success or failure.[85] For it is the many, not just the few, who will ultimately benefit from technocratic rule.

In essence, Bell's hopes for a post-industrial society conforming to the best features of social progress requires a new scientific ethos that does not degenerate into ideological distortion of reality, as both the Protestant ethic of capitalism and the socialist ideal of communist systems did. This will happen only if the scientific elite can perform its acknowledged role as the true arbiter of value and interest con-

215

flicts in a pluralist democracy.[86] Bell is aware that a meritocracy like the one he envisions can become another way of perpetuating the privileges of a few, or simply an incentive to greater bureaucratization of society. His answer to this problem is to insist that <u>earned</u> authority and status must determine the exercise of power and decision-making. This means individual achievement must be promoted and rewarded, and professional authority recognized as the chief legitimizer of status.[87] Bell, it seems, wants desperately to retain the incentive-reward features of an out-moded Protestant ethic, even as he embraces the need for a scientific-technocratic ethic that unites the individual to communal norms and thus avoids an unconscionable gulf between a privileged few and less privileged many. Bell is realistic enough to question whether a society based upon the principle of abundance for most or all citizens is a viable socio-economic goal, but he anticipates sufficient progress in the form of an expanding GNP to insure improved benefits for the masses. This is how Bell analyzes this crucial problem, but he leaves out any attempt to reconcile this proposition to even a modified capitalistic order:

> The political ethos of an emerging post-industrial society is communal, insofar as social goals and priorities are defined by and national policy is directed to the realization of those goals. It is sociologizing rather than economic...insofar as the criteria of individual utility and profit maximization become subordinated to broader conceptions of social welfare and community interest—particularly as the ancillary effects of ecological devestation multiply social costs and threaten the amenities of life.[88]

In <u>The Cultural Contradictions of Capitalism</u>, Bell proposes a new approach to social analysis in place of Marxist and functionalist methodological perspectives by breaking the concept of "society" into three analytical concepts: techno-economic structure, polity, and culture.[89] Discordance, not congruence, characterizes these aspects of change, and until more attention is paid to the need for a more integrated process of change, legitimacy will continue to erode, and instability will become the rule rather than the exception in the American system.[90] It was the Protestant-Puritan ethic which kept individualism within bounds and fused it with the larger national purpose. Now that capitalism has shifted its emphasis to easy credit and instant gratification, there are no restraints upon individual wants and no means of regulating human desire in the interests of a larger social good.[91] The inflation which plagues modern economies is a structured outgrowth of insatiable consumer demand.[92] With government playing an ever more dominant role in all national economies, the relationship between the private and public sectors has to assume a new and changed perspective. Since scarcity cannot be eliminated, the determination of who gets what shifts away from market considerations to governmental decision-making.[93] The danger is that social-political-economic conflict will intensify in the absence of acceptable social restraints that once existed but now have all but disappeared. The contemporary ideal of social pluralism seems to be the main culprit in Bell's critique, for it converts a consensual into an adversarial culture and such rampant discontinuity is too high a price to pay for social coherence.[94]

The great strength of a middle-class ethos is in its commitment to moderation and standards of civility in manners and morals. Its loss leaves "capitalism with no moral or transcendental ethic,"[95] when delayed gratification was in force, before instant gratification became the norm.[96] This new hedonism threatens to deprive capitalism of its traditional legitimacy; in the process, the moral supports of the society crumble.[97] No society, according to Bell, can long survive a severe rupture between its social structure and the culture—which is what is happening to America today.[98] Self-indulgence is the chief contemporary characteristic of art in all its forms of expression—another indication of how little evidence remains of social responsibility as a cultural norm.[99] When nothing is forbidden and everything is allowable, the uninhibited becomes the norm, the self is liberated; but a loss of the true self ensues, since a present arbitrarily divorced from the past is like a ship without a rudder, drifting away on an endless ocean of unfulfillable expectations and unknowable destinations.[100]

The alternative to this disastrous course is an economy oriented to human needs rather than to human wants. Somehow—and Bell is not at all helpful in showing how it might be effectuated—a better balance between economic growth and consumer demand must be achieved, and the contradictions within our capitalistic economy, which now promise to get out of hand, must be contained. "The foundation of any liberal society is the willingness of all groups to compromise private ends for the public interest."[101] A restoration of bourgeois civilization is still the only way this vital objective can be realized. And what Bell asks for, without being too clear as to how it might be accomplished, is a new normative commitment to "the public household." In effect, "what is needed is that balance of the private and public spheres—of public care for private needs—which enhances liberty and equity."[102]

There are many difficulties with Bell's prospectus, but the central one relates to a confusion between descriptive analysis and the normative assumptions which underly his liberal-conservative stance. Even if he is correct about the current transformation of industrialized societies—and there have been serious challenges to the empirical foundation of Bell's analysis—he is much less convincing in defending the merits of a non-ideological, scientific-technocratic elite as the proper custodian of power in the post-industrial society.[103] It is doubtful whether any elite can be trusted not to subvert the real requirements of a democratic society, or whether democratic pluralism will safeguard the monopolization of power and authority by the few at the expense of the many. The fact is, however, that democratic pluralism has never really protected the American system from its own undemocratic excesses, and the economic power structure has largely controlled the socio-political structure. Bell feels this is no longer the case; conditions of the post-industrial era will place a premium upon political rather than economic control. Yet his case is weak exactly where it needs to be strong. There is little evidence that the pursuit of profit or of economic power has been tamed or is likely to become dependent upon scientific management; more evidence supports the opposite contention. Neither changing conditions nor the national purpose are likely to make the capitalistic system either more humanistic or more committed to the public good, if this means reducing its insatiable need for expansion and profitability or giving up a controlling influence over the political sector. Self-restraint has never been a notable feature of capitalism.

There is also some question whether Bell has drawn the proper conclusions from contemporary statistical data. Much of his analysis stands or falls on this assertion:

> The United States today is the only nation in the world in which the service sector accounts for more than half the Gross National Product. It is the first service economy, the first nation, in which the major portion of the population is engaged in neither agrarian nor industrial pursuits. Today about 60 percent of the United States labor force is engaged in services; by 1980, the figure will have risen to 70 percent.[104]

Presumably, this shift away from manufacturing and agricultural occupations to a "service" economy implies upgrading all along the line, wherein the working conditions and recompense for the vast majority of working people will gradually improve thanks to a reduction in "blue collar" manual labor and a subsequent increase in "white collar" mental labor.[105] Andrew Levison, in his well-received The Working-Class Majority, drawing upon the same census and governmental data, refutes Bell's prognosis, insisting that "for the rest of this century, the majority of Americans will be essentially manual, rather than professional or managerial, workers."[106] Of course, the sharp disagreement between Bell and Levison depends a good deal upon how terms like "white collar" and "blue collar" are defined; as Levison argues, much that is classified as "white collar" or "service" occupation really involve manual or rote skills and is far removed from professional or managerial status, not to mention the number of married women who are included, supplementing the husband's income. Levison concludes: "America is not a white-collar or middle-class society. Sixty percent of American men still work in essentially rote, menial jobs,"[107] and this means generally "low pay and low prestige jobs."[108] From this perspective, Bell's post-industrial society looks a lot more like the past and present than the future.

There is no attempt here to question either the value or

solidity of Daniel Bell's work. He is a political sociologist of uncommon ability and genuine intellectual achievement. He can be read with profit, regardless of one's ideological predisposition. But there is good reason to conclude that he represents the best and the worst of the liberal-conservative stance in a paradoxical way. In contrast to many conventional liberals, he pays greater attention to the interrelatedness of economic, social, and political phenomena and places less reliance upon solving problems by allocating more money to the public sector and forcing the rich to pay more for their privileges. At the same time, the liberal-conservative has no real solution to the problem of an essentially inequitable society except to argue that things are not really as bad as they have so often been painted by the literary intelligentsia; and that capitalism, if left alone without excessive government interference, will adopt a more responsible role in an increasingly integrated political economy, to the degree that a scientific ethic based upon meritocracy is encouraged to prevail. There is certainly much evidence to show that such an appeal rests more on blind faith than on empirical data, contrary to the professed aims of liberal-conservatism. In fact, Bell may be faulted for thinking the greatest benefit of a more cautious, yet scientifically-calibrated approach to public policy is to defuse the danger of a distorted perception of complex reality. Bell asserts: "Any issue that becomes ideological distorts reality."[109] This may well be true, but it is not self-evident that there is any alternative to ideological behavior when change is needed. Bell is a prime example of what he rails against. The problem may not be simply eliminating ideology from the assertion of human value preferences, but determining what value assumptions and preferences are better than others in dealing with extremely difficult socio-economic-political problems. And this is inevitably a matter of interpretation, not just of fact.

Nathan Glazer

Nathan Glazer is a Harvard University sociologist who has specialized in patterns of ethnic assimilation in American society and has become a co-editor, with Irving Kristol, of The Public Interest, replacing Daniel Bell in that capacity. He has been a regular contributor to the magazine since its first issue. If there is one theme that unites his concern with educational, health, housing, and ethnic problems, it is that the American system does much better in regard to public policy than it is given credit for by its liberal-radical critics. When compared with other advanced industrialized nations, the United States does better than just about anyone else.

In an article which appeared in the magazine's first issue, "The Paradoxes of Poverty," Glazer made this interesting observation: "We deal with a statistical artifact when we speak of poverty in the United States" because "income that would spell comfort in some countries is actually poverty in

America."110   In other words, the poor do not have it so bad
when they can afford to own automobiles and television sets;
and although the funding level of public services directed to
alleviating poverty varies considerably across the country, "we
also have higher plateaus of income, on which very substantial
numbers are located."111   It is the same for housing—if the
definition of what constitutes "adequate housing" is framed realistically, then "on the whole, desperately inadequate housing
is infrequent in this country outside the rural areas."112   He
is convinced "voluntary" change is much to be preferred over
government-induced change, whether one is talking about "forced
busing," "opening up the suburbs," or extending free health care
to those in need.113   In Glazer's view, the explosion in welfare
dependency that occurred in New York City during the relatively
affluent 1960's was a disastrous consequence of a misbegotten
liberalism, fostered by bureaucratic vested interests, and destructive of "commitment to work and the strengthening of family
ties."114   He is not opposed to relief per se, but is against
the rhetoric of "welfare rights" which led to an unrealistic
explosion of the welfare rolls at a time of relative national
prosperity.

The term "affirmative action" is now part of the language.
It is comparatively new, and hotly controversial.   Although few
would dissent from its overt meaning, many reject its covert
meaning.   Nominally, affirmative action means that publically-
funded government agencies and those institutions, such as universities, which receive any form of federal funding, must not
discriminate in hiring practices; in fact, they should make every effort to provide opportunities for historically discriminated against racial minorities and women.   However, the real
significance of affirmative action, according to some of its
critics, is that bureaucrats and even, sometimes, the courts,
have exceeded this rather limited purpose of affirmative action
by actually mandating "hiring quotas," "suburb busting," "cross-
town busing," "special treatment" of individuals who share minority group status, and other forms of "reverse discrimination."
It is far from clear, however, how much or how little affirmative action of the latter sort is a calculated element in much
recent public policy—nor is it clear whether these two meanings of affirmative action can be distinguished.   But it is certainly true that affirmative action does symbolize the effort
of some public agencies and officials to use the power of the
federal government to expand opportunities for "minority group"
individuals, even if it may result in some unfairness to other
individuals and groups.   What is less easily ascertained is
the degree to which such policies cross the line into a less
defensible—from the standpoint of traditional democratic values—form of reverse discrimination.

Nathan Glazer has already made up his mind on this issue,
as the title of his recent book, _Affirmative Discrimination_,
attests.115   It is a book which deserves close attention, because it presents quite ably the negative case for affirmative
action, a policy which the author feels is widely employed by

government officials and judges to weaken, not strengthen, democratic values.

The first thing Nathan Glazer does is to applaud the steady progress that Black Americans have been making in reducing discrimination and improving their status as Americans. He attributes such continuing progress to political and legal efforts directed at liberating individuals as individuals, not as mythical members of special interest groups.[116] In effect, Glazer is quite hopeful that his gradual and yet substantial improvement will continue, because public consciousness has changed and the normal workings of democratic politics is asserting itself. The overly-zealous desire of liberal reformers to convert affirmative action into an instrument of coercion in behalf of an instant integration policy, according to Glazer, has produced infinitely more harm than good, has contributed to increasing social division, and what is worse, has eroded democratic principles of fairness and consensus. Ethnic assimilation has been one of the enduring facts in American life and history, but it cannot be force-fed. This is exactly what affirmative action advocates seek to do, however, in respect to both Black Americans and other so-called disadvantaged groups, including women.

Respect for human diversity, coupled with a concern for defining individual rights and opportunity in a manner that enhances personal responsibility and freedom rather than social coercion and conformity, has been the hallmark of the American experience. Thus, individuals are encouraged to retain ethnic ties and attributes while also adapting to the norms of nationality and citizenship. Neither need proceed at the expense of the other. Unfortunately, there is never a straight line between policy-making by legislatures and executive department officials, and the actual implementation of policies and programs. Under the American system, bureaucratic administrators and the courts have extraordinary leeway in interpreting the law all along the line, and here is where conflicts of interest and value come into play; for unlike politicians, bureaucrats and judges do not usually need to be concerned about the next election and constituency concerns.[117] In regard to affirmative action, this situation permits bureaucratic implementors and constitutional custodians to shape policies in accordance with their values and interests, and has led to the following questionable turn of events:

> 'Affirmative action' originally meant that one should not only not discriminate, but inform people one did not discriminate; not only treat those who applied for jobs without discrimination, but seek out those who might not apply. This is what it apparently meant when first used in executive orders. In the Civil Rights Act of 1964, it was used to mean something else—the remedies a court could impose when some employer was found guilty of discrimination, and they could be severe. The new concept of 'affirmative action' that has since emerged and has

221

been enforced with ever greater vigor combines both elements: it assumes that everyone is guilty of discrimination; it then imposes on every employer the remedies which in the Civil Rights Act of 1964 could only be imposed on those guilty of discrimination.[118]

The result of all this, according to Nathan Glazer, has been a widespread tendency to impose "preferential treatment" in hiring practices respecting minority-group individuals, frequently at the expense of better qualified and equally deserving non-minorities, and always under the sanctioning power of government edict.[119] Thus "racism" has become a weapon in the hands of liberal reformers who see racist attitudes in every instance where minority-group individuals are rejected, and automatically discount the possibility that personal responsibility and adequacy may enter into the picture.[120]

Two assumptions vitally affect Glazer's approach to public policy. First, he feels that government action cannot solve social problems that are linked to lower-class conditions rooted in the social structure and in historical forces; and efforts to do so are most likely to exacerbate rather than alleviate the problem. Second, the closer government is to the people, the more democratic it is likely to be, and the more free choice it is likely to offer; on the other hand, when decision-making is monopolized by professionals and so-called experts, there is less prospect that policy-making can be made accountable to the people. Both these assumptions are characteristics of conservatism today. They enjoy wide support, perhaps justifiably. The liberal rejects these assumptions because, in his assessment, the situation requires remedial action, no matter how difficult or intractable the problem, and because he believes disadvantaged individuals are human beings with considerable potential that can be aided by government policies that strive to close, rather than widen, the gulf between the better and less well off. And as for the old Jeffersonian idea—that government is best which is closest to the people—the contemporary liberal sees more myth than reality in this attitude, since government performance tends to improve as one moves up the ladder, and since, when pressing problems are left to solve themselves, the few tend to benefit at the expense of the many. The policy implications of these two divergent views of the proper role of government marks the very real cleavage that separates liberals from conservatives.

There is no evidence, however, that Nathan Glazer would not like to see liberal ends predominate, provided that conservative means are also honored. He is a pragmatic realist who would like to see progress made in improving the lot of disadvantaged Americans, but not by disregarding the time-table already established through the normal workings of consensus democracy.[121] Such an approach will bring about progress without excessive strain on the tenuous socio-economic fabric:

The integration of blacks proceeds, and at a pace related to their rise in income and occupation level.

The segregation of other minority groups is based more on income and occupation than on racial and ethnic discrimination and will decline with rising incomes and related changes in occupation and culture. The integration of the poor is quite another matter, and is hardly likely to be much advanced whatever measures of public policy we adopt. The poor are constrained in their movements by limited income, are resisted by the middle classes because of the social problems they bring, and further, it is not at all clear that the poor will be better off if distributed through an active public policy—even if it were possible—among the middle classes.[122]

The mistake liberals make is to substitute "statistical distribution" for "equal opportunity."[123] The result has been contrary to expectations. Endowing an abstraction, "minority group," with metaphysical meaning, subverts the individual as the basis of social justice and equity and opens the way for serious encroachments upon everyone's freedom.[124] Society is simply not equipped to compensate previously oppressed groups without creating greater harm than good to its democratic integrity.[125] When the individual person ceases to be an end, and becomes instead a means to an abstract idea of distributive justice, there will be only losers, not real winners. If Glazer is correct, everybody loses, when government becomes the "great equalizer." But this can hardly placate those whose hardship and suffering are real, less because of their own individual failings than because of a man-made social structure that is much less equitable than it could be.

Finally, in a Commentary article, Nathan Glazer raises a poignant question: "How does a radical—a mild radical, it is true, but someone who felt closer to radical than to liberal writers and politicians in the late 1950's—end up by early 1970 a conservative, a mild conservative, but still closer to those who now call themselves conservative than to those who call themselves liberal?"[126] First of all, he sees some convergence between late 50's-early 60's radicalism and conservatism in a growing distrust of bureaucratic government as a problem solver and rejection of the Soviet system as the beacon light of socialism. Then he became less certain that democratic pluralism and radical prescriptions for instant change were compatible, and acquired more respect for the continuity that institutions embodied. Diversified, complex interests needed to be accommodated somehow, if democracy were to survive. By the mid-sixties, radicalism, especially on campus, had grown ugly and threatening, in Glazer's view, and the divorce between frequently legitimate ends and illegitimate means became pronounced. Leadership in the Negro Rights Movement shifted away from Martin Luther King's brand of responsible idealism to the separatist extremism of black power advocacy. When the university itself became the main casualty of the student revolt, even moderate radicalism no longer seemed a viable stance.[127] And as the egalitarian revolution advanced, the price to be paid seemed too

223

high: increasing social control was gained at the expense of individual rights and freedom. So Nathan Glazer experienced a slow but perceptible shift of personal ideology as events moved too rapidly in a direction he could not accept. Yesterday's friend is today's enemy. And things are not nearly as bad as they may sometimes appear to be.

And Some Others...

Ideological classification lacks precision. In fact, it frequently distorts more than it illuminates. Just as prejudicial behavior has a tendency to lump all individuals of a certain type indiscriminately together, so does an ideological designation open up the possibility for distorted evaluation based on inflexible labels. Ideological typology is the least satisfying part of historical and social science analysis; yet somehow it is unavoidable. Good thinking does need a certain quality of consistency and conceptualization. And inevitably, this spells ideological conviction, for where certain bedrock assumptions or principles are an integral part of a person's thought and actions, there is a baseline which influences the selective way ideas, facts, and relationships are perceived.[128] Of course, there is much variation among individuals who think conceptually in the intensity of their ideological beliefs and how closely specific values affect actual conduct. But the point that needs emphasizing is how similarity, as well as difference, characterizes the thinking of individuals whose basic assumptions about the nature of man, society, and the state more or less coalesce. The beliefs of liberal, conservative, and radical thinkers diverge on the key issues of liberty, e- quality, and social justice, at least in terms of issues and priorities among these sometimes incompatible values. Ideological classification can be helpful in understanding where individuals stand on significant issues and values: and as a first step in evaluating the intellectual validity of different positions. Recognizing the limited value and the danger of over-simplification in all ideological classification, it is nevertheless a necessary adjunct to the study of man in society. With this in mind, a number of additional contemporary thinkers who have either written regularly for The Public Interest, or reflect a liberal-conservative socio-political orientation, will be identified; and a brief account of their individual contributions to a liberal-conservative ideological stance will be presented.

Irving Kristol was one of the founders of The Public Interest, shared early editorial responsibilities with Daniel Bell, and was one of the original founder-editors of the English based monthly journal of opinion, Encounter. In recent years, he has been a somewhat disillusioned critic of the declining quality of American civilization, but a strong supporter of the capitalistic system itself. In his book, On the Democratic Idea in America, Kristol takes note of the slippage in "republican morality and virtue," which he detects

224

as a movement away from the "original, animating principles" of the early days of the Republic.[129] He argues for a "conservative reform," which would seek to forestall the often negative results of unanticipated consequences of social action.[130] He deplores the inexorable spread of urban values throughout the culture, and looks to a restoration of an older morality; but he is not too explicit regarding the means and substance of such a recovery.[131] What America needs is to install a sense of higher purpose in the public arena. He attacks liberals for preferring their illusions to reality.[132] And in a _Psychology Today_ interview, he questions the value of the egalitarian thrust of contemporary liberalism:

> It may be that an egalitarian society is not a dynamic one economically. It may also be that a society that is equal economically becomes very unequal politically. It may be that one of the functions of inequality of wealth is to create political pluralism by creating many different centers of power—many different interest centers. It is perfectly conceivable to imagine a society in which everyone has equal pay but in which political power is so unequally distributed that, in fact, individual liberty becomes almost meaningless. One has to balance off all these terms; equality, liberty, religious values. And then look at the whole. In our experience, countries that become more equal don't necessarily become more contented, more self-assured or more optimistic about the future.[133]

Kristol believes that American democracy is in trouble mainly because such pivotal institutions as the family, the church, and the school have lost much of their traditional moral authority; the vacuum has been filled by political action-oriented ideologies of both Right and Left, which have little to offer and inhibit any real coming to grips with the contemporary "value crisis."[134] Yet American capitalism, even when it falls short of its promise, still represents the ideal for a liberal society that can achieve material abundance for all its citizens, freedom of choice, and individual striving that promotes the common good.[135] Those who reject this ideal, especially a segment of today's radical youth, do so out of ignorance, self-indulgence, and an inability to offer anything better in its stead.

Peter F. Drucker is primarily a political economist and authority on managerial theory and practice. In _The Age of Discontinuity_, he focuses upon the forces of change in contemporary society, and examines the potential impact of advanced technology on the socio-political structure. Like Daniel Bell, he foresees the emergence of new industries, which will be based upon the central role of knowledge in future productivity.[136] Humanists and businessmen will have to become more knowledgeable about technology. The managerial sector holds the key to real future progress. Conservatism and status quoism no longer represent a desirable working model for industrial entrepreneurs; technical innovation demands an openness to new ideas that converts traditional companies into change-responsive organizations.[137] This will also necessitate major changes in institutions, especially government and organized labor; the tax structure will have to be modified to encourage incentive, and labor will have to develop greater mobility.[138] Planning for tomorrow must replace day-to-day decision-making.[139] An interdependent world economy will gradually develop an institutional structure, replacing competing national entities,[140] unless political sectors fail to respond adequately to the challenge of a new era in international relations.[141]

Speaking of rich versus poor nations, Drucker offers this stark warning: "Either the poor will become richer, or the rich will not long remain rich."[142] This will happen only by harnessing human resources and capital to the new technology, not through foreign aid or other kinds of subsidy.[143] In Drucker's view, Japan, not the United States, or the Soviet Union, or Communist China, offers the best model for modernization to the Third World.[144] Better productivity depends upon better management of existing resources.[145] And to go along with this, there needs to be a "new pluralism" of organizational interdependence.[146] This is not just a matter of functional interdependence, but involves an integrated moral and political awareness.[147] Only forward-looking organizations will be successful in the new climate of technological innovation.[148] But the chief stumbling block to progress, according to Peter Drucker, remains the impotency of the governmental sector everywhere. In a now famous passage, he states the problem succinctly:

> There is mounting evidence that government is big rather than strong; that it is fat and flabby rather than powerful; that it costs a great deal but does not achieve much. There is mounting evidence also that the citizen less and less believes in government and is increasingly disenchanted with it. Indeed, government is sick— and just at the time when we need a strong, healthy, and vigorous government.[149]

At the root of this widespread political failure is the fact that modern government tries to <u>do</u> too much, and has become too involved in management, where it has no real competency. Drucker wants to see a new attempt at decentralizing government, not from a policy-making standpoint, but in respect to policy implementation. "We do face a choice between big and impotent government and a government that is strong because it confines itself to decision and direction and leaves the 'doing' to others."[150] This means reprivatizing the public sector, but does not mean a reversion to laissez-faire political economy. Although he does not specify how this can be accomplished, Drucker does suggest that policy-making and administration must be separated, with the former the sole province of government, and the latter a private sector responsibility.[151]

The strength of Drucker's analysis is his acute awareness of how socio-economic change is challenging old assumptions and placing great strain on existing political structures. Its weakness lies in the excessive claims that are made for rapid transition to "the knowledge economy," in which the manual worker will be displaced by the computer attendant. "Scientific management" cannot replace politics if democratic pluralism is to survive. Drucker errs in thinking the "knowledge worker" is a superior kind of human being, immune to the ordinary temptations of human greed and status superiority.[152] When it comes to the point that a majority of "haves" will have to subsidize a substantial minority of "have-nots," power factors will take over, and those who "have" will be inclined to look to their own interests rather than to the larger public interest. Drucker offers no prescription for changing the way the power game is played, or for taking care of the losers in the power struggle. Everyone cannot be a winner, as we have long known.

James Q. Wilson is a political scientist whose speciality is local urban politics. He has produced an impressive body of work, including a major study of the role of interest groups in the American political process, Political Organizations. Above all, he is sensitive to the complexity of contemporary government and policy-making, and usually adopts a judicious, balanced view of the phenomenon he is dealing with. For example, he cautions fellow analysts to avoid both the "pluralist fallacy" and the "Marxist fallacy," or "the error of assuming either that every social interest has one or more organizations representing it or that every organization represents the underlying objective interests or social conditions of its members."[153] Being a liberal-conservative, Wilson is very much on the side of change and reform; but he also sharply delimits the possibilities for improving either society or politics from the traditional liberal perspective that "everything is possible."[154]

Perhaps his most significant and controversial formulation, jointly shared with his colleague, Edward C. Banfield, is the dichotomy they found to exist in many urban areas between an upper-middle-class, Anglo-Saxon Protestant, professionally inclined, civic-minded political ethos and a lower or working-class ethos, highly reflective of the era of heavy immigration, family-based, strongly addicted to personal loyalty and to individual competition for scarce resources and opportunities, a contest in which the public interest gets short shrift.[155] This emphasis upon culturally-induced attitudes and values seemed to favor the ethos which reinforced larger community norms and to denigrate the one which conflicted with such interests, thus equating "good government" with high income and educational attainment. However valid this may be in some respects, it offers no comfort to those who might favor a more positive role for the underclass in social and political policy-making. In effect, Wilson insists that social scientists need

227

to pay more attention to class-bound attitudes and values,
which are much more resistant to change than other factors.[156]

In a short but brilliant essay, entitled "The Riddle of
the Middle Class," Wilson digs deeper than most other critics
into the contemporary malaise and value crisis that has spawned
such internal division in America during the past decade; he
concludes that this has occurred mainly because the Madisonian
model of slow constitutional change and majority coalition-
building has not been able to cope with the unprecedented demands placed upon it. The homogeneity of middle-class America
has broken apart on issues—like race, war, crime, campus un-
rest—that normally would not create such disharmony; conflict
within the middle-class itself represents the unprecedented aspects of contemporary value conflicts. Instead of viable pluralism, there is bureaucratic ascendancy, and instead of middle-
class leadership, there is middle-class weakness. Here is Wilson's evocative analysis of the problem:

> The animating spirit of the American democracy is the
> desire for equality. It is the middle class—not the
> poor—that historically has carried forward this de-
> sire. As the middle class grows in size, inequality
> lessens, but as inequality lessens, the demand that
> it disappear altogether grows louder. Vast inequali-
> ties and great social ills are tolerated, but as priv-
> ilege becomes less and problems become fewer, the ef-
> fort to abolish the last trace of privilege and to
> solve the last remaining (and therefore most intract-
> able) problem intensifies. But by this time, the gov-
> ernment itself has become a source of privilege and a
> creator of many problems, and thus to meet these new
> demands old gains would have to be abandoned—a pros-
> pect which no one relishes. In a middle-class democ-
> racy, the middle classes will inevitably be frustrated.[157]

Edward C. Banfield, formerly of Harvard, later a Profess-
or at the University of Pennsylvania, has written the most controversial, yet widely read scholarly study to appear in years.
In a 1970 publication, The Unheavenly City, and an up-dating
of it in 1974, entitled The Unheavenly City Revisited, Banfield
attacks the liberal view of poverty, the urban crisis, and government's responsibility for alleviating these problems. He
has taken account of the scholarly criticisms of his work, and
clarified meanings, but admits that there is still insufficient empirical data to either prove or refute his thesis. Yet
the thesis stands, much as it was originally stated: the 1960's
crisis of the cities was unjustly blamed on an indifferent
white power structure, neglect of urban poverty conditions,
and policy failures. Banfield asserts that the reality was
as follows:

> The plain fact is that the overwhelming majority of
> city dwellers live more comfortably and conveniently
> than ever before. They have more and better housing,

more and better schools, more and better transportation, and so on. By any conceivable measure of material welfare the present generation of urban Americans is, on the whole, better off than any other large group of people has been anywhere. What is more, there is every reason to expect that the general level of comfort and convenience will continue to rise at an ever more rapid rate through the foreseeable future...A great many so-called urban problems are really conditions that we either cannot eliminate or do not want to incur the disadvantages of eliminating.[158]

The problem is one of definition. If living standards and expectations are measured in relative rather than absolute terms, then there can be no limits set on what constitutes adequate welfare. In Banfield's view, this is generally what happened. As long as national policy helps the middle-class to leave blighted urban areas through taxation and housing subsidies and invites the poor to take its place by offering higher welfare benefits, the urban crisis will continue to be a politically inspired crisis rather than a genuine economic one. It is also psychologically rooted, and thus not likely to respond to even the most liberal sort of reform efforts or welfare subsidies, because the lower-class person is naturally irresponsible, present rather than future oriented, and incapable of taking advantage of opportunity for self-improvement even when it is offered to him.[159] If left alone, Negroes will do just as well climbing out of poverty as they would if there were no substantial government assistance.[160] Banfield is strenuously opposed to minimum wage laws which exacerbate unemployment in menial work. Better schools in slum areas will not compensate for the cultural deprivation that is a more severe constraint on self-improvement among poor people.[161] The exceedingly high crime rate in poor areas is less a reflection of need than of cultural and psychological factors, which substitute destructive for constructive inducements.[162]

In a chapter enticingly labeled "Rioting Mainly for Fun and Profit," Banfield argues that the widespread rioting that occurred in Negro areas of many Northern cities in the 60's was not caused by conditions so much as by media exploitation, a permissive judicial system, and the fact that it had acquired a kind of legitimacy in liberal circles.[163] In essence, Banfield feels that "so long as the city contains a sizable lower class, nothing basic can be done about its most serious problems."[164] The mistake underlying the theory behind the Johnson Administration's "war on poverty" was to expect that lower-class conditions could be eliminated entirely and that the lives of everyone below the poverty line could be upgraded to a decent living standard—and that from this only good would follow. Banfield rejects such thinking as being unrealistic and actually pernicious, for it generates expectations that cannot be fulfilled and that are bound to do more harm than good for all concerned.[165]

229

Whether or not one agrees with Banfield's anti-liberal and rather pessimistic view of the "urban-poverty problem," it is presented with considerable skill and resourcefulness. The scholarly verdict has been understandably mixed, and more reflective of ideological differences than is the case with most recent social science studies.[166] The liberal-conservative dichotomy, usually somewhat muted, did not speak with a soft and forgiving voice when The Unheavenly City was published.

Seymour Martin Lipset is an historian, sociologist, and political scientist. His main interest has been the relationship between political traditions and social structure. Change and continuity in relation to the nature and functioning of democratic societies have been the leading themes of his work. In his 1960 book, Political Man, Lipset presented one of the earliest analyses underscoring the paradox of "working class authoritarianism" going hand-in-hand with "economic liberalism." In Lipset's view, that bulwark of Marxian-Socialist movements, the working class (at least in Europe, with the United States something of an exception here), seemed also much more predisposed toward non-democratic, extremist, authoritarian attitudes than did the bourgeoisie:

> The poorer strata everywhere are more liberal or leftist on economic issues; they favor more welfare state measures, higher wages, graduated income taxes, support of trade-unions, and so forth. But when liberalism is defined in noneconomic terms—as support of civil liberties, internationalism, etc—the correlation is reversed. The more well-to-do are more liberal, the poorer are more intolerant.[167]

Parochialism, psychological insecurity, and lower educational attainment combine to make this class of people less tolerant of ambiguity and thus more inclined to evaluate other people and events in either/or terms.[168] In fact, characteristics that Banfield later found to be typical of ghettoized urban slum dwellers were identified much earlier in the working class by Lipset. Only the level of economic development keeps the situation in check, and reduces this potential threat to democratic stability.

In his studies of the American national character, Lipset sees greater continuity than change in respect to the chief values he postulates as animating principles: achievement and equality. In contrast to many social critics, who have noted strain and loss in contemporary value conflicts, Lipset sees mainly beneficial consequences, especially a strengthening of pluralist democracy.[169] He sanctions the ascendancy of political elitism as a counterweight to the "excesses inherent in the populist assumptions of democracy."[170] He notes that while radicalism flourished in the late sixties and created great turmoil on campus and in the streets, the "non-college populations...gradually moved in a more conservative direction."[171] Despite support from many moderates, the radicalized few never did represent more than a small minority of students and youth.[1]

The system remains sound at the core.

Lipset's most valuable work has been in comparative cultural analysis and in his continued search for an interdisciplinary methodology. Commitment to egalitarian-achievement values serves a unique function in American society: it reduces class stratification and virtually ensures stability within change.[173] For Lipset, America has achieved the distinctive position of having an ideology that works for change and does not divorce means from ends.[174] Needless to say, this is no longer such a widely-held view of the American political system, and it reflects the dilemma of a thoughtful liberal-conservative who blurs the normative and empirical modes of inquiry.

Individually and collectively, the thinkers spotlighted in this chapter are among the most perceptive and knowledgeable one is likely to encounter in the social science literature. They favor effective reform, but they are equally convinced that the liberal tradition has failed to realize its promise. The intellectuals have betrayed the masses. Liberal reform has proven to be both too little and too much. Compared to what was promised, results have been meagre, thanks to bad politics and faulty social science, while government itself has grown in size but not in either efficiency or effectiveness. Something else is needed, such as replacing politics-as-usual by a non-political elite that places professional values and respect for scientific rationality in the driver's seat. The only difficulty with this outlook is that it assumes greater competency and idealism among the meritocracy than seems justified on the evidence at hand. Professional bureaucracies are no better than other bureaucracies, and the scientific approach is not immune from ideological manipulation.

In their desire for greater realism and rationality in policy formulation and implementation, liberal-conservatives are certainly to be commended. But at the same time, they are unhappy with the usual messiness and unpredictability of popular democracy, and would like to believe some improvement would be forthcoming if a non-economic professional elite could be somehow given the authority now exercised by an alliance of economic and political elites. Even if this should occur, it is doubtful whether it would be either a beneficent or a democratic elitism, since the dependency of the many on the good auspices of the few would surely weaken the foundations of democracy itself. There would be no way of safeguarding the intimate relationship between power and ethics.

Liberal idealism and conservative realism are two sides of the same coin, but the coin has had long use and is now quite tarnished. At a time when American leadership has been so badly battered in domestic and foreign affairs, the public will have to finally decide what it wants and what it will accept. What has changed most obviously is that the public, rather than any elite, may now hold the key to America's future.

CHAPTER 9

AMERICAN AND EUROPEAN CONSERVATISM: SOME COMPARATIVE NOTES

"Truth" is one of those words which has gone out of fashion. A scientific, secular, relativistic age shies away from any claim that portends a universality or certainty which neither history nor man's nature can verify. The only trouble with this approach, which eschews certitude for contingency, is that, carried to its logical conclusion, it seems to sanction a might-makes-right, essentially purposeless, and ultimately nihilistic view of man's world. Although many philosophers and intellectuals go along with this world view, while seeking to restrict its more negative implications, there are a few who reject totally such unmitigated relativism, and dedicate their scholarly efforts to counteracting this modern trend and demonstrating the reality of universal truth.

Eric Voegelin, Bertrand de Jouvenel, Ortega y Gasset, Jacques Ellul, and Michael Oakeshott are five notable European thinkers whose work has been generally well-received and widely read in America. Their inclusion in this study is desirable to the extent one aims for an adequate survey of contemporary American conservative thought, for too rigid a separation of interrelated influences among political cultures makes little sense.

What ties all conservative political thinkers together is belief in an objective moral order, in which certain preferred values have universal validity for human conduct.[1] Although conservatives may differ on the importance they attach to specific values, such as hierarchy, tradition, order, authority, morality, and liberty, they are united in seeking a restoration of the Christian ethic and of humanistic moral standards, whose guidelines are to be found through a rediscovery of classical literature and classical political thought.

European conservatives have been especially concerned with combatting modern leveling tendencies and the egalitarian ideal; they fear that it destroys the ideal of excellence and substitutes in its stead a pernicious mediocrity. Thus the growing incidence of a mass culture throughout the industrialized world is looked upon as a most severe threat to moral standards and to the qualitative aspects of human existence. From their perspective, effective freedom depends upon a society which honors individual creativity and individual excellence, even if only a select few can achieve this cultivated life style. These few would establish a mood and uphold standards that others might emulate. Whether or not such qualitative elitism can be translated into actual governance, it at least ensures a social structure whose values would advance the spiritual content of human existence and counteract the insidious threat to man's spiritual aspirations represented by the increasing dominance of secularism, relativism, and scientism. Although conservatives entertain few illusions that this will

be an easy task to accomplish, they are adamant in their conviction that only such a reversal of present value tendencies
can save Western civilization from a growing moral sterility
and eventual self-destruction.

What is reality, and how is it to be apprehended? This
epistemological question is what most distinguishes American
from European conservative thinkers. The search for unitary
knowledge of the mind/body, spirit/matter, essence/existence
split has been the major preoccupation of contemporary European conservative thinkers. They thus tend to be more histor-
ically-oriented, more profoundly philosophical in their political analysis, and more interested in normative questions than
native-born American conservatives. This is evident even when
one considers transplanted Europeans such as George Santayana,
Leo Strauss, Hannah Arendt, and Hans Morgenthau. Having received their early education and training in European universities, they experienced a deeper exposure to classical literature and languages than is the usual situation at American
colleges and universities. In addition, these European and
ex-European scholars cut their intellectual teeth on a heavy
dose of German idealist philosophy, especially Kant and Hegel,
with an assist from Heidegger in the more recent period. These
reasons alone explain the lingering epistemological dualism
and continuing commitment to a metaphysical cosmology that has
marked European thinkers, in sharp contrast with their American co-conservatives, who tend more toward nominalism, in
which the objective and subjective realms are not so readily
distinguishable, and reality is defined as an existential continuum. This distinction is significant only insofar as it
highlights the differing preoccupations of European-born and
American-born thinkers. The former tend to assume a dualistic
cosmology, and thus devote their intellectual labors to heal-
ing the split. The latter are less sure this is a feasible
assumption to start with, and view the power/ethics problem
as a matter of individual and social morality, rather than
the right kind of metaphysics.

Historical and cultural differences largely account for
the differences between American and European conservative
thought. The predominance of feudalism in the European past
and the absence of feudalism in the American past, the prev-
alence of a monarchical-aristocratic phase in the evolution
of European political institutions and its absence in America, along with the early ascendancy of the middle-class in
America and the accompanying muting of class division, affected these respective political cultures in quite different
ways.[2] A conservative defense of the status quo, in Europe,
meant the outright acceptance of severe social stratification
and a glorification of values which gave little comfort to
the masses, who were hopelessly mired in a bottom-rung existence. Thus the path of genuine improvement for the many involved the kind of radical change, which exacerbated class
conflict and gave movements of the Left a solid basis of popular support. In the process, the Right responded by oppos-

ing changes which they felt engendered an illusory progress and threatened to tear the social fabric apart at great cost to a humanistic moral order. In England, conflict between Left and Right was re-channeled into a relatively constructive accommodation that hinged upon the nearly universal acceptance of procedural democracy by all rival camps. In continental Europe, ideological conflict sometimes assumed a more dangerous form, and Left-Right opposition struck at the foundations of democratic governance, especially in pre-World War II Italy, France, and Germany. Conservative thought had a role to play in either case, and maintained a substantial following in spite of all its ups and downs.[3]

America, in contrast, developed a political culture which forged a popular value consensus behind the basic constitutional-institutional structure and thus endowed a libertarian system with conservative coloration. As a result, political differences seldom acquired ideological content, and mainstream conservative-liberalism established the boundaries within which ideological conflict was permissible. Both radical and conservative thought were left out in the cold. Only rarely, and then only in a crisis atmosphere, could either radical or genuinely conservative ideas get a hearing. So the political consciousness of the public in America has been largely unresponsive to the extreme Left or Right. By thus narrowing the parameters within which discourse and debate could take place, pragmatism and the politics of self-interest liberalism carried the day. Not only have Americans been inhospitable to conservative and radical critiques of the social and power structures; at least until recently, they have also been highly successful in suppressing ideas and the individuals who exemplify them that do not reinforce the dominant value consensus. This is why political philosophy has not flourished in America as it has in Europe. Empirical theory and preoccupation with methodology have been the most pronounced characteristics of the social sciences in contemporary America. The who, what, and how, in America, take precedence in the pursuit of knowledge. European thinkers, on the other hand, still seem to care most about the why questions. This is an important difference. Knowledge translated into better policy-direction is the major preoccupation among American social scientists. Knowledge that is morally meaningful and enriches understanding is still the major preoccupation of European social scientists. In America, the main emphasis is directed at political theory. In Europe, the main emphasis focuses upon political philosophy.

Eric Voegelin

Political philosophy has come on hard times. The increasing emphasis within the social sciences on scientific methodology, empirical research, and policy-oriented studies leaves little room for the traditional historical, rationalistic, normative, and value-oriented approach to political analysis. Those few important thinkers who remain committed to the traditional approach seem like embattled, esoteric, and even irrelevant antagonists vis à vis the great bulk of contemporary social scientists trained to devote all their energies to a science of man, society, and the state. As a result, such thinkers tend to attract a small but fervid band of acolytes— students who have been exposed, either directly or indirectly, to their special brand of scholarship, and whose own conservative values are substantiated by an eloquent and learned spokesman. This is not to say, however, that these thinkers do not merit the highest consideration. It may well be that what is regarded as anachronistic, irrelevant, and esoteric by a majority of other scholars may indeed have more true relevance and substance in a larger time perspective. This possibility at least deserves to be left moot. The point to be underscored here is that there are a number of political philosophers who reflect this traditional approach which a large proportion of contemporary social scientists find dismissable either because the philosophers reject the canons of a scientific study of man, or because they pay too much attention to the past and not enough to the present and future in the quest for knowledge.

Eric Voegelin is such a thinker. Although seldom mentioned in current periodicals and generally overlooked in the ratings game, his multi-volume _Order and History_ is surely one of the more notable examples of the traditional approach in political philosophy. Dante Germino, who enjoys a solid standing among his professional colleagues, has been making a concerted effort in recent years to introduce Voegelin's work to a larger public, and refers to Voegelin's achievement in the following terms: "...with him we are in the presence of one of the most creative, sensitive, erudite and profound philosophical minds of our century. He has played a leading role in the revival of political thought in our time."[4] One can question the usefulness of Germino's tendency to equate theory and political philosophy, and the lack of evidence for his "revival theory" judgment, but one must respect the intellectual quality and extraordinary achievement that has marked Eric Voegelin's work.[5] Although a European by birth and education, Voegelin taught for many years at Louisiana State University, as well as at the University of Vienna and the University of Munich, where he retired as Professor Emeritus of Political Science. There is still one volume to go before he completes a projected five-volume study of the historical origins of political ideas and their relevance for the present age. He has also published other studies in the history of ideas.

The theme that unifies Voegelin's corpus is the search for transcendental truth.[6] His major presupposition is that political principles require a philosophy of history, for only in this way can the conflicting claims of power and ethics finally be reconciled; this insight was very much understood by earlier thinkers, but has since been largely abandoned. The task is one of restoration.[7] There is an overriding need for a new intellectual synthesis, comparable to Plato's and

Aristotle's, St. Augustine's and Hegel's achievements, if the right political principles are to be reclaimed from the quagmire of a power-obsessed age like the present.[8] He deplores the modern tendency to divorce fact from value, the positivistic fallacy. It is Voegelin's strongest belief that the scientific ideal is a dead-end in political inquiry, highlighted by Max Weber's heroic failure to reconcile scientific and humanistic values.[9]

The next step, therefore, is to lay the foundations for a "new science of order."[10] Objective truth exists. Man lives by symbols. Truth can be known philosophically. History can serve as the medium for revealed truth.[11] Theory is to meaning as existence is to action; they represent dual activities, and only when the former dictates the latter can man be sure he is on the right track.[12] Truth is dependent upon the proper relationship between man and God:

> The truth of man and the truth of God are inseparably one. Man will be in the truth of his existence when he has opened his psyche to the truth of God; and the truth of God will become manifest in history when it has formed the psyche of man into receptivity for the unseen measure.[13]

The source of man's fall from grace lies in the myopia of modern man's rejection of transcendental truth. The arrogance of power has replaced the earlier humanistic understanding of human limits and the Christian teachings concerning man's spiritual aspirations.[14] The Church's loss of hegemony in the late medieval period marked the decline of the spiritual power in human affairs.[15] This has been accompanied by the rise of what Voegelin calls Gnosticism, or the secularization of modern society. And this is tantamount to confusing an illusory progress with an actual decline, for "the life of the spirit is the source of order in man and society," and "the very success of a Gnostic civilization is the cause of its decline."[16] The loss of Christian unity and the suppression of transcendental truth has opened the floodgates, enabling disharmony and disorder to prevail in the world.[17] A restoration of rationality in politics and order in the world depends upon the defeat of Gnosticism and a renewal of the original Christian vision.

In From Enlightenment to Revolution Voegelin traces the spiritual decline of Western man from the Reformation in the sixteenth century.[18] The evidence is clear to Voegelin that the modern attempts to substitute a scientific for a spiritual approach to human knowledge and understanding have been disastrous.[19] All forms of utilitarian ethics are destructive of objective truth, because relativism fosters a might-makes-right value system, and divorces ethical from power considerations.[20] Such secular faiths are traceable to the misconceptions spawned by the Age of Reason, and to the false belief that man is master of his fate and that collectivism poses no threat to individual freedom.[21] Existential man cannot be separated from spiritual man, "for the problem of human history is precisely the tension between the historical existence of man and his transcendental distinction."[22] As a result of the decline of religion and the triumph of secularism, man's existence has been plunged into a severe crisis; what is unprecedented about this crisis is "that the spiritual substance of Western society has diminished to the vanishing point, and that the vacuum does not now show any signs of refilling from new sources."[23] It is clear that Voegelin is pessimistic about the chances for any major reversal of the pattern of deterioration he has discovered in his study of history.

But Voegelin's pessimism is not absolute. He has directed his intellectual labors toward a systematic examination of pre-modern historical and theoretical developments in his search for the outline of an alternative to existing tendencies and a philosophy of history that might offer a constructive replacement of destructive currents of thought that predominate today. History is neither willed nor determined, but is a complex structured process where meaning transcends actuality. At the very start of his study of history, Voegelin announces the guiding assumption of his work: "The order of history emerges from the history of order."[24] The past reveals itself through appropriate symbols of failure and success in man's effort to know himself and his world.[25] Reality is multi-dimensional: it is both immanent and transcendent at the same time. Order itself has assumed many different forms throughout history, but its most significant manifestations are to be found in Ancient Near Eastern civilization, early Israel, the Greek Polis, the rise of Christianity, and modern nation-statehood. Each of the volumes revolves around these watershed developments, except that there has been some revision of the original scheme in the later volumes. Voegelin acknowledges encountering greater complexity than he initially expected; and the coexistence of peak moments of spirituality with troughs of mundanity proved hard to decipher. Still, his purpose has not changed: he analyzes contrasting perspectives upon historical manifestations of spiritual truth and secular (or Gnostic) untruth, and searches for a new balance integrating symbolic and existential values or a re-divinization of human existence.[26]

According to Voegelin, history does not have a meaning in the usual sense of representing a record of human activities. The meaning of history resides in a structure of order that is a reflection of the divine presence in human existence.[27] The following passage expresses this central element in Voegelin's thought:

Human existence in society has history because it has a dimension of spirit and freedom beyond mere animal existence, because social order is an attunement of man with the order of being, and because this order can be understood by man and realized in society with increasing approximation to its truth.[28]

Only Western history, and only a brief interlude during the ancient period, truly qualifies for this award. Only Greek philosophy and the Judaeo-Christian tradition really approximate this highest form of human spirituality.[29]

A time of political crisis is good for political philosophy, but bad for the people who happen to live in such a period.[30] Man lives by myths. Science is the destroyer of myths.[31] History has neither beginning nor end—it is an eternal mystery that requires revelation for unlocking its nerve center.[32] Thus meaningful change occurs in history as a result of noetic (or spiritual) advances, not of the mere existential chronology of events.[33]

One of Voegelin's key concepts is "the in-between" state, linking subjective particularity and objective universality.[34] It is openness to the divine presence in the face of other enticements.[35] Neither idealism nor materialism offers a satisfactory metaphysics. Both these philosophical modes of inquiry substitute either the part for the whole or the whole for the part.[36] So the philosopher is needed to explore the depths of human consciousness, just as the deep-sea diver is needed for revealing the secrets of the ocean floor. There is an obvious meaning and a less obvious meaning inherent in political reality.[37] All ideological movements distort reality and undermine truth, because they violate the rule of order and disregard that sense of human limits which is the essence of ethical curbs on power. Only when a particular society is open to the God-like spirit can it rise above itself and achieve a high level of human excellence.[38] It has happened, occasionally, and it can happen again. This is the one hopeful note in what is otherwise a somber recital of the failure of mankind to realize its true potential:

> The 'absolute epoch,' understood as the events in which reality becomes luminous to itself as a process of transfiguration, is indeed the central issue in a philosophy of history. For without the noetic and pneumatic differentiation, there would not be a history in which man's humanity achieves its rational and spiritual consciousness, nor would there be a philosopher's intellect to be concerned with this structure in history.[39]

In other words, faith is more important than reason, and truth is wired to universality. Man is as he believes. And belief is a form of truth-seeking only insofar as it partakes of the divine presence.[40] Since Christianity has come closest in historical time to revealed truth, it is to a revitalized Christianity that man must turn if he is to be innoculated against the poisons of a raging anti-humanistic value virus. Voegelin does not really hold out much hope for man, but the right road is knowable if only the right choice can be executed.

239

One can respect Eric Voegelin's scholarly attainments and appreciate the richness of his probing intelligence without necessarily being persuaded that his claims are justified or his basic assumptions are valid. Like all philosophical conservatives, he displays a compulsive need to eliminate social conflict, curb political disorder, and ignore the economic injustices that have plagued human history. The quest for order is another name for the need for security, and what is possible for the few may not be possible for the many under existing power realities. So harmony and hierarchy become principles endowed with spiritual content. However, it is not easily demonstrated whether man benefits more when a religious mode of thought is enhanced or when it abates. The spirit/matter, essence/existence, subject/object dichotomy may be a false one, and just as troublesome as the fact/value dichotomy is in scientific parlance.

The relevance of Eric Voegelin's political philosophy, and its ultimate appeal, depends upon an arbitrary decision that can be asserted, but not proved, and whose implications for conduct are mired in ambiguity. This is the exact opposite of what he maintains is the truth of the matter.[41] An either/or dichotomy is perhaps the weakest place to start in the search for meaning in history. Yet without this either/or dichotomy, Voegelin would have nothing to say.

Once again, the conservative dilemma cannot integrate diagnosis of the disease with the right remedy, but there is good reason to conclude it is a false certainty and a questionable diagnosis to start with. For instance, a more truthful view of modernism, secularism, and the scientific mode of inquiry may well require a more balanced and less one-sided conceptualization of man, society, and the state. However disputable such an approach may be in the quest for better understanding, truth, and knowledge, it may have more to offer in the long run, for political disorder can be a creative force as well as a destructive force in advancing human welfare. The unwillingness, if not inability, of conservative thinkers to appreciate this possibility must surely distort their perception of political reality. Eric Voegelin's quest for greater order in history may be more a reflection of his own subjective needs than an objective portrayal of meaning in history. Whatever may be the case, one can appreciate Eric Voegelin's intellectual accomplishments without at the same time accepting the rather dubious thesis he propounds.

Bertrand de Jouvenel

There is a profound paradox that touches the heart of conservative political thought. The conservative has been quite distrustful of power in all its forms. Not only does power corrupt—it also interferes with individual rights and freedom, and must be curbed if there is to be any hope for good government. At the same time, there is a pronounced tendency for conservatives to favor some form of political authoritarianism and to exhibit a distaste for democracy. The mass public, or the average person, is unfit to rule, or even to participate substantially in the decision-making process. Not only does too much democracy pose an ever-present threat to property ownership and rights, it also opens the floodgates to mob rule, disorder, and demagoguery. So democracy, when defined as broad-based participation in the ruling process, gets an instant dismissal from conservatives. On the other hand, conservatives do respect authority and seem to welcome a dependency relationship between ruler and ruled. They are willing to grant inordinate power to the few as long as they can have confidence that their own values and interests are being looked after, and are mirrored in the designated authority. The heart of the paradox is a negative view of political power, which conservatives tend to adopt at the same time that they sanction a substantial delegation of power to a central authority. In their concern to free the individual from governmental interference over his life, conservatives are equally anxious to have a strong, authoritative, and powerful ruler who will do whatever needs doing in order to maintain social order, hold high the banner of individual freedom, and preserve the status quo. In a way, it is like trying to have one's cake and eat it, too.

Bertrand de Jouvenel, a distinguished French political philosopher, is a case in point. In a series of historical and analytical studies, he seldom strays far from a preoccupation with power, especially the question: Who should rule? Yet his pro-monarchical, aristocratic, and anti-democratic bias is never concealed. He is a bitter antagonist of all forms of collectivism, and a steady defender of the right kind of authoritarianism. There is a quaint, even courageous quality to his pro-monarchist leanings in an age of egalitarian ascendancy. When he surveys the field of recent political history, he sees nothing but loss and decline, because false gods, democracy and totalitarianism, have been permitted to usurp the role which should legitimately be given to an aristocratic tradition in the art of governance. Although Jouvenel has no illusions that current historical trends can be readily reversed, he does have some hope that, when survival is finally at stake, man will return to the wisdom of the past and reclaim a misplaced birthright, the validity of benevolent authoritarianism. He would accept political authority in order to maximize social freedom. The trick is to weld one to the other. The means to this end, according to Jouvenel, is to endow authority with legitimacy.

As long as voluntary consent and not coercive control is at issue, authority itself is de-clawed and government achieves legitimacy.[42] Authority is good when it is preservative; change is good only in slow accretion, not in sudden leaps.[43] Society is more than the sum of its parts; it is the social bond of friendship, community, and mutual respect which transforms quantity into quality and endows society with a balance of authority and freedom.[44] The chief end of rulership is to advance the common good by insuring the superiority of moral standards and slowing the pace of social change.[45] Social justice is an empty ideal; human progress comes through individual, not collective effort.[46]

Jouvenel turns to the pre-modern period, from the 16th through the 18th century, for his ideal of society, and finds it in a form of monarchy that was less than absolute and more than nominal. It is not the people, but a higher reason, that determines sovereign legitimacy.[47] And true individual freedom depends upon a sense of obligation to what is highest and best in man. It is not outward authority which is the controlling factor, but individual conscience. "A man is free when and to the extent that he is his own judge of his obligations, when none but himself compels him to fulfil them."[48] That government is best which interferes least in the life of the individual citizen.[49]

Jouvenel's most important book is On Power, first published in 1945, wherein he investigates "its nature and the history of its growth."[50] It is both a defense of monarchy as a potentially benevolent institution and a critique of Rousseauistic democracy. The thesis is that the coercive power of the state has increased with the growth of democracy in the world, while no monarchy ever commanded the kind of centralized power now characteristic of so-called democracies.[51] Power is neither evil nor good per se; it can be used for either good or evil purposes.[52] The best check on arbitrary abuse of power is a society where routine and habit and custom hold sway.[53] Revolutions invariably bolster the claims of power.[54] And democracy invariably distorts power, because the people are in no position to handle the authority thrust upon them:

> It is possible, with the help of prudently balanced institutions, to provide everyone with effective safeguards against Power. But there are no institutions on earth which enable each separate person to have a hand in the exercise of Power, for Power is command, and everyone cannot command. Sovereignty of the people is, therefore, nothing but a fiction, and one which must in the long run prove destructive of individual liberties.[55]

Real liberty is for the few, not for the many, for it has to be carefully cultivated and not simply tied to hedonistic pleasure-seeking.[56] This leads Jouvenel to opt for elitism, and to defend an aristocratic class structure as the proper insurance for true liberty, which is, at root, moral and qualitative.[57] Established religion is the main bulwark against a debased value system, for "whenever the current concepts of right conduct are disturbed, the social harmony is in danger."[58] Once again, the value priorities of conservative thinkers are in evidence: harmony, order, and authority are all of a piece, and without these, man cannot hope to improve his condition or to achieve excellence. Both social conformity and obedience to authority are good.[59] Man needs order and structure in his life.[60] The liberal notion that the chief end of government is to solve problems strikes Jouvenel as the height of absurdity. Social problems are not soluble. At best, they can be contained, and agreement reached, but not to everyone's satisfaction or benefit.[61] This is additional testimony to the efficacy of government in doing less rather than more. When it tries to do too much, it ends up doing the wrong thing.

In a slim volume entitled The Ethics of Redistribution, Jouvenel attacks the current emphasis upon income redistribution via socialism.[62] Any government scheme which aims to improve the lot of lower income segments suffers from two main defects: first, by taking from the rich and giving to the poor it reduces total income, and there is that much less for everyone; second, it raises expectations that cannot be fulfilled, for government hand-outs are bound to fall short of actual need, let alone desire.[63] The best hope for improved living standards in general lies in better productivity, which in turn rests on the incentive motive.[64] The fact that some have too much and others too little may be deplorable, but it is not remediable. For the government to impose remedial policy in the interests of income equalization, the total society would be the loser, for mediocrity would be elevated and creativity diminished.[65] Worst of all, "the more redistribution, the more power to the State."[66] And in Jouvenel's view, there is little prospect that this enhanced power will be wielded wisely. But the most serious argument against the state moving into the area of national wealth redistribution is what it would mean to the cultural life of the nation, for "it is clear enough that progress is linked with the existence of elites, the production and upkeep of which are costly, and the incomes of which could not be flattened out without great social loss."[67] In sum, the cost to the taxpayer, no matter how progressive the rate may be, would be excessive "in all ranges," not just to the wealthy few.[68] The poor or the many do not benefit from redistribution schemes; instead, everyone suffers, because it requires a "redistribution of power from the individual to the State."[69]

Even among conservative thinkers, Bertrand de Jouvenel seems old-fashioned and a poor guide for getting one through the thick jungle of policy and value conflicts. His political values are so anti-modern and anti-change that it is hard to see how history could be reversed in a manner that would accommodate Jouvenel's cherished beliefs. Even his understanding of power can be considered suspect, for it nowhere partakes of nuance; power is never a question of degree but of difference in kind—it is defined as command, never influence. Although he claims to view power in both positive as well as negative terms, it is almost always couched in negative tones and his use of historical example reflects this one-sided either/or-ism. His conservatism is more a matter of personal taste and

temperamental need than of intellectual analysis. Politically,
Jouvenel would have to be listed as a reactionary; socially, he
is a thinker who seldom rises above the level of self-indulgence. One might agree with his critiques of contemporary socialism and liberalism, but it is unlikely that one can recommend a defense of conservatism that sweeps aside so much current history and distorts the meaning of democracy in the world.
Few conservatives would support Jouvenel's contention that democratic rule and conservative values are incompatible, even if
the term democracy is itself open to varied interpretations.
European conservative thought is not seen in its best light in
the writings of Bertrand de Jouvenel. He has done little to
repair the split between power and ethics, which has continued
to challenge the best conservative minds of this century.

Jose Ortega y Gasset

The main thrust of a democratic society is to reduce, and
hopefully to eliminate, all gradations of superior-inferior relationships. The average person is king, because he embodies
that irreducible quality of human dignity and moral worth and
human potentiality that constitutes the essence of democracy.
The good life in the good society must be open to everyone,
regardless of circumstance, inheritance, or achievement. Fundamentally, no one is better than anyone else. No human being,
a priori, is more valuable to himself and/or society than any
other human being. Everyone is equally valuable, equally important, equally a moral asset. A democratic society must do
as much as it can to promote equality, and to create conditions
which foster greater equality, because true evil resides not
in basic human nature, but in defective institutions and structures which allow gross inequalities to exist and to become
self-perpetuating. A democratic ethos insists that human beings, in general, are capable of responding creatively and constructively to life, if given a genuine opportunity to free
themselves from the burdens of insecurity and disadvantaged
social situations. The ideal which propels democracy is to
maximize both personal freedom and true equality; together they
represent an irresistible force for good. However, the historical evidence suggesting that equality and liberty are also
frequently at odds with each other is substantial: the more
egalitarian the society, the less personal freedom. It is
this dilemma that has compelled conservative thinkers to reject equality in favor of liberty. The problem is that such
a choice also means rejecting democracy and accepting in its
place a kind of benevolent authoritarianism.

Jose Ortega y Gasset, who died in 1955, was a Spanish philosopher and man of letters who continues to be one of the most
widely read writers of our time. Nearly a dozen of his books
remain in print, and are frequently used in various college
courses. He is a graceful writer, and has the rare ability
to make normally abstruse philosophical concepts understandable to the average reader. Critics might say he is too much

the over-generalizer, who talks incessantly about man but seldom with either precision or objectivity. There are only a few
basic ideas or themes which are repeatedly explored and elabor-
ated upon in his numerous books, which are mainly essays rather
than systematic philosophical treatises. This accounts for
their popularity, but the price is high: a closer inspection
would necessitate a lower estimate of Ortega's intellectual
achievement.

Ortega's life was an exemplary tribute to the democratic-
liberal ideal. As a leading figure in the pre-Franco Spanish
Republican government, he was forced to give up his position
as a philosophy professor at Madrid University and the editor-
ship of a prestigious journal of opinion, to leave his native
land, and to spend the rest of his life in exile, later returning only as a visitor. His most famous and influential book
is <u>Revolt of the Masses</u>, originally published in 1930. Although
he did not consider himself a conservative in the usual sense,
since he was not opposed to reform or change, he certainly
can be considered an important European conservative thinker
in his personal values; the entire thrust of his writings was
to denigrate the equalitarian strand in democratic thought.

Ortega was, at heart, an aristocrat; all his judgments reflect this initial bias. Only a small minority of the human
race is capable of true self-realization, for few individuals
make cognitive and moral demands on themselves that enable them
to rise above the herd mentality and to experience life quali-
tatively.[70] A specter is haunting man, threatening to destroy
all that is best in civilized society. This is the rise of
"mass man," accompanied by the triumph of the political; ethics,
individual creativity, and privacy are casualties of the transition to mass conformity and a popular culture that has no respect for high standards of individuality.[71] The reason for
this unfortunate development is the ill-founded popularity of
mass democracy—or that definition of democracy which would
sacrifice liberty to equality. Although Ortega sees a positive
side to the improved circumstances of the masses in Western nations, and is not opposed to better living standards for all
or to a more cosmopolitan world-outlook, he feels that the price
has been too high, for it is destroying the elitist basis of a
rationally ordered society, and is unleashing a new barbarism
across the land.[72] If this trend should continue for any
length of time, then the results are likely to be catastrophic
for civilization:

> The mass crushes beneath it everything that is differ-
> ent, everything that is excellent, individual, quali-
> fied and select. Anybody who is not like everybody,
> who does not think like everybody, runs the risk of
> being eliminated.[73]

The model which Ortega sets forth in contrast to "mass
man" is the "exceptional man" who will not settle for less
than is best, since "nobility is defined by the demands it
makes on us—by obligations, not by rights."[74] The current

prooccupation with science and technology as a panacea that may ultimately bring the good life to everyone is completely misdirected and illusory, according to Ortega.[7] For as we progress scientifically, we regress morally.[76] "...Our time, being the most intensely technical, is also the emptiest in all human history."[77] Only the exceptional person is capable of self-transcendence; that is, only he can be true to himself, while remaining sufficiently self-disciplined to maximize his sense of rationality and responsibility.[78] Western Europe has experienced a decline from a past golden age, a time when excellence was rewarded and mass man was the underdog.[79] In this respect, Ortega looks to antiquity, especially to Ancient Greece, for inspiration and a possible source for a "new revelation."[80] Yet he also sees a profound tension between what man is and what man might be, especially the facts that just being alive is risky business, and that contingency interferes with man's need for ultimate certainty.[81]

Perhaps the main source of Ortega's continuing appeal to a contemporary public, which is probably unsympathetic to his political values, is the social philosophy that undergirds his thought and strikes a responsive chord in many people today. At a time when life is becoming overly-organized, overly-socialized, and overly-permissive, Ortega stands firm behind an older ethic that may not have a name, but does have a history rooted in tradition. The individual is essentially alone in the world. Society is the enemy.[82] Each human being is essentially alone in the carapace of his/her individual existence.[83] Unlike many conservatives, who feel that the individual fulfils himself through an accommodation with social traditions, Ortega resists any theory that might encourage the individual to be swallowed up by society, however defined. Life is a "radical solitude."[84] And the socialization process is an ever-present danger to the integrity of the self.[85] Therefore Ortega's thought is a glorification of the introspective and contemplative side of life, and an unabashed paean to self-centeredness. Personal life is really all there is. The self is an absolute.[86] "Life is what we do and what happens to us."[87] But not all aspects of life are equally valuable. Here is where Ortega takes issue with what he believes is a pernicious democratization of contemporary life in the West. There is an obvious and sharp distinction between the qualitative and quantitative aspects of life. "And so the terrible gap which began at least a century ago continues to grow, the gap between living culture, genuine knowledge, and the ordinary man..."[88] There is a pronounced existential quality to Ortega's thought which has kept him in tune with the times even as his substantive achievement comes more and more into question.[89]

Does Ortega postulate a false dichotomy, a questionable either/orism, which cannot really be sustained when reviewing either man's history or nature? Is "mass man" really all that bad—and is the "exceptional man" all that good," a term that may encompass all of the human race from a certain standpoint, can also be a very unaverage person at the same time. From a democratic standpoint, the average man is a myth. No one is average; everyone has dignity and unique human potential. From an aristocratic standpoint, the average man represents a threat to all that is best and qualitative in life. But at the same time, the best enjoy privileges that the many can only aspire toward, and mostly with a sense of hopelessness, futility, and powerlessness. It may well be that, descriptively speaking, Ortega is perfectly correct: there are the few and the many and an insuperable chasm separates these two components of society. But he is not correct in asserting, with virtually no factual evidence, that a large segment of the total human race is incapable of rising to the heights of individuality and creativity that he proclaims to be the ultimate ideal. In fact, the entire edifice Ortega has constructed has a rotten foundation. If the "sanitation worker" is a good father and husband and worker, then, no matter how lowly his position in the socioeconomic scheme of things, it is quite likely this makes him a superior human being in any scale of values. And he may be writing a good serious novel on the side! Likewise, if the great writer is something of a failure in his/her human relationships, then it is doubtful that person qualifies as a superior human being. Not only does Ortega postulate a false dichotomy to begin with, but he robs man of his birthright— the right to strive for a society that does not legitimize or sanctify superior-inferior relationships.

Still, there is a positive quality to Ortega's intellectual achievement. In an age that seems to deny man's basic claim to subjectivity, he argues unceasingly and eloquently for a renewal of man's inward being, as something that deserves respect and nourishment. If it is true that those forces that are usually designated "mass culture" tend to drive a wedge between the inner and outer man, making it less possible to integrate one's personality and to harmonize one's relationship with the world, then one must conclude that Ortega was on to something important. Unlike most conservative thinkers, he trusts emotion more than intellect. He favors the concrete over the abstract. Each person has a core of authenticity that is the source of true self-realization. In this respect, Ortega's dichotomy is a qualified one: everyone is capable of exceptionality. The reason why so few finally make the grade is a matter which Ortega both over-simplifies and evades. His conservatism comes through in the pro-elitist, anti-democratic, and past-oriented value assumptions that permeate his outlook on life. In this respect he is preeminently the product of a European background, which displays more sensitivity to the tragic dimension of the human condition and human aspirations than does the American tradition, which can still face the future with muted optimism. There is no room for much hope in Ortega's vision. Man may survive, but there is little prospect that a humanistic ethic will prevail.

Jacques Ellul

In contrast to their American counterparts, European conservatives tend to be a good deal more anti-modern. That is to say, they find little to commend and much to condemn in the emergence of an advanced industrial-technological society; and, in large measure, their writings revolve around critiques of modernism from social and political, not just economic, standpoints. The impact of modernism on social change and on the quality of contemporary civilization is deemed an even more serious threat to cherished values than what is occurring in the political and economic spheres, although these aspects are not disconnected. Whereas American conservatives appear to accept both the inevitability, and the occasional beneficial consequences of across-the-board higher living standards and upward mobility, European conservatives would like to set back the clock, and to reestablish a cultural milieu in which social values are rooted in class differences and an acquiescent mass public "knows its place" in the general scheme of things.

Jacques Ellul is representative of this particular approach to conservative values. He has been a professor of social history and the history of law at the University of Bordeaux since 1946. English translations of five of his numerous output of politico-sociological analyses, have made Ellul as well-known on this side of the Atlantic as he is throughout Western Europe. Two of his books, The Technological Society (1964), and Propaganda (1965) are classic studies of two of the most important modern developments: the impact of technology on man's nature and well-being, and the pervasive role that propaganda plays in contemporary life. Three lesser studies, The Political Illusion (1967), A Critique of the New Commonplaces (1968), and Autopsy of Revolution (1971) round out the presently available English translations of Ellul's prolific writings.

The Technological Society defends this thesis: the onset of the technological society is a revolutionary event in modern history. According to Ellul, the individual is becoming a helpless victim of forces he can no longer control; technology, a necessarily dehumanizing and change-producing phenomenon, now dominates virtually all aspects of modern life, and this will prove to be progressively more true as time goes on.[90] All human ends and purposes are now at the mercy of technological power.[91] The split between the natural world of human experience and the artificial world of technological control is all but complete: "The two worlds obey different imperatives, different directions, and different laws which have nothing in common."[92] Those nations which monopolize the new sources of technology—Russia and America—are destined to rule the world,[93] since they are the only ones capable of adapting even partially to technological necessities.[94] But even in these two cases, their similarities will be greater than their differences, for centralization of political power, planned economies, and totalitarianism are indelible characteristics of modern technological societies.[95] The complete merging of the public and private sectors is inevitable, even in democratic systems. Efforts to resist the centralizing thrust of technology through various forms of decentralization are an exercise in futility.96 Liberal values cannot withstand the inevitable triumph of efficient ends and technological means: "Technique is the boundary of democracy. What technique wins, democracy loses."97

Perhaps the most harrowing aspect of Ellul's vision of a completely technological society is his conviction that the human element will be squeezed dry and only the rind will remain.98 Technology strikes directly at the unconscious wellsprings of human psychology and human behavior; individuality is sacrificed to collective necessity.99 No form of human intervention or political structure can reverse this process of technological change and dominance.

Ellul is not alone in this preoccupation with the negative consequences of modern technology. Lewis Mumford, among others, has written in this vein, and countless contemporary social critics have emphasized the de-humanizing dangers implicit in a society dominated by technology. Marxist theory is based upon this vision of human alienation deriving from machines controlling man rather than the reverse. On the other hand, Ellul goes a step beyond most other critics in endowing technology with a metaphysical content and an irresistible power for doing only harm and no good. As William Kuhns has noted, such mechanistic determinism is reflective of a nineteenth-century frame of reference; twentieth-century electronic technology poses a more complex man-environment relationship that has prompted many thinkers, like Marshall McLuhan and Harold Adams Innis, to favor an organic rather than mechanistic view of technology.100 This creative-tension approach leads to less simplistic conclusions, and seems more attuned to contemporary historical reality.

Despite strong argumentation and provocative analysis, Ellul's study is seriously flawed, since he is so intent upon building up a massive case for the evil results of technology that he completely discounts the possibility that technology can be beneficial for man and responsive to political direction. For example, improvement in health care and life expectancy are just a few of the fruits of modern technology.

According to Ellul, the main political consequences of a technological age is that everywhere, eventually, politics becomes subordinate to technology; technology displaces ideology; bureaucracy expands at the expense of politics; and democracy expires.101 All distinction between means and ends disappears; power increases at the expense of humanistic values, and man finds that he lives for power, or is victimized by it.102 There is, furthermore, no escape from the collectivist requirements of technology; the average person gains security, but gives up both liberty and equality.103 Thus modern society becomes more totalitarian, regardless of whether it is democratic or non-democratic:

Unconsciously, modern man knows himself to be the
victim of forces over which he has no control. The
modern state has become the coldest of all monsters.
Nobody can do anything against it: it _is_. It develops for reasons of its own, regardless of governments, constitutions, institutions. Modern technology has acquired perfect autonomy from all af-
firmations and philosophies...[104]

More individualism was possible under authoritarian regimes prior to this century than is possible today, and democratic systems are a pale copy of original democratic ideals.
Mass democracy has displaced individualist democracy, and true
personal freedom has been sacrificed to a false egalitarianism.[105] In historical analysis of the meaning and central importance of modern political revolutions, Ellul concludes that
revolutions can no longer be instigated by, and primarily for,
the few; the technological imperative necessitates mass involvement and statism, which favors stability over change.[106]
In fact, the older form of the nation-state is giving way to
an entirely new form:

The modern state is no longer the symbol of 'political
power,' or of a class or social group; it has been the
motor of a globalized, unitary, and all-embracing society of which it is also the inseparable expression.
Technology and the state combined influence and mold
individuals, too—through psychological and psychoso-
ciological processes (e.g., propaganda).[107]

Jacques Ellul's major contribution to political thought
rests less on his excessively one-sided conceptualization of
"technological society" than on his systematic treatment of
the increased importance of "propaganda" as the means by which
elites and masses are locked into a symbiotic relationship.
Even though it exemplifies Ellul's propensity toward sweeping
metaphysical statements, Propaganda: The Formation of Men's
Attitudes is probably one of the best analytical studies of
this increasingly important concept. For Ellul, propaganda
is less a matter of manipulating language to persuade large
numbers of people to think in a certain way or buy products
they normally do not need, than a subliminal means to achieve
behavior modification linked to the power of the state. By
adopting this approach, Ellul sees the uses of propaganda as
not just an expression of a totalitarian need to indoctrinate
the masses in accordance with regime goals, but as a universal
trait of modern technology, which sweeps together all political systems, regardless of their political structures.[102]
With propaganda the means, and technology the end, the individual soon becomes swallowed up in a mass culture that releases the unconscious irrationalism that underlies rational
consciousness. It is not so much thought, but action itself,
that is the real index of the effects of man's exposure to
propaganda:

The aim of modern propaganda is no longer to modify

ideas, but to provoke action. It is no longer to change adherence to a doctrine, but to make the individual cling irrationally to a process of action. It is no longer to lead to a choice, but to loosen the reflexes. It is no longer to transform an opinion, but to arouse an action and mythical belief.[109]

The secret power of propaganda resides in its capacity to convert individual responsens into collective action.[110] The mythological aspiration that at one time was the prerogative of religion is now monopolized by society and the state via the instrument of propaganda. The average person's attitudes and values are so conditioned by propaganda, that group life becomes the standard by which individuals view and measure themselves.[111] Ultimately, all behavior becomes politicized, and emotions subvert reason.[112] Since thinking involves disciplined effort, it is always easier to accept stereotyped images in its place.[114] People do not respond passively to propaganda; it fulfils psychological needs which engage the masses actively in political affairs.[115] However, it feeds on irrational, not rational, predispositions; and in this respect the average citizen becomes addicted as he is exposed to more propaganda.[116]

The real nature of propaganda, therefore, is obscured by the tendency to concentrate upon its surface manifestations. Propaganda, in essence, is a substitute religion: it provides explanation, release from uncertainties, and a justification for life's meaning and purpose.[117] It fills an emotional void. It gives the alienated individual an identification with the community and culture of which he is a part. Only through collective action can modern man assuage his sense of loneliness, powerlessness and isolation. But group life alone cannot give a person the sense of self-identity he craves. An overly organized and repressive society provides an opportunity for propaganda to afford a release from tension and anxiety.[118] It is the means by which self and society are integrated:

Man, eager for self-justification, throws himself in the direction of a propaganda that justifies him and this eliminates one of the sources of his anxiety. Propaganda dissolves contradictions and restores to man a unitary world in which the demands are in accord with the facts. It gives man a clear and simple call to action that takes precedence over all else. It permits him to participate in the world round him without being in conflict with it, because the action he has been called upon to perform will surely remove all obstacles from the path of realizing the proclaimed ideal.[119]

Unfortunately, the price is high. Propaganda drives a wedge between the inner and outer man; it substitutes artificial desires and values for what is most needed—a life of rational control.[120] The chief casualty of propaganda is thought itself.[121] And who benefits from all this? The state, naturally—or the rulers. Since most people, at the very least want the truth sugar-coated, and will tend to choose illusion over truth, the state becomes the interpreter of truth; this means that the ruler's interests need not coincide with the public interest. This immense power is a convenient tool for manipulating mass opinion and insuring the supremacy of might over right.

Throughout this substantive study, Jacques Ellul shifts attention away from the content of propaganda to its effects, especially the psychological predisposition of a technolog- ically-oriented society to need the emotional sustenance that only propaganda can provide. One can quarrel with Ellul's tendency to over-state his case and to present his message in a strictly negative light. But despite such serious pitfalls, one can still admire the cumulative impact of his analysis from book to book, and the fact that much of what he says is undoubtedly true and disturbing, although hardly as all-encom- passing as he claims. As a thinker, he has the defects of his virtues: he presents an unbalanced picture of the technologi- cal society, propaganda, and modern revolutionary activity, yet manages to enlighten us at the same time.

The contemporary conservative exhibits two strong fears: popular control of government, and popular control of culture. Much of his negativism toward government and mass culture stems from these two fears. Jacques Ellul is certainly preoccupied, perhaps even obsessed, by these fears. This is why so much of his analyses attacks these interrelated developments. By high- lighting the source and implications of these distinctive trends of modern society, he hopes to find a way to tame po- litical power in behalf of individual autonomy. The only trouble is that there appears to be little hope of any such reversal, given the growing strength of the coalition of state power and dynamic technology.

Are such fears really justified? Any answer to this ques- tion necessarily involves another value judgment; and there is no way of proving the validity of anyone's value judgments. The empirical evidence can take one just so far, but never quite far enough. The fact is, however, that the differences be- tween totalitarian and democratic political structures are sig- nificant; Ellul is at least partly incorrect in maintaining the opposite. And when Ellul refers to the average man, mass pub- lic opinion, and technological society, he is indulging in myth- making. Even in modern society, in which political, social, and economic power have become ever more concentrated, the individ- ual has retained some control over his own life. Society and the state are still a long way from swallowing up the individ- ual, at least in democratic systems, and perhaps non-democrat- ic systems as well. But there are problems that do require more concerted attention if individual autonomy is to be pre- served. In this regard, Ellul has made a substantial contri- bution to our knowledge and understanding. In other words, Jacques Ellul is a more trustworthy guide than he is a proph- et.

Michael Oakeshott

Realism has been the great strength and the great weakness of conservative thought. The conservative thinker desires, above all, to see things as they are, without illusion and without false sentimentality; man is as he is, not as he would like to be, and it is always better to recognize limitations than to force changes that are bound to do greater harm than good. For the realist, morality is tested self-interest. Skepticism is his natural stance. The concrete is preferred over the abstract. Experience is more reliable than are ideas. Politics, which thrives on conflict and disagreement, should be replaced by some form of imposed harmony—in effect, a benevolent authoritarianism. But realism can also be blind: blind to injustice, blind to things being different from what they are, and blind to the power of ideals in helping to solidify the connection between means and ends. The conservative is a realist who shuns illusion and appreciates complexity, but at the same time seeks to inspire a one-dimensional view of reality purged of any sense of self-transcendence. Conservatism, therefore, contrary to the intent of its practitioners, creates an atmosphere wherein morality becomes strictly a matter of "isness," not "oughtness." And power is where it is found, not where it may need to be. Untempered skepticism contains the seeds of its own extremism: thus, England's outstanding exponent of conservative thought, Michael Oakeshott, is the perfect example of conservatism's paradoxical mixture of weakness and strength.

Michael Oakeshott, until his recent retirement from teaching, held the prestigious chair as University Professor of Political Science at the London School of Economics for twenty years. Prior to that, he had been, for many years, a lecturer in history at Cambridge University. Although his writings have been limited to essays and two philosophical treatises, Experience and Its Modes (1933) and On Human Conduct (1975), Oakeshott has acquired a substantial reputation as a critic of liberalism and as an authority on the political philosophy of Thomas Hobbes. He does not easily fit the conservative label, if only because he carries a conservative world-view to such extreme lengths that one critic, the late Bernard Crick, has referred to him as "the lonely nihilist."[122] He is a traditionalist who has difficulty indicating what is good in tradition. He is a political philosopher who seems to see little use in politics per se. Instead of putting back the clock, he would sooner dispense with clocks altogether. Perhaps the following passage captures best the unique quality of Oakeshott's vision and style:

> In political activity, then, men sail a boundless and bottomless sea; there is neither harbour for shelter nor floor for anchorage, neither starting-place nor appointed destination. The entrerprise is to keep afloat on an even keel; the sea is both friend and enemy; and the seamanship consists in

using the resources of a traditional manner of behavior in order to make a friend of every hostile occasion.[123]

There are two political philosophers who rank exceedingly high in the estimation of many conservative thinkers: Edmund Burke and Thomas Hobbes. It was Burke who elevated traditionalism to a normative principle; it was Hobbes who showed how liberty and authority could be reconciled in the interests of an ordered society and polity. Michael Oakeshott's major intellectual efforts have focused upon these two thinkers, and much of his work is a re-interpretation of their enduring legacies.

He equates modern liberalism with what he refers to as a pernicious Rationalism with a capital R; it is the main reason for a decline in civilization, or the art of civility. He blames both the American and French Revolutionary traditions for unleashing the forces of change which continue to undermine the sanctity of tradition, habit, custom, and authority and to replace them with a false ideological Rationalism.[124] The notion that every political problem has a solution and that progress is inevitably good strikes Oakeshott as being the height of irrationality.[125] One of the least commendable attributes of Rationalism is that it makes a fetish of methodology and technique, while short-circuiting the efficacy of revealed religious truth.[126] "Rationalism has ceased to be merely one style in politics and has become the stylistic criterion of all respectable politics"; Oakeshott believes the result has been disastrous, making government responsible for redistributive justice via the welfare state at the expense of the wisdom and authority of the past, which are the only sources of meaning and purpose to human life.[127]

The present trend toward ever greater collectivism must surely destroy the libertarian tradition which made political democracy possible.[128] Oakeshott equates pluralism and democracy, and finds that both are losing ground in the contemporary world.[129] The power of government must be severely limited, because "collectivism and freedom are real alternatives—if we choose one we cannot have the other."[130] This is one reason why there has been so much warfare in this century: the increase in coercive power is incompatible with democratic politics.[131]

Oakeshott is a firm believer in the importance of education as a prime source of moral training and of the willingness to translate ethical concerns into political management. But such formal education is not for everybody, and its value is in direct relationship to how intellectually demanding it is.[132] The right habit of mind finds morality in tested experience, not in abstract ideas that seek to impose arbitrary goals and questionable procedures upon reality.[133] Oakeshott advocates a return to a practical morality that makes the pursuit of excellence the guiding light of human endeavor.[134] Neither Reason nor Conscience are the true sources of moral conduct—only that which establishes a basic harmony between the individual and society can be considered truly moral.[135]

The main problem one encounters in trying to assess Oakeshott's thought processes is that his writing style has a way of disarming the unwary reader into thinking there is more substance than may well be the case. For someone who relishes concreteness, he is curiously remiss in clarifying his key terms, like Rationalism, and relating them historically to men, ideas, and movements of thought. His mind is a highly selective filter which ignores more than it sees. For example, the egalitarian rhetoric of the Declaration of Independence receives his scorn as a major embodiment of "the politics of Rationalism," but he makes no mention of the American Constitution, and of the fact that it represents political principles that a conservative thinker might well applaud.[136] He nowhere grapples with the problem of how to maintain effective government under contemporary conditions of advanced industrialization and population increase. It is as though nothing much has really changed since the eighteenth century, except for the hegemony of Rationalism-Liberalism. He seems perfectly content to have democracy for the few, even if the many should suffer from a lack of minimal justice. He distrusts all abstract ideas, and defines ideology in strictly negative terms, refusing to consider the possibility that ideology is one of the chief mechanisms for constructive change.[137] Nothing is valued more than Burkean traditionalism, and nothing is better than simply maintaining the status quo.[138] Here is a passage from his essay, "On Being a Conservative," that perfectly summarizes Oakeshott's value assumptions:

> To be conservative, then, is to prefer the familiar to the unknown, to prefer the tried to the untried, fact to mystery, the actual to the possible, the limited to the unbounded, the near to the distant, the sufficient to the superabundant, the convenient to the perfect, present laughter to utopian bliss. Familiar relationships and loyalties will be preferred to the allure of more profitable attachments; to acquire and to enlarge will be less important than to keep, to cultivate and to enjoy; the grief of loss will be more acute than the excitement of novelty or promise. It is to be equal to one's own fortune, to live at the level of one's own means, to be content with the want of greater perfection which belongs alike to oneself and one's circumstances. With some people this is itself a choice; in others it is a disposition which appears frequently or less frequently, in their preferences and aversions, and not itself chosen or specifically cultivated.[139]

Next to Burkeanism, Michael Oakeshott has been most attracted to the political philosophy of Thomas Hobbes. He believes that "Leviathan is the greatest, perhaps the sole, masterpiece of political philosophy written in the English

language."[140] In an effort to correct what he feels to have
been mostly distorted interpretations of Hobbes's achievement,
Oakeshott presents Hobbes as a true libertarian thinker, and
not as the authoritarian he is frequently portrayed. Along
with Leo Strauss, Oakeshott regards Hobbes as the pivotal
thinker dividing pre-modern from modern political philosophy;
Hobbes was the first major thinker to separate the contrasting claims of theological and scientific, and empirical and
rationalistic, modes of inquiry.[141]

However, Oakeshott differs with other commentators in his
insistence that Hobbes managed to integrate, not to divorce,
the rationalistic and empirical strands in the history of Western thought.[142] In partially rejecting the traditions of natural rights and natural law that provided the rationale for
constitutional government in the eighteenth century, Hobbes
made individual will the centerpiece of his political philosophy, and gave sovereignty its strongest standing as the seat
of both moral and political authority.[143] As the originator
"of a new tradition in political philosophy," Hobbes elevated
individualism to a preeminent position and showed how freedom
could also be reconciled with a responsible authority.[144]
Hobbes argued that no such concept as the common purpose or
public interest exists; man is what he wills and society is
a conflict of interests. Therefore, in order to insure adequate peace, harmony, and stability, a strong authority is
needed to represent sovereign power. This authority creates
conditions of freedom through necessity.[145] The individual
surrenders partial freedom, but never total freedom, via the
social contract, and the Sovereign, as law-maker, is also the
custodian for both the limits and extent of authority and liberty. As Oakeshott maintains, "Hobbes, without being himself
a liberal, had in him more of the philosophy of liberalism
than most of its professed defenders."[146]

Both liberty and authority can be carried to an extreme.
Hobbes solved the dilemma by making civil obligation both a
voluntary and a moral act, whereby some rights are given up
to the Sovereign while others are retained by the individual.
Man accepts constraint over his fondest wishes in order to
survive in a dog-eat-dog world. Law is the cement which binds
society together, and the law is man-made. But it is grounded
in free choice and can be changed. The highest form of moral
conduct is found in one's sense of obligation to one's civic
duty.[147] In effect, Hobbes's preferred values are also Oakeshott's: harmony, accommodation, social order, personal security, and respect for institutionalized authority.[148] Mutual
trust cannot be mandated, but under certain conditions, which
can be encouraged, these values will be more likely to prevail.[149] By marrying Burke to Hobbes, Michael Oakeshott has
found what he considers to be the best hope for arresting the
process of decline in public morality and preventing the destruction of all that is best in Western civilization.

Nowhere is it revealed more strikingly than in Oakeshott's

writings that at heart, the true conservative adopts an ideology to meet a psychological need, and does not simply choose an ideological preference in a reflective spirit. Conservatism is rooted in temperament, not in consciousness. This is why a dedicated conservative cannot afford to be wrong. From a personal standpoint, too much is at stake. Always, need displaces desire. The final irony of conservatism is that it cannot truly confront the consequences of repression. The conservative is the servant, not the master, of ideas. In this respect, the strongest exponent of individual autonomy is at the same time the greatest threat to individual autonomy.

PART III   IDEOLOGICAL VERSUS NON-IDEOLOGICAL CONSERVATISM

"Emotional attitudes are the great under-
water segment of the iceberg of political
culture."

—William T. Bluhm

"The individual's pattern of thought, whatever its content, reflects his personality
and is not merely an aggregate of opinions
picked up helter-skelter from the ideological environment."

—Daniel J. Levinson

"Always remember, others may hate you, but
those who hate you don't win unless you
hate them, and then you destroy yourself."

—Richard M. Nixon

"Ideology is moralizing on a grand scale.
And whenever ideology is expanding, the
need for political man will be contract-
ing."

—Theodore J. Lowi

CONSERVATISM AND THE AMERICAN PUBLIC

In chapter two, certain assumptions relating to the nature of man, society, and the state were designated the common value-assumptions of a conservative tradition in American political thought. Yet it is obvious that there has been no neat correlation between the contributions of individual thinkers and a definitive conservatism. What emerges is a good deal of complexity and variation within the conservative tradition, and too many different voices, making it difficult, if not impossible, to recognize a dominant species of conservatism. Despite a major transformation within American liberalism in the twentieth-century, the Lockean origins of an essentially individualistic value system still give consensual legitimacy and ideological potency to the liberal tradition.[1] This cannot be said of the conservative tradition, whose value-assumptions have maintained a minority status, mainly because conservatives have always tended to be critical of the overly optimistic, egalitarian, and pragmatic liberal ethos. In this respect, the larger public plays a significant role, for it has been a singular fact that, throughout American history, the public-at-large has accepted this prevailing liberal outlook and rejected, virtually without reflection, any alternative stance. Yet, paradoxically, this has not been the entire story either. For the majority of Americans take pride in being non-ideological, prefer to be middle-of-the-road or centrist, however imprecise and deceptive this concept may be, and apply liberal ends to conservative means.[2]

The role of ideology, however, cannot be so easily dismissed, even if it is true that the average American eschews ideology. Conscious rejection may be one thing, unconscious ideological predilection may be another. As William T. Bluhm has indicated: "It has been demonstrated that the political world of the average man is not formless but does have ideological structure."[3] Even the middle-of-the-roader, in other words, exhibits a non-rational predisposition toward conservatism or liberalism, and everyone's personality structure influences his ideological behavior to a greater or lesser degree. A person's values are not just assorted personality traits, but intimately connected with individualized needs, and function as a guidance system for personal conduct. The social psychologist, Milton Rokeach, has provided this illuminating summary of the role values can serve in promoting ideological behavior:

> They (1) lead us to take particular positions on social issues, and (2) predispose us to favor one particular political or religious ideology over another. They are standards employed (3) to guide presentations of the self to others, and (4) to evaluate and judge, to heap praise and fix blame on ourselves and

others. (5) Values are central to the study of comparison processes; we employ them as standards to ascertain whether we are as moral and as competent as others. (6) They are, moreover, standards employed to persuade and influence others, to tell us which beliefs, attitudes, values, and actions of others are worth challenging, protesting, and arguing about, or worth trying to influence or change. Finally, (7) values are standards that tell us how to rationalize in the psychoanalytic sense, beliefs, attitudes, and actions that would otherwise be personally and socially unacceptable so that we will end up with personal feelings of morality and competence, both indispensable ingredients for the maintenance and enhancement of self esteem.[4]

If Rokeach is correct, then it follows that all human actions are basically ideological in nature. And individuals vary as to whether their personal value systems serve self-justifying ego-defense functions in the psychoanalytical sense, or allow for a higher degree of rationality, personality integration, and self-actualization. Various segments of any nation's political culture may reflect either strategy, but the point that should be emphasized is that a patterned attitude response underlies what appears to be a person's disparate opinions.[5] Every person represents a system of values that may undergo change or modification over time, but which nevertheless is deeply rooted in personality structure.[6] Personality and culture interact in establishing a person's value system, but not always to enhance either personal or social well-being. Various manifestations of prejudicial behavior, for example, may well be psychologically motivated, rather than a response to objective reality. As the monumental post-World War II study, The Authoritarian Personality, revealed, the American public is more susceptible to fascistic appeals than would appear to be the case; and other studies have raised the question as to whether conservatism itself, in its more extremist form, does not represent a deviation from democratic norms. Herbert McClosky, in a new famous 1958 article based upon interview sampling data, made this startling announcement:

> Conservatism, in our society at least, appears to be far more characteristic of social isolates, of people who think poorly of themselves, who suffer personal disgruntlement and frustration, who are submissive, timid, and wanting in confidence, who are uncertain about their values, and who are generally bewildered by the alarming task of having to thread their way through a society which seems to them too complex to fathom.[7]

In contrast, the liberal tends to be better informed and more autonomous in his value orientation.[8] McClosky's methodology and interpretation have been challenged, of course, but not completely refuted.[9] The main weakness of this particular

study is a tendency to lump all variants of conservatism together under a single rubric, which few scholars will any longer defend. A more acceptable approach is to distinguish a moderate or principled conservative outlook from pseudo-conservatism, which clearly does have psychopathological overtones.
At any event, it is quite evident that any attempt to analyze
the relationship between conservatism and public opinion in
general will need to tread carefully through a jungle of conflicting interpretations.

Elites and Masses

Classical democratic theory emphasized the crucial role
of mass public opinion in making democracy workable and bridg-
ing the inevitable gulf between democratic norms and practices.
A certain level of voter choice and rationality could be anticipated, and a competitive party system would evolve as the
instrument for translating mass public opinion into viable democratic politics. But expectation exceeded actuality. Although the debate continues unresolved, there is today much
less confidence in the ability of the larger electorate to
support democratic norms or to make wise electoral choices of
leaders.[10] To cover up this troublesome discrepancy between
democratic theory and practice, many contemporary political
scientists simply applaud the fact that barely a majority of
eligible voters actually exercise their franchise rights in
national elections and that frequently less than a majority
vote in state-local elections; many political scientists argue
that it is better when poorly informed or weakly motivated citizens do not go out to the polls and that, anyway, the political elite can be better trusted to abide by the "rules of the
game," and is more responsive to democratic norms. The system works better with less public participation and involvement in electoral politics then it would if it were the other
way around.

Of course, not everyone agrees with this point of view,
but it has acquired considerable acceptance among both political scientists and the general public. It accounts for the
basic stability of American political institutions, an acceptable mixture of change and continuity, and a needed curtail-
ment of the ideological factor, which inevitably invites divisiveness and instability. The only trouble with this analysis
is that it does not square with reality. Ideological conflict
may be muted from time to time, but it continues to exist underground as well as above-ground, and there are limits to the
value of consensus in a democratic society. Too much consensus is as dangerous to a democratic system as too little. If
the Hartz thesis is correct, then America has suffered more
from too much than too little consensus, for it ultimately distorts the lens through which Americans view the rest of the
world, as well as their own society, and leads to the breakdown in institutional structures that now threatens to rob consensus of its enduring legitimacy.[11] Ideological homogeneity

and ideological suppression are two sides of the same coin, and their main casualty is ideological pluralism. Democracy can function better when ideological pluralism occupies a sanctioned role in the socio-political process. This has not been the case for a long time. A good part of the problem is continuing confusion regarding the proper roles of elites and masses in a democratic society.

If it is true that the majority of the American public prefers a middle-of-the-road stance in politics, can this be considered a virtue or defect? As Time magazine once aptly expressed it, "The middle is the natural hiding place of the uninvolved," suggesting perhaps that as an ideal, a non-ideological stance is less a virtue than an evasion.[12] Still, it has been reliably reported that "only 12 to 15 percent of the American electorate can be classified as ideological in their voting habits, while a fifth appear to lack even a minimal issue content."[13] This would tend to confirm the weak ideological proclivities of the American public. To further complicate the situation, numerous empirical studies reveal the fact that those of higher socio-economic income, education, and status tend to be conservative on economic issues, but more liberal on political and social issues, whereas lower-class public opinion reflects the inverse of this general tendency. In addition, Lloyd A. Free and Hadley Cantril pointed out in The Political Beliefs of Americans that the American public presents a split personality in the matter of ideological outlook:

The majority of Americans remain conservative at the ideological level in the sense that they continue to accept the traditional American ideology, which advocates the curbing of Federal power. Yet, at the practical level of Government operations, there has been an apparently inexorable trend in liberal directions in the United States since the days of the New Deal. This has been reflected in the increased size of the Federal government and the Governments willingness to use its power for social purposes.[14]

A Gallup poll survey made just prior to the 1972 congressional elections issued this confusing verdict on the public's current ideological profile:

The survey indicated that a majority of Americans take a liberal position on such issues as limiting Federal spending for health, education and welfare programs, re-establishing relations with Cuba and gun registration. But they voice strong conservative sentiment on such issues as busing to achieve better racial balance in schools, the death penalty and unconditional amnesty for draft evaders, according to the survey.[15]

In its August 26, 1974 issue, Time magazine reported "slightly more than half (of the American people) now qualify as conservatives, though what they mean by the label varies widely." This would appear surprising, given the substantial electoral success of liberal congressional candidates in the 1972 national election, and the generally low Republican Party affiliation even before the ravages of Watergate set in. The article offered this interesting explanation for the conservative trend in the country-at-large:

> The pollsters found that most Americans now connect conservative more with social morality than with political ideology. Such traditional benchmarks as attitudes toward capitalism and big business no longer help much to define the country politically. While three out of four of the conservative majority said that they were willing to make sacrifices to preserve the free enterprise system, 54% expressed anger and hostility toward big business—as did 58% of the non-conservatives.16

This development has raised hopes among conservative thinkers that a real opportunity exists to unite this "conservative majority" behind a new, revitalized, mass-based conservative party, displacing what many consider to be a moribund Republican Party hobbled by its liberal wing. In the past, it has been liberals who have usually raised the cry for "more responsible, policy-oriented, disciplined major parties"; now it is the turn of conservatives.17 But there are grave doubts among most political scientists when it comes to contemplating more ideologically-oriented major parties. Instead of fostering stability and more effective government, it would likely have a reverse effect, since the heterogeneity and conflict-prone character of the American polity could probably not survive the loss of institutional stability and legitimacy such a change might entail. The question remains, however, whether this has not happened anyway, in spite of centrist party coalitions. The existing form of party politics remains more part of the problem than a solution to present difficulties.

So given this strange mixture of a dominant ideological conservatism and operational liberalism, one may well ask: Is there any practical importance to liberalism or conservatism as ideological movements in the American political context? The answer can be affirmative if distinctions are made among three separate concepts: pragmatic, ideological, and philosophical conservatism/liberalism. In a sense, one may speak of three different levels of increasing intellectual value, but decreasing practical value, for each of these concepts. Accepting the fact that the vast majority of Americans are pragmatic about their political values, this means that habit, opinion, and self-interest are the main motivating factors influencing the average person's belief outlook. Another relatively small segment of the total population exhibits a marked ideological predisposition along liberal, conservative, reactionary, or radical lines. An even smaller group seeks a philosophical underpinning for their political values. The latter represents most of the thinkers included in this study. Practically speaking, therefore, neither ideas nor meaningful issues play an important conscious role in the average person's general outlook. But in a deeper sense, the philosophical formulations of a nation's intellectual elite become an important and influential force in developing the attitudes and values which become embedded in the national character.[18] The ideologue plays an equally necessary role as the active proponent of alternate courses of action.

Thus the pragmatic conservative or liberal may count most in sheer numbers; the ideological conservative or liberal, radical or reactionary, may keep things stirred up and lively; but the philosophical conservative or liberal is the keeper of the nation's conscience. Despite incessant disagreement on the meaning of basic values, the need exists for developing a coherent view of the meaning of American democracy, and this need can only be met by a careful attention to this level of thought. At best, the relationship between elites and masses in a democratic society will reflect a persistent tension and unresolvable conflict between better- and less-informed segments of the populace. Yet no one segment can claim a monopoly on truth. A workable relationship, even if it misses out on mutual trust, can be maintained as long as ethical constraints on the abuse of power are built into the system. The conservative, no less than the liberal, has an obligation to recognize this need. Unfortunately, it is the conservative, more often than the liberal, who is most likely to overlook this fact.

Personality and Ideology

In August 1974, when Richard Nixon resigned as President of the United States on the eve of impeachment proceedings that almost surely would have led to his conviction by the Senate in the wake of the Watergate revelations, there was, understandably, a great desire in the country to probe for the answer to the perplexing question: "How could it have happened?" A man who had seemingly won the most decisive electoral victory in the history of the American presidency a year and a half earlier, a man who was widely respected for his conduct of the nation's foreign policy, and a man whose activist conservatism seemed to correspond quite well with the dominant mood of the American public at the time, was literally forced to resign in utter disgrace from the office he had so long coveted—perhaps the greatest single failure of presidential leadership in the nation's history. Was it really nothing more nor less than a man's willingness to do anything to insure his electoral victory, because he sincerely believed that the country needed him? Was it personal selfishness and insensitivity on the part of a man who was a capable leader, except for a single personality flaw? Was it the political system, itself, which was seriously defective? Or was it the weakness of a man who encouraged his associates to place loyalty to him above loyalty to the Constitution and the law of the land? One could go

266

on raising the questions that the Watergate Affair inevitably inspired, but one would find no better source for an insightful answer than a 1950 study, The Authoritarian Personality, researched and written by a group of social scientists, including T.W. Adorno, Else Frankel-Brunswik, Daniel J. Levinson, and R. Nevitt Sanford. This was a pioneer empirical study conducted in the mid-1940's, based upon extensive questionnaire samples and in-depth interviews with over five thousand members of the American public.[19] The result, although open to the usual scholarly criticism on its methodology and analysis, certainly has to be considered a major contribution to human understanding.[20]

The authors discovered that a small, though significant, percentage of individuals in the general populace had a "potentially fascistic" character, marked by a strong addiction to prejudice and bigotry, and reflective of certain psychopathological ego-defense mechanisms traceable to destructive early childhood-family behavioral patterns. Thus, certain individuals needed the ideological release of an authoritarian syndrome as protection against otherwise self-destructive personality tendencies. The authors at the time were mainly interested in finding out to what extent such anti-democratic tendencies existed in the general public, and they could hardly be aware that the most disturbing aspect of their findings was the possibility that such a person might someday become President of the United States!

Underlying this study was the assumption "that the political, economic, and social convictions of an individual often form a broad and coherent pattern...and that this pattern is an expression of deep-lying trends in personality."[21] Richard Nixon, in the view of some commentators, exemplified this connection between personality and politics. Such a person can be a victim, rather than the master, of his psychological structure. Some of the characteristics set forth in the study purporting to establish an "authoritarian personality" syndrome can be noted as follows:

(1) Ethnocentrism, or a compulsive need to classify people into two categories, those who qualify as part of one's own ingroup identification and those who represent an outgroup, who pose a threat to one's well-being, and who must be opposed at all cost. "The ingroup-outgroup distinction thus becomes the basis for most of his social thinking, and people are categorized primarily according to the group to which they belong."[22] Those minority groups which a particular culture normally discriminates against become likely candidates for ethnocentric animosity and rejection. One of the authors, Daniel J. Levinson, also offers this observation: "There is considerable evidence suggesting a psychological affinity between conservatism and ethnocentrism, liberalism and anti-ethnocentrism."[23]

(2) Conventionalism, or uncritical acceptance of the dominant middle-class value ethos, and antagonism toward those

who seemingly violate these values. Suppressed aggressive impulses are readily transferred to "deviants," who deserve what may happen to them as members of the "outgroup." There is thus moral justification for striking out against "offenders" of the standards which are being violated, regardless of the objective truth of the situation.[24]

(3) Anti-introceptivism, or repressed emotions, whereby a split occurs between the inner and outer man for fear that acting as one feels will mean losing control of one's deeper feelings. "Out of touch with large areas of his own inner life, he is afraid of what might be revealed if he, or others, should look closely at himself."[25] Human relationships can be dealt with only if the situation can be depersonalized and manipulated. Such a person has an ambivalent attitude toward power: he has a strong need to dominate others and to seek a position of power; but at the same time he is reluctant to actually use power, and prefers the trappings of power to the exercise of power. These contradictory impulses force this kind of individual to see human relationships in strong-weak, dominant-submissive, leader-follower terms.[26] Such a view is readily applied to ingroup-outgroup, inferior-superior racial groupings.[27]

Theodore H. White, certainly one of the more sympathetic defenders of Richard Nixon in the past, in his post-Watergate study of Nixon, Breach of Faith, mentioned the possibility that Nixon's undoing was the result of "an unstable personality,"[28] but White then proceeded to write a book touching upon innumerable political and social factors contributing to the rise and fall of Richard Nixon, without again alluding to the psychological aspects of the situation.[29] Others have been less constrained, and what emerges is a striking parallel between the "authoritarian personality" and Richard Nixon's character deficiencies.[29] As James David Barber has pointed out, "no President of the twentieth century experienced such an incredible series of hard knocks in childhood as Richard Milhous Nixon did." The result, according to Barber, was an "active-negative" personality structure which might not have interfered with a successful life in almost any other career except politics.[30]

An American politician who cannot accept the give-and-take, compromise nature of the American governmental system, and instead sees politics as a form of total war, where the enemy has to be vanquished, humiliated, and utterly defeated, neither understands nor is capable of respecting democratic norms, where the unwritten rules of the game require a basic trust among the antagonists in the political arena. Only authoritarian systems allow for this personality defect—and the cost is usually high for the cause of human justice. Speaking of Nixon and his entourage, a writer for Encounter magazine made this telling comment: "They began to lose the sense of politics as the art of the possible, and to believe that nothing was impossible so long as one is tough and ruthless enough."[31] Whether or not a democratic society can protect itself from this happening in its top leadership position cannot be determined. What is to be hoped is that the public will become more alert to the fact that there is such a phenomenon as "the authoritarian personality," and that it represents the greatest possible danger to the internal stability of any democratic system.

Although there is much more to the study than has been indicated above, including considerable attention to the interrelatedness of anti-Semitic, authoritarian, anti-democratic, and psychopathological factors contributing to an "authoritarian personality" syndrome, the authors are cautious about extrapolating their findings onto the national scene, emphasize the potential over the actual incidence of this flawed personality structure, and consider how much of a danger it may represent in a democratic polity. Perhaps the most controversial aspect of the study, yet the most suggestive one for present purposes, is the close connection between a conservative political orientation and certain internal psychological needs that individuals may externalize, causing them to distort their perception of reality while relieving inner anxiety. Although other studies have reinforced this possible insight, there is insufficient evidence to either prove or disprove it.[32] Perhaps the most that can be said is that the relationship between political ideology and personality structure, especially if the ideology is relatively strong, coherent, and consistent, may indeed serve a much less rational function than is ordinarily assumed to be the case. This may be true of any ideological belief system. Yet the evidence does point toward the possibility that the dividing line between rational and irrational conservatism needs to be recognized for what it is: the dividing line between democracy and authoritarianism.

Conservatism versus Liberalism

Is it true that conservatism and liberalism, as "self-consistent ideological positions," are much more characteristic of elites than the general public, which fails to conform to this traditional polarization?[33] And is it also true that ideological elites are "more perfectly committed than their pragmatic followers to the large principles of liberal constitutional process that form the conception of authority that in turn underpins the political system as a whole?"[34] If so, then Professor William T. Bluhm is stating a widely supported belief that the conservative/liberal cleavage in American politics is strictly a difference over means, not over "the legitimacy of ends or basic philosophic principles."[35] A good deal of empirical research in the 1950's and 1960's seems to confirm this hypothesis.

Yet there are signs that this may no longer be quite so accurate a rendition of contemporary trends or future prospects. Everett Carll Ladd Jr., in his recent study, _Ideology in America_, sees the likelihood that conflict, rather than consensus, will come to characterize American society and politics; one indication of this, according to Ladd, is that "the mass-exten-

269

sion of higher education seems now to be having the entirely predictable effect of expanding tremendously the constituency for
ideological appeals."[36] Another study by Norman H. Nie and
Kristi Andersen reinforces Ladd's thesis:

> The average citizen may not be as apolitical as has
> been thought...We have located a substantial and wide-
> spread increase in the consistency of political atti-
> tudes in the post-1960 era and we have argued that
> this finding is indicative of the growth of a more
> ideologically-oriented mass public.[37]

In 1950, Arthur Schlesinger Jr. equated "the vital center"
of the political spectrum with "the politics of freedom."[38]
Leonard Freedman continues this theme:

> The centrist category comprises the largest body of
> opinion in the country. It includes many political
> scientists, sociologists, economists, and historians.
> Most high school and several college texts on Amer-
> ican history and government speak from a Centrist
> context. The larger number of opinions expressed
> in the media are Centrist views, and most elected
> public officials are Centrists.[39]

A 1972 Harris Survey reported this profile for a "self-
attributed political philosophy of the public":[40]

Position	Percentage Accepting Label
Conservative	29%
Middle-of-the-Road	35%
Liberal	19%
Radical	4%
Not sure	13%

But once again, one should remind oneself that if "only
a small percentage of the electorate can be classified on the
liberal-conservative dimension on the basis of its position on
issues," the elites reflect a more ideological orientation,
and have substantially greater influence on political activities.[41] And even if ideological division plays a minor role
in political results, there is a "dominant liberal ideology"
which exerts strong influence, and glorifies certain values,
such as the virtues of hard work, getting ahead in the world,
respecting property, and political democracy defined as a maximization of individual freedom.[42] Whether this ideology also
justifies excessive inequality, social stratification, and e-
litism is presently the major bone of contention separating
liberal and conservative opinion in the United States.[43]

There is ample evidence that a conservative/liberal split
does vitally affect the nation's life and well-being, although
it would be impossible to favor one side against the other without indulging in subjective bias.[44] And even if Martin Diamond
is correct when he argues, "in the vast majority of Americans
the tendencies of liberalism and conservatism are hopelessly

intermixed," the labels do mirror significant facets of reality.[45] This persistent tendency among some contemporary scholars to overlook the significant differences that do exist between conservative and liberal value assumptions needs at the very least a second look. These can be singled out as some of the main areas of disagreement:

(1) Conservatives and liberals disagree on the kind of democracy America should be and on basic philosophical principles. Conservatives are aristocratic elitists; liberals are democratic elitists.

(2) It is probably correct that only the elites reflect ideological differences, and that the general public tends to be either non-ideological or confusedly ideological in a moderate, or weak sense; but ideology exerts more influence on public policy than would otherwise be the case if "consensus within cleavage" were more consistently applied. Its effect is to dilute liberalism and to enhance the negative power of conservatism to slow-down change. In other words, veto power is the rule in American government, innovation the exception to the rule.[46] Cleavage is more effective than consensus in the policy area, and its main consequence is to help maintain a high degree of political stability.

(3) Even if it is true that the various divergent elites are more attuned to the "democratic rules of the game" and the constitutional system than the general public is, this has been more the result of necessity than of real interest or desire. Contrary to the conventional view, there is more agreement over means, among liberals and conservatives, than over ends. It is simply that the opportunity for a real battle over ends will not arise as long as the system continues to place a premium upon stability and pseudo-consensus. This is not to say, however, that conservatives and liberals are permanently locked into an ends-means strait-jacket.

(4) Philosophical conservatism and ideological conservatism have parted company in the American context. Politician-activists like Senator Barry Goldwater and Ronald Reagan, for example, are really nineteenth-century Jeffersonian-Lockean liberals, while philosophical conservatives are Burkeans, who place the needs of the social good over individual self-interest. This transposition has created a more pronounced cleavage within the conservative tradition than exists between contemporary conservatives and liberals. Here the difference over ends is profound and irremediable. But the political impotence of philosophical conservatives has defused the potential importance of such decided divergence over philosophical differences and assumptions.

(5) The liberal and conservative traditions have crisscrossed in this century in their respective views of the self-society relationship. The liberal now tends to emphasize man's social needs and relationships to such a degree that the rights of the individual are sometimes subordinated to the rights of

society; while the conservative now tends to emphasize the rights of the individual and downgrades the rights of society. This switch is not absolute, but the tendency has been quite pronounced.

Finally, in one important respect there is a fundamental disagreement that does highlight differences between conservatives and liberals respecting policy choices and the role of government. Although there may be little disagreement any longer between conservatives and liberals regarding the central place personal and political liberty holds in the value system, as much cannot be said of that other great ideal of American democracy: equality.[47] Certainly Milton Rokeach is on target when he says:

> ...the liberalism-conservatism dimension in American politics is really an _equality_ dimension: The major ideological differences evident in American politics are reducible to variation in one value alone—_equality_—rather than in two values. What seems to be missing from the present American scene are political groupings large enough to support viable political candidates for the presidency who place a low value on freedom.[48]

This being the case, the next chapter, which will attempt to identify some of the more valuable recent contributions to conservative thought, will also focus upon the deepening cleavage that is presently emerging over the egalitarian ideal. Perhaps for the first time in American history there will be a fundamental divergence between liberal and conservative perspectives on the meaning of the American democratic creed. If this should indeed happen, it will probably mean the demise of the traditional value consensus that has for so long kept the system in relative equilibrium. The consequences, needless to add, could be momentous, especially in terms of continuity and stability.

CHAPTER 11

IDEOLOGICAL POLITICS: A SEARCH FOR NEW DIRECTIONS

It is the function of ideology to fuse together morality, legality, and legitimacy. In effect, a political ideology projects a vision of the good society.[1] Despite all its various permutations in the course of American history, liberalism has provided the underlying consensus that has enabled American society to perform this ideological function reasonably well. Some would argue too well. Despite all the changes that have taken place and the rapid pace of modernization, America has managed to couple an experimental, dynamic, pragmatic world outlook with an ideology that continues to place a high premium upon individualism, property rights, and limited government.[2] Now, at long last, it appears that this ideological consensus is breaking down, partly because of unprecedented stresses and strains imposed by contemporary conditions, but mostly because of escalating failures of the system, highlighted by a lost war, a faltering economy, and severe social malaise. By the mid-seventies, America was experiencing withdrawal symptoms that some intellectuals have referred to as a "failure of nerve," and which others have called "the democratic distemper.[3] What all such criticism has in common is a recognition that the ideology that once united morality, legality and legitimacy has broken asunder, and unless something can be done soon to put it back together again, a temporary setback will surely become a permanent decline.[4]

For some, this new situation calls forth feelings of perplexity and a sense of despair. Liberals are particularly prone to this pitfall, since it is largely a failure of the liberal tradition that seems in evidence at the moment: so much money, so much government effort, so many good intentions directed at the cause of redistributive justice, and so little to show for it. Radicals are also now on the defensive, since the euphoria of the late sixties, which accompanied the growth of a counter-culture and the critiques of capitalism which drew support from a substantial segment of moderate opinion, has since dissipated; and the "Movement" is very much in decline, all but extinct politically.

This leaves a vacuum, and while ideological liberals and radicals can only lick their wounds and wait it out, ideological conservatives are suddenly confronted with their best opportunity in ages. Not only do the opinion polls report a dramatic shift away from liberalism and toward conservatism within the larger public, but conservatives, themselves, are gaining renewed confidence in their ability to provide a philosophical foundation for their ideological vision. In fact, the mid-seventies saw the publication of a number of books which, taken together, may mark the beginning of a renaissance for conservative political philosophy, and represent the initial stages of a concerted endeavor: the forging of a new, comprehensive, and relevant conservative political philosophy capable of replacing the reigning, and somewhat discredited, liberal ideology. These new spokesmen for conservatism include Alexander M. Bickel, Robert Nisbet, M. Stanton Evans, Kevin P. Phillips, and George F. Kennan. Space does not permit extended analysis of these writers, but a brief summary of some of their most recent publications underscores the importance and value of this search for new directions in pursuit of a "new American ideology."

Alexander M. Bickel, whose death in 1974 at the age of 49 can be looked upon as one of the great losses to both the conservative tradition in American thought and to American scholarship, had only a short time to begin an enterprise that might have given a major impetus to the creation of a new American ideology. Certainly, his posthumous book, The Morality of Consent, can be regarded as a remarkable achievement in its own right; and at the very least it lights the way for others to follow. Robert H. Bork, former solicitor general of the United States, captured the Bickel legacy best in this passage from a review of the above-mentioned book:

> To be conservative in the sense that Alex increasingly became is not to be a doctrinaire adherent to particular principles, whether they be liberty or the primacy of the free market or some other. In his sense conservatism was a habit of mind and a quality of spirit—thoughtfulness, prudence, respect for established values and institutions.5

The spirt of Edmund Burke permeated Alexander Bickel's thought. He criticizes what he calls the "contractarian tradition in American politics," which he associates primarily with Locke and Rousseau, and which he contrasts with the Whig tradition of Burke and the American Founding Fathers. Whereas the former creates values, seeks to impose them under the rubric of majority rule, and frequently violates the democratic respect for minority interests, the latter finds its values in history, tradition, and morality, and is manifested through an evolving legal structure. "Law is the principle institution through which a society can assert its values."6 Like contemporary liberal theorists, Bickel sees consensus rule, not majority rule, as the centerpiece of the American political system.7 Yet he accuses the liberal of being a moral absolutist, and applauds the conservative view as being on the side of moral relativism—an argument which may not stand close scrutiny.8 The main thrust of his analysis is to show how liberals are the real ideologues, while true conservatives are just the opposite—unmoralistic, unauthoritarian, and unlegalistic—and therefore less susceptible to "the totalitarian tendency of the democratic faith."9 Taking a leaf from Burke's lexicon of political wisdom, Bickel declares: "the business of politics is not with theory and ideology but with accommodation."10

For Bickel, the key problem is relating the uses of power to moral considerations. And this means not a present or future oriented ideology but one that locates "our visions of good and evil and the denominations we compute where Burke told us to look, in the experience of our past, in our traditions, in the secular religion of the American republic."11 Bickel is not against change; he is against imposed change, especially under the auspices of governmental authority. This is why Bickel, as one of the country's leading constitutional scholars, has been one of the strongest critics of the Warren Court political legacy.12 He has been a leading supporter of judicial self-restraint against the tendency of the Court majority, from time to time, to assert "judicial supremacy" in areas that he feels should devolve upon legislative discretion.13 He has also been a consistent critic of the Black-Douglas view of First Amendment freedoms: that they pose absolute prohibitions upon government vis à vis the protection of individual rights. Bickel believed that First Amendment freedoms represent just as ambiguous a problem for constitutional interpretation as does the Constitution in general, and that a balance of conflicting rights, involving institutional, individual, and community opinion factors, can only be reconciled when circumstances are weighed against constitutional principles, and not in accordance with ideological preconceptions, a tendency he finds all too evident in the liberal camp.14

Among other things, Bickel presents a brilliant analysis of the limits of civil disobedience in a democracy, and whether or not one agrees with his rather narrow and unpermissive view of the problem, one can readily respect the manner in which he upholds the integrity of the legal process. A critic of Bickel's position might say that the "withholding of consent" is just as legitimate under the American constitutional system as the necessity of obeying the law and of working through "normal channels" to change it when there is sufficient concern about its failings.

Means always count more than ends in Bickel's hierarchy of values, and this is the hallmark of his conservatism. This is not, however, characteristic of a good proportion of the conservative thinkers treated in this study. Before Bickel's neo-Burkeanism can become the basis of a new American ideology, it will have to satisfy the anti-pragmatic bias of most conservatives. This is unlikely as long as liberals maintain their monopoly on consensual politics--a matter that Bickel fails to deal with adequately. Principled conservatism still represents a minority outlook in the country-at-large and within the intellectual establishment. Only as this situation changes--as it may indeed--can one anticipate the political ascendancy of conservative ideology. But if this should happen, then Alexander Bickel will have been one of its severest critics, for the governing principle of his political thought is reflected in this statement from his book: "...the highest morality almost always is the morality of process."15

Robert Nisbet is a distinguished sociologist and historian of ideas who has already engaged our interest in a previous
chapter of this book dealing with "liberal-conservatism."[16]
His recent book, <u>Twilight of Authority</u>, constitutes another
important contribution to the resurgence of conservatism. Employing broad brush-strokes, Nisbet digs deep into history—
ancient, modern, and contemporary—for illustrative material
to reinforce his belief that Western civilization has been in
a steady decline since at least the late medieval period, and
possibly since the 6th century B.C., because ever more concentrated political, economic, and military power is destroying
the pluralist structures that alone can ensure a condition of
maximum human liberty.

The twin evils, in Nisbet's view, are hedonism and egalitarianism. Both these forces threaten to destroy the social
bond of community, authority, tradition, and hierarchy. Western culture has reached an advanced stage of "cultural decay,
erosion of institutions, progressive inflation of values in
all spheres, economic included, and constantly increasing centralization—and militarization—of power."[16] In short, all
power is evil; good comes from restoring communal ties and re-
laxing the grip of power that is now so overwhelmingly lodged
in the governmental sector. The problem, as Nisbet sees it,
is that control over people's lives has shifted away from the
family, ethnic, neighborhood, and local sources to highly organized collectivities, primarily national governments.[17]
This spells breakdown, and a rapid rise in the incidence of
individual alienation and constituted authority. Unless arrested, this process will lead inevitably to "the decline of
the West." People everywhere have lost confidence in government and political leaders. Public morality is a mockery of
professed Christian ideals. There is no longer anything worth
believing in.

On top of everything else, once efficacious ideologies
have lost credibility, so that only the pursuit of self-interest and of power for its own sake characterizes contemporary
political and social reality.[18] "Politics in our era has become nearly devoid of genuinely ideological divisions as is
possible to conceive of."[19] The ethical basis of democracy
has literally evaporated. Even conservatism, historically an-
ti-power, has become a victim of the craze to control everything.[20] Personal freedom has become a casualty of limitless
bureaucratization.[21] The state dominates all intermediate social bodies, so that pluralism and diversity are undermined.[22]
Nothing is sacred any longer; everything is politicized. The
more affluent modern societies become, the less respect they
show for humanistic values.[23] War, or military adventurism,
becomes almost a surrogate for the lack of traditional authority.[24] Moral standards always lose ground under conditions
of major war, and these conditions have been the rule, rather
than the exception, throughout this century.[25] More than anything else, Nisbet blames the "spirit of Rousseau" and the contemporary infatuation with equality for the inability of democratic nations to put a brake on expanding power at the expense

of individual liberty.[26]

Nisbet's solution to the power-ethics problem is "a restoration of authority," which means reversing present trends in favor of "the values of localism, regionalism, voluntary association, decentralization of authority..."[27] While Alexander Bickel looks to Burke as the inspiration for a revitalized conservatism, Nisbet draws his inspiration from Tocqueville.[28] But it is a one-dimensional Tocqueville, devoid of that worthy thinker's perspicuity. Tocqueville saw good, as well as bad, in egalitarianism. Nisbet sees only its leveling side, rejecting completely its claim to advancing social justice.

The problem with Robert Nisbet's analysis and prescription is that what he is for gets confused with what he is against; this is typical of contemporary conservatives, and is the main reason why they are so much better at explaining the nature of the problem than at presenting a satisfactory solution.[29] All the blame for the ills of contemporary society and politics are ascribed to the failures of a predominantly liberal ideology and to governmental intervention in areas such as public education, health, welfare and business enterprise. Presumably, the solution lies in a contraction of political power and a laissez-faire attitude toward the individual-government relationship.

At the same time, conservatives like Robert Nisbet would strengthen the power of society, through its institutional structures, to favor the exceptional person over the so-called unexceptional person, and to convert the individual-society relationship into a kind of benevolent dictatorship of the few over the many. That the personal freedom which is so important in contemporary conservative political philosophy probably means little to those who have to struggle day by day just to keep their heads above water does not seem to matter: such people are not important enough to justify the higher taxes which invariably accompany expanded welfarism. The size of this less advantaged group may or may not be large in the total scheme of things, but it is large enough. And until a conservative philosophy can convince this sizeable segment of the population that their interests will be better served by a drastic reduction in government services, a conservative solution to contemporary social and economic problems is not likely to take root.

M. Stanton Evans is a newspaper editor and a long-time contributor, as well as a former associate editor, of National Review. After writing a series of books lauding the conservative view on affairs of state and attacking all things liberal, he has recently written a textbook type study, Clear and Present Dangers: A Conservative's View of American Government, which fills a long-standing need: an institutionally-oriented, comprehensive treatment of policy failures from a conservative perspective. It is a well-documented, clearly written, and effectively argued critique of liberalism's "failures," accompanied by a strong implication that a less-government-the-better conservatism would correct most of the harm done by the reigning liberalism. Coming at a time when the record favors a more critical appraisal of the government's role in human affairs, Evans's book can be recommended to anyone who would like an anti-liberal critique that transcends mere polemics, although there is a good deal of this also.

According to Evans, liberalism has betrayed its libertarian origins, for it "is drawn by the logic of its assumptions increasingly further from humanitarian social goals toward the repressive and elitist practices of the totalitarian governments."[30] Strong medicine indeed. And although it is questionable whether Evans substantiates these startling charges, there is much else in his analysis that does ring the bell. He discusses the anti-majoritarian vision of the Founders, emphasizing especially the _federal_ nature of the system.[31] In view of the fact that "limitations on the monopolization of power" were the central concern of the early constitutionalists, he accuses contemporary liberals of violating this sacred principle by encouraging government assertions of power and authority in virtually all areas of public life.[32] A whole series of questionable Supreme Court decisions, "misinterpreting" the "separate but equal" clause of the Fourteenth Amendment, has seriously weakened the states' role under the constitutional system—another reflection of misguided liberalism.[33] Since liberals have been mainly responsible for the excessive expansion of presidential power in this century, Richard Nixon was more victim than victimizer when he was forced to resign his office under the cloud of Watergate.[34] It is the liberal's "zeal for collectivist planning" which created the "imperial presidency."[35] Secrecy, deception, and executive privilege were all employed quite systematically under Democratic presidents going back to FDR's time.[36] Evans cites numerous specific instances, although he does not show convincingly that it was a calculated and systematic operation. He does, however, make these telling points:

> When the exercise of presidential power conflicts with what liberals want, then it is both immoral and illegal; when the exercise of presidential power conforms to what the liberals want, it is right and proper... The liberals have blandly changed the rules of the game, opposing the Court when it hurt their cause, supporting it when their cause was helped.[37]

Compared with the escalating costs of varied welfare subsidies, Evans argues that the costs of defense have actually declined as a proportion of the total budget.[38] The burden of all this on the taxpayer has become intolerable. He argues that it is an expanded middle-class professional bureaucracy that has benefited most from welfare programs, not the poor.[39] The same is true for federal aid to schools, since a teacher-administrative class benefits far more than do the pupils themselves. In short, Evans refers to "the regressive state" as a prime example of liberal failures. The real need in tax reform is not to force the rich to pay "a fairer share," since "unfairness" is a myth promulgated by the liberal establishment, but to close the "loopholes" enjoyed mainly by the lower income taxpayers, "since three-quarters of the untaxed income in our country...consists of personal exemptions, social benefits, mortgage interest, and the like—with the result that 97 percent of non-taxable returns belong to the people with annual incomes of $5,000 or less."[40] Like Edward Banfield, he feels that minimum wage legislation is the main cause of high unemployment in poverty areas, and suggests that eliminating such legislation would go a long way toward alleviating the problem.[41]

According to Evans, "there is no urban crisis." in housing, transportation, and education, the problem is too much government intervention and not enough private or local incentive. And the nation's major problem—inflation—is the result of "continual expansion of the money supply."[42] It would appear that Evans is a down-the-line disciple of the conservative economist, Milton Friedman. Here is Evans's analysis of the "cause and cure of inflation":

> Inflation, in sum, is the creation of government itself—a method of financing continued spending programs while diffusing the costs so widely that taxpayers have trouble assessing blame for the resultant discomfort. Because the process is generated by government expansion of the money supply, it cannot be halted by controls or exhortations to consumers to change their buying habits. The cure for inflation, and the only cure, is to make certain that the national pool of money and credit is not expanded more rapidly than the annual increase in the volume of production.[43]

In sum, Evans sees the liberal's addiction to "social engineering" pushing the American system in a totalitarian-authoritarian direction. The conservative corrective to this trend is to de-regulate the economy, return public education to local financing and control, de-federalize welfare, reduce the federal government's intervention in all aspects of medical care, place a freeze upon the income tax and move toward rolling it back over a period of years, and most important of all, shift more of the burden of government back to the states and away from Washington.[44]

All these ideas and policy reversals add up to one phrase: laissez-faire. Nothing would probably make M. Stanton Evans happier than a magic eraser that would take the nation back to the nineteenth century and would let him make believe that the past three-quarters of a century never happened. There may be some justification for his nostalgia, but it is hard to imagine how it would be workable, given the nature of the changes to the American society and economy that have taken place since that time. It reflects the fact that conservatives like Evans do tend to have just one answer to every problem: restore the private enterprise system to its former pristine character and substantially reduce government intervention in the socio-economic sphere. It is doubtful whether there are any longer such simple answers to exceedingly complex problems.[45]

Kevin P. Phillips is a young man who created something of a stir with the publication of his The Emerging Republican Majority in 1969.[46] As a political analyst in the 1968 Nixon campaign, he presented his mentor with a blueprint for converting the 1968 hair's breadth electoral victory into a more enduring conservative coalition, thus ensuring an era of Republican Party ascendancy in national politics. The so-called "Southern strategy" was one of the features of this prospective party re-alignment. In a new book, Mediacracy: American Parties and Politics in the Communications Age, Kevin Phillips modifies, extends, and deepens his previous analysis.[47] Even though the Republican Party is probably today in worse shape in regard to "registered voters" than at any time in its history, Phillips sees a continuation of the same trends that he identified earlier; and he blames Nixon's inability to help push these trends to favor the Republican Party's future political fortunes on political myopia, faulty conceptualization, and the Watergate fiasco.

There is no doubt that Phillips has done his homework well: both his books are replete with maps, election data, and sophisticated quantification. What makes this an important book is the careful way that he blends ample historical analysis with contemporary forces of change to present a convincing portrait of the party system in flux, and to analyze the implications for "ideological politics." In addition, he propounds an interesting thesis that may prompt a new examination of the changing pattern of liberal-conservative support within the electorate itself.

According to Phillips, there is a new political and ideological cleavage in the making, with profound implications for the future of American politics. Drawing upon the work of the political scientist, Walter Dean Burnham, Phillips takes note of a cyclical phenomenon in the evolution of the American party system: every 32-36 years since 1800, the parties have gone through a major re-alignment, affecting electoral coalitions and ideological shifts.[48] 1968 was the most recent due date, and, as might be expected, this election heralded the break-up of the old New Deal coalition and the onset of significant shift in electoral behavior. But unlike past cyclical changes, when the two-party system emerged stronger than ever, this time around other factors have fostered the emergence of an entirely new situation: the decline of both major parties as the repository of most of the electorate's party allegiances, a rapid increase of non-affiliated, so-called independent voters, much evidence of ticket-splitting, a more dominant role for the communications media, and decreased organizational need for the party itself among future candidates in all levels of politics.

In addition, following the lead of the sociologist, Daniel Bell, Phillips emphasizes the emergence of a new post-industrial society, which is the fruit of the communications revolution and of advanced technology, and analyzes the changes this will bring to traditional political attitudes and values. The chief new development is a "knowledge elite"—"lower class" alliance, committed to a liberal ideology favoring change and an expanded role for a governmental-public sector, and increasingly estranged from, and opposed to, a vast middle-class that is still wedded to traditionalist social values and is growing ever more conservative in ideology. This group of Americans, which constitutes 60% to 70% of the total population, is already showing signs of deepening resentment over the costs of a welfare state that does little for them and benefits mostly upper-middle-class professionals, with some trickle-down benefits going to the poorest class. Not only is the middle-class becoming more conservative in outlook, but it also is becoming resentful of the new intellectual elite, tied to the communications media and to major corporate interests that wish to perpetuate their vested interests via an ever more powerful central government which they can dominate. This is how Phillips introduces his thesis:

> During the previous century, the nation's economic elite was conservative, and liberal-conservative struggles were rooted in that economic context. This book will examine the rise of a 'new class' of affluent liberals—and the impact of that rise. A new correlation is arising—among education, wealth, and liberalism—to replace the old one—among education, wealth, and conservatism. And, on a number of issues, opposition to liberal elitism is strongest among the groups historically in the vanguard of opposition to conservative-economic elites. Upheaval has also undermined or reversed many of the loyalites rooted in the industrial era—Civil War orbit of American politics.[49]

The two factors that have marked the difference between two eras of American history are the powerful role the communications media now asserts over all aspects of American life, and the shift to a knowledge economy, in which "roughly 35 per cent of the U.S. gross national product is now accounted for by the production, consumption, and dissemination of knowledge."[50] This new elite is change-oriented, and contrasts sharply with older elites, which had more of a vested interest in maintaining the status quo.[51] The media, supposedly neutral, is anything but this, and it became clear in the late sixties that "the New York-Washington media axis (had become) closely linked, in succession, to the liberal integration, anti-poverty, anti-hunger, anti-war, and anti-ecology causes."[52] This "adversary culture" has become a persistent critic of "the prevailing middle-class values of work, patriotism, and traditional morality."[53] Furthermore, this new liberal elite feeds off and depends heavily upon the service-state, where consultants, pollsters, public relations experts, and bureaucrats are in high demand.[54] "Change keeps up demand for the product (research, news, theory, and technology). Post-industrialism, a knowledge elite, and accelerated social change appear to go hand in hand."[55]

In consequence of the above development, Phillips detects a "traditionalist counterreformation" in the making, a decline in liberal support within the general electorate, and a rise in conservatism.[56] Regionally, this translates itself into two Americas: one made up of the South, the Rockies, the Great Plains, Southern California and scattered areas of rural-small town complexion, the other with its center of gravity in the Northeast, upper Middle West, and Pacific Northwest. Furthermore, it is the southern rim that has been gaining population and the northern rim which continues to lose population. Thus the older labels, "liberal" versus "conservative," no longer have much meaning. The new cleavage does not pit "haves" against "have nots" so much as new elite versus the middle-class. The liberal commitment to equality is another reflection of this upper-class—lower-class alliance against the interests of middle-class Americans.[58] Yet if this is so, then how can one explain the fact that there is still little evidence of slippage and loss of support for liberalism, as may be seen in the 1974 off-year congressional elections which sent to the House a large number of liberal-oriented freshmen Congressmen and women, most of whom retained their seats in 1976? Phillips explains the situation as follows:

> On one hand, the new class seems out of kilter with the beliefs of the majority. And on the other hand, the traditionalist coalition seems to lack the technical and intellectual capacity to turn things around within the political, administrative, and communications framework established by liberal forces in basic control of Washington since the New Deal.[59]

Kevin Phillips provides a good deal of historical example and empirical data to substantiate his interpretation of current trends and changes in American politics. In short, Phillips foresees a complete reversal in the composition of traditional party coalitions; the politics of liberalism will become more closely identified with elitist interests, and the politics of conservatism will reflect anti-elitist attitudes within the predominantly middle-class electorate.[60] Also, the median voter age will advance considerably over the next few decades, and this should further strengthen the prospects of an emerging conservative majority. But Phillips does not believe that the Republican Party is in a position to capitalize on these new changes, for it may not be able to adjust to the Populist side of the emergent conservatism; instead of a new majority party realignment, the prospects point toward a radical reconstruction of the party system—in effect, either a multi-party or non-party system.[61] The key factor may well be the role played by the media, and whether or not it can detach itself from its present involvement with the politics of liberalism in favor of a more neutral stance.[62] Chances are, however, that ideology will mean much less, and that regional, ethnic, middle-class interests will coalesce in support of candidates whose personal attributes will count for more than what they seem to stand for.[63]

There are two problems that caution one to go slow before accepting the Phillips analysis at face value. First, he downplays ideology to such an extent that his thesis verges on a neo-Marxist kind of economic determinism. Self-interest undercuts ideology, according to this assumption, and does not have independent power in its own right. This problem is reflected in the fact that Phillips pays little attention to the growing split within the Republican Party between ultra-conservative ideology and the pragmatic conservatism that is more characteristic of the general electorate. Ideologues, or true-believers— to use Eric Hoffer's famous term—exert influence in inverse proportion to their limited numbers.[64] This is not likely to change. Second, elitism is a term that is hard to demonstrate, let alone to quantify. Elitism involves a combination of economic wealth, political power, and ideological control that is not easily achieved in a pluralist society. Phillips uses the term in a loose, self-serving way to build his case, but does little to clarify the problem or convince the reader that it goes beyond this.

There is no doubt that Kevin Phillips has written one of the most informative, insightful, and empirically sound studies of present electoral tendencies. That it contains unequivocal reassurance of an emerging conservatism is more debatable. Ideology is not so neatly tied to socio-economic self-interest as Phillips would have us think it is.

George F. Kennan exemplifies the conservative mind at its best—ironical, illusionless, and concerned about revitalizing standards of public morality in an age of debased secularism and relativism. He is without peer as diplomat and historian, having had a notable career in the United States Foreign Service from 1926 through 1963, culminating in stints as Ambassador to Russia and Yugoslavia. His <u>American Diplomacy 1900-1950</u>, published in 1951, has been a singularly important contemporary critique of American foreign relations, and he is generally regarded as the true author of cold war U.S. containment policy.[65] As a scholar, he has written important studies of Soviet-American relations since the turn of the century.[66] His two volumes of <u>Memoirs</u>, published in 1967 and 1972, are without doubt a most valuable contribution to an understanding of the American mind at mid-century.[67] All in all, he is a man who had a close-up view of historical events that changed all our lives, and whether or not one agrees with his views in retrospect, one cannot but respect the thoughtful and authoritative quality of his political philosophy.[68]

In commemorating the famous "Mr. X" article, which George F. Kennan wrote over 30 years ago for <u>Foreign Affairs</u> while he was still a government official, and which presented the initial analytical justification for a "containment of communism" policy, <u>Encounter</u> magazine published an extensive interview with Mr. Kennan, perhaps as good an up-dated revelation of his personal and political views as is available.[69] And it is quite evident that Kennan's disillusionment with the present state of America and the world is profound and devastating:

> I do not think that the United States civilization of these last 40-50 years is a successful civilization; I do not think that our political system is adequate to the needs of the age into which we are now moving; I think this country is destined to succumb to failures which cannot be other than tragic and enormous in their scope.[70]

Interestingly, the author of "containment" is now one of its severest critics; the strong advocate of a realpolitik approach to foreign policy is now looking to re-introduce moral values to the conduct of human affairs; the earlier defender of activist internationalism is now an avowed neo-isolationist.[71] Of course, George Kennan would deplore the use of such imprecise terminology; he is, above all, a believer in doing only what has to be done, not what one would like to do; and in this respect he is very much the realistic foe of all forms of ideological activism. His conservatism, therefore, is rooted in a painful disenchantment with what he sees as the disastrous historical results of a mindless Americanism and an equally destructive Marxism. The only hope he entertains for future betterment lies in structural changes that might encourage a more responsible elitism as a counterweight to what he regards as an irresponsible populist democracy.

The main source of his discouragement is the conviction that the wrong conclusions were drawn from his analysis of Soviet behavior during the war years and immediately thereafter, and that decisions made by top government officials led to a series of foreign policy diasters.[72] Above all, the tendency to neglect political factors in favor of military considerations, and the overly-charged moralism which surrounded the enunciation of the Truman Doctrine and Korean War interventionism receive Kennan's strongest censure. It is no wonder that neither the American government nor the American people were prepared to handle the Joe McCarthy phenomenon with rationality. The persistent foolishness since FDR's days to over-estimate the importance of mainland China and misjudge Russian intentions also gains Kennan's unqualified disapproval. He questions the policy of establishing American military bases and keeping troops stationed throughout the world on the periphery of Soviet territory, for this, too, convert political problems into military ones.[73] The failure to recognize Com-

munist China, along with the irrational support of Chiang
Kai-shek's Formosa regime, is another of Kennan's major re-
grets concerning U.S. policy in the post-war period.[74]

George Kennan's criticism of the foreign policy establishment is equally severe. There is too little evidence of imagination and creativity, too much evidence of bureaucratic stod-
giness and rigidity.[75] Americans are simply incapable of understanding the nature and requirements of "limited war," since
there has always been that seeming need of leaders to placate
public opinion and to universalize (e.g., moralize) actions
that should have been seen in more restrained terms with due
regard to political complexity.[76] This either/orism continues
to be the Achilles heel in the conduct of U.S. foreign affairs.[77]

McCarthyism, in the early 1950's, virtually deciminated
foreign service morale, led to the harrassment and persecution
of those China "experts" who, if they had been heeded, might
have prevented the tragic intervention in Vietnam in the 60's,
and left the public unprepared to grasp the true dimension of
the "cold-war" situation.[78] But even more poignantly, Kennan
marks this failure as the decisive experience of his public
life:

> What the phenomenon of McCarthyism did do, in
> my case, was to implant in my consciousness a last-
> ing doubt as to the adequacy of our political system,
> and the level of public understanding on which it
> rested, to the role of a great power in the modern
> age. A political system and a public opinion, it
> seemed to me, that could be so easily disoriented
> by this sort of challenge in one epoch would be no
> less vulnerable to similar ones in another. I
> could never recapture, after these experiences of
> the late 1940s and early 1950s, quite the same faith
> in the American system of government and in tradi-
> tional American outlooks that I had, despite all
> the discouragements of official life, before this
> time.[79]

From a conservative standpoint, elitism is the critical
issue for democratic government. Most of what is inadequate
and dysfunctional in government can be attributed to too much
democracy; for the majority will is untrustworthy, wedded to
mediocrity, and incapable of rising above self-interest. This
is why democratic politics so seldom permits the best qualified and most capable individuals to ascend to leadership positions in the polity; and on the rare occasions when this
does happen, the system itself cannot respond to such leadership. In essence, democracy is its own worst enemy, for the
anti-elitist bias which has been the main legacy of liberal
ideology deprives democracy of its one hope for success: "A
minority which has enough confidence in itself to act boldly
and lead, rather than follow, public opinion."[80] Only in
this way might enough self-discipline, sense of responsibility

to the public good, and applied intelligence come to the fore.
Only if and when the American people begin to realize and to
accept the fact that a "natural aristocracy of intellect and
merit" represents the best hope for making democracy effective
and responsible rather than irresponsible and ineffectual can
present self-destructive tendencies be reversed. Kennan is
not optimistic that such a reversal of traditional attitudes
and values is likely to occur under present conditions. The
egalitarian ideal may be more myth than reality, but it is
still a powerful force, blocking any real progress toward a
democratic elitism based upon a professional and intellectual
meritocracy.

Is the conservative right about this? Is it true that
only benevolent elitism can save democracy from its own excesses? Is the great defect of democratic government really
that politicians cater to popular whim and popular ignorance
and to a mistaken idea of what consent of the governed is all
about? Are democracy and elitism incompatible? Is government
by the few in behalf of the many necessarily anti-democratic?
Would democracy benefit if populism were curtailed and a meritocracy superimposed upon a non-involved mass public? These
questions no longer can be considered to be irrelevant or in
opposition to a democratic society.

Conservative answers to these questions may not finally
be acceptable or as helpful as George Kennan would have it,
but the fact remains, at a time when liberalism has stumbled
badly and radicalism has short-circuited, conservatism may
have a good deal more to offer than at any other time in American intellectual history. At the very least, conservative
values and the conservative critique of liberal democracy deserves to be listened to with renewed attentiveness.

CHAPTER 12

CONCLUSIONS

Liberalism, Radicalism, and Conservatism: Contrasting Perspectives

Although there is no doubt there are as many perspectives on the meaning of American democracy and the American experience as there are thinkers who ponder this intriguing subject, the purpose for this study has been to underline the significance of one of the three main perspectives in American thought—the conservative perspective. Liberalism, whatever else it may represent, enunciates an on-going concern about bringing democratic norms into closer harmony with power relationships and distributive justice. Radicalism, recognizing the universality of class division and conflict, differs from both the liberal and conservative perspectives by questioning the effectiveness of democracy in America in the absence of greater popular control over power resources, and seeks to displace the established elites by an elite presumably more responsive to the larger public good.

Conservatism, in all its mutations, is by no means uncritical of the existing social, political, and economic structure, but it repudiates the kinds of change usually advanced by liberals and radicals on the grounds that it would invariably lead to worse situations than presently exist. The conservative is no less critical of the discrepancy between democratic norms and practices, but he is more inclined than the liberal to prefer individual effort over collective effort, and if this makes for lesser effort in behalf of change, so be it. The radical, meanwhile, struggles hopelessly against the deadweight of a vast American public enamored of the "politics of moderation" and, from his viewpoint, suffused with a false sense of complacency that most Americans "never had it so good." On the level of thought, conservatism shares with radicalism a perplexing lack of legitimacy and the want of a really viable outlet for its ideological position on the political spectrum. This means that both these ideological stances must necessarily be limited to peripheral and secondary status in contrast to liberalism, which enjoys legitimacy but only sporadic efficacy. Historical factors, such as the consensual nature of the American Revolution, as well as institutional factors, such as the strong conservative character of the constitutional and political systems, combine with a resource-and-land-rich country to make America an intricate, and perhaps even perplexing, blend of conservative-liberal-radical components.

Despite their secondary roles, radical and conservative perspectives have played an important part in shaping the country's institutional structure. The two dominant ideals of American democracy—liberty and equality—would have be-

287

come much less significant instruments of social, economic, and political change, if a conformitarian liberalism had not had to cope with radical and conservative alternatives from time to time. A Thomas Paine, Frederick Douglass, or Malcolm "X" may have changed nothing, but their "radical" visions of a better America seeped into the national consciousness and helped to enrich democracy in America. A John Adams, John Calhoun, or Henry Adams may be honored more as statesmen or literary figures than as political philosophers, but their "conservative" critiques of the power structure in their time still offer valuable instruction for measuring the gap between democratic norms and actuality.

The dominant liberal perspective exhibits both the weaknesses and strengths of any effort designed to integrate potentially conflictful values, like liberty and equality. And where the radical would be more likely to sacrifice liberty to achieve greater equality, and the conservative would definitely favor liberty over equality, the liberal must balance one against the other, trying not to tilt either way, for fear that failure to integrate these two preeminent values will weaken the cause of democracy itself. It is mainly because liberalism has not been able to do nearly as well in advancing both political and socio-economic democracy as the national need requires, that the conservative and radical perspectives deserve a place in the ideological firmament. All three perspectives have been, and will continue to be, distinctively important contributors to a viable democratic society.

There are, however, important differences which demarcate liberal, radical, and conservative value preferences, offering conflicting guidelines for policy choices and contrasting conceptions of the public good. These differences can best be understood by reference to their divergent answers to three major questions: (1) How much popular participation is desirable in a democratic political system? (2) Who should rule? (3) Which of the two leading values—liberty or equality—should be emphasized in relation to public policy?

As to the first question, "how much popular participation is desirable in a democratic political system?", the three perspectives are markedly divergent. Normatively speaking, the conservative distrusts public opinion in general, and would therefore seek to minimize the role of the public in democratic governance by such mechanisms as a restrictive franchise, greater reliance upon expertise, and deference to elite authority. The radical has great confidence in the potential, if not actual, capacity of the public to perform well as a participatory citizenry in self-governance; and he blames the ideological manipulation of a class-biased power structure for the present low estate of popular participation.[1] Although the classical liberalism of a Thomas Jefferson also placed a high premium upon the need and potential ability of average citizens to participate meaningfully and rationally in the political process, contemporary liberals take a more realistic view of the prospects for a responsible, broad-based, issue-oriented participatory citizenry, and tend to feel that it is more important that the activist political stratum and the elites abide by the democratic rules of the game than that the larger public do so.

The fact is, these divergent views are resolved by trans-posing theory and practice. In theory, the myth persists that public opinion does insure a more responsive and responsible democracy. In reality, those in the upper range of socio-economic status and income exercise a far greater influence on the "authoritative allocation of values for a society," to use David Easton's famous formula, than does the larger public.[2] The weight of a vast amount of empirical evidence reveals that active participation is a virtual monopoly of upper-class Americans, at least in national politics, and that the potential influence of the mass public is seldom heard or felt by politicians in any meaningful way, contrasted with the continuing and effective voice of the upper stratum of the populace.[3] Why this is so, and what might be done to even things out, is open to the usual speculative disagreements and uncertainties. What is of interest, however, is that "participation remains a powerful social force for increasing or decreasing inequality, (for) it depends upon who takes advantage of it."[4] The fact is that this power is actual, rather than merely potential, among the elite at the top of the socio-economic order, even though it is the many who are supposed to be the real source of authority in democratic theory. The discrepancy is real, not apparent. Whereas the radical deplores this situation and feels that it can be corrected, the conservative applauds it, but complains that the public still exercises too much pernicious authority. The liberal simply overlooks the discrepancy between democratic theory and practice and adjusts his theory to fit a dubious reality.

The conservative has good reason to be concerned about the low level of knowledge, skill, and sustained interest which the general public usually exhibits. The radical may be on to something when he exposes the gulf between present passivity and the potential for political effectiveness in respect to the larger public, while asserting the necessary dependence of meaningful opportunity upon enhanced participatory democracy. The contemporary liberal occupies the less defensible position, because of a short-sighted tendency to misread the real message: there is an obvious relationship between individual self-worth and political effectiveness. Feelings of powerlessness lead to anomie and apathy—both of which can cause a substantial erosion of the democratic foundation if carried too far.

The question, "who should rule?", is another area of considerable disagreement among conservatives, radicals, and liberals. The conservative has the greatest difficulty here, for he defends a certain kind of elitism, but is still attached to the democratic system. It is an elitism based upon merit, not ascribed status; but the conservative is vague about who can qualify for positions of authority and how the sorting out process can be accomplished with a minimum of damage to democratic accountability. When pressed for an answer to this question, a conservative response will look beyond the usual opportunistic and pragmatic political figure to single out the person who appears to be more at home with conservative principles. These conservative principles may vary from time to time, but the main tenets will remain; and in the contemporary context, these will be anti-Government, anti-welfarism, and anti-compromise when principles are at stake. In effect, the conservative ruling class will be neither political nor economic in affiliation but cultural, if this is understood to mean that they will be well-educated, religious, and well above average in I.Q.

How such a transfer of power can be effectuated is left open; the conservative is sufficiently realistic to accept the fact that it is not likely to happen given the nature of American traditions. Therefore, his main efforts are directed at attacking and opposing liberals, who represent the real enemy, since radicals are too impotent to count for much, and it is the constant torment of principled or ideological conservatives in America that all they really have to offer is negativism. They are sometimes close enough to actual power to sample the taste, but remain unable to advance their cause without serious compromise of their principles—a truly anguish-filled situation—since the American political system requires leadership that is comfortable with the art of compromise. A Richard Nixon or Gerald Ford may receive grudging support, but when the chips are down, a principled conservative prefers a tantalizing, if unrealistic, alternative. This is the explanation behind Ronald Reagan's unsuccessful near miss in capturing the Republican Party nomination from President Ford in 1976.

A radical response to the leadership question, "who should rule?", contemplates major structural changes in the existing socio-economic-political system, in behalf of substantial egalitarianism. The chosen leader must be a "man of the people," who champions the rights of the underprivileged class and would compel sacrifices from those at the top in the interests of greater equity. The problem for the radical is that, in order to achieve a more just society, a good deal of coercive power will be necessary, and this must inevitably threaten the very nature of the democratic process; good ends cannot justify evil means. Although the radical believes whole-heartedly in broad-based, meaningful, and effective participatory democracy, his ideology inevitably tempts him to substitute one form of elitism for another. There is no way out of this dilemma; for like the conservative, the radical rejects the view that politics is the art of the possible. Compromise is surrender; therefore, ends are more important than means. Democracy cannot flourish under such a political philosophy.

The liberal would answer the question by suggesting that the current situation is quite acceptable. He is a strong defender of political competition and the two party system. While the attendant chaotic system of primaries, national conventions, and media exposure should be improved and made to work in a more responsibly democratic manner, the basic institutional structure should be preserved intact. The liberal would undoubtedly like to see better caliber leadership than the existing system usually provides, and will marshall support for reforms that promise to strengthen the democratic tendencies already built into the system, but he cannot see any good reason to jettison the cargo on hand. The liberal experiences a large measure of frustration and disgust with the snail's pace tempo of change, especially with the way special interests can so regularly subvert the liberal's conception of the public interest; he accepts the far more common bitter defeats with the occasional sweet victory, and regards this as the price paid for safeguarding the means-ends interrelationship. For the liberal, compromise is the tribute of politics—and principles have to be held loosely. Only those who are willing to bend—and bend, and bend—deserve to rule.

The third question—"which of the two leading ideas, liberty or equality, should be emphasized in relation to public policy?"—may well be the area of sharpest difference among conservatives, radicals, and liberals today. Liberty presents less of a problem than equality, since few Americans would not agree to the primacy of political democracy and the historic legacy of individual rights, the rule of law, and limitations on the power of government. Applying this value to contemporary conditions, especially to problems relating to the legitimacy of dissent, national security requirements versus the protection of individual rights, and freedom of the press versus the right to privacy, fair trial, and the needs of government, it can produce sticky questions concerning the relationship between power and fairness. But equality presents more special difficulties, since its meaning has always been fraught with ambiguity and conflict. From the moment the Declaration of Independence became a documentary cornerstone of American democracy, the meaning of equality has been suspended in air. "We hold these truths to be self-evident, that all men are created equal, that they are endowed by their Creator with certain unalienable rights, that among these are life, liberty and the pursuit of happiness..." A newspaper item of June 12, 1975, announced the results of a poll of 2,3000 federal workers among 12 government agencies conducted by the Peoples Bicentennial Commission, a rather unofficial anti-establishment group: 47% of those polled could not identify the above passage from the Declaration of Independence, 32% agreed to endorse the words, and 68% apparently disapproved of the passage. Needless to add, this was a most unreliable and trivial sort of poll, and as a news item it confirms Daniel Boorstin's depiction of a pseudo event.[5] But it does highlight the fact that there is very little consensus on the meaning of equality in the American historical context.

The interpretations of equality which probably have lasted longest and have dominated the popular understanding of this concept are "equality under the law" and "equality of opportunity." Although not quite the same, they are mutually-reinforcing concepts. As an ideal, equality has meant equal rights, equal justice, and equal opportunity. Morally, each person is an end, not a means. Inequality may be inherent in human nature from the standpoint of genetic inheritance. Some are weak, others are strong. Some are successful, others are unsuccessful. Some uphold, others try to destroy, the social fabric. But democratic equality supposedly implies a "rule of fairness" and "equal treatment" when it comes to legislative and legal standards; and even when these principles are violated, the ideal remains untarnished, part of the central meaning of American democracy. So far so good.

What leads to complications and uncertainty over the meaning of equality is a contemporary version of equality which is not universally accepted, but has become a major source of social and political change, to the extent that political and judicial elements of the political system have adopted this interpretation of equality. Sometimes called "equality of condition," or "equality of result," this view of equality, when backed up by the coercive power of government or the courts, seeks a redress of past, present, and future inequalities via "affirmative action" policies, such as school busing in the interest of minority group and opposite sex favoritism.[6] The cries of "reverse discrimination" and "unfairness" echo across the land; and however erratic, even sporadic, the application of this new meaning of equality by such instrumentalities as the Department of Health, Education and Welfare, or state court judges, may be, the impact has been substantial. And what one sees emerging is a growing split between radicals and some liberals on one hand, who tend to unite behind the idea of having government assume greater responsibility for promoting a more egalitarian society, and conservatives on the other, who see all such efforts as designed to sacrifice liberty on the altar of a dubious equality.[7]

When cherished ideals clash, reasoned discussion goes flying out the window. However simplified, conservatives, liberals, and radicals can be identified by their positions on the meaning of equality: the conservative wants less, the liberal wants more, and the radical will not settle for less than absolute equality.

Conservatism and the American Mind

The American mind has exhibited a split personality from

the very beginning. America has been conservative in social thought and liberal in political thought.[8] While a conservative outlook and values have predominated on the institutional-cultural-social level, a moderately liberal reform outlook has generally prevailed in politics. As Clinton Rossiter has stated in his lively and provocative <u>Conservatism in America</u>: "The American political mind has been a liberal mind, for change and progress have been the American way of life."[9] The unifying ideal, liberty, has proved stronger than the contentious voices of disagreement over means.

This has not meant, however, that harmony has triumphed over dissension, or that there has been any lack of conflict in the ideological arena. On a deeper level, the confusions and ambiguities in this lack of coherence between political and social thought has been the most pronounced feature of American thought. Individualism and social conformity have co-existed in great tension and contradiction throughout the course of American history. Liberty and equality have often appeared to be at cross-purposes and antagonistic to one another. The role of government has perplexed and divided Americans of the same and different ideological persuasions. Conservatives have defended and opposed socio-political-economic change from time to time and liberals have applied the brakes on change as often as they have released them.[10]

These confusions and reversals have not only made it difficult to define what these concepts really mean, but have made it equally difficult for those Americans predisposed toward an ideological position to understand exactly what the ideology was about. Even if it is true that most Americans would prefer to be considered non-ideological, middle-of-the-road, and flexibly pragmatic in their response to political, social, and economic issues, it is doubtful whether an ideological stance, no matter how slight or incoherent, can be avoided. And to further compound the confusion, there is clear evidence that Americans are capable of entertaining liberal views regarding the role of government, while retaining conservative views regarding the self-society relationship.

At least three factors account for the strong current of conservatism in American social thought. First, the legacy of Puritanism has long sanctioned the right of the community— or at least of a temporary majority of its members—to set forth rules, embodied in legal statute and reinforced by "community standards," that presumably regulate behavior and exact conformity from all citizens alike, with any deviation appropriately punishable. Second, the Protestant ethic has made hard work, individual effort, and self-restraint exalted ideals that mark the dividing line between success and failure, emphasize individual over social opportunity, strengthen competition while weakening cooperation, and equate morality and success. Third, the lack of uniformity in the establishment of legal sanctions throughout the nation due to the tripartite system of federal, state, and local jurisdiction has generally shifted the major responsibility for determining the rights and wrongs of individual behavior to thousands of semi-independent governmental authorities, which incline toward greater conservatism than the national temper would probably support.

The right of the state to "legislate morals" has always been a widely accepted feature of the American scene; and since various vested interests have frequently been able to control the situation to their advantage in defiance of changing social need, the power to set "standards" and to "legalize" proper (i.e., expected) versus improper (i.e., deviant) behavior has been the greatest single factor maintaining a conservative social structure in America and preventing change, no matter how much it might be needed or desired. Eventually, yesterday's minority becomes today's majority, and new social conditions warrant readjustment of the institutional structure to reflect historical realities. Public apathy, minority tyranny, institutional rigidity, and lack of responsiveness to democratic processes have insured a wide strain of conservatism in social thought and behavior throughout the entire course of American history, preserving continuity, while also creating strains and stresses that have not always been in the nation's best interest.[11]

At the same time, pradoxically, certain features of political liberalism have usually fostered moderate reform and concessions to the needs of the many, despite an economic structure geared more to the interests of the few. The political structure has been generally more liberal, democratic, and responsive to change than the social structure, even though the intellectual tradition drawing sustenance from Lockean-Jeffersonian liberalism has expressed a decided anti-government bias, a distrust of ideas, or theory, in favor of supposedly non-ideological practicality, and an equally pronounced antipathy toward aristocratic elitism. In the latter decades of the nineteenth-century, when Social Darwinism was dominant, political liberalism and social conservatism momentarily coalesced; Lockean-Jeffersonian liberalism found itself representing a questionable defense of laissez-faire economic theory; liberty was translated into an unqualified defense of property rights; faith in progress was reduced to materialistic considerations; and the highly esteemed commitment to individualism and independent-mindedness masked a powerful conformitarianism.[12] The strains of World Wars I and II, and the intervening decade of economic Depression destroyed this tenuous linking of conservative and liberal ideology; only a central government more responsive to the widening discrepancy between democratic ideals and practices, and to the public's growing awareness that America was drifting away from the egalitarian ideal, could save American democracy from its deepening failures and prevent a turn toward authoritarianism of the Left or Right.

Franklin Roosevelt's New Deal, and the transformation of

liberalism it brought about, may have been another typical example of liberal ends tied to conservative means, but it did succeed in reversing the trend toward directionless government. When one recalls the vehemence and sense of betrayal that Roosevelt encountered from the Right in response to his rather moderate efforts to save capitalism from its own foolishness, it is easy to see why liberalism and conservatism again began to diverge and move along separate paths. Only this time, it was conservatism which faced an impossible dilemma, and which subsequently fragmented into disparate movements more divided than united by conservative principles.

The New Deal-Fair Deal-New Frontier-Great Society tradition retained a basic continuity as the standard-bearer of political liberalism and proved quite successful in controlling the Executive branch of government from 1933 to 1968, except for the eight Eisenhower years; however, conservatism disintegrated as a viable political movement, splitting three ways, into ideological, pragmatic, and philosophical forms. By the 1950's, ideological conservatives found a cause in anti-Communism and a spokesman in the late Wisconsin Senator, Joseph McCarthy; but in the process they discredited the movement in the eyes of other conservatives, who were just as appalled and uncomfortable with the undemocratic excesses of McCarthyism as were most liberals, and who were certainly concerned about the betrayal of conservative, as well as liberal, values in what they concluded was a mindless subversion of democratic ends by undemocratic means. Meanwhile, Robert Taft, Dwight Eisenhower, and Richard Nixon, politically ambitious and anxious about their standing with the wider public, played both ends against the middle. At first they cautiously supported McCarthy's irresponsible behavior for political advantage; but finally they turned away from him when it was no longer so politically sound to support him. There was no effort by Republican administrations to repeal the New Deal, although some reduction in federal support for welfarism did occur.

Philosophical conservatives had a more difficult time of it, for they could never accede to the blandishments of the ultra-conservative ideologues for a General MacArthur-type "man on a white horse" and the fascistic overtones of this alternative, nor could they identify with the evasions and compromises of the pragmatic conservatives in defense of certain long-held principles regarding the nature of man, society, and the state. Caught in this sort of dilemma, a philosophical conservative-liberal like Walter Lippmann travelled a lonely road, trying to reconcile as best he could the liberal and conservative ideals of the good society and government. This breakdown in conservatism dissipated its strength, just when it appeared that a revival of popular support was in the offing.

Clinton Rossiter provides an accurate and valuable analysis of this development, but fails to draw the proper conclusion, clinging to the notion that what conservatives believe in common is stronger than what divides them.[13] More than a

295

decade after his revised edition of <u>Conservatism in America</u>
was published, the situation has hardly improved, and his hope
that philosophical conservatism, or "Conservatism with a capital C," as he liked to put it, would serve as a rallying
point for a newly minted re-affirmation of conservative principles, seems less and less probable.[14]

However, the disorganization and splitting apart of the
New Deal liberal coalition that occurred in the late 60's,
looms as a continuing problem for the cause of liberalism and
the Democratic Party, despite Jimmy Carter's successful electoral victory in 1976, which reflected to some extent a partial reformulation of the old New Deal coalition. As a result
of shifting allegiances and the enhanced unpredictability of
the electorate, the erosion of the New Deal political coalition of a formerly "solid South," organized labor, urban minorities, and liberal publicists, and the rapid social changes
that have accompanied the rise of a dissident counterculture
to challenge the hegemony of the Puritan-Protestant-Religious
ethic over the nation's life-style and social values, liberalism remains divided within itself.

The split personality in the American mind remained latent and comparatively benign for most of the country's life,
because the ambiguity of social conservatism and political
liberalism could be integrated through the actual and symbolic
importance of the libertarian tradition and the achievement of
political democracy. It is becoming clear, however, that this
split personality contains elements of disease and derangement,
and unless the American people can bring themselves to accept
the reality of cultural pluralism—marked by diversity in life-
styles and a sharp reduction in the state's right to interfere
in a person's private life—it is quite possible that the unresolved tension between political liberalism and social conservatism could cause irrevocable havoc to the stability and viability of the American system.

There are formidable obstacles blocking the way toward a
resolution of this conservative-liberal dilemma. The first is
the slowness in which the Puritan-Protestant-Religious ethic
has been disintegrating, the conflicts and divisions that are
muddying the water, and the intensification of "generation gap"
problems resulting from this situation. By and large, the
post-World War II generation has embraced cultural pluralism,
while the older generation has either resisted it through
greater political clout and resources or joined forces with
the younger element to fight for changes in the social structure of legal sanctions and community mores. Those who have
fought for change have done so without great success. A more
relativistic and open-minded social ethic is surely in the
making, for better or for worse, but the period of transition
between one ethos and the other is proving to be long and ar-
duous, as note the fate of the Equal Rights Amendment.

A second obstacle is the fluctuations in public opinion
and the popular mood, which respond to upsetting events rather

than to the forces of change, pushing the pendulum from one extreme to the other. The upsurge of "radicalism" in the late 1960's, spewing forth campus disruption and violence, a seeming breakdown in manners and morals, torn-apart cities, and a political reaction that devastated the Democratic Party's moderately liberal coalition, is one of the main reasons for the conservative mood that dominates public consciousness in the mid-seventies, coupled with the inflationary spiral and the rise of big government. Since former President Nixon made no concessions whatever to the former problem, and upheld with prestige and power the sanctity of a restored Puritan-Protestant-Religious-ethic, the clock was set back rather than forward, and neither liberalism nor conservatism came out a winner. Although Jimmy Carter appears to be of a different mind and temperament, it is still unclear just what positions he will take on this issue. It will surely take extraordinary leadership to achieve a viable integration of these conflicting values and interests.

A third obstacle requires a longer perspective to explain. As the late historian, Richard Hofstadter, and others have pointed out, there was always another side to the liberal tradition, at least through the turn of the century, that revealed an illiberal underside to its liberal structure. The so-called Populist-Progressive-New Deal era of reform between 1890 and the Second World War sponsored a political revolution in behalf of a restoration of political democracy and a more responsible capitalism, but at the same time tried to dampen the fires of revolutionary social change. In his important study, The Age of Reform, Hofstadter laments the fact: "Somewhere along the way a large part of the Populist-Progressive tradition has turned sour, become illiberal and ill-tempered."[15] Hofstadter goes on to spell out the reasons for this charge: the threat posed to the dominant White-Anglo-Saxon-Protestant-Yankee middle-class ethic of public service, self-discipline, and social morality by the waves of "alien" immigrants, mostly poor, Catholic, and conditioned to authoritarian subserviance.[16] Out of this clash of values came the corrupt old-style big-city political machine, and the cleavage between rural and urban America. Also, despite an idealistic and selfish concern for improving American political democracy, turn-of-the-century reformers did not find progressive and reactionary social ideas incompatible:

Such tendencies in American life as isolationism and the extreme nationalism that usually goes with it, hatred of Europe and Europeans, racial, religious, and nativist phobias, resentment of big business, trade-unionism, intellectuals, the Eastern seaboard and its culture—all these have been found not only in opposition to reform but also at times oddly combined with it. One of the most interesting and least studied aspects of American life has been the frequent recurrence of the demand for reforms, many of them aimed at the remedy of genuine ills, combined with strong moral convictions and with the choice of hatred as a kind of creed.[17]

In other words, isolationism, ultra-nationalism, anti-Semitism, nativism, and anti-urbanism were all aspects of reform-oriented liberalism tied to reactionary social attitudes. And even the New Deal tradition took little positive action to develop a liberal social philosophy to go with a political liberalism that often confused principle with expediency. Conservatives, meanwhile, gained a measure of respectability and honor under the aegis of such presidents as William Howard Taft and Herbert Hoover, who embodied the qualities of meritorious reward and individualism, until events transpired to show how virtue can be defeated by political ineptness.

It is this ambivalent legacy which has caused the dilemmas of liberalism-conservatism to continue to plague any concerted effort to untangle the strands of means and ends. The dilemma of liberalism continues to be an inability to integrate means and ends around a continuum of political and social philosophy. The dilemma of conservatism continues to be an inability to ride herd on an irresponsible ultra-Rightist hard core of "know-nothing" ideologues and to solidify the end-means relationship behind the traditional conservative's desire for a reconciliation of ethical and power considerations. The dilemmas of each, however, are less significant than the failure of both conservatism and liberalism to come to terms with the radical tradition in America. Surely this has to be the higher price exacted by the contradictions, impurities, and downright confusions of the conservative-liberal tradition. The American public has been conditioned to regard any serious threat to the established order or to orthodox thinking as reprehensible. The worst thing a public official can be called is a "radical." Few survive the label, whether or not it is deserved—and in many instances it is not. William Jennings Bryan ran unsuccessfully for the Presidency three successive times, and although many complex factors can be blamed for his successive failures to gain a majority of electoral votes, not least was the fact that he ran in 1896 against William McKinley as a would-be reformer and "radical." The labor leader Eugene Debs, who never displayed an ounce of leadership irresponsibility, was an avowed Socialist whose "radicalism" put him in jail during World War I. The presidential ambitions of Barry Goldwater in 1964 and of George McGovern in 1972 were irreparably damaged by the fact that they appeared to be too "radical," although in these instances one was on the Right and the other on the Left of the political spectrum.

These historical figures, and thousands of less notable individuals, have experienced harsh repression at the hands of elected public officials supported by a substantial segment of public opinion so often and so repeatedly, that it raises disturbing questions as to whether American democracy is more than superficially rooted.[18] Even if one makes allowance for the historical background of external threat to the national security that has frequently accompanied such repressive measures, such behavior leaves a large reservoir of betrayed democratic ideals in its wake.[19] Even liberals and conservatives, from time to time, have been forced on the defensive, and have been hard put to defend their reputations and honor against the charge of being too "radical." Collectivism, creeping Socialism, Fascism, and authoritarianism are terms that Left and Right often find applied indiscriminately as labels of denigration. A healthy democracy should not only accommodate, but also welcome, a responsible "radical" viewpoint and tradition—it is the only way conservatism and liberalism can be kept honest and aware of differences.

Tom Paine was a "radical" who contributed more than anyone else toward creating a sense of unity and purpose in the revolutionary movement in 1776 through his writings; he later paid a high price for his "radicalism" when the need for a radical symbol gave way to its opposite, and his burial monument was a pauper's grave. Just as there is irresponsible "liberalism" and "conservatism," so there is irresponsible "radicalism." But the utter failure of the American political tradition to make room for "responsible radicalism," that is, for those who argue for major structural change in the light of an intellectually respectable diagnosis of the discrepancies between democratic norms and practices, must surely be a failure that affects the integrity and viability of the liberal and conservative traditions equally. Not only has it had a cost in wasted lives and damaged reputations, but it has frequently served to cut off meaningful debate over issues of importance, and has handicapped the cause of reform and social justice.

Success breeds complacency, and complacency has been a perennial problem for both liberalism and conservatism. Times change, however, and America, for the first time in its history, is confronted with the fact of failure on a scale that is without precedent. Economic dislocation, misplaced priorities, such as a hundred billion dollar military budget in peacetime, unresolved racial problems, and a political system that seems less and less capable of making democracy work—all this and much more can be enumerated, and while there is also much that can be said on the positive side, the crisis of legitimacy which now afflicts all the major political, social, and economic institutions of the United States will not be solved or even alleviated without a revitalized and more responsible conservatism, liberalism, and radicalism—which would provide options for alternate solutions to the institutional crises.

An acceptable conservative response to the crisis has been handicapped for a number of reasons. In social philosophy, the persistence of the Puritan-Protestant-Religious ethic in the face of increasing internal stress is one problem. Another is the fact that in social philosophy, a conservative approach tends to be reactionary and anti-democratic. One sees this especially revealed in such artist-writers as the literary critics, Irving Babbitt and Paul Elmer More, and the poet, T.S. Eliot, who also wrote two of the most relevant essays in this tradition.[20] The search for a more appealing and useful conservative political philosophy has also been handicapped by the need to reconcile liberal democracy with conservative principles. The political system functions in the context of compromise; and it is hard for thoughtful conservatives to sacrifice principles on the altar of expediency.

The single biggest problem standing in the way of a widely acceptable conservative political philosophy is the public's complete rejection of aristocratic ideals—such as the pursuit of excellence for its own sake, public service as a duty and not just a career option, and the necessity of social hierarchy—and worship of the common man. Only when the uncommon man pretends to have feet of clay and plays a role that endows him with familiar traits will he be accepted by the people. Such compromising is seldom successful. So the conservative philosopher or politician-statesman faces a dilemma which has no solution. He believes in elitist democracy because he knows that virtue and honesty are in short supply, and there is no true alternative to rule-by-the-best. Yet democracy abhors a self-chosen meritocracy, and it is hard to see any other method for achieving this objective. Democracy also requires a pluralist political system, where competing interests can vie with one another and opportunity is reasonably open. Whether or not this is ever the case in practice is debatable, but the norm has to be respected. Meanwhile, conservative thinkers do their best building a case for a viable democratic elitism, knowing in their hearts the futility of the exercise.

Conservatism: Assets, Liabilities, and Prospects

By the 1970's, one thing was clear: the climate of the times was again swinging away from one dominant ideological stance to another. After nearly four decades of reform-minded liberalism, and the expansion of government in all directions, the American people were ready to call a halt; distrust of government has never been so widespread or so serious a problem in American history as now appears to be the case. It is surely one of the ironies of the times that the two outstanding conservative statesmen of the first half of this century—Herbert Hoover and Robert A. Taft—can now be seen as wiser prophets and better analysts of the national purpose than those liberal leaders and pundits who subjected them to such unrelenting scorn all those years. Both argued strenuously that America was too big, too diverse, too unrly, to be governed exclusively from Washington; when government tried to do too much, it quickly lost its effectiveness. Also, they were opponents of "globalism," and feared both the "imperial presidency" and the extension of American power in areas of the world where it would be most difficult to achieve American purposes. After considerable failure in each of these policy spheres during a long liberal reign, Hoover-Taft conservatism looks quite good indeed—at least in retrospect.[21]

Although he opposed most of the progressive legislation backed by the Democratic Party leadership and advocated a neo-isolationist foreign policy on the eve of cold war polariza-- tion, Taft did have cogent reasons for his position: the means were inadequate to the projected ends, and expanded governmental power was bound to weaken the moral underpinning of a democratic society. As Richard Rovere argues in an article cited earlier in this study, if the legitimacy of American democracy is based upon an ever tenuous consensus, then Taft understood quite well the unintended consequences, mostly non-beneficial, of any major effort by government to deal with social change. Whether doing less was any solution either, is, of course, equally problematical.

It is not the least of recent ironies that so-called radical revisionist historian-critics of the Truman Doctrine, and in their view all it portended for an economic imperialism disguised as anti-communism, are now in the forefront of a re-evaluation of conservatism that is much more appreciative than one would ordinarily expect, and at the same time much more critical of liberal cold war perceptions.[22] The revisionist Ronald Radosh, in his <u>Prophets on the Right: Profiles of Conservative Critics of American Globalism</u>, provides this new assessment of Robert A. Taft:

> But at a moment in our history when the policy makers and crisis managers believed firmly in 'uniting the free world against Communism,' Taft had the foresight to know that such a course would prove fruitless and costly. At a time when advocates of an American Century urged negotiations from positions of strength, and piled armaments on anti-Communist nations, Taft saw such measures as violations of the best elements of the American tradition...From the perspective of the 1970s Taft's views seem sober, wise, and realistic.[23]

Herbert Hoover's reputation as a statesman and thinker has never quite recovered from the "leadership failures" which exacerbated the economic collapse of the early 1930's and the "laissez-faire individualism" he continued to preach at a time when millions of Americans were helpless in the face of escalating unemployment and economic depression. FDR's "take charge" personality and willingness to experiment did a good deal to restore public confidence in the system at a perilous time, and ever after, there was a notable tendency among historians to magnify Hoover's failures while perhaps overestimating Roosevelt's success.[24] With the publication of a new biography of Herbert Hoover by Joan Hoff Wilson in 1975, as well as other recent studies by "radical revisionists," it will be easier to note the extraordinary degree of "progressivism" in his thought, the basic soundness of his foreign policy views, and the caricature of his libertarian social, economic, and political philosophy that the "liberal establishment" so long popularized. After leaving the presidency, Hoover became one of the more consistent critics of the New Deal, but his objectivity was obviously suspect and the liberal's contempt for Hooversism held sway. Joan Wilson does a good job of reopening the Hoover file, and a more "balanced assessment" may well restore his name to the front rank of responsible conservative critics of American domestic and foreign policy in the second quarter of this century.[25]

Is it true that conservatives are "stricken with a moral blindness which unites a lack of compassion for their fellow men—those especially who are on the lower rungs of socio-economic achievement—with a rationalized commitment to human diversity and inequality?[26] Is poverty the result of individual character failure or of a faulty social structure? The conservative would favor the former view, but most social scientists tend to take the latter view. D. Stanley Eitzen, for instance, states emphatically in a recent sociological text: "The weight of sociological evidence suggests strongly that the inequalities of society are to blame for poverty, not the traits of individuals."[27] This on-going debate has been one of the more obvious differences dividing liberals and conservatives, and when either premise has been applied to social policy options, it has had serious consequences. It affects such issues as abolition or reinstatement of the death penalty, rehabilitation versus punishment of individuals who commit anti-social acts, and the responsibility of public policy for the poor. The academic-intellectual community is overwhelmingly liberal in its value premises, and this puts conservatives at a decided disadvantage in getting their views across to a wider audience.[28] Jeffrey Hart, one of the more vocal spokesmen for conservatism, complains that liberal and radical ideas have more media appeal generally, which makes conservatism seem dowdy by comparison:

> Conservatives stress things like the essential unchangingness of human nature, and its flawed character. They speak of the limitations that reality imposes on the human will. They point to the lessons of history and experience. I think it is true to say that liberal-radical thinkers from Rousseau through Marx and Sartre possess a powerful appeal because what they purpose is speculative and novel, whereas conservative thought—precisely because it describes reality—has about it an air of the commonplace...We thus arrive at the following paradox. The liberal-radical idea is interesting because it describes an unreality. The conservative idea often seems banal because it describes reality. But the very novelty of the liberal-radical idea gives it tremendous impetus in a media oriented culture which thrives on the marketing of novelty.[29]

However true this observation may be, it does pinpoint the difficulty conservative views encounter seeking a "fair" and "generous" treatment in the mass media or academia. This has been a source of genuine concern and frustration among those who would like to see conservative ideas evaluated on merit, rather than subjected to the vagaries of distorted "image" considerations.

Nicholas O. Berry has written a tantalizing essay which detects a pattern in the politics and thought of the twentieth-century that reveals a paradoxical competence-incompetence performance record for Democratic versus Republican administrations.[30] Republican leadership seems to be so much better handling foreign policy, while its greatest failures have been in domestic policy. Democratic leadership responds better to public need in domestic policy, but has precipiated all the major warfare and a good deal of questionable foreign interventionism. This is how Berry states the matter:

> To put it simply, the conservative Republican can operate effectively in international politics because international politics occurs in a conservative environment. Their conservative orientation fails in domestic politics because the domestic political environment is overwhelmingly liberal. Again, the opposite applies to Democratic administrations. As liberals, they fail to adapt to the conservative international political environment but they succeed in the compatible arena of domestic politics.[31]

Liberal positivism and conservative negativism toward change favors the liberal in domestic affairs, where the less privileged outnumber the more privileged; but when it comes to assessing the national interest, the conservative tends to be more realistic, less moralistic, and is consequently more likely to be effective in dealing with other nations than the liberal. The inability of the two major political parties to coordinate their domestic and foreign policy skills and values has been a serious weakness of American leadership throughout this century, according to Nicholas Berry. Although over-generalized and under-documented, his thesis does offer a suggestive insight into one of the peculiarities of the conservative-liberal relationship in the United States.

On the conceptual, or theoretical level, in contrast to the policy implications of conservative versus liberal value premises, the picture is equally cloudy.[32] During the course of this study, the writer has made two discoveries about the conservative political tradition that surprised him and considerably changed the structure of the book from what had been initially contemplated. First, any narrow characterization of what constitutes conservative political philosophy is invalid. The range and variety of conservative thinking, and the peculiar amalgam of conservative-liberal values in the history of American thought, rules out any recognizable commonality or consistency in the conservative tradition. Instead, what one notices is the persistence of certain themes, particularly a realistic sense of human limits and a concomitant distrust of mass public opinion and of the corruptions of power, which lead to a faith in some form of elitist democracy. The more systematic conservative thinkers, especially those featured in chapter 4, also reveal more dissimilarity than similarity; but they all present a contrast to their more liberal or radical opponents in rejecting a naturalist, relativist, secularist rationale for democratic theory in favor of a continuing search for a metaphysical rationale that might give the ethical component of the means-ends relationship greater objectivity, universality, and authority. Although it can hardly be said that their individual and collective achievement has been widely accepted, or even welcomed, there is not a one who cannot be read today for insight and stimulation.

Second, so-called conservative thinkers do not deserve either the neglect or contempt they have generally received at the hands of a predominantly liberal intellectual establishment. Liberalism itself would have been better and more responsible if it had dealt more honestly with the conservative critique of liberalism. When artificial roadblocks are erected to forestall a reasoned re-examination of basic assumptions, little is gained and much is lost. This has been the main flaw in a liberal tradition that all too often has preferred rhetoric and myth to reality. A liberal or radical view of man, society, and the state, however defined, may still have more to offer and make more sense than the conservative outlook; but in the give and take of the free marketplace of ideas, it is the liberal who usually employs his power advantage to reduce the impact of conservative or radical critiques of liberal orthodoxy. Perhaps this is inevitable, and if conservative or radical ideology were in the ascendancy, the situation would be much the same. But the fact remains, the health of any democratic society depends upon a free flow of ideas and self-criticism. Anything that impedes this should be deplored and resisted. As a number of historians have pointed out, a viable conservatism can be a valuable complement to an equally viable liberalism and radicalism.

Ideas do have consequences. Some assumptions are better than others. It is a difficult undertaking to assess accurately and knowledgeably the conceptual underpinning of policy choices. There is never enough proof; facts seldom speak for themselves. Ideology is the hidden mainspring of individual conduct. If the day ever comes when ideologies can be subjected to objective assessment, a major advance in human knowledge and understanding will have been accomplished. At the moment, however, that day seems far away.

THE TRANSFORMATION OF LIBERALISM

Classical Liberalism (18th-19th centuries)	Contemporary Liberalism (20th century)
1. Concept of passive or least government the best	1. Concept of positive or activist government
2. Economic laissez-faire based upon private enterprise	2. Increased control of government over economy; mixed capitalism
3. Basically agricultural economy	3. Industrial-technological economy
4. Fairly equitable society— minimal gap between rich & poor, but at a generally modest living standard for most citizens	4. Substantial maldistribution of wealth and income despite expand ed middle-class and social secu ity programs
5. Widespread popular distrust of, & independence from, central government	5. Increased dependence of masses upon central government for the well-being and security
6. Individualism both in theory and practice characterizes the political-social system	6. Individualism in theory, but a good deal of collectivism in practice, characterizes the political-social system
7. Main liberal achievement of this period: political democracy; equality depends upon maximizing personal freedom	7. Main liberal aspiration of this period: socio-economic democrac genuine liberty depends upon a more egalitarian society

Meaning of American Democracy
1. Government based upon consent of the governed—representative democracy
2. Constitutionalism—power limited and accountable via institutional separation of powers, checks and balances, and an electoral system with widened franchise and competitive party politics
3. Protection of individual rights against the coercive power of government; especially the Bill of Rights and the Fourteenth Amendment
4. Federalism—shared power and authority between central government and state-local governments
5. Rule of law—independent judiciary, judicial review, and fair trial procedures

Classical Liberalism
1. The best government is that which interferes minimally in the private sector
2. Pursuit of individual self-interest equals the public good— private sector takes precedence over the public sector per se
3. The achievement of political democracy will promote socio-economic democracy and equity

Contemporary Liberalism
1. Government has certain responsibilities or obligations to improve the lot of all the people, especially the underclass
2. The public sector is just as important as the private sector and cannot be left to take care of itself
3. Liberty (or political democracy) has become increasingly reliant upon greater socio-economic democracy; the social structure and public policies should promote greater equity

THE RISE AND FALL OF AMERICAN LIBERALISM

Liberalism-Capitalism
1. Faith in progress and ever higher standard of living for the majority via an ever expanding Gross National Product
2. Moderate reform and pluralist, or consensus, democracy
3. It is a responsibility of government to advance the welfare of the masses and seek greater equity in the distribution of wealth

Decline of Liberalism-Capitalism (as alleged by many critics)
1. Periodic prosperity interspersed with recession-depression is an endless phenomenon of capitalism (16 such cycles over the past 100 years); leads to persistent insecurity for lower income groups
2. Failure of moderate reform to cope with deepening socio-economic-political problems; greed and the rip-off society seem to be the rule throughout the system
3. Persistent pattern of inequity; high percentage of minority-group poverty and unemployment; increase in self-interested corporate power over the political and economic system

Neo-Marxist Critique of Liberalism-Capitalism (Gabriel Kolko, Edward S. Greenberg, Michael Parenti, William A. Williams among some of the leading spokesmen for this position)
1. Progressive-New Deal liberalism was mainly designed to save capitalism from its own excesses, and had the effect of solidifying its control over the market economy while permitting benefits to trickle down to the disadvantaged via a less-than-adequate welfare-social security system
2. The business sycle was stabilized mainly through the rise of the warfare state and a bi-partisan foreign policy geared to American militarism-globalism-economic imperialism
3. Business-government collaboration to enhance and perpetuate the privileges of the few at the expense of the many has been characteristic of American liberalism-capitalism. Liberalism has really been a disguised conservatism for better than a century now

What Are The Alternatives?
1. Greater public regulation of the corporate structure and a more equitable tax system; a revitalized liberalism via a new Democratic Party coalition minus the Southern conservatives and "reactionary" blue-collar elements; the New Politics of radicalized youth, minorities, intellectuals, and liberated women
2. Major structural changes—a shift to a socialist economy, including nationalization of key industries, and a systematic attack upon "bigness" and excessive technology that leads to dehumanization
3. Politics as usual—just muddle through

Purported Failures of Contemporary Liberalism
1. Succeeded in maximizing political democracy in the 19th century but failed to curb monopolistic economic power in 20th century
2. Failed to advance the cause of social democracy and a more equitable society except for piecemeal (i.e., incremental) reforms
3. Failed to curb the expansion of Executive and bureaucratic power at the expense of constitutional accountability; critics claim that liberalism has been a major contributor to this trend

Appendix IIb

TYPOLOGY FOR RECENT CONSERVATIVE POLITICAL THOUGHT

LEFT ← | CENTER | → RIGHT

Liberalism	Conservative Liberalism	Liberal Conservatism	Pragmatic Conservatism	Philosophical Conservatism	Ideological Conservatism	Ultra Conservatism	Libertarian Conservatism
(Left wing of Democratic Party and welfare state egalitarianism)	Sidney Hook Reinhold Niebuhr	Edward C. Banfield Daniel Bell Peter Drucker Nathan Glazer Irving Kristol Seymour M. Lipset Patrick Moynihan Robert Nisbet James Q. Wilson	(Right wing of Democratic Party and moderate wing of the Republican Party)	Hannah Arendt Alexander Bickel Jacques Ellul Friedrich A. Hayek Bertrand de Jouvenel Willmoore Kendall George F. Kennan Walter Lippmann Hans J. Morgenthau Michael Oakeshott George Santayana Leo Strauss Peter Viereck Eric Voegelin	(Right wing of Republican Party) William F. Buckley, Jr. James Burnham M. Stanton Evans Russell Kirk Kevin Phillips	John Birch Society Various single-issue rightist movements and politico-religious fundamentalist organizations	Raoul Berger Milton Friedman Frank Meyer Robert Nozick Ayn Rand Murray Rothbard William E. Simon
← strongly ideological → Emphasis on change and reform via concept of positive government	← moderately ideological → Limited reform and change plus reduced role for government and strengthening of private sector		← middle of the road → Politics of stalemate and deadlock	← moderately ideological → Some resistance to change and reform plus restoration of traditional values and reduced role for government	← strongly ideological → Emphasis on turning back the clock via concept of minimal government for ideological and libertarian conservatives; strong government authoritarianism for ultra-conservatism →		

Explanatory note: Any placement of individual writers under such loose and imprecise labels as indicated above is bound to be somewhat arbitrary and subjective. This is offered as a tentative schematization reflecting the analysis presented in this particular book.

Moderately ideological = means more important than ends

Strongly ideological = ends more important than

309

Appendix III

LIBERALISM versus CONSERVATISM

A. Basic Assumptions (20th Century Post-New Deal Liberalism)

	LIBERALISM (idealism & optimism)	CONSERVATISM (realism & pessimism)
MAN (What is the true nature of man?)	1. Improvable 2. Nurture more important than Nature 3. Capable of transcending selfishness if external conditions are conducive to this end	1. Relatively stable 2. Nature more important than Nurture 3. Selfishness is endemic to the human condition and irremediable
SOCIETY (What is the proper relationship between the individual & society)	1. Man's social being determines the quality of his individual being 2. Society should not try to regulate human social behavior; strong commitment to "cultural pluralism" 3. By improving social conditions one expands the opportunities for individual self-fulfillment	1. Man's individual being takes precedence over his social being 2. Society should impose some degree of uniformity regarding mass moral behavior by "legislating morals" 3. Promoting incentive and success depends less on conditions than on individual ability and initiative
STATE (What is the proper relationship between the rulers & the ruled?)	1. Gov't should play a positive role in fostering equity & should place a floor under the deprivations of the underclass 2. Indiv. human rights tied to the quest for greater social justice takes precedence over the rights of property 3. Gov't should regulate the corporate economy in behalf of the liberal's view of the public interest	1. The less gov't intervention the better; individual incentive & responsibility require a minimum of gov't control over the private sector 2. Individual property rights remain the main bulwark of a viable capitalistic system 3. Gov't regulation of the corporate economy should be minimized because the health of the economy depends upon maximum self-regulation

B. Policy Preferences (The preferred means for achieving ideological goals)

1. Majority Rule Democracy	1. Consensus Democracy
2. Protection of individual rights	2. Respect for authority
3. Emphasis on equality of opportunity for all	3. Emphasis upon property rights
4. More power to the central gov't in the interests of higher performance standards & equity	4. More power to the state & local governments—less centralization & greater decentralization of power
5. Meaningful liberty depends upon greater equity	5. Equality depends upon liberty & economic growth as an end in itself

311

NOTES AND REFERENCES

Introduction

1. See Ronald Radosh and Murray N. Rothbard (eds.), A
New History of Leviathan: Essays on the Rise of the American Corporate State (New York: E.P. Dutton paperback, 1972),
especially Murray N. Rothbard's essay, "Herbert Hoover and
the Myth of Laissez-Faire," wherein it is argued: "Herbert
Hoover, far from being an advocate of laissez-faire, was in
every way the precursor of Roosevelt and the New Deal, that,
in short, he was one of the major leaders of the twentieth-
century shift from relatively laissez-faire capitalism to
the modern corporate state." (p. 111)

2. See Russell Kirk, The Conservative Mind: From Burke
to Eliot (New York: Avon Books, Equinox Edition of 1973, originally published in 1953) for what is sometimes referred
to as 'the definitive study of conservative political
thought.' It is a wide-ranging survey of English and American thinkers who 'qualify' as conservatives, and sets forth
the following criteria by which to judge same: "(1) Belief
that a divine intent rules society as well as conscience,
forging an eternal chain of right and duty which links great
and obscure, living and dead. Political problems, at bottom,
are religious and moral problems...(2) Affection for the pro-
liferating variety and mystery of traditional life, as distinguished from the narrowing uniformity and equalitarianism
and utilitarian aims of most radical systems...(3) Conviction that civilized society requires orders and classes.
The only true equality is moral equality; all other attempts
at leveling lead to despair...(4) Faith in prescription...
Tradition and sound prejudice provide checks upon man's anarchic impulse...(6) Recognition that change and reform are
not identical, and that innovation is a devouring conflagra-
tion more often than it is a torch of progress." (pp. 17-18)
There are a number of problems in accepting Kirk's characterization of conservative thought as definitive. His itemiza-
tion of conservative values in the above passage is rather
esoteric and even idiosyncratic; he makes little attempt to
distinguish political from social philosophy nor does he
show how both liberal and conservative traditions have undergone mutations in the development of American institutions
and thought; but the most serious problem is a drastic either/
orism, in which all ideas that do not conform to his version
of conservatism are labeled 'radical' and summarily rejected.
The analysis is brilliant in spots but uneven in quality and
quite uncritical in judging the relationship of conservative
to other ideological tendencies.
See Clinton Rossiter, Conservatism in America: The Thank-
less Persuasion (New York: Random House Vintage Books, 1955).
Rossiter's study is stronger where Kirk's study is weakest,
and makes a better connection between ideas and their consequences for institutional developments, although it lacks
Kirk's deep sense of historical perspective and a satisfac-

tory basis for evaluating conservative values as a belief
system. Although Rossiter does present twenty-two specific attributes of the conservative outlook, throughout his
book he finds so many ways of applying conservative values
to historical happenings that distinctions blur and it is
difficult not to conclude that every political stance has
more conservative coloration than any other ideological proclivity, which in the American historical experience can
hardly be true if liberalism is as dominant and all-pervasive as has been indicated, even if liberalism is shown to
have a substantial conservative underpinning. Rossiter may
be correct when he stresses the non-ideological content of
conservative thought in America; on the other hand, he could
just as easily have called his book "Liberalism in America"
and it would not have done violence to his analysis.

An impressive, and largely neglected, study tracing conservatism from its origins in Greek philosophy to contemporary American "New Conservatism" is M. Morton Auerbach's The
Conservative Illusion (New York: Columbia University Press,
1959). It is a devastating critique of conservative ideology from a radical perspective which stands out because of
the forcefulness of its argumentation. According to Auerbach, internal contradictions and the backward-looking
thrust of historical conservatism consigns it to the grave-
yard of inoperable political ideologies, and since it "cannot avoid contradiction and alienation from history...it
offers nothing to historical man except submission to necessity, resignation to defeat." (p. 311) Auerbach finds
"the unifying thread of Conservatism in its underlying value of harmony through minimizing individual desires and maximizing affection for the community." (p. 252) The primary
attachment to welfare and income improvements for the masses and a maximum of personal freedom in democratic systems
pulls the rug from under meaningful Conservatism. According to Auerbach, "Conservatism has no way of making the crucial transition from values to reality, from theory to practice; and in the limited periods of history when it seemed
to make this transition, it was able to do so only for reasons which contradicted its premises." (p. vii) There is
obvious difficulty with Auerbach's attempt to define Conservatism as limiting wants and maximizing affection, for it
presupposes a division of society between "haves" and "have
nots" and the ideology has the effect of perpetuating a privileged class at the expense of general improvement for the
many. Is harmony truly the chief value of a conservative outlook? It is true that conservative elitism is based principally upon social and moral values rather than upon economic
privilege per se. Yet freedom for economic striving has not
been an absent factor in shaping conservative values. By requiring reality to match ideology rather than allowing for
the adjustments every ideology concedes to reality, Auerbach
puts the cart before the horse. A society can be more or
less conservative-liberal, not necessarily completely one or
the other, and this could be a legitimate ideal. Auerbach
denies that this can be a viable alternative. Paradoxically,

the strength of any ideology resides in the way it is perceived, not in its capacity to unify theory and practice.
What Auerbach says of conservatism is true of every political ideology: theory and practice will be dysfunctional.
Auerbach refuses to accept the fact that this is inevitable
and his book is thus more a criticism of ideology per se than
of any particular ideology.

See Ronald Lora, Conservative Minds in America (Chicago:
Rand McNally, 1971 paperback edition). This book has great
merit, but in painting a broad canvas which focuses upon literary and cultural aspects of conservative thought there is
a tendency to do less than justice to the political dimension.

Allen Guttmann's The Conservative Tradition in America
(New York: Oxford University Press, 1967) also finds more to
say about the cultural aspects of conservatism than the political side, explaining the problem in these terms: "The democratization of American society has made Conservatives increasingly feeble as an institutionalized force, but the Conservative dream of a hierarchically structured society of pre-
scribed values and restrained liberty has continued on as
an important and usually unrecognized aspect of American
literature." (p. 11)

See George H. Nash, The Conservative Intellectual Movement in America Since 1945 (New York: Basic Books, 1976) for
a very sympathetic analysis of contemporary conservative
thinkers, most of whom were at one time or another associated with the conservative bi-monthly, National Review. This
is excellent descriptive intellectual history but weak in
respect to critical analysis.

See also N.J. O'Sullivan, Conservatism (New York: St.
Martin's Press paperback, 1976), for the best available short
study of historical and contemporary conservatism that provides not only a valuable conceptual analysis, but also devotes separate chapters to French, German, and British conservatism, as well as recent developments in American conservative thought. However, little is done on individual
thinkers except for illustrative purposes. O'Sullivan includes this helpful definition of conservatism: "Conservative ideology, accordingly, may be defined as a philosophy
of imperfection, committed to the idea of limits, and directed towards the defence of a limited style of politics."
(pp. 11-12)

3. From Colony to Country: The Revolution in American
Thought 1750-1820 (New York: Macmillan Co., 1974), p. x,
Preface.

Chapter 1

1. Note especially the legacy of "The Progressive Historians" who exercised such enormous influence over the interpretation of American thought during the second quarter
of this century, especially Turner, Beard, and Parrington.
Although their respective reputations were under sustained
attack by the 1960's as a later historiography found serious fault with their tendency to accept a too simplistic
equation of liberalism and democracy, there is no question
but that conservative values received a heavy pounding when
Progressivism held sway on the intellectual front. See
Richard Hofstadter, The Progressive Historians: Turner,
Beard, Parrington (New York: Random House Vintage Books,
1970 edition), p. xv.
     Vernon Louis Parrington's Main Currents in American
Thought (New York: Harcourt, Brace, 1932) provided the
seemingly definitive documentation for such a view of the
American historical experience. Yet when Hofstadter came
to write his book in the late 1960's, Parrington's great
study no longer seemed so relevant or defensible. Although
primarily designed as literary history and criticism, Parrington's three volume survey of American thought contains
an ample amount of political and social analysis. His concern to give even relatively minor and neglected thinkers
their due commands respect; but the sparkling style, adept-
ness in personality portraiture, and always insightful literary evaluations which still make this a worthwhile contribution to cultural history have stood up less well as
an interpretive synthesis of American thought. The liberalism Parrington glorified has come on rather hard times
of late; the conservative currents he denigrated have experienced at least a modest revival. At a time when America's self-image and self-confidence have sustained shock
after shock, neither liberalism nor democracy appear to be
on quite such easy terms as appeared to be the case in an
age when the agrarian ideal still had visibility and was
not just a receding mirage. Ironically, the progressive
liberalism of Turner, Beard, and Parrington now seems downright conservative in its major value premises.
     It was another group of historians, spearheaded by
Louis Hartz and Daniel Boorstin, who exposed the inadequacy
of the Progressive version of liberalism on the grounds of
its having read too much ideological conflict into American
history and not enough consensus on basic values. Not democratic ideals, but unique environmental conditions, held
the key to an interpretation of the American mind and character. While Hartz was lamenting the reactionary underside
of traditional Lockean-Jeffersonian liberalism, Boorstin discovered "the genius of American politics" in the very same
consensual basis of a non-ideological continuity with European traditions and a unique historical experience. See
Louis Hartz, The Liberal Tradition in America (New York:

316

Harcourt, Brace & Co., 1955) and Daniel J. Boorstin, The Genius of American Politics (Chicago: University of Chicago Phoenix Press, 1959 paperback edition). Although Boorstin elevates institutions over ideas, and applauds the conservative roots of the liberal tradition in America, Hartz sees more harm than good in this development, for it resulted in a debased individualistic ethic which retarded needed social progress. In both instances, however, liberal assumptions are severely criticized and found wanting.

Actually, the real division between a conservative and liberal interpretation of history revolves around whether belief in some sort of progressive improvement in the human condition is affirmed or denied as a desiradatum. The conservative not only distrusts political and social change, for fear that it will weaken stability, continuity, and established institutional arrangements, but also accepts the essential irreversibility of hierarchy and inequality. The liberal, on the other hand, believes that the masses deserve a greater share of the national wealth than is usually available to them under existing power configurations and that only a governmental system more responsive to the needs of the less privileged many rather than the privileged few can and should be promoted. As Marion J. Morton has pointed out in her recent study, The Terrors of Ideological Politics: Liberal Historians in a Conservative Mood (Cleveland: The Press of Case Western Reserve University, 1972), one cannot really have it both ways. Either one has confidence in man's inherent capacity for rationality and the transforming power of ethical ideals or one takes irrationality as the norm and limits ethics to individual rather than social purposes. Applying this insight to the conservative-liberal dichotomy, one recognizes the fundamental disagreement between those historians who define democracy in reference to conservative or liberal values: "Progressive historians described the American past from the Revolution onward as a continuous struggle between economic interest groups—merchants versus farmers, rich versus poor, East versus West, debtors versus creditors. This conflict was headed ultimately and inevitably toward the progressive goal of a more genuinely participatory democracy, a goal based, first, on the belief that man as a rational, moral being was capable of self-government, and second, on the idea that economic equality was a precondition for equal political participation. These reformers, therefore, advocated government regulation of the economy in order to achieve economic justice. The Progressive tradition offered a corrective to free enterprise and strengthened the faltering faith in democracy." (p. 8)

2. The classic statement of this theme can be found in Louis Hartz, The Liberal Tradition in America, op. cit.: "There has never been a 'liberal movement' or a real 'liberal party' in America: we have only had the American Way of Life, a nationalist articulation of Locke, which usually does not know that Locke himself is involved..." (p. 11)

See also Samuel P. Huntington, The Soldier and the State: The Theory and Politics of Civil-Military Relations (New York:

Random House Vintage Books, 1970 edition): "Liberalism has always been the dominant ideology in the United States..." (p. 143)

See also Donald J. Devine, The Political Culture of the United States: The Influence of Member Values on Regime Maintenance (Boston: Little, Brown, 1972): "It is the contention of this work that a consensual political culture has existed in the United States, essentially unchanged, during its entire history (p. 47)...Stress in America has not been the result of conflict over the worth of the fundamental values but over their precise meaning and their relationship to each other. It appears that there has been relatively severe conflict in interpreting these values in every generation in American history. Indeed, the major conflicts seem to reduce to five—federalism; popular rule; the specific role of government in regard to property and its regulation; the nature of equality as applied to the Negro; and the interpretation of the necessities of national identiy as applied to foreign policy." (p. 364)

See also Raymond E. Wolfinger, Martin Shapiro, Fred I. Greenstein, Dynamics of American Politics (Englewood Cliffs, N.J.: Prentice-Hall, 1976): "The point here is that both those who think of themselves as liberals and those who think of themselves as conservative share a basic common ideology. This ideology derives from a specific historical body of thought that is commonly described as liberal because it emphasizes the rights of the individual against the powers of government." (p. 67)

For a sharp dissent from this "conventional wisdom" see Garry Wills, Inventing America: Jefferson's Declaration of Independence (New York: Doubleday & Co., 1978), wherein he argues brilliantly, based upon a close textual analysis and a fresh exploration of the 18th century intellectual background, that Lockean-Smithian individualism was a good deal less significant in shaping Thomas Jefferson's thought "than the Scottish school" which stressed fraternity and the social bond. (p. 238) Although one may grant Wills' main contention that Jeffersonian ideas as embodied in the Declaration and elsewhere have been grossly distorted and misrepresented, the fact still remains, perceptions and interpretations shape reality regardless of original intentions, and the "conventional wisdom" certainly supports this development.

3. See Zbigniew Brzezinski and Samuel P. Huntington, Political Power: USA/USSR (New York: The Viking Press, 1964): "In the United States, on the other hand, power and ideology seldom meet. Those who wield power are un-ideological or anti-ideological. Those who hold firmly to political principle or have definite ideologies rarely scale the heights of power. The two compete rather than reinforce each other as they do in the Soviet Union. The separation weakens each. Power divorced from ideology becomes dissolved in compromise. Ideilogy divorced from power degenerates into negative extremism." (p. 42)

4. A much quoted passage reinforcing this point is to

be found in Gunnar Myrdal, The American Dilemma: The Negro Problem and Modern Democracy (New York: Harper & Row, 1962 Twentieth Anniversary Edition): "But taking the broad historical view, the American creed has triumphed. It has given the main direction to change in this country. America has had gifted conservative statesmen and national leaders, and they have often determined the course of public affairs. But with few exceptions, only the liberals have gone down in history as national heroes. America is, as we shall point out, conservative in fundamental principles, and in much more than that, though hopefully experimentalistic in regard to much of the practical arrangements in society. But the principles conserved are liberal, and some, indeed, are radical." (p. 7)

See also William R. Brock, The Evolution of American Democracy (New York: The Dial Press, 1970): "There is a tendency to regard American history as a steady progress along the middle road, interrupted only by the tragedy of the Civil War. In reality, and throughout two centuries of national existence, there has been criticism and disquiet, and the illusion of agreement has been created by the paradox that the men most convinced of the essential justice of the American system have been the most dissatisfied with its practice. There has been consensus in accepting the revolutionary and constitutional heritage, but much argument about its meaning... Each generation has engaged in a discourse with the revolutionary traditions of American democracy, and history has been made by the outcome." (pp. 245-246)

5. See Daniel J. Boorstin, The Genius of American Politics, op. cit.: "The marvelous success and vitality of our institutions is equaled by the amazing poverty and inarticulateness of our theorizing about politics. No nation has ever believed more firmly that its political life was based on a perfect theory. And yet no nation has ever been less interested in political philosophy or produced less in the way of theory. If we can explain this paradox, we shall have a key to much that is characteristic—and much that is good—in our institutions." (p. 8)

See also Hans J. Morgenthau, The Purpose of American Politics (New York: Random House Vintage Books, 1964 edition): "What makes America unique among the nations is that it has achieved at least in a certain measure what other nations—by no means many—have aspired to. It has created a society that is still today radically different from the other societies of the modern world." (p. 34)

See also James P. Young, The Politics of Affluence: Ideology in the United States Since World War II (Scranton, Pa.: Chandler Publishing Co., 1968 paperback edition): "Thus both the conservative and the liberal traditions in America have common roots in a highly individualistic conception of the nature of society. They have differed largely over the means by which the individual is to be saved..." (p. 7)

6. See H. Mark Roelofs, Ideology and Myth in American Politics: A Critique of a National Political Mind (Boston: Little-Brown, 1976 paperback edition): "America's particular ideolog-

319

ical commitments are narrow, they lack key elements that
would encourage political adaptability and, above all, they
are largely and inherently unresponsive to elementary demands
of social justice..." (p. 37)

See also George C. Lodge, The New American Ideology (New
York: Alfred A. Knopf, 1975): "The significance of what I call
Lockeanism is that, particularly as practiced in America, this
ideology has tended to sever economic activities from their
political and social context, allowing economic ends to dominate. Political and social institutions have thus come to
be assigned the task of cleaning up the mess left in the wake
of economic undertakings." (p. 44)

See also Jonathan Schell, The Time of Illusion (New York:
Alfred A. Knopf, 1976). This is a devestating critique of the
Nixon Administration which underscores the way imagery and substance have become inverted so often in recent American politics: "The Nixon Administration was characterized by, among
other things, fragmentation. What the Nixon men thought was
unconnected to what they said. What they said was unconnected to what they did. What they did or said they were doing
was unconnected to what they did or said they were doing the
next moment. And when they were driven from office, they left
behind them not one but several unconnected records of themselves..." (p. 6)

See also Michael Parenti, Power and the Powerless (New
York: St. Martin's Press, 1978 paperback edition): "The traditional conservative view that social problems, by their
nature, have no solutions ('The poor shall always be with us')
allows little room for rational change. The modern scientist-
ic view that almost all problems are subject to solution by
rational investigation and manipulation seemingly allows all
the room in the world. Yet both views have certain things in
common: both avoid the political reality; both fail to draw
any link between the social problems of the have-nots and
their powerlessness, or more generally, between social problems and power distribution; both accept the existing politico-economic social order as an immutable given, operating
with neutral effect...One reason they fail to find solutions,
then, is that they are part of the problem." (p. 25)

7. See Theodore J. Lowi, The End of Liberalism: Ideology,
Policy, and the Crisis of Public Authority (New York: W.W.
Norton, 1969 paperback edition): "Even when the purpose of
the program is the uplifting of the underprivileged, the administrative arrangement favored by interest-group liberalism tends toward creation of new privilege instead..." (p. 90)

See also Robert Nisbet, The Twilight of Authority (New
York: Oxford University Press, 1975): "The once proud ideologies of liberalism, radicalism, and conservatism have dissipated themselves into often mindless devotions to this or
that individual, this or that issue, irrespective of the relation of either to any seriously held body of belief." (p. 49)

See also Robert Paul Wolff, The Poverty of Liberalism
(Boston: Beacon Press, 1968 paperback edition): "The most significant fact about the distribution of power in America is
not who makes such decisions as are made, but rather how many

320

matters of the greatest social importance are not objects of anyone's decision at all." (p. 118)

See also Robert Paul Wolff, Barrington Moore, Jr., and Herbert Marcuse, A Critique of Pure Tolerance (Boston: Beacon Press, 1969 paperback edition).

See also Alan Wolfe, The Limits of Legitimacy: Political Contradictions of Contemporary Capitalism (New York: The Free Press, 1977).

8. See Michael Parenti, Democracy for the Few (New York: St. Martin's Press, 1974 paperback edition): "The central theme here is that our government represents the privileged few rather than the needy many and that elections, political parties and the right to speak out are seldom effective measures against the influence of corporate wealth. The laws of our polity operate chiefly with undemocratic effect—first, because they are written principally to protect the haves against the claims of the have-nots and, second, because even if equitable in appearance, they usually are enforced in highly discriminatory ways." (p. 2)

See also Charles E. Lindblom, Politics and Markets: The World's Political-Economic Systems (New York: Basic Books, 1977): "In the polyarchies, it is widely believed that the trend is in the direction of income equality. If so, it is a slow movement, so slow that it is now being debated whether the movement has quietly expired in the last few decades, while the U.S.S.R., by contrast moves significantly toward more equality. In all the polyarchies a barrier to substantial equalization of income, if it were desired, is inequality in the distribution of wealth. Beyond some point wealth has to be collectivized or redistributed if more income equality is desired. The possibilities of further income redistribution or redistribution of wealth then turn not on technical features of market system but on polyarchal politics, especially on the constraints on popular control...In private enterprise systems, moves toward equality are a threat to a large and disproportionately influential segment of the population. Political obstacles to equalization are often much reduced in some authoritarian systems." (p. 273)

9. For an interesting survey of some leading conservative spokesmen in politics and economics who seem to be in the forefront of a revivified conservatism, see Gerald R. Rosen, "The New Conservative Idea Men," Dun's Review, April, 1976: "Conservatism is on the march again...Conservative views, pushed by a new generation of idea men, and some long-ignored, middle-aged intellectuals, are making a measurable impact on public policy." (p. 39)

See also Louis Rukeyser, "Capitalism Could be Coming Back," New York Daily News, August 9, 1978: "It's not only the increasingly undeniable worldwide evidence that the socialist alternative to capitalism is an economic and human flop: discouraging initiative, limiting production...and curbing individual freedom...Don't look now, but just possibly capitalism is coming back into style." (p. C16)

As for the "crisis of liberalism," see particularly the

following:

Arthur M. Schlesinger, Jr., The Crisis of Confidence:
Ideas, Power and Violence in America (Boston: Houghton Mifflin
Co., 1969): "The crisis of American confidence comes in part
from a growing sense of the dissociation between ideas and power. On the one hand, the spread of violence challenges the old
belief in the efficacy of reason; on the other, the new structures brought into existence by modern industrial society intensify the feelings of individual impotence. The great organizations which tower over us seem to have a life and momentum
of their own; they consume human beings and human ideas as
they consume steel and electricity. Above all, the accelerating pace of social and technological change heightens the impression of a world out of human control. We all today are
constrained to see ourselves as helpless victims of the vel-
ocity of history." (p. 53)

See also James MacGregor Burns, Uncommon Sense (New York:
Harper & Row, 1972): "Potentially, the most powerful instrument we have to control change...is the government. It is the
failure of government over the past century to anticipate and
manage the enormous social change of that century that most
directly lies at the source of our difficulties..." (pp. 7-8)

See also Peter F. Drucker, The Age of Discontinuity:
Guidelines to Our Changing Society (New York: Harper & Row,
1968): "Modern government has become ungovernable. There is
no government today that can still claim control of its bureaucracy and of its various agencies. Government agencies
are all becoming autonomous, ends in themselves, and directed
by their own desire for power, their own narrow vision rather
than by national policy and by their own boss, the national
government." (p. 220)

See also Christopher Lasch, The Agony of the American
Left (New York: Vintage Books, 1969): "It is clearer than ever
that radicalism is the only long-term hope for America. The
erosion of the liberal Center makes it difficult for liberals
to undertake even palliative reforms...The liberal values of
self-reliance, sexual self-discipline, ambition, acquisition,
and accomplishment, while often admirable in themselves, have
come to be embodied in a social order resting on imperialism,
elitism, racism, and inhuman acts of technological destruction.
They have therefore lost their capacity to serve as a guide to
any but individual conduct. As a social philosophy, liberalism is dead; and it cannot survive even as a private morality
unless it is integrated into a new moral and philosophical
synthesis beyond liberalism..." (pp. 208-210)

10. This, of course, is the great hope and promise of that
paragon of conservatism, William F. Buckley, Jr. See Up From
Liberalism (New Rochelle, N.Y.: Arlington House, 1968 revised
edition, originally published in 1959). Although he can be
critical of what passes for conservatism in America today, he
is also quite convinced that the only hope for improvement is
the displacement of a dominant liberalism by a dominant conservatism: "There is no commonly acknowledged conservative
position today...Yet there is to be found in contemporary

conservative literature both a total critique of liberalism, and compelling proposals for the reorientation of our thought." (p. xvii)

11. "The New Conservatism Versus American Traditions: Ideals, Institutions, and Responsibilities," in Varieties of Political Conservatism (ed.) by Matthew Holden, Jr. (Beverly Hills: Sage Publications, 1974), p. 48.

12. "The New Conservatives," New York Review of Books, February 5, 1976.

13. See Louis Hartz, The Liberal Tradition in America, op. cit., pp. 14-15.

See also the great classic study of the American character, Alexis de Tocqueville's Democracy in America (ed.) by J.P. Mayer (New York: Doubleday & Co Anchor Books, 1969 edition), and his opening statement: "No novelty in the United States struck me more vividly during my stay there than the equality of conditions." (p. 9)

See Irving Louis Horowitz, Ideology and Utopia in the United States 1956-1976 (New York: Oxford University Press, 1977 paperback): "Conservatism is a movement, an ideology, but it has no class to give it support. The middle classes— this is especially true in the United States—are liberal... All ideologies face dilemmas in America, but none more so than conservatism because it singularly makes a claim to political relevancy yet has no real claim or relevance. It must accept the framework set by a cosmopolitan liberalism...Historically, with the exception of its use by southern slaveholding class, the conservative philosophy has always played a secondary role in American thought." (pp. 133-161, "The New Conservatism in America," 1956 essay.

14. See Max Lerner, America as a Civilization: Life and Thought in the United States Today (New York: Simon and Schuster, 1957): "Unlike the Europeans, Americans have never turned traditionalism into a major political and social philosophy and a party movement." (p. 44)

See also David M. Potter, People of Plenty: Economic Abundance and the American Character (Chicago: University of Chicago Press Phoenix Books, 1954 edition): "Essentially, the difference is that Europe has always conceived of redistribution of wealth as necessitating the expropriation of some and the corresponding aggrandizement of others; but America has conceived of it primarily in terms of giving to some without taking from others." (p. 118)

See also Samuel P. Huntington, Political Order in Changing Societies (New Haven: Yale University Press, 1968 paperback edition): "In Europe the conservative is the defender of traditional institutions and values, particularly those in society rather than in government. Conservatism is associated with the church, the aristocracy, social customs, the established social order. The attitude of conservatives toward government is ambivalent: it is viewed as guarantor of social order; but it is also viewed as the generator of social change. Society rather than government has been the principal conservative concern. European liberals, on the other hand, have had a much more positive attitude toward government...In America, on the other hand, these liberal and conservative attitudes have been thoroughly confused and partly reversed. Conservatism has seldom flourished because it has lacked social institutions to conserve. Society is changing and modern, while government, which the conservative views with suspicion, has been relatively unchanging and antique...(pp. 32-33)

15. Samuel DuBois Cook, _Varieties of Political Conservatism_, _op. cit._, p. 49.

16. See John P. Diggins, _Up From Communism: Conservative Odyessys in American Intellectual History_ (New York: Harper & Row, 1974): "Ultimately what vitiates American conservatism is not so much a lack of unity as a lack of historical continuity. To be a conservative means to become aware of the historical dimension of knowledge, to nurture, revere, and defend those values and institutions that belong to the past. Knowledge of the American past, however, is precisely the paradox of American conservatism. The same problem of American 'exceptionalism' that confronted the Old Left in the thirties confronted the New Right in the fifties. For the same country that failed to produce a revolutionary proletariat failed to produce a conservative aristocracy. The Right, no less than the Left, must come to terms with the bourgeois ethos of Lockean individualism that resounds throughout American history like a choral fugue on the theme of liberal 'consensus.' Indeed, the dilemma is greater for the neo-conservative, for even while attacking contemporary liberalism and radicalism he is forced to defend America in terms of its liberal tradition." (p. 453)

17. _The Evolution of Liberalism_ (New York: Collier Books, 1963), p. 380.

18. See Michael Kammen, _People of Paradox: An Inquiry Concerning the Origins of American Civilization_ (New York: Alfred A. Knopf, 1973): "Once the Revolution had been reduced to a maudlin memory, politics in the United States turned moderately conservative—accompanied, nevertheless, by a liberal, progressive, popular ideology. Despite our behavioral conservatism in public affairs, however, we have never developed a sound and substantial tradition of conservative thought." (p. 252)

See also Seymour Martin Lipset and Earl Raab, _The Politics of Unreason_ (Harper & Row, 1970 paperback edition): "The genius of the American society is that it has legitimized ambiguity. The American ideology embraces contradictory values; the Constitution is a hot house of ambivalence; the political parties are amalgams of inconsistency. But these are not stains on America as much as they are the stains that have made America America." (p. 20)

19. Samuel P. Huntington, _The Soldier and the State_, _op. cit._, p. 145.

20. See Edgar Litt, _Democracy's Ordeal in America_ (Hins-

dale, Ill.: The Dryden Press, 1973), p. 55.

See also Michael Harrington, The Twilight of Capital-ism (New York: Simon & Schuster, 1976): "The preference for the unplanned, and even the irrational, as opposed to conscious government policy. This is a fundamental conservative theme, the nostalgia for the vanished Gemeinschaft, the suspicion of the contemporary Gesellschaft. From Burke to Dostoyevsky to Spengler it has been at the very center of conservative thought." (p. 290)

See also William Pfaff, "The Decline of Liberal Politics," Commentary, October, 1969, pp. 45-51.

See also Louis Hartz, The Founding of New Societies (New York: Harcourt, Brace & World Harbinger Book, 1964), especially Part One, "A Theory of the Development of New Societies."

21. See Doris Kearns, Lyndon Johnson and the American Dream (New York: Harper & Row, 1976): "Johnson's most trusted advisers on Vietnam, Robert McNamara and McGeorge Bundy, contended that step-by-step escalation would allow continuous monitoring of the reactions of China and Russia; it would emphasize America's limited objective; it might press Hanoi to negotiate in order to prevent the terrible damage which large-scale bombing would inflict. Johnson chose gradual escalation. It was a predictable choice, based, as it was, on the type of approach he found most congenial; limited bombing represented the moderate path between the competing extremes of widespread destruction and total withdrawal. Of course sometimes, as every automobile driver knows, the middle of the road is the most dangerous place to be." (p. 262)

22. See William T. Bluhm, Ideologies and Attitudes: Modern Political Culture (Englewood Cliffs, N.J.: Prentic-Hall, 1974 paperback edition): "We have described the leading ideals of a political culture marked by broad areas of historical agreement and cloven only by moderate ideological diversity and conflict." (p. 78) As the present study attempts to show, the over-emphasis upon the consensual character of American thought may not be altogether justified.

23. Kenneth M. Dolbeare and Patricia Dolbeare with Jane A. Hadley, American Ideologies: The Competing Political Beliefs of the 1970's (Chicago: Markham, 1973 paperback 2nd edition): "Conservatism has many problems in the United States, not least of which is that of gaining a fair hearing. On many occasions, its principles are seized upon by reactionaries or by others who seek merely to defend a particular status quo that happens to serve them well at the moment. Without adopting its values or goals, and certainly without following its consistent principles or even appreciating its real qualities, those who so use conservatism as a rallying point do it a major disservice. But its principles themselves do lend themselves to this use and contribute to this effect because they run contrary to the mainstream of American egalitarianism, majoritarianism, and idealism." (p. 107)

24. See Donald Atwell Zoll, <u>Twentieth Century Political Philosophy</u> (Englewood Cliffs, N.J.: Prentice-Hall, 1974 paperback edition): "The main impact of twentieth century conservatism has been its opposition to the growth of popular democracy. The primary attack mounted by traditional conservatives has been ethical in nature: the accusation that popular democracy is possible, but not desirable, because it debauches moral values. The cardinal faults of popular democracy are seen as moral relativism, licentiousness, mediocrity, and egocentricity." (p. 131)

See William A. Rusher, "Letters from Readers," <u>Commentary</u>, May, 1977: "I...believe that conservatism can constitute a united and fully effective majority in contemporary America only if the 'social conservatives' (many of them former Democrats) can be effectively allied with the 'economic conservatives' (most of whom are presently Republicans) in a new political vehicle reflecting, as any major party in this country must, not only broad areas of agreement but others on which compromise will be required." (p. 16)

25. <u>The Promise of Politics</u> (Englewood Cliffs, N.J.: Prentice-Hall, 1966 paperback edition), p. 91.

26. <u>The Poverty of Liberalism</u>, <u>op</u>. <u>cit</u>., p. 118

27. <u>The End of Liberalism</u>, <u>op</u>. <u>cit</u>., p. 18.

28. See Jeanne Kirkpatrick, <u>Commentary</u>, May, 1977, "Letters from Readers" section, in reply to criticisms of a recent article she wrote for <u>Commentary</u>, Jeanne Kirkpatrick made this telling point: "The Goldwater, McCarthy, McGovern, Wallace and Reagan campaigns illustrate how an effective candidate can mobilize issue-enthusiasts to support a candidate-centered rather than a party-centered campaign, and more impressive still, President Carter's pre-convention campaign demonstrated how an 'outsider' could mobilize support and win his party's nomination <u>without</u> an issue or an issue constituency. But it is worth noting once again that though McCarthy, McGovern, Wallace, Goldwater and Reagan were able to muster intense support among a minority of voters, no candidacy based on a relatively narrow ideological appeal has so far won the support of a majority of the electorate." (p. 25)

29. "Conservatism as an Ideology," <u>The American Political Science Review</u>, vol. LI, No. 2, June, 1957, p. 457.

30. See Reo M. Christenson, Alan S. Engel, Dan N. Jacobs, Mostafa Rejai and Herbert Waltzer, <u>Ideologies and Modern Politics</u>, 2nd edition (New York: Dodd, Mead & Co., 1975 paperback edition): "Political ideology is a belief system that explains and justifies a preferred political order for society, either existing or proposed, and offers a strategy (processes, institutions, programs) for its attainment. Political ideology includes a set of basic propositions, both normative and empirical, about human nature and society which in turn serve to explain and judge the human condition and to guide the development of or preserve a preferred political order. An ideology offers an interpretation of the past, an explanation of the present, and a vision of the future. Its

principles set forth the purposes, organization, and boundaries of political life and power." (p. 6)

31. See H.M. Drucker, The Political Uses of Ideology (New York: Barnes & Noble, 1974)" "Taken strictly, Conservatives would deny that they have a picture of an ideal political world. Such pictures strike them as suspiciously ideological. All the same, there is a deeper level at which they do have an ideal, and this ideal gives them a model against which to hold the present ideology-intoxicated world." (p. 121)

32. "Conservatism," The Annals, vol. 344, November, 1962, p. 14.

33. See Eric F. Goldman, "The Liberals, the Blacks, and the War," The New York Times Magazine, November 30, 1969: "Through all the ups and downs in the long history of American liberalism, its bedrock strength has been its moral authority...But the performance of many liberals on the issues of the black revolution and the Vietnam war has permitted the left and the right to mount a criticism which adds up to a challenge to this very moral authority..."
See also William V. Shannon, "Liberalism Old and New," The New York Times, October 2, 1976: "The nation only turns to liberalism when it wants major social problems solved, whether the problem is mass unemployment in the 1930's or racial equality in the 1960's. But if liberalism is discredited as well as radicalism and conservatism, then the society is adrift. The renewal of liberalism is therefore essential if the nation is to confront its social problems. What is in doubt about liberalism is not its good intentions but its competence." (p. C25)

34. See Aaron Wildavsky, "Government and the People," Commentary, August, 1973: "...My thesis is that the problems being allocated to government are not just a random sample of those ordinarily associated with governing, some of which, at least, are eminently soluble, given hard work and good judgment, but that government is increasingly getting a skewed distribution of problems that are insoluble precisely because people demand of government what government cannot do." (p. 32)

35. See news item, "More Conservatives Share Liberal Views," The New York Times, January 22, 1978: "At a time when the American people are thinking of themselves as increasingly conservative, and when a political shift to the right is widely perceived, a look beneath the surface at political attitudes discloses a landscape dotted with Americans who do not use the words and concepts of politics the way the experts do. In the latest quarterly New York Times/CBS News poll of political attitudes taken earlier this month it was found that most self-styled conservatives are as ready to accept bread and butter concepts like jobs for all who want them as are self-styled liberals..."
See also Amitai Etzioni, "Societal Overload," Political Science Quarterly, Winter 1977-78, vol. 92, pp. 607-

631: "Americans have difficulty reaching a consensus in part
because millions are philosophically conservative yet pro-
grammatically liberal..." (p. 611)
    See also Wolfinger, Shapiro, Greenstein, Dynamics of Am-
erican Politics, op. cit., p. 81: "...Both the liberal and
the conservative believe in individual rights. This is why
we remarked earlier that Americans are fundamentally liberal
regardless of their political persuasion. Both sides want to
protect the liberties of the individual citizen. But each
sees the threats to individual liberties as coming from a
different direction, and therefore each adopts a different
strategy aimed at what is essentially the same end. Those
we call liberals typically want the government to aid the
needy, control the powerful, and leave free the critics and
nonconformists. Those we call conservatives typically want
the government to aid business enterprise, control those who
threaten the good order of society, and leave free the business and professional leaders whom they see as contributing
most to our prosperity."
    See also Henry Fairlie, "The Mobile Home of Republican-
ism," The New Republic, September 4, 1976, pp. 21-28: "One of
the weaknesses of the conservative position is that it rests
on the belief that there are unnumbered—but enough—conservatives 'out there' who are just waiting to vote if they are
given what Goldwater called an 'alternative.' But this is
untrue. Every election study and statistic emphasizes that
it is the Republicans—and especially the conservatives—who
are most likely to go to the polls. They are better educated, have more time..." (p. 21)
    See also Peter P. Witowski, "A Place for All," in a re-
view of Andrew Gamble's A Conservative Nation (London: Rut-
ledge & Kegan Paul, 1974), The New Republic, March 8, 1975,
pp. 26-28: "One can also say, among other things, that conservatives are—for all their differences—generally ideologies of crisis and opposition. They are reaction ideologies that respond to the crises engendered by opposing both
the change and the forces that brought it about in the first
place. Therefore, there can be no real conservatism in relatively calm and happy times."
    See also Paul H. Weaver, "Do the American People Know
What They Want," Commentary, December, 1977, pp. 62-67: "Or
consider, as another example, the much heralded, long await-
ed new 'conservatism' that now is said finally to have aris-
en in the electorate. Today, more than twice as many Americans identify themselves as 'conservatives' as identifiy
thenselves as 'liberals.' And on the surface, at least,
these numbers would indeed seem to portend a major shift toward the Right. Yet a closer inspection suggests that what
they demonstrate is not so much a resurgence of conservatism
as an upwelling of confusion. For the self identified conservatives, though they narrowly preferred Gerald Ford to
Jimmy Carter in the 1976 presidential election, identify
more with the Democratic party than with the Republicans...
(p. 63)
    36. (New York: Basic Books, 1971), p. 65.

37. (Princeton, J.J.: Princeton University Press, 1973 paperback edition), p. 191.

38. (New Haven: Yale University Press, 1977).

39. "The Death of Liberalism," _Playboy_ magazine, April, 1977, pp. 99-122 and pp. 246-253, with the quotation from p. 99.
     See also Jack Newfield, _A Prophetic Minority_ (New York: The New American Library, 1966).

40. _Ideology and Utopia in the United States_, _op. cit._, p. 8.

41. "Liberalism According to Galbraith," _Commentary_, October, 1967, pp. 77-87, quotation from p. 77.

42. "The Decline of Liberal Politics," _Commentary_, October, 1969, pp. 45-51.

43. (New York: Bantam Books, 1975).

44. _Toward a Planned Society: From Roosevelt to Nixon_ (New York: Oxford University Press, 1977 paperback edition), pp. 296-297.

45. _The New York Times_, December 28, 1975, "Michigan Senator and His Wife See Liberalism Faded."

46. _Crooked Paths: Reflections on Socialism, Conservatism and the Welfare State_ (New York: Harper & Row, 1977), p. 81.

47. See Arthur A. Ekirch, Jr., _Ideologies and Utopias: The Impact of the New Deal on American Thought_ (Chicago: Quadrangle Books, 1969 paperback edition): "Clearly Roosevelt, in pursuing a middle way, was able at once to preserve capitalism and at the same time disarm both its revolutionary and reactionary critics." (p. 104)
     See also John D. Buenker, _Urban Liberalism and Progressive Reform_ (New York: W.W. Norton & Co., 1978 paperback edition): "The inauguration of the national welfare state during the New Deal Era was not a sudden departure from the nation's past history. The programs it embodied were essentially a broadening of those that had been developed in most of the industrial states during the Progressive Era..." (p. 42)

48. (Caldwell, Idaho: The Caxton Printers, 1959).

49. (Chicago: Henry Regnery Co., Gateway Editions, 1969).

50. (New York: Van Nostrand Co., 1959).

51. "Letter from Washington," _The New Yorker_, July 18, 1970, pp. 72-80.

52. _Ibid._

53. See chapter 7 of this book.

54. Irving Louis Horowitz, _Ideology and Utopia in the United States_, _op. cit._, p. 149.

55. See Dsvid Caute, <u>The Great Fear: The Anti-Communist Purge Under Truman and Eisenhower</u> (New York: Simon & Schuster, 1978).

56. See Otis L. Graham, Jr., <u>Toward a Planned Society</u>, <u>op. cit.</u>: "For in the end he presided over a more rapid evolution toward Planning than any other president since FDR. Perhaps Nixon himself would be surprised to see these actions summarized: encouragement to national growth policy, encouragement to population policy including appointment of a population commission, establishment of a national goals research staff with suggestions that it become a base for social reporting, a proposed reorganization of executive agencies by function, establishment of the Domestic Council for integrated policy consideration, support for national land use policy, and a dozen lesser actions to encourage forecasting and long range projections. These are the building blocks of the planning modes, and if pursued far enough, must lead to comprehensive planning." (p. 256)

57. See Ann Crittenden, "The Economic Wind's Blowing Toward the Right—for Now," <u>The New York Times</u>, Sunday, July 16, 1978, section 3: "The prevailing wind in economic thinking is clearly blowing from the right. After a long post-war period characterized by a liberal, Keynesian consensus that government can and should be used to correct the imperfections of the market system, the critics of government intervention in the economy now dominate the intellectual debate."

58. (New York: Macmillan Co., 1973).

59. <u>Ibid.</u>, p. 40.

60. <u>Ibid.</u>, p. 93.

61. <u>Ibid.</u>, p. 116.

62. <u>Ibid.</u>, p. 117.

63. <u>Ibid.</u>, p. 167.

64. <u>Ibid.</u>, p. 308: "In the deepest sense, then, the libertarian doctrine is not utopian but eminently realistic, because it is the only theory that is really consistent with the nature of man and the world."

65. (New York: McGraw Hill & Readers Digest Press).

66. <u>Ibid.</u>, p. 41.

67. He notes, for instance, the following: "It is only fair to say that it was not entirely the fault of the Congressmen that I finally grew allergic to them. There is something distinctly abnormal about have to testify so frequently, on the same subjects, and often in the same words before small, competitive groups of politicians. By my count, the number of such Capitol Hill appearances was close to 400... Most of these hearings were an abysmal waste of time." <u>Ibid.</u>, p. 2.

68. <u>Ibid.</u>, p. 73.

69. Ibid., p. 75.

70. Ibid., p. 111 and p. 123

71. Ibid., pp. 126-180

72. (New York: Basic Books, 1978).

73. Ibid., p. 15.

74. Ibid., p. 167.

75. Ibid., p. 243.

76. Ibid., p. 269.

77. See "Understanding the 'New Conservatives,'" Polity, vol. X, No. 2, Winter, 1977, pp. 261-273; quotation is from p. 262.
For an opposite view, see Robert Shrum, "The Neo-Conservative Cop-out," New Times, December 9, 1977, pp. 16-16: "The Neo-Conservative analysis of the Great Society is half-right. It was indeed a case of overpromising—but the underperforming was primarily a matter of underfunding...The presumed failure of liberal government has an effect, and a purpose...It tends to allow private, corporate interests a freer hand." (p. 16)

78. "Is America Turning Right," November 7, 1977, pp. 34-44; quotation from p. 42.

79. "The Neo-Conservatives," Partisan Review, vol. XLIV, No. 3, 1977, pp. 431-437; quotation from p. 432.

80. See Impeachment: The Constitutional Problems (New York: Bantam Books, 1973); Executive Privilege: A Constitutional Right (New York: Bantam Books, 1975); Congress v. The Supreme Court (New York: Bantam Books, 1975).

81. See Walter Berns, The First Amendment and the Future of American Democracy (New York: Basic Books, 1976), pp. 232-233.

82. See Ronald Dworkin, Taking Rights Seriously (Cambridge: Harvard University Press, 1977).

83. Government by Judiciary: The Transformation of the Fourteenth Amendment (Cambridge: Harvard University Press, 1977).

84. See Raoul Berger, "Academe vs. The Founding Fathers," National Review, April 14, 1978, pp. 468-471.

85. Ibid., p. 471.

86. Raoul Berger, Government by Judiciary, op. cit., p. 214.

87. Ibid., p. 296.

88. Ibid., p. 315.

89. "The Chains of the Constitution," Commentary, December, 1977, pp. 84-86; quotation from p. 86.

Chapter 2

1. See Rossiter, Conservatism in America, op. cit.:
"The American political mind has been a liberal mind, for
change and progress have been the American way of life.
The American political tradition is basically a liberal tradition, an avowedly optimistic, idealistic, even lighthearted
way of thinking about man and government. It is stamped with
the mighty name and spirit of Thomas Jefferson, and its articles of faith, a sort of American Holy Writ, are meliorism,
progress, liberty, equality, democracy, and individualism."
(pp. 69-71)
Yet the triumph of liberalism has often been the opposite of what it was supposed to be. See Merrill D. Peterson,
The Jefferson Image in the American Mind (New York: Oxford
University Press, 1960): "As the light falls on Jefferson,
he appears less radical and more conservative, less theoretical and more practical, less universal and more national."
(p. 450)
For a study which deplores the weakening of this liberal tradition resulting from the contemporary trend toward
collectivism and centralization of power in the United States,
see Arthur A. Ekirch, Jr., The Decline of American Liberalism (New York: Longmans, Gree & Co., 1955).
For another critical view of this thesis see David E.
Price, "Community and Control: Critical Democratic Theory
in the Progressive Period," The American Political Science
Review, vol. LXVIII, No. 4, December, 1974: "Louis Hartz and
other historians have too often maintained their monolithic
portrayal of America's liberal tradition by ignoring the
communitarian strains in Progressive political theory."
(p. 1673)
See also Everett Carll Ladd, Jr., and Seymour Martin
Lipset, The Divided Academy: Professors & Politics (New York:
McGraw Hill, 1975): "The basic record would seem to sustain
Richard Hofstadter's generalization that for almost all of
the past century, the political weight of American intellectuals, including leading academics, has been disproportionately on the progressive, liberal, and leftist side...This
bias, to a considerable extent, reflects the absence or
weakness of a legitimate national conservative tradition in
America. National identity and national ideology are linked
to a value system, stemming from an elaboration of those
principles enunciated in the Declaration of Independence,
that emphasizes egalitarianism and populism..." (p. 15)

2. See Bernard Sternsher, Consensus, Conflict and American Historians (Bloomington: Indiana University Press, 1975):
"A main theme in consensus historiography is that essential
ideological conformity emerged in American politics sometime
between 1776 and 1840, and that the development of widespread
conformity in political thought soon became evident in political behavior." (p. 19)
See also Morton, The Terrors of Ideological Politics,

op. cit., p. 141.

3. See Gordon S. Wood, The Creation of the American Republic 1776-1787 (Chapel Hill: University of North Carolina Press, 1969): "In 1776 the solution to the problem of American politics seemed to rest not so much in emphasizing the private rights of individuals against the general will as it did in stressing the public rights of collective people against the supposed privileged interests of their rulers." (p. 61)
See also Donald S. Lutz, "Bernard Bailyn, Gordon S. Wood, and Whig Political Theory," The Political Science Reviewer, Vol. VII, Fall, 1977, pp. 110-144.
See also A.J. Beitzinger, A History of American Political Thought (New York: Dodd, Mead & Co., 1972), p. 3.
See also David W. Minar, Ideas and Politics: The American Experience (Homewood, Ill.: The Dorsey Press, 1964), p. 147.
See also Paul K. Conkin, Self Evident Truths: Being a Discourse on the Origins and Development of the First Principles of American Government—Popular Sovereignty, Natural Rights, and Balance & Separation of Powers (Bloomington: Indiana University Press, 1974), p. 159.

4. See Henry Bamford Parkes, The American Experience: An Interpretation of the History and Civilization of the American People (New York: Vintage Books, 1959 edition), pp. 120-121.

5. See the masterful four-volume biography of Washington by James Thomas Flexner: George Washington: Forge of Experience 1732-1775 (Boston: Little, Brown, 1965); George Washington: In the American Revolution 1775-1793 (Boston: Little, Brown, 1967); George Washington: And the New Nation 1783-1793 (Boston: Little, Brown, 1969); George Washington Anguish and Farewell 1793-1799 (Boston: Little, Brown, 1972).

6. See Charles Francis Adams (ed.), The Works of John Adams, vol. IV (Boston: Little, Brown, 1851).
See also John R. Howe, Jr., The Changing Political Thought of John Adams (Princeton, J.J.: Princeton University Press, 1966 paperback edition), p. 90.
See also Peter Shaw, The Character of John Adams (Chapel Hill: University of North Carolina Press, 1976), p. 216.

7. See Jacob E. Cooke, (ed.) The Reports of Alexander Hamilton (New York: Harper Torchbooks, 1974).
See also Alexander Hamilton, John Jay and James Madison, The Federalist (New York: The Modern Library, 1937 edition).
See also Broadus Mitchell, Alexander Hamilton: A Concise Biography (New York: Oxford University Press, 1976).
See also John C. Miller, Alexander Hamilton & The Growth of the New Nation (New York: Harper Torchbooks, 1959).

8. See Linda K. Kerber, Federalists in Dissent: Imagery and Ideology in Jeffersonian America (Ithaca: Cornell University Press, 1970), p. 4.

333

9. See Richard Hofstadter, The Idea of a Party System: The Rise of Legitimate Opposition in the United States, 1780-1840 (Berkeley-Los Angeles: University of California Press, 1969), p. xi.

There is a tendency among many later historians, however, to mute the conflict aspect of ideological differences during this period of nation-building. See Marcus Cunliffe, The Nation Takes Shape 1789-1837 (Chicago: University of Chicago Press, 1967 paperback edition, originally published in 1959), p. 161.

See also Carl N. Degler, Out of Our Past: The Forces That Shaped Modern America (New York: Harper Colophon Books, 1962 edition, originally published in 1959), p. 94.

See also Clinton Rossiter, The American Quest 1790-1860: An Emerging Nation in Search of Identity, Unity, and Modernity (New York: Harcourt, Brace, Jovanovich, 1971), p. 123.

10. See Leonard W. Levy, Judgments: Essays on American Constitutional History (Chicago: Quadrangle Books, 1972) and Leonard W. Levy, Jefferson and Civil Liberties: The Darker Side (New York: Quadrangle Books, 1973 paperback edition).

11. See Samuel J. Konefsky, John Marshall and Alexander Hamilton: Architects of the American Constitution (New York: The Macmillan Co., 1964), p. 21.

12. See Rush Welter, The Mind of America 1820-1860 (New York: Columbia University Press, 1975), p. 6.

13. See David Hackett Fischer, The Revolution of American Conservatism: The Federalist Party in the Era of Jeffersonian Democracy (New York: Harper Torchbooks, 1965 paperback edition), p. 180.

See also Donald L. Robinson, Slavery in the Structure of American Politics 1765-1820 (New York: Harcourt, Brace, Jovanovich, 1971), p. 429.

14. See Michael Paul Rogin, Fathers and Children: Andrew Jackson and the Subjugation of the American Indian (New York: Alfred A. Knopf, 1975), p. 4.

15. See the essays which re-evaluate the Turner Thesis in Richard Hofstadter and Seymour Martin Lipset (eds.) Turner and the Sociology of the Frontier (New York: Basic Books, 1968).

See also Thomas L. Hartshorne, The Distorted Image: Changing Conceptions of the American Character Since Turner (Cleveland: The Press of Case Western Reserve University, 1968), p. 192.

See also Robert H. Wiebe, The Segmented Society: An Introduction to the Meaning of America (New York: Oxford University Press, 1975), p. 176.

16. See I'll Take My Stand: The South and the Agrarian Tradition by Twelve Southerners (New York: Harper Torchbook, 1962 edition, originally published in 1930).

17. See Harry V. Jaffa, The Conditions of Freedom: Essays

in Political Philosophy (Baltimore: The Johns Hopkins University Press, 1975).

18. See Robert Green McCloskey, American Conservatism in the Age of Enterprise 1865-1910 (New York: Harper Torchbooks, 1964 edition, originally published in 1951), p. 169.

19. See Sidney Fine, Laissez Faire and the General-Welfare State: A Study of Conflict in American Thought 1865-1901 (Ann Arbor: The University of Michigan Press, 1966 paperback edition; originally published in 1956), p. 29.
   See also Richard Hofstadter, Social Darwinism in American Thought (1860-1915) (Philadelphia: University of Pennsylvania Press, 1945), p. 174).
   See also Paul F. Boller, Jr., American Thought in Transition: The Impact of Evolutionary Naturalism 1865-1900 (Chicago: Rand McNally & Co., 1969 paperback edition), p. 200.

20. The Education of Henry Adams: An Autobiography (Boston: Houghton Mifflin Co., Sentry Edition, 1961).

21. See Everett Carll Ladd, Jr. and Charles D. Hadley, Transformation of the American Party System: Political Coalitions from the New Deal to the 1970s (New York: W.W. Norton Co., 1975), p. 89.

22. See Stephen J. Tonsor, "The Second Spring of American Conservatism" National Review, September 30, 1977, pp. 1103-1107: "Conservative intellectuals are particularly well-placed to exert their influence in the search for order and community. They are virtually the only political theorists of any importance today. Increasingly, they are playing an important role in the fields of sociology and law. In theology there has been a swing away from the pop-theology and the social gospelism of the Sixties to a concentration on traditional questions pursued by conventional methods. In the natural sciences, ethology and socio-biology have opened up important new areas of knowledge which are of the utmost importance to conservative social theory." (p. 1106)

23. See Lloyd A. Free and Hadley Cantril, The Political Beliefs of Americans: A Study of Public Opinion (New York: Simon & Schuster Clarion Book, 1968), pp. 5-6.
   See also William H. Form and Joan Huber, "Income, Race, and the Ideology of Political Efficacy," Journal of Politics, August, 1971, pp. 661-662.
   See also Gerald Pomper, Voters' Choice: Varieties of American Electoral Behavior (New York: Dodd, Mead & Co., 1975 paperback edition), pp. 109-110.

24. A good indication of the growing interest in this approach can be found in almost any issue of The Public Interest and Commentary magazine. See chapter 7 of this book for an analysis of some leading exponents of this approach to ideology and policy.

25. See Robert E. Lane, Political Ideology: Why the American Common Man Believes What He Does (New York: The Free Press, 1962), p. 60.

26. Huntington, "Conservatism as an Ideology," op. cit., has presented the following as the common elements of the conservative creed, but I think many conservatives would have difficulty accepting (1) and (4):

"(1) Man is basically a religious animal, and religion is the foundation of civil society. A divine sanction infuses the legitimate, existing, social order.

"(2) Society is the natural, organic product of slow historical growth. Existing institutions embody the wisdom of existing institutions. Right is a function of time.

"(3) Man is a creation of instinct and emotion as well as reason. Prudence, prejudice, experience, and habit are better guides than reason, logic, abstractions, and metaphysics. Truth exists not in universal propositions but in concrete experience.

"(4) The community is superior to the individual. The rights of man derive from their duties. Evil is rooted in human nature, not in any particular social institutions.

"(5) Except in an ultimate moral sense, men are unequal. Social organization is complex and always includes a variety of classes, orders, and groups. Differentiation, hierarchy, and leadership are the inevitable characteristics of any civil society.

"(6) A presumption exists 'in favor of any settled scheme of government against any untried project.' Man's hopes are high, but his vision is short. Efforts to remedy existing evils usually result in even greater ones." (p. 456)

27. See Robert Mangabeira Unger, Knowledge and Politics (New York: The Free Press, 1975): "The liberal doctrine fails to provide a coherent view of knowledge, personality, and society (p. 192)...Thus, the separation between self and the world is the tie that unites liberal theory, the dominant consciousness of the liberal state, and its characteristic type of organization. It is the approach to life they share, the principle of common meaning that joins them together, and the source of both their power and their weakness." (p. 229)

28. Huntington, "Conservatism as an Ideology," op. cit. For example, Huntington calls conservatism a 'positional ideology,' since it does not reflect "the continuing interests and needs of a particular social group." (p. 468) He goes on to make this interesting point: "Conservatism develops to meet a specific historical need. When the need disappears, the conservative philosophy subsides. In each case, the articulation of conservatism is a response to a specific social situation. The manifestation of conservatism at any one time and place has little connection with its manifestation at any other time and place. Conservatism thus reflects no permanent group interest...Consequently, the conservative ideology is not developed and transmitted with alterations, elaborations, and revision from one age to the next. Nor does it

have a set of basic writings to be annotated, interpreted, and argued over by contending sets of disciples...The substance of conservatism is essentially static." (pp. 468-469)

In a sense, this study is an effort to refute this interpretation of conservatism and stress the continuity, rather than discontinuity aspects, of conservative political and social thought, especially in America. Policy preferences may change, but not so the basic conservative value structure.

29. See Suzannah Lessard, "The Real Conservatism," in Readings in American Government 76/77 (Guilford, Ct.: The Dushkin Publishing Group, Inc., 1976), p. 22.

See also Ralph P. Hummel, The Bureaucratic Experience (New York: St. Martin's Press, 1977 paperback edition): "What characterizes the apolitics of bureaucracy is not only that decisions made on behalf of the public are no longer open to participation by the public, but that these decisions are enforced by a new form of power. Traditional political power rests at least minimally on the citizen's belief that orders given by government are just and proper because they were arrived at through just and proper means, generally approved by the citizenry. Political power of this sort rested on legitimacy; it was authority. The power of enforcing bureaucratic decisions, however, rests ultimately on the psychological dependency of subordinates and on the system at large. Such power is the power of psychological coercion, resting not on ideas, but on mere survival impulse. Just as bureaucracy reduces citizens to functionaries, it reduces authority to force." (pp. 166=167)

30. See Thomas A. Spragens, Jr., Understanding Political Theory (New York: St. Martin's Press, 1976 paperback edition): "The strength of the conservative theorist is his 'realism.' His careful grounding in the concrete experience of the past protects him against falling prey to utopian delusions. Because he relies upon the resources of tradition, the possibilities that he envisions are in fact possible. The corresponding weakness of this approach to political theory is its susceptibility to stagnation and reaction. The conservative theorist may tie his view of the possible too closely to the contingent features of the past. He may not be able to see the new possibilities—or even new necessities—that changing historical circumstances open up." (pp. 87-88)

31. See Stuart Hampshire, "The Conservative Dilemma," The New York Review of Books, February 24, 1972, pp. 23-25: "The Burkean belief that a just social order with its inherited degrees and subordinations reflects a deeper natural order can scarcely have much hold in a freely competitive and socially mobile capitalism. On the contrary, the conservative philosophy of a society which has not been preoccupied with legitimacy and which has had no aristocracy, as in the United States, will rather stress that inequality is the natural result of competition, and will try to justify the inequalities by a strictly utilitarian argument: that is, that the social order ought to be an efficient instrument for maximizing welfare and happiness; and justice and

337

fairness in distribution ought to be no more than useful means to this end. Thus it is argued by conservatives in the U.S. that over-all economic growth has been worth its costs in inequality and injustices."

32. See Gerald Kent Hikel, <u>Beyond the Polls: Political Ideology and Its Correlates</u> (Lexington, Mass.: D.C. Heath & Co. Lexington Books, 1973): "Reanalysis of Survey Research Center data, however, suggest that there is indeed a liberalism-conservatism dimension underlying, and cutting across, issue areas, and La Ponce's success in using this dimension with college samples suggests that it is indeed meaningful, at least to educated subgroups. Moreover, Rice's earlier research indicates that for educated populations the distribution of this dimension may indeed be bell shaped." (p. 4)

See also Michael Novak, <u>Choosing Our King: Powerful Symbols in Presidential Politics</u> (New York: Macmillan Co., 1974): "Being a liberal rather than a conservative is not like belonging to a church. But it is like living within a different sense of reality, living out a different story with one's life, responding to a different set of symbols. Being a liberal or a conservative—or radical—is not merely a matter of having different facts at hand or of holding different moral principles. One's whole imagaination, person, life-project are involved. It is more like cherishing a different understanding of the nation and the self." (p. 17)

Chapter 3

1. See the many essays in Gordon J. DiRenzo, (ed.) Personality and Politics (Garden City, N.Y.: Doubleday Anchor
Books, 1974): "...only a few modern scholars seem willing
to entertain the hypothesis that political behavior is a
function, at least in part, of the personality of its
agents." (p. 4)
    See Milton Rokeach, The Nature of Human Values (New
York: The Free Press, 1973): "(The data) suggest that the
liberalism-conservatism dimension in American politics is
really an equality dimension: the major ideological differences evident in American politics are reducible to variations in one value alone—equality—rather than in two values. What seems to be missing from the recent American
scene are political groupings large enough to support viable political candidates for the presidency who place a
low value on freedom." (p. 181)

2. See Peter L. Berger, Pyramids of Sacrifice: Political Ethics and Social Change (New York: Basic Books, 1974:
"...it is safe to assume that the old optimism and self-
confidence have been disturbed even among large groups who
never felt that the country was in desparate crisis...What
it spells is, precisely, the 'loss of innocence.' Even in
these groups one may speak of a crisis of the 'American
creed.'" (p. 203)

3. See Richard J. Whalen, Taking Sides: A Personal
View of America from Kennedy to Nixon to Kennedy (Boston:
Houghton Mifflin Co., 1974): "The conservatives have not
yet evolved anything resembling a coherent, systematic program for implementing their avowed principles." (p. 124)

4. See Barry Holden, The Nature of Democracy (New York:
Barnes & Noble, 1974), pp. 231-232.

5. See Nisbet, Twilight of Authority, op. cit.: "Politics in our era has become as nearly devoid of genuinely
ideological divisions as is possible to conveive." (p. 47)

6. See Harold L. Wilensky, The Welfare State and Equality: Structural and Ideological Roots of Public Expenditures
(Berkeley: University of California Press, 1975 paperback
edition): "The welfare state is a major structural tendency
of modern society. With economic growth all countries develop similar social security programs. Whatever their economic or political system, whatever the ideologies of elites
or masses, the rich countries converge in types of health
and welfare programs, in increasingly comprehensive coverage,
and, to a lesser extent, in methods of financing. The frac-
tion of national resources devoted to these programs climbs,
eventually at a decelerating rate." (p. 86)
    See also Henry Steele Commager, The American Mind: An
Interpretation of American Thought and Character Since the
1880's (New Haven: Yale University Press, 1950), p. 41.

7. See The Crisis of Democratic Theory: Scientific Naturalism and the Problem of Value (Lexington: The University of Kentucky Press, 1973).

8. Ibid., p. 5.

9. See Morton White, Social Thought in America: The Revolt Against Formalism (Boston: Beacon Press, 1964 paperback edition, originally published in 1949): "The movements of thought with which we shall be most concerned cannot be fully understood without some sense of their relation to the ideas which dominated the nineteenth century. That century transcended the eighteenth through its concern with change, process, history, and culture. It was the century of history, evolutionary biology, psychology and sociology, historical jurisprudence and economics; the century of Comte, Darwin, Hegel, Marx, and Spencer. It is not surprising, therefore, to find American intellectuals ranging themselves, in the eighteen-nineties, against formalism, since they had been convinced that logic, abstraction, deduction, mathematics and mechanics were inadequate to social research and incapable of containing the rich, moving, living current of social life..." (p. 11)
See Harrington, The Twilight of Capitalism, op. cit.: "Capitalism, it has been shown, is outrageously unjust; it requires a continuing maldistribtuion of wealth in order to exist. But more than that, it is also self-destructive. This is why we live in the twilight of an epoch, one that has lasted more than four centuries." (p. 320)

10. See John Dewey, Liberalism and Social Action (New York: Capricorn Books, 1963 edition, originally published in 1935): "But the majority who call themselves liberals today are committed to the principle that organized society must use its powers to establish the conditions under which the mass of individuals can possess actual as distinct from merely legal liberty. They define their liberalism in the concrete in terms of a program of measures moving toward this end..." (p. 27)

11. See Rossiter, Conservatism in America, op. cit.: "In a country as large and richly varied as the United States, a social movement of any size must of necessity be a loose confederacy of other-minded interests rather than a tight union of like-minded individuals, and it is hardly necessary to point out that conservatism, like progressivism, must bear the burden of variety and dissent so long as it aspires to influence and authority in the land." (p. 245)

12. See Richard H. Pells, Radical Visions and American Dreams: Culture and Social Thought in the Depression Years (New York: Harper & Row, 1973): "Niebuhr began by attacking liberalism on grounds that had become fairly familiar among radicals...he argued that liberalism conveniently overlooked the extent to which man's imagination and intelligence were inevitably frustrated by economic interests, class biases, political conflict, an inveterate desire for power, and the inherent 'limitations of human nature.'" (p. 142)

13. See Charles W. Kegley and Robert W. Bretall, (eds.) Reinhold Niebuhr: His Religious, Social, and Political Thought (New York: Macmillan paperback edition, 1961; originally published in 1956), p. 5.

14. Gabriel Fackre, The Promise of Reinhold Niebuhr (Philadelphia: J.B. Lippincott Co., 1970), p. 7.

15. Reinhold Niebuhr, The Nature and Destiny of Man: Human Nature (New York: Charles Scribner's Sons, 1964 paperback edition; originally published in 1941), p. 12.

16. Ibid.

17. Ibid., p. 17.

18. Ibid., p. 122.

19. Reinhold Niebuhr, Moral Man and Immoral Society: A Study in Ethics and Politics (New York: Charles Scribner's Sons, 1960 paperback edition; originally published in 1932), p. xx.

20. Ibid., p. xxiii.

21. Ibid., p. xxv.

22. Ibid., p. 2.

23. Ibid., p. 9.

24. See the series of special feature articles in the July 6, 1970 issue of Newsweek, especially the following:
Andrew Hacker, "We Will Meet as Enemies": "We no longer possess the qualities upon which citizenship depends. To be specific: we cannot bring ourselves to make the personal sacrifices required to sustain domestic order or international authority. We have, in short, become a loose aggregation of private personal pleasures than to collective endeavors. Americans no longer display that spirit which transforms a people into a citizenry and turns territory into a nation. There eventually arrives a time when a preoccupation with self-centered concerns deflects a population from public obligations, when a willingness to be governed stands less in evidence. We have reached that time."
Richard Hofstadter, "The Age of Rubbish": "But the desire to perform well, the feeling of craftsmanship, the sense of vocation, which has been quite intense in this society for a long time, has, it seems to me, begun to fade in the last ten, perhaps twenty, years. And it seems to be fading faster and faster. Young people don't have anything they want to do. Our culture hasn't been able to perpetuate from one generation to the next, as it used to, the desire to do this or that or the other thing, and I think this is one of the roots of the dissatisfaction in college. Students keep saying that they don't know why they are there. They are less disposed than they used to be to keep order partly because the sense that they are leading a purposeful life has gone..."

341

25. Niebuhr, <u>Moral Man and Immoral Society</u>, <u>op</u>. <u>cit</u>., p. 46.

26. <u>Ibid</u>., p. 81.

27. <u>Ibid</u>., p. 129.

28. <u>Ibid</u>., p. 160.

29. <u>Ibid</u>., p. 167.

30. <u>Ibid</u>., p. 171.

31. <u>Ibid</u>.

32. <u>Ibid</u>., p. 234.

33. <u>Ibid</u>., p. 254.

34. <u>Ibid</u>., pp. 173-174.

35. Reinhold Niebuhr, <u>The Irony of American History</u> (New York: Charles Scribner's Sons, 1952 paperback edition), p. 5.

36. <u>Ibid</u>., p. 10.

37. <u>Ibid</u>., p. 31.

38. <u>Ibid</u>., p. 34.

39. <u>Ibid</u>., p. 74.

40. See Senator J. William Fullbright, <u>The Crippled Giant: American Foreign Policy and Its Domestic Consequences</u> (New York: Random House Vintage Books, 1972).
See also David Halberstam, <u>The Best and the Brightest</u> (Random House, 1972).

41. <u>The Irony of American History</u>, <u>op</u>. <u>cit</u>., p. 88.

42. <u>Ibid</u>., p. 101.

43. <u>Ibid</u>., p. 149.

44. Reinhold Niebuhr, <u>The Children of Light and the Children of Darkness: A Vindication of Democracy and a Critique of its Traditional Defence</u> (New York: Charles Scribner's Sons, 1947), p. xi.

45. See Arthur Schlesinger, Jr., <u>The Politics of Hope</u> (Boston: Houghton Mifflin Co., 1962), pp. 97-125.

46. Purcell, Jr., <u>The Crisis of Democratic Theory</u>, <u>op</u>. <u>cit</u>., p. 253.

47. Charles W. Kegley and Robert W. Bretall, (eds.) <u>Reinhold Niebuhr</u>, <u>op</u>. <u>cit</u>., p. 434.

48. Charles Frankel, <u>The Case for Modern Man</u> (New York: Harper & Bros., 1957), p. 101.

49. White, <u>Social Thought in America</u>, <u>op</u>. <u>cit</u>., p. 258.

50. <u>Ibid</u>., p. 259.

51. Wilson Carey McWilliams, "Reinhold Niebuhr: New Orthodoxy for Old Liberalism," <u>The American Political Sci-</u>

ence Review, vol. LVI, No. 4, December, 1962, pp. 875-885.

52. Kegley and Bretall, Reinhold Niebuhr, op. cit.

53. See Christopher Lasch, The New Radicalism in America 1889-1963: The Intellectual as a Social Type (New York: Alfred A. Knopf, 1965): "Hook's 'critical support' of American culture was hard to distinguish from unconditional acceptance." (p. 307)

See also Henry David Aiken, "Yes Men," review of Sidney Hook's Academic Freedom and Academic Anarchy and Daniel J. Boorstin's The Decline of Radicalism: Reflections on America Today, The New York Review of Books, February 12, 1970, pp. 5-11: "Plainly, Hook's theory of academic freedom, were it consistently enforced, would increase the very anarchy he deplores. Why does he fail so completely to see this? The generic reason, I believe, is that Hook's own mind has lost its old power of thinking problematically and concretely. He announces principles which, abstractly considered, have an air of reasonableness, but which, when applied, merely intensify the issues they are presumed to resolve. More specifically, Hook cannot, or will not, relate the problems of academic freedom to the realities of academic power."

54. See Pells, Radical Visions and American Dreams, op. cit.: "There was at least one writer in the 1930s, however, who believed that such a philosophy could emerge from a synthesis of Dewey and Marx without sacrificing or distorting the ideas of either man. Few were better equipped for this task than Sidney Hook..." (p. 131)

See Sidney Hook, The Quest for Being: And Other Studies in Naturalism and Humanism (New York: St. Martin's Press, 1961).

Lewis S. Feuer, however, feels that John Dewey's influence has waned in Hook's thought. See "The Pragmatic Wisdom of Sidney Hook," Encounter, October, 1975, pp. 37-45: "Few of the distinctive tenets of pragmatism remain in his philosophy...After many years of reflection, Sidney Hook departs from Dewey's philosophy in two basic respects. He finds a basic difference between the quest for truth and the quest for good; and second...he now recognizes that moral courage is not necessarily bred by the pragmatic philosophy or any other. As far as truth and good are concerned, Hook holds that an asymmetry characterizes their relations." (pp. 38-44)

55. See John P. Diggins, The American Left in the Twentieth Century (New York: Harcourt Brace Jovanovich, Inc., 1973 paperback edition: "The Stalinization of the American Left was the end of radical innocence." (p. 95)

56. See Sidney Hook, Revolution, Reform, and Social Justice: Studies in the Theory and Practice of Marxism (New York: New York University Press, 1975): "As a system Marxism is now invalid..." (p. 52)

57. See Sidney Hook, Pragmatism and the Tragic Sense of Life (New York: Basic Books, 1974): "No human person can read history without being moved more by man's failures to use the

knowledge he has had to remove the evils and sufferings which were remediable than by this attempt to achieve too great a control or power over nature." (p. 22)

58. <u>Ibid.</u>: "There is no substitute for intelligence... Pragmatism, as I interpret it, is the theory and practice of enlarging human freedom in a precarious and tragic world by the arts of intelligent social control." (pp. 23-25)

59. <u>Ibid.</u>, pp. ix and x.

60. See Alvin W. Gouldner, <u>The Coming Crisis of Western Sociology</u> (New York: Basic Books, 1970): "To say that an action should be judged by its consequences does not <u>per se</u> indicate <u>how</u> those consequences should be evaluated. Utilitarian culture might be characterized, therefore, as having a standpoint which, while insistently focusing on the consequences of actions, does so without an equally insistent concern with the standards in terms of which these consequences will themselves be judged." (p. 68)

How would a pragmatist respond to this criticism? See Charles Kadushin, <u>The American Intellectual Elite</u> (Boston: Little, Brown, 1974): "Pragmatism denies that means can be separately evaluated from ends. There are no absolute ends or goals because the very search for such ends may involve people in undesirable actions or activities...In one sense, because it is a system of ideas dealing with human preferences, pragmatism, too, is an ideology. But the system deals with how to go about solving problems, that is, it is about method, not substance, and so pragmatists claim that they have no ideology." (p. 163)

61. See Sidney Hook, <u>The Paradoxes of Freedom</u> (Berkeley: University of California Press, 1964 paperback edition): "Moral rights develop out of the marriage of interests and intelligence. They are nurtured and strengthened by shared interests." (p. 5)

62. Sidney Hook, <u>Heresy Yes, Conspiracy No</u> (New York: John Day Co., 1953), p. 36.

63. See Sidney Hook, <u>Political Power and Personal Freedom: Critical Studies in Democracy, Communism, and Civil Rights</u> (New York: Collier Books, 1962 edition): "Ritualistic liberalism is the reliance upon rhetoric rather than logic, slogans rather than analysis of problems in defense of freedom. It does not rethink situations afresh but makes a ritual of phrases, principles, and solutions which have come down from the past as if they were sufficient guides to complex and novel issues..." (p. 319)

64. <u>Ibid.</u>

65. See Sidney Hook, <u>Reason, Social Myths and Democracy</u> (New York: Harper & Row, reprinted Torchbooks 1966 edition; originally published in 1940 by the John Day Co.): "The upshot, then, of our analysis is that just as political democracy is incomplete without some form of economic democracy, so there can be no genuine economic democracy without polit-

ical democracy." (p. 291)

66. See Revolution, Reform, and Social Justice, op. cit., pp. 286-287.

67. In Defense of Academic Freedom (New York: Pegasus Bobbs-Merrill, 1971), pp. 18-20.

68. "What the Cold War was About," Encounter, March, 1975, pp. 86-88: "Whatever form detente takes with powers like China and the Soviet Union, so long as they are wedded to their ideologies we must not abandon the use of the moral weapons of education and propaganda against these systems of organised terror. If we fight this kind of cold war, it may not be necessary, if we retain our defensive capacity, to fight any other." (p. 66)

69. See Pragmatism and the Tragic Sense of Life, op. cit.: "One of the great weaknesses of the democratic socialist movement of the past was its uncritical faith in institutional change. They were accepted because they promised to remove some existing evil, but they were not examined for their own possibilities of even greater evil." (p. 39)

70. See Michael Novak's review of Pragmatism and the Tragic Sense of Life, "In Defense of Reason," Commentary, June, 1975, pp. 86-88: "If there is a failing in Hook, it is some failing of sensibility: he finds it hard to feel himself into the intellectual horizon of others. He is generous enough about attributing good intentions, fair in reporting what others actually say. But he is so wrapped up in his own horizon that he cannot feel the force of their arguments, and as a result he often evinces irritation at their own perspicacity...Ironically, this at once mild and stern man, a life-long enemy of fanaticism, a despiser of dogmatism, a celebrator of openness and pluralism and variety, has a certain narrow range of sympathies." (p. 88)

71. See Paul Kurtz (ed.), Sidney Hook and the Contemporary World: Essays on the Pragmatic Intelligence (New York: John Day Co., 1968).

72. See John Westergaard and Henrietta Resler, Class in a Capitalist Society: A Study of Contemporary Britain (New York: Basic Books, 1975): "'Equality' has come to mean different things in America and in Europe. In the United States the notion for long has been conventionally thought of as 'equality of opportunity'. The ideal then is seen as a state of affairs where each individual would find his own level in the hierarchy of inequality, according only to his abilities and drive, regardless of his parentage and the circumstances of his early life. There is no challenge in that notion to the existence of hierarchy itself. The European conception of equality, by contrast, incorporates just such a challenge. In some interpretations here, too, equality has been narrowly defined, to mean only equal opportunity. But other interpretations have pushed the definition well beyond that. The ideal then is 'equality of condition': the eradication of all significant divisions of power, wealth and security." (p. 282)

See also Kenneth J. Arrow, "Taxation and Democratic Values," _The New Republic_, November 2, 1974, pp. 23-25: "Perhaps the most important recent intellectual event in the area of distributive justice has been the publication of John Rawls' _A Theory of Justice_, followed by attacks on Rawls and on the desirability of equality in general by Irving Kristol, Robert Nisbet and others. Among other strands of the debate is the old idea of a conflict between liberty and equality. The debate occurs against the background of a presumed common acceptance of the ideals of a democratic society, and democracy clearly includes in its sayings both these ideals. I want to argue here that a commitment to democratic values strongly implies an ideal of redistribution of income and wealth."

See also Charles Frankel, "The New Egalitarianism and the Old," _Commentary_, September, 1973, pp. 54-61.

73. See Goodwin, _The American Condition_, op. cit.: "The principal source of today's alienation is not a ruling class, but a social process dominated by bureaucratic institutions which have...transcended traditional concepts of ownership—which are unowned." (p. 15)

74. See _Pragmatism and the Tragic Sense of Life_, op. cit.: "But if the history of our time can establish anything, it is that freedom is not safe when enthusiasm is undisciplined by concern for others, when conscience rather than intelligence is king, and when the fanaticism of virtue scorns to discriminate between degrees of achievement, between lesser evils in a world in which all human action falls short of ideal intent." (p. xv)

75. See _Revolution, Reform, and Social Justice_, op. cit.

76. _Ibid._, p. x.

77. See "Loving America," _Time_ Essay, July 5, 1976, pp. 35-36: "Both American conservatives and liberals are embodiments of this paradox. Liberals are forever asking state intervention in the economy for the sake of social justice, while insisting on hands-off in the private area of morals. Conservatives take the opposite view. They demand self-determination in politics, but suspect self-determination in morals. They demand laissez-faire in business, but hate laissez-faire in behavior. In theory, there is no contradiction between these positions. For freedom to be workable as a political and social system, strong inner controls, a powerful moral compass and sense of values, are needed. In practice, the contradiction is vast. The compass is increasingly hard to read, the values hard to find in a frantically open, mobile, fractioned society. Thus a troubling, paradoxical question: does freedom destroy the inner disciplines that alone make freedom possible?" (p. 36: essay written by Henry Grunwald)

78. See Anthony Lewis, "Liberals Now Worry About Federal Power," _The New York Times_, April 12, 1975, section E, p. 18.

For an opposite view, see Henry Fairlie, "In Defense of Big Government," _The New Republic_, March 13, 1976, pp. 24-27.

Chapter 4

1. "A Symposium; What is a Liberal—Who is a Conservative?" Commentary, volume 62, No. 3, September, 1976, Jervis Anderson, p. 35.

2. Ibid., Robert L. Bartley, p. 39.

3. Ibid., David T. Bazelon, p. 40.

4. Ibid., Arnold Beichman, p. 42.

5. Ibid., Norman Birnbaum, p. 45.

6. Ibid., Edith Efron, p. 51.

7. Ibid., Eugene D. Genovese, p. 58.

8. Ibid., Walter Goodman, p. 65.

9. Ibid., Carey McWilliams, p. 80.

10. Ibid., Diane Ravitch, p. 92.

11. Ibid., Thomas Sowell, p. 98.

12. Ibid., Ernest van den Haag, p. 102.

13. Ibid., Paul H. Weaver, p. 104.

14. Ibid., Peter P. Witonski, p. 108.

15. See Henry Fairlie, The Spoiled Child of the Western World: The Miscarriage of the American Idea in Our Time (Garden City, N.Y.: Doubleday & Co., 1976), p. 282.
See also J.R. Pole, The Pursuit of Equality in America (Berkeley: University of California Press, 1978); this is a richly detailed, scholarly historical analysis of the central importance of this ideal in American history.

16. William E. Arnett, George Santayana (New York: Washington Square Press, 1968 paperback edition), p. 3.
See also David L. Norton, Personal Destinies: A Philosophy of Ethical Individualism (Princeton, N.J.: Princeton University Press, 1976 paperback edition): "By his love of ideals and his refusal to petrify them by an effort of precise description, Santayana awakens in us the recognition that life is immensely richer with meanings than any of us take it to be." (p. 338)

17. George Santayana, Dominations and Powers: Reflections on Liberty, Society and Government (New York: Charles Scribner's Sons, 1951), p. 327.

18. Ibid., p. 17.

19. Ibid., p. 45.

20. Ibid., p. 66.

21. Ibid., p. 110.

22. George Santayana, The Life of Reason or the Phases of Human Progress, one volume edition, revised by the author

in collaboration with Daniel Cory, (New York: Charles Scribner's Sons, 1955), p. 148.

23. *Dominations and Powers*, *op. cit.*, p. 300

24. *Ibid.*, p. 315.

25. *Ibid.*, p. 334.

26. *Ibid.*, p. 422.

27. *Ibid.*, p. 434.

28. *Ibid.*

29. See George Santayana, *Character and Opinion in the United States* (New York: W.W. Norton & Co., White Oak Library edition); George Santayana, *Persons and Places: The Background of My Life* (New York: Charles Scribner's Sons, 1942).

30. Charles Wellborn, *Twentieth-Century Pilgrimage: Walter Lippmann and the Public Philosophy* (Baton Rouge: Louisiana State University Press, 1969), p. 27.

31. Walter Lippmann, *The Good Society* (New York: Grosset & Dunlop, A Universal Library paperback, 1943), p. 14.

32. *Ibid.*, p. 35.

33. Walter Lippmann, *The Public Philosophy* (New York: The New American Library Mentor Book, 1955), p. 19.

34. *Ibid.*, p. 25.

35. *Ibid.*, p. 27.

36. *Ibid.*, p. 31.

37. *Ibid.*, pp. 34-39.

38. *Ibid.*, p. 40.

39. *Ibid.*, p. 48.

40. *Ibid.*, p. 54.

41. *Ibid.*, p. 61.

42. *Ibid.*, p. 75.

43. *Ibid.*, p. 79.

44. *Ibid.*, p. 80.

45. *Ibid.*, p. 82.

46. *Ibid.*, p. 107.

47. *Ibid.*, p. 102.

48. *Ibid.*, p. 103.

49. *Ibid.*, p. 105.

50. *Ibid.*, p. 116.

51. *Ibid.*, p. 118.

52. *Ibid.*, p. 136.

53. Charles Forcey, <u>The Crossroads of Liberalism: Croly,
Weyl, Lippmann and the Progressive Era 1900-1925</u> (New York:
Oxford University Press, 1961 paperback edition), p. 118.

54. Morton White, <u>Social Thought in America</u>, <u>op</u>. <u>cit</u>.,
p. 272.

55. Benjamin F. Wright, <u>5 Public Philosophies of Walter
Lippmann</u> (Austin: University of Texas Press, 1973), p. 135.

56. See "Lippmann" Philosopher-Journalist," <u>Time</u>, December 23, 1974, pp. 56-57.

57. For an excellent analysis of this model see John C.
Livingston and Robert G. Thompson, <u>The Consent of the Governed</u> (New York: Macmillan Co., 1966, 2nd edition), although
what I call consensus model the authors refer to as the "Broker Rule" model: "Its major assumptions and arguments include
the following: (1) Politics is a struggle for power. (2) The
elements in this struggle in a democracy are organized interest groups. (3) The stability of democratic politics requires overlapping membership in groups and the selection of
legislators, administrators, and judges who will define their
roles as mediators of group compromise. (4) Democracy cannot
operate under other than brokerage techniques." (pp. 121-22)

58. See Robert A. Dahl, <u>Who Governs? Democracy and Power
in an American City</u> (New Haven: Yale University Press, 1961):
"...the stability of a political system, even a democratic
one, is not merely a matter of the <u>numbers</u> of persons who
adhere to it but also of the <u>amount of political resources</u>
they use—or are expected to use—in acting on their beliefs..."
(pp. 314-315)

59. See Darryl Baskin, <u>American Pluralist Democracy: A
Critique</u> (New York: Van Nostrand Reinhold Co., 1971 paperback edition), p. 174.
See also G. David Garson, <u>Power and Politics in the
United States: A Political Economy Approach</u> (Lexington,
Mass.: D.C. Heath & Co., 1977 paperback edition), pp. 53-56.

60. See Sidney Hook's review of <u>The Essential Lippmann:
A Political Philosophy of Liberal Democracy</u> (eds.) Clinton
Rossiter and James Lane (New York: Random House, 1963), <u>New
York Times Book Review</u>, July 14, 1963: "Lippmann's criticisms
of democracy bite much deeper. They go to the quick of the
entire conception of the role of popular rule in the democratic or parliamentary process itself. He holds that belief in
the sovereignty and supremacy of the will of the people is a
perversion of democracy. Worse still, he believes, it has
led logically and historically, to the totalitarian state."
Section 7, p. 1.
See also Richard W. Rovere, "Walter Lippmann," <u>The American Scholar</u>, Autumn, 1975: "Lippmann was an elitist. When
he was misled, it was almost always because of an undue respect for established authority." (p. 601)

61. See Walter Lippmann, <u>Public Opinion</u> (New York: Harcourt, Brace & Co., 1922).

62. See "Myrdal and von Hayek Share a Noble Prize," The New York Times, Thursday, October 10, 1974, p. 1 and p. 81.

63. Friedrich A. Hayek, The Constitution of Liberty (Chicago: Henry Regnery Co., Gateway edition, 1960), p. 401.

64. Ibid., p. 403.

65. See Philip W. Dyer and R. Harrison Hickman, "Hayek and American Conservatism," paper delivered at the 1976 Annual Meeting of the American Political Science Association, The Palmer House, Chicago, Illinois, Sept. 2-5, 1976, p. 18.
See also Fritz Machlup (ed.), Essays on Hayek (New York: New York University Press, 1976).
See also Emily R. Gill, "Detours on the Road to Serfdom: Private Interests and the Rule of Law in F.A. Hayek," paper delivered at the 1978 Annual Meeting of the American Political Science Association, New York Hilton Hotel, Aug. 31-Sept. 3, 1978: "Liberalism for Hayek, then, is both a method of procedure, one which affords the greatest possible scope for the individual, and also substantial set of goals. It offers a program which could be a focal point for at least some of those who want to see a reduction of group influence upon government." (p. 31)

66. See Nash, The Conservative Intellectual Movement, op. cit.: "The Right consisted of three loosely related groups: traditionalists or new conservatives, appalled by the erosion of values and the emergence of a secular, rootless, mass society; libertarians, apprehensive about the threat of the State to private enterprise and individualism; and disillusioned ex-radicals and their allies, alarmed by international Communism. No rigid barriers separated the three groups. Traditionalists and libertarians were usually anti-Communist, while ex-Communists generally endorsed free-market capitalism and Western traditions. Nevertheless, the impulses that comprised the developing conservative movement were clearly diverse." (p. 131)

67. Ibid. Nash does not agree with my viewpoint here: "...after some fierce polemics, Meyers' synthesis was, in effect, accepted (p. 179)...Conservatism in America in the 1950s and 1960s was not, in its essence, a speculative or theoretical enterprise. It was an intellectual movement with definitive political implications. It sought not just to understand the world but to preserve, purify, even restore some of it. The crucial question therefore became: were the terms of cooperation sufficiently clear and consistent on the intermediate level of intelligent action to justify an alliance of thoughtful men and women in defense of their civilization and its dearest values? For most conservatives the answer to this question was resolutely affirmative." (p. 185)
I think the problem with Nash's conclusion is that he sees the National Review as the clearing-house and focal point for all these disparate varieties of conservatism, whereas many reputable conservative thinkers, and many who have no use for the National Review brand of "fusionism" cannot be brought under this single umbrella. The internal conflicts and divergencies within contemporary conservatism are much greater and more

consequential than Nash is willing to accept. My own research, as brought out in this book, coincides more with the judgment of Philip W. Dyer and R. Harrison Hickman, "Hayek and American Conservatism," op. cit., wherein they conclude: "...the practical successes of Meyers' fusionism were impressive while the philosophical deficiency is deficient." (p. 8)

68. Friedrich A. Hayek, The Constitution of Liberty, op. cit., p. 26.

69. Ibid., p. 31.

70. Ibid., p. 32.
See also Friedrich A. Hayek, Individualism and Economic Order (South Bend, Indiana: Gateways Editions, Ltd., 1977 edition; originally published by University of Chicago Press in 1948): "There is all the difference in the world between treating people equally and attempting to make them equal." (p. 16)

71. Hayek, The Constitution of Liberty, op. cit., p. 38.

72. See Friedrich A. Hayek, The Road to Serfdom (Chicago: University of Chicago Press Phoenix Books, 1967 paperback edition, originally published in 1944).

73. Hayek, The Constitution of Liberty, op. cit., p. 49.

74. Ibid., p. 57.

75. Ibid., p. 63.

76. Ibid., p. 83.

77. Ibid., p. 101.

78. Ibid., pp. 109-110.

79. Ibid., p. 120.

80. Ibid., p. 205.

81. Ibid., p. 209.

82. Ibid., pp. 232-233.

83. Ibid., p. 262.

84. Ibid., p. 283.

85. Ibid., p. 298.

86. Ibid., p. 304.

87. Ibid., p. 321.

88. Ibid., p. 322.

89. Ibid., p. 430.

90. Ibid., p. 337.

91. As this is written, two of the three-volumes have been published. See Friedrich A. Hayek, Law, Legislation and Liberty, volume 1, Rules and Order (Chicago: University of Chicago Press, 1973 paperback edition) and F.A. Hayek, Law, Legislation and Liberty, volume 2, The Mirage of Social Justice (Chicago: University of Chicago Press, 1976).

92. F.A. Hayek, New Studies in Philosophy, Politics, Economics and the History of Ideas (Chicago: University of Chicago Press, 1978), p. 116.

93. Friedrich A. Hayek, Studies in Philosophy, Politics, and Economics (New York: Simon & Schuster Clarion Book, 1967), p. 81.

94. Ibid., p. 90.

95. Ibid., p. 222.

96. Hayek, The Road to Serfdom, op. cit., p. 13.

97. Ibid., p. 70.

98. Deyer and Hickman, "Hayek and American Conservatism," op. cit., pp. 8-11.

99. The conservatives referred to in the next chapter as "libertarian-individualists" are an exception to this generalization.

100. See Richard M. Weaver, Ideas Have Consequences (Chicago: University of Chicago Press, 1971 paperback edition, originally published in 1948).
See also John H. Hallowell, The Moral Foundation of Democracy (Chicago: The University of Chicago Press, 1974 Midway Reprint edition, originally published in 1954).
See also Francis Graham Wilson, The Case for Conservatism (Seattle: University of Washington Press, 1951).

101. See Allan Bloom, "Leo Strauss: Sept. 20, 1899-October 18, 1973," Political Theory, vol. 2, No. 1, November, 1974: "A survey of Strauss's entire body of work will reveal that it constitues a unified and continuous, ever deepening, investigation into the meaning and possibility of philosophy..." (p. 376)
See Milton Himmelfarb, "On Leo Strauss," Commentary, August, 1974, pp. 60-66.

102. See William T. Bluhm, Theories of the Political System (Englewood Cliffs, N.J.: Prentice-Hall, 1965), pp. 98-103.

103. See Charles A. McCoy and John Playford (eds.) Apolitical Politics (New York: Thomas Y. Crowell, 1967 paperback edition).
See also James C. Charlesworth (ed.), Contemporary Political Analysis (New York: The Free Press, 1967 paperback edition).
See also Fred M. Frohock, "Notes on the Concept of Politics: Weber, Easton, Strauss," The Journal of Politics, May, 1974, vol. 36, no. 2, pp. 379-408.

104. Leo Strauss, What is Political Philosophy? And Other Essays (Glencoe: The Free Press, 1959), p. 14.

105. Ibid., pp. 10-14.

106. Ibid., p. 17.

107. Ibid., p. 18.

108. Ibid., p. 26.

109. _Ibid._, p. 24.

110. _Ibid._, p. 66.

111. Leo Strauss, _The City of Man_ (Chicago: Rand McNally, 1964), pp. 1-2.

112. _Ibid._, p. 8.

113. _Ibid._, pp. 9-10.

114. _Ibid._, p. 12.

115. Leo Strauss, _Natural Right and History_ (Chicago: University of Chicago Press, 1974 paperback edition, originally published in 1953), p. 3.

116. _Ibid._, p. 5.

117. _Ibid._, p. 7.

118. _Ibid._, pp. 33-36.

119. _Ibid._, p. 41.

120. _Ibid._, p. 61.

121. _Ibid._, p. 118.

122. _Ibid._, Chapter 5, "Modern Natural Right," pp. 165-251.

123. _Ibid._, Chapter 6, "The Crisis of Modern Natural Right," pp. 252-323.

124. Leo Strauss, _The Political Philosophy of Hobbes: Its Basis and its Genesis_, translated by Elsa M. Sinclair (Oxford: The Clarenden Press, 1936), p. 160.

125. Herbert J. Storing (ed.), _Essays on the Scientific Study of Politics_ (New York: Holt, Rinehart & Winston, 1962), p. 309.

126. _Ibid._

127. _Ibid._, p. 310.

128. _Ibid._

129. _Ibid._

130. _Ibid._, p. 311.

131. _Ibid._, p. 320.

132. _Ibid._, p. 322.

133. _Ibid._, p. 326.

134. Strauss, _What is Political Philosophy?_, _op. cit._, p. 91.

135. See Dante Germino, _Beyond Ideology: The Revival of Political Theory_ (New York: Harper & Row, 1967): "Although Strauss's determination to understand the great minds of the past on their own terms is wholly admirable, and although his insistence on digging out of ·the major works the consistency at the root of apparent contradictions is a much-needed corrective to the widespread habit of lazily ascribing to the thinker under scrutiny an eclectic attitude which the inter-

preter himself might favor, nonetheless Strauss's method is subject to abuse. On occasion, as in the interpretation of Machiavelli as a 'teacher of evil,' he appears to have gone so far as to impose a straightjacket of consistency upon a man who surely saw his own inner tension too clearly to come up with a doctrine free of self-contradiction..." (p. 152)

For a harsher critique of Strauss's political philosophy, see John H. Gunnell, "The Myth of the Tradition," The American Political Science Review, vol. 72, no. 1, March, 1978, pp. 122-134: "It is indeed strange that Strauss's account of the tradition...seems to reflect the very historicism which he so vehemently repudiates..." (p. 337)

136. Leo Strauss, Thoughts on Machiavelli (Glencoe: The Free Press, 1958), pp. 9-12.

137. Storing, Essays on the Scientific Study of Politics, op. cit., p. 318.

138. Leo Strauss, Liberalism Ancient and Modern (New York: Basic Books, 1968), pp. 5-19.

139. Willmoore Kendall, Contra Mundum, edited by Nellie D. Kendall (New Rochelle: Arlington House, 1971), introduction by Jeffrey Hart, p. 9.

140. "Conservative Iconoclast: The Intellectual Oddyssey of Willmoore Kendall," paper delivered at the American Political Science Association annual meeting, The Palmer House, Chicago, Illinois, Aug. 29-Sept. 2, 1974.

141. "The Political Thought of Willmoore Kendall," pp. 201-239; quotation from p. 201.

142. Kendall, Contra Mundum, op. cit., Introduction by Jeffrey Hart, p. 13.

143. Ibid., p. 572.

144. Ibid., p. 454.

145. It should be noted, however, that George W. Carey collaborated on the writing of this essay.

146. Ibid., pp. 213-22 and pp. 266-281.

147. See James MacGregor Burns, The Deadlock of Democracy: Four Party Politics in America (Englewood Cliffs, N.J.: Prentice-Hall, 1963).
See also Robert A. Dahl, A Preface to Democratic Theory (Chicago: University of Chicago Press Phoenix Books, 1956).

148. Kendall, Contra Mundum, op. cit., p. 368.

149. See Thomas R. Dye and L. Harmon Zeigler, The Irony of Democracy: An Uncommon Interpretation of American Politics, 2nd edition, (Belmont, Calif.: Wadsworth Publishing Co., Duxbury Press Book, 1972, originally published in 1970).

150. Kendall, Contra Mundum, op. cit., p. 470.

151. Ibid., p. 474.

152. Ibid., p. 475.

153. *Ibid.*, p. 479.

154. *Ibid.*, p. 487.

155. *Ibid.*, p. 491.

156. *Ibid.*, p. 497.

157. *Ibid.*, p. 501.

158. *Ibid.*, pp. 504-505.

159. Willmoore Kendall, *John Locke and the Doctrine of Majority Rule* (Urbana: University of Illinois Press, 1965 paperback), p. 90.

160. *Ibid.*, pp. 92-93.

161. *Ibid.*, p. 101.

162. *Ibid.*, p. 103.

163. *Ibid.*, p. 111.

164. *Ibid.*, p. 113.

165. Willmoore Kendall, *The Conservative Affirmation* (Chicago: Henry Regnery Co., 1963), p. x.

166. Willmoore Kendall, *Contra Mundum, op. cit.*, p. 67.

167. *Ibid.*, p. 565.

168. *Ibid.*, p. 566.

169. *Ibid.*

170. See Willmoore Kendall and George W. Carey, *The Basic Symbols of the American Political Tradition* (Baton Rouge: Louisiana State University, 1970): "As we shall see in due course, we have come to have two traditions: one which holds to a rather extreme view of equality; the other, an older one, which holds that our supreme symbol is to rule the deliberate sense of the community. This accounts for the fact that we are somewhat schizophrenic today about our tradition. Beyond this is a graver matter; the two traditions are not compatible with one another, and the manifestations of this are quite apparent in our contemporary world." (pp. 94-95)
See also Willmoore Kendall and George C. Carey, eds., *Liberalism versus Conservatism* (Princeton, N.J.: D. Van Nostrand Co., 1966), pp. 66-74.

171. Kendall, *Contra Mundum, op. cit.*, p. 577.

172. *Ibid.*, pp. 571-612.

173. *Ibid.*, p. 586.

174. Nash, "Conservative Iconoclast," *op. cit.*, p. 11.

175. See Nelson Polsby's review of George H. Nash's *The Conservative Intellectual Movement in America: Since 1945* and John P. Diggins' *Up From Communism, Commentary*, August, 1976, pp. 62-65: "If I am right in thinking that American conservative intellectuals have on the whole, been neither especially persuasive nor powerful, what accounts for the view

that somehow conservative thinking has recently had a resurgence in this country? I'm afraid the best answer is
that present-day intellectual 'conservatism' has been taken
over by liberals. If not taken over, then strongly infiltra-
ted." (p. 64)

176. Hannah Arendt, The Life of the Mind, vol. 1 Thinking
and vol. 2 Willing (New York: Harcourt Brace Jovanovich, 1978).
See Greil Marcus, "Eichmann Was the Spur, Freedom Must
Be Willed," The Village Voice, May 15, 1978, pp. 87-90, for
a negative appraisal of The Life of the Mind by a critic who
otherwise has a high regard for Arendt's body of work: "Hannah
Arendt's last work suggests that the philosophical tradition,
by valuing necessity over contingency, is more on Eichmann's
side than ours. But the work is too timid, too divorced from
events, to serve as an indictment." (p. 87)

177. Hannah Arendt, Between Past and Future: Six Exercises
in Political Thought (New York: The Viking Press, 1961), p.
25.

178. Ibid., pp. 26-27.

179. Ibid., p. 29.

180. Ibid., p. 28.

181. Ibid., p. 40.

182. Ibid., pp. 52-53.

183. Ibid., p. 53.

184. Ibid., p. 64.

185. Ibid., pp. 66-69.

186. Ibid., p. 79.

187. Ibid., p. 90.

188. Ibid., p. 43.

189. Ibid., p. 106.

190. Ibid., p. 111.

191. Ibid., p. 127.

192. Ibid., pp. 128-141.

193. Ibid., p. 141.

194. Hannah Arendt, Crises of the Republic (New York: Harcourt, Brace, Jovanovich, Inc., Harvest Book, 1972), p. 69.

195. Ibid., pp. 70-71.

196. Ibid., p. 94.

197. Ibid., p. 96.

198. There is considerable disagreement among critics regarding this point of whether Arendt is elitist, and thus unreliable as a democratic theorist. See, for example, the
contrasting views of Martin Jay and Leo Botstein, "Hannah
Arendt: Opposing Views," Partisan Review, vol. SLV, No. 3,

1978, pp. 348-380. Martin Jay states as follows: "...despite the bredth of her knowledge and the unquestionable ingenuity of her mind, the political thought of Hannah Arendt is ultimately as problematic as her historical scholarship. Built on a foundation of arbitrary definitions and questionable, if highly imaginative, interpretations of history and previous political thought, her system is vulnerable to many of the objections that led to the shipwreck of her political existentialist predecessors." (p. 361) Leo Botstein refutes Jay as follows: "If extreme economic optimism, a belief in the primary need for politics in the modern age, and an admiration for virtuosity, performance, and excellence make Arendt an elitist, then perhaps the label is not as significant or damaging as Jay thinks. Certainly, Arendt's admiration for participatory democracy and for workers' councils hardly corresponds to what we normally associate with elitist democratic theory." (p. 378) For reasons cited in this section of the book, I favor Martin Jay's evaluation of Hannah Arendt over that of Leo Botstein.

199. Lewis A. Coser and Irving Hoew, (eds.) The New Conservatives: A Critique from the Left (New York: Quadrangle Books, 1973). This quotation derives from Hanna Fenichel Pitkin's essay, "The Roots of Conservatism: Michael Oakeshott and the Denial of Politics," p. 268.

200. Daniel Bell, The End of Ideology: On the Exhaustion of Political Ideas in the Fifties, revised edition (New York: The Free Press, 1962 paperback, originally published in 1960), p. 30.

201. "Hannah Arendt's America," Commentary, September, 1975, pp. 61-67, quotation on p. 64.

202. See Judith Shklar, "Hannah Arendt's Triumph," The New Republic, December 27, 1975, pp. 8-10.
    See also Hans J. Morgenthau, "An Appreciation," Political Theory, vol. 4, no. 1, February, 1976, pp. 5-8.

203. See George Kateb, "Freedom and Worldliness in the Thought of Hannah Arendt," paper delivered at the 1976 Annual Meeting of the American Political Science Association, The Palmer House, Sept. 2-5, 1976: "The fact is that her work as a whole is usually found shocking and foreign whenever it is seriously attended to—certainly in America." (p. 1)
    See also Richard J. Bernstein, "Hannah Arendt: Opinion and Judgment," paper delivered at the 1976 Annual Meeting of the American Political Science Association, The Palmer House, Chicago, Illinois, Sept. 2-5, 1976: "We can deepen our grasp of Arendt's vision of politics by exploring how it is closely related to freedom and power. The political realm is the only realm where men can be free. Freedom is essentially public freedom." (p. 5)

204. The Political Thought of Hannah Arendt (New York: Harcourt Brace Jovanovich, 1974), p. 124.

205. Commentary, June, 1963, pp. 506-516: "Mr. Morgenthau, in fact, shares with Niebuhr and others the habit of appeal-

ing to something called 'the Western tradition' which on inspection turns out to be the conservative tradition.   Its
chief pillars are Aristotle, the Church Fathers, and the
theorists of absolutism, down to and including Hobbes, plus
of course Edmund Burke...All radical thinkers are ipso facto
outside 'the Western tradition.'   As for liberalism, it stands
revealed as an illusion, and for the rest it is to be considered as a middle-class ideology." (p. 511)

206. See Kenneth Thompson and Robert Myers, Truth & Tragedy: A Tribute to Hans J. Morgenthau (New York: New Republic
Press, 1977).

207. (New York: New American Library, 1972), p. 125.

208. Ibid.

209. Ibid., p. 168.

210. Ibid., p. 13.

211. Ibid., p. 18.

212. Ibid., p. 72.

213. Ibid., especially Chapter Two.

214. See Kenneth W. Thompson, Political Realism and the
Crisis of World Politics: An American Approach to Foreign
Policy (Princeton, N.J.: Princeton University Press, 1960).
    See also Kenneth W. Thompson, Interpreters and Critics
of the Cold War (Washington, D.C.: University Press of America).
    See also Cecil V. Crabb, Jr., and June Savoy, "Hans J.
Morgenthau's View of Real-Politik," The Political Science Reviewer, vol. V, Fall, 1975, pp. 189-228: "Morgenthau and other modern political realists supplied as essential and extremely useful perspective on international politics and on
America's role in them since World War II.   In the absence
of the realist approach, two orientations—isolationism and
Wilsonian-New Deal idealism—were available to American policy-makers.   Alone, neither was capable of providing the kind
of guidance required by the United States in its new role as
a Super Power.   The same point can also be made of Realpolitik: this perspective exhibits numerous deficiencies, contradictions, and weaknesses—fully as many as isolationist or
idealistic thought.   Careful examination of America's post-
war diplomatic record, however, would reveal that most major
decisions in foreign affairs have involved some combination
of two or more of these approaches to problems in the outside
world." (p. 223)

215. Hans J. Morgenthau, Politics Among Nations: The Struggle for Power and Peace, 4th edition, (New York: Alfred A.
Knopf, 1967).

216. Hans J. Morgenthau, The Decline of Democratic Politics, vol. 1 of Politics in the Twentieth Century, (Chicago:
University of Chicago Press, 1962), p. 75.

217. Hans J. Morgenthau, Truth and Power: Essays of a Decade, 1960-70 (New York: Praeger Publishers, 1970), p. 27.

218. Ibid., p. 29.

219. Ibid., p. 81.

220. Hans J. Morgenthau, A New Foreign Policy for the United States (New York: Praeger, 1969 paperback), pp. 15-16.

221. Hans J. Morgenthau, "The New Diplomacy of Movement," Encounter, August, 1974, pp. 52-57; quotation from p. 56.

222. Hans J. Morgenthau, "Decline of Democratic Government," The New Republic, November 9, 1974, p. 9.

223. Ibid., p. 11.

224. Hans J. Morgenthau, Science: Servant or Master, op. cit., p. 45.

225. Hans J. Morgenthau, The Restoration of American Politics, vol. III of Politics in the Twentieth Century (Chicago: University of Chicago Press, 1962), p. 29.

226. Morgenthau, The Decline of Democratic Politics, op. cit., p. 1.

227. Ibid., p. 59.

228. Hans J. Morgenthau, The Purpose of American Politics (New York: Random House Vintage Books, 1964).

229. Ibid., p. 346.

230. Morgenthau, The Decline of Democratic Politics, op. cit., p. 38.

231. Rene DuBois, Saturday Review/World, December 14, 1974, p. 76.

232. See Hans J. Morgenthau, "Goldwater—The Romantic Regression," Commentary, September, 1964: "A conservatism of philosophy and method is intrinsic to the American political tradition. The Federalist is its greatest literary movement, Alexander Hamilton is its greatest theoretician, John Quincy Adams and Abraham Lincoln are in different ways its greatest practitioners. This kind of conservatism holds that the imperfections of the world as seen from the rational point of view are the result of forces inherent in human nature. To improve the world, one must work with these forces, not against them. The world being by nature made up of conflicting interests, abstract principles can never be fully realized; they can at best be approximated through the ever temporary balancing of interests and the ever precarious settlement of conflicts. This kind of conservatism, then, sees in a system of checks and balances a universal principle for all pluralist societies. It appeals to historic precedent rather than abstract doctrine and aims at the realization of the lesser evil rather than of the absolute good."

233. Ibid.

234. Ibid.

Chapter 5

1. See Kenneth M. and Patricia Dolbeare, <u>American Ideol-ogies: The Competing Political Beliefs of the 1970s</u>, 3rd edi-tion, (Chicago: Rand McNally, 1976 paperback), pp. 56-71.
See also George H. Nash, <u>The Conservative Intellectual Movement</u>, <u>op</u>. <u>cit</u>.: "While libertarians tended to emphasize economic arguments against the State, the new conservatives were more concerned with what they saw as the ethical and spiritual causes and consequences of Leviathan. On the whole, the new conservatives were little interested in economics— particularly what they regarded as abstract and doctrinaire economics. Instead, they were fundamentally social and cul-tural critics, for whom conservatism meant the restoration of values, not the preservation of material gains." (p. 82)

2. See "Freedom, Tradition, Conservatism," <u>Modern Age</u>, vol. 4, no. 4, Fall, 1960: "There is no real antagonism. Con-servatism, to continue to develop today, must embrace both: reason operating within tradition: neither ideological <u>hu-bris</u> abstractly creating utopian blueprints..." (p. 359)

3. Kenneth M. and Patricia Dolbeare, <u>American Ideologies</u>, <u>op</u>. <u>cit</u>., p. 69.

4. Ayn Rand, <u>The Fountainhead</u> (New York: The New Ameri-can Library Signet Book, 1968 edition, originally published 1943), p. xi.

5. See Ayn Rand, <u>For the New Intellectual: The Philos-ophy of Ayn Rand</u> (New York: The New American Library Signet Book, 1961 edition).

6. <u>Ibid</u>., pp. 11-12.

7. Ayn Rand, <u>Capitalism: The Unknown Ideal</u> (New York: The New American Library Signet Book, 1966 edition), p. vii.

8. <u>Ibid</u>., p. 37.

9. <u>Ibid</u>., p. 328.

10. See Rand, <u>For the New Intellectual</u>, op. cit.

11. Ayn Rand, <u>The Virtue of Selfishness: A New Concept of Egoism</u> (New York: The New American Library Signet Book, 1964 edition), p. 22.

12. <u>Ibid</u>., p. 27.

13. Ayn Rand, <u>Atlas Shrugged</u> (New York: The New American Library Signet Book, 1957), pp. 936-993.

14. <u>Ibid</u>., p. 943.

15. <u>Ibid</u>., p. 944.

16. (New York: The New American Library Signet Book, 1959), p. 80.

17. See "The Self-centered Generation," <u>Time</u>, Sept. 23, 1974.

18. Rand, *Capitalism: The Unknown Ideal*, *op. cit.*, p. 254.

19. *Ibid.*, p. 256.

20. *Ibid.*, p. 259.

21. See Richard L. Strout, "Economic Fundamentalist: Chairman Greenspan," *The New Republic,* September 14, 1974 and "Super-Capitalist at the CEA," *Time*, August 5, 1974.

22. Rand, *Capitalism: The Unknown Ideal*, *op. cit.*, p. vii.

23. Ayn Rand, *The Ayn Rand Letter*, October 25, 1971, vol. 1, no. 2.

24. See *Time* magazine cover story, December 19, 1969: "Friedman is the Leading Iconoclast of U.S. Economists," p. 66.

25. *The Academic Scribblers* (New York: Holt, Rinehart & Winston, Inc., 1971 paperback edition), p. 225.

26. See Leonard Silk, *The Economists* (New York: Basic Books, 1976, pp. 47-93: "Friedman's methodological insistence on the free market as the basic hypothesis of positive economic analysis conveniently dovetailed with his ideological faith in laissez-faire and his opposition to government controls and planning." (p. 74)

27. (New Haven, Yale University Press, 1949).

28. *Ibid.*, p. 3.

29. See Ludwig von Mises, *Omnipotent Government* (New Haven: Yale University Press, 1944) and *Bureaucracy* (New Haven: Yale University Press, 1944).

30. *The Conservative Intellectual Movement in America*, *op. cit.*, p. 13.

31. *Capitalism and Freedom* (Chicago: University of Chicago Press, 1972 paperback edition, originally published in 1962), pp. 2-3.

32. *Ibid.*, p. 3.

33. *Ibid.*, p. 4.

34. *Ibid.*, p. 5.

35. *Ibid.*, p. 9.

36. *Ibid.*, p. 23.

37. Milton Friedman and Anna J. Schwartz, *A Monetary History of the United States, 1867-1960* (Princeton, N.J.: Princeton University Press, 1963), p. 300.

38. See Milton Friedman and Walter W. Heller, *Monetary vs. Fiscal Policy: A Dialogue* (New York: W.W. Norton & Co., 1969 paperback edition).

39. *Capitalism and Freedom*, *op. cit.*, p. 46.

40. *Ibid.*, p. 50.

41. *Ibid.*, p. 64.

42. Ibid., pp. 66-67.

43. Ibid., p. 68.

44. Ibid., pp. 76-77.

45. Ibid., p. 79.

46. See Chapter VI, "The Role of Government in Education," and chapter XII, "Alleviation of Poverty," Capitalism and Freedom, op. cit.

47. Ibid., p. 109.

48. Ibid., pp. 132-133.

49. Ibid., p. 135.

50. Ibid., p. 169.

51. Ibid., p. 176.

52. Ibid., pp. 178-179.

53. Ibid., p. 180.

54. Ibid., p. 182.

55. Ibid., p. 188.

56. Ibid., pp. 199-200.

57. See Henry Hazlett, "Where the Monetarists Go Wrong," The Freeman, vol. 26, no. 8, August, 1976: "It rests on greatly over-simplified assumptions (p. 470)...This brings us to what I consider the fatal flaw in the monetarist prescriptions. If the leader of the school cannot make up his own mind regarding what the most desirable rate of monetary increase should be, what does he expect to happen when the decision is put in the hands of the politicians?" (p. 477)
See also "A Socialist Sounds Like a Conservative," interview with Joan Robinson, Business Week, October 20, 1975, pp. 83-84: "There is an unearthly, mystical element in Friedman's thought that the mere existence of a stock of money somehow promotes expenditures. The idea that with the correct monetary policy everything will be O.K. is only a daydream." (p.80)

58. It is true, of course, that Milton Friedman, as a critic of liberal reformers, directs his criticism at their overly rationalistic approach to what can be accomplished in the face of intractable reality and human nature. In this respect he is very much in the conservative mold. See, for example, his Newsweek column, February 19, 1973, p. 70): "The error of supposing that the behavior of social organism can be shaped at will is widespread. It is the fundamental error of most social reformers..." Yet when it comes to his unswerving confidence in the ability of market capitalism to function according to principles of rationality, Friedman is on thin ice indeed. In this crucial matter, the empirical-historical evidence does not support his assumption.

59. One could note the fact that Milton Friedman, like so many of his fellow conservatives, is quite sympathetic to authoritarian regimes, regardless of their ruthless suppress-

ion of internal dissidents, such as the white minority rule regime in South Africa and its apartheid policies, or the Chile military dictatorship, to which he became an ad hoc advisor for a time. The anti-democratic, pro-elitist bias that underlies Friedman's political-social philosophy should at least be noted.

60. Diggins, *Up From Communism*, *op. cit.*, p. 3.

61. *Ibid.*, p. 14.

62. *Ibid.*, p. 398.

63. See George H. Nash, *The Conservative Intellectual Movement in America*, *op. cit.*, pp. 334-342.

64. See Frank Meyer, "Conservatism," in *Left, Right and Center: Essays on Liberalism and Conservatism in the United States* (ed.) by Robert A. Goldwin (Chicago: Rand McNally & Co., 1969 paperback edition), p. 2.

65. *Ibid.*

66. *Ibid.*, p. 4.

67. *Ibid.*, p. 5.

68. *Ibid.*, p. 6.

69. *Ibid.*

70. *Ibid.*, p. 7.

71. *Ibid.*

72. *Ibid.*, p. 8.

73. *Ibid.*

74. *Ibid.*, p. 11.

75. *Ibid.*, p. 12.

76. See Frank S. Meyer, "Principles and Heresies," *National Review*, September 25, 1962, p. 223.

77. *Ibid.*

78. *Ibid.*,: "I have thought that the rigid positions of doctrinaire traditionalists and doctrinaire libertarians were both distortions of the same fundamental tradition and could be reconciled and assimilated in the central consensus of American conservatism."

79. Nash, *The Conservative Intellectual Movement in America*, *op. cit.*, pp. 339-340.

80. Frank S. Meyer, *In Defense of Freedom: A Conservative Credo* (Chicago: Henry Regnery Co., 1962), p. 28.

81. *Ibid.*

82. *Ibid.*, pp. 44-45.

83. *Ibid.*, p. 55.

84. *Ibid.*, p. 65.

85. *Ibid.*, p. 70.

86. _Ibid._, p. 101.

87. _Ibid._, p. 124.

88. _Ibid._, p. 133.

89. _Ibid._, p. 135.

90. _Ibid._, p. 155.

91. _Ibid._, p. 154.

92. See Frank S. Meyer, "Principles and Heresies," _National Review_, January 25, 1966, p. 71.

93. See Glenn Tinder, "Community: The Tragic Ideal," _The Yale Review_, Summer, 1976: "Even though community is unattainable, it is seemingly true that a person is fully himself only when united with others and that the longing for community is inherent in men." (p. 554)

94. See Sanford A. Lakoff, "The Liberal Revival," paper delivered at the 1976 Annual Meeting of the American Political Science Association, The Palmer House, Chicago, Illinois, Sept. 2-5, 1976: "Like Hayek, Nozick is clearly working the classical or laissiz-faire vein of the liberal mother lode..." (p. 2)

95. See Josiah Lee Auspitz's review, "Libertarians Without Law," _Commentary_, September, 1975, pp. 76-84: "Two errors which Nozick makes are so widely shared that they stamp not only the character of his book but of much American discourse about politics. He rigorously uses legitimacy as a concept which excludes coercion and, more loosely, treats liberty as a concept which excludes equality." (p. 82)
   See also Sheldon S. Wolin's review, "Proposed: That the Best Government is the Least Government," _The New York Times Book Review_, May 11, 1975, pp. 31-32: "That the book is wholly devoid of political sense is evident in the dichotomy from which it begins: the State defined as the monopoly on violence versus the individual endowed with near-absolute rights." (p. 32)
   See also Ernest Van Den Haag, "The Libertarian Argument," _National Review_, July 4, 1975, pp. 729-731: "Unless individuals are tied together by affectional social bonds, rights can no more exist than societies can. Rights are but the rationalization of these materially prior affectional ties." (p. 731)
   See also George Kateb, "The Nightwatchman State," _The American Scholar_, Winter, 1975, pp. 816-826: "Nozick's conception of the person is mangled by an almost absolute right of property..." (p. 825)
   See also Michael J. McGrath, "On Radical Individualism and Social Justice: A Critique of Robert Nozick's Political Theory," paper delivered at the 1976 Annual Meeting of the American Political Science Association, The Palmer House, Chicago, Illinois, Sept. 2-5, 1976: "Simply put, Nozick's minimal state caters to self-interested, acquisitive beings always on the make to increase their private holdings, but lacking any concern for the public situation except when their rights are threatened." (p. 4)

96. See review of Anarchy, State and Utopia, Political Theory, Vol. 3, No. 1, August, 1975, pp. 331-336: "Justice for Nozick, as for Thrasymachus, is the interest of the stronger. Any contract that anyone makes, so long as he is not actually threatened with deliberately produced harm by the person with whom he makes it, is just, even if he is facing a de facto monopoly seller of goods, a de facto monopoly buyer of labor, or a defacto monopoly supplier of physical security. Conversely, if the weaker propose to club together to use the coercive machinery of the state to control contracts or redistribute resources, that is unjust. If Nozick is discontented to find that his views put him in nasty company, he should, I suggest, reflect on the possibility that the reason is that these are nasty views." (p. 334)

97. Robert Nozick, Anarchy, State and Utopia (New York: Basic Books, 1974), p. ix.

98. Ibid., p. 6.

99. Ibid., p. 12.

100. Ibid., p. 24.

101. Ibid., p. 52.

102. Ibid., p. 90.

103. Ibid., p. 94.

104. Ibid., p. 118.

105. Ibid., p. 133.

106. Ibid., p. 149.

107. See John Rawls, A Theory of Justice (Cambridge, Mass.: Belknap Press of Harvard University Press, 1971 paperback edition).
See also Norman Daniels, (ed.) Readings Rawls: Critical Studies of a Theory of Justice (New York: Basic Books paperback, 1974).

108. Nozick, Anarchy, State and Utopia, op. cit., p. 190.

109. Ibid., p. 193.

110. Ibid., p. 195.

111. Ibid., p. 219.

112. Ibid., p. 274.

113. Ibid., pp. 333-34.

114. See Philip P. Witonski, "New Argument," review of Robert Nozick's Anarchy, State and Utopia, The New Republic, August 26, 1975, pp. 29-30: "There is something of the Social Darwinist in Nozick, and one cannot fail to notice the specter of Herbert Spencer's Man versus the State in his pages." (p. 29)
See also Herbert Spencer, The Man versus the State (Caldwell, Idaho: The Caxton Printers, Ltd., 1969, originally pub-

lished in 1892).

115. Although he now calls himself a "left-wing libertarian," Karl Hess, former top speechwriter for Barry Goldwater in his 1964 presidential bid and supporter of rightist causes, has written a semi-autobiographical essay explaining why he now thinks of himself as a libertarian of the Left. See Karl Hess, _Dear America_ (New York: William Morrow & Co., 1975). What he now seeks is democracy from the "bottom-up" rather than from the "top-down." And he repudiates his earlier conservative affiliations because "conservative politics... is corporate politics. In my long years of service to that politics it was conformity to corporate norms...that dominated, and not loyalty to—or even interest in—self in any deep sense." (p. 63)

NOTES AND REFERENCES

Chapter 6

1. See Seymour Martin Lipset & Everett Carll Ladd, Jr., "College Generations—from the 1930's to the 1960's," *The Public Interest*, No. 25, Fall, 1971, pp. 99-113. See also Kenneth Keniston, *Youth and Dissent: The Rise of a New Opposition* (New York: Harcourt, Brace, Jovanovich, 1971: "Opposition among today's young, far from springing from deprivation, poverty, or discrimination, springs from affluence, wealth, and privilege. Never before have so many who had so much been so deeply disenchanted with their inheritance." (p. ix)

2. See Richard Sennett, *The Uses of Disorder: Personal Identity and City Life* (New York: Random House Vintage Books, 1970); Joseph Bensman and Arthur J. Vidich, *The New American Society & The Revolution of the Middle Class* (Chicago: Quadrangle Books, 1971); Louis Harris, *The Anguish of Change* (New York: W.W. Norton paperback, 1973); Warren G. Bennis and Philip E. Slater, *The Temporary Society* (New York: Harper & Row Colophon Books, 1968); Michael Novak, *The Experience of Nothingness* (New York: Harper & Row Colophon Books, 1971); Edgar Z. Friedenberg, *Coming of Age in America: Growth and Acquiescence* (New York: Random House, 1965); William Braden, *The Age of Aquarius: Technology and the Cultural Revolution* (Chicago: Quadrangle Books, 1970).

3. See Alvin W. Gouldner, *The Dialectic of Ideology and Technology: The Origins, Grammar, and Future of Ideology* (New York: The Seabury Press, 1976): "In industrial countries, there is considerable tension between the 'cultural apparatus,' largely influenced by the intelligentsia and academicians, and the 'consciousness industry,' largely increasingly integrated with political functionaries and the state apparatus." (p. 171)

4. See David Wise, *The Politics of Lying: Government Deception, Secrecy, and Power* (New York: Random House Vintage Books, 1973): "The vast, interlocking federal information machine has one primary purpose: the selling of the government. The machine markets its one product—the President and his administration—by distributing an official, and often misleading, version of truth to the voters. It does so with the help of the system of secrecy and classification, combined with government control over access to military and diplomatic news events...The major objective is to enhance and preserve the Presidential image." (p. 273)

5. See James MacGregor Burns, *Uncommon Sense* (New York: Harper & Row, 1972): "Potentially, the most powerful instrument we have to control change in this fashion is the government. It is the failure of government over the past century to anticipate and manage the enormous social change of that century that most directly lies at the source of our difficulties..." (pp. 7-8)
See also Arthur M. Schlesinger, Jr., *The Crisis of Confi-

dence: Ideas, Power and Violence in America (Boston: Houghton
Mifflin Co., 1969): "The crisis of American confidence comes
in part from a growing sense of the dissociation between ideas
and power. On the one hand, the spread of violence challenges
the old belief in the efficacy of reason; on the other, the
new structures brought into existence by modern industrial society intensify the feelings of individual impotence..." (p. 53)

6. See Richard Hofstadter, The Paranoid Style in American
Politics and Other Essays (New York: Alfred A. Knopf, 1965);
Murray B. Levin, Political Hysteria in America: The Democratic
Capacity for Repression (New York: Basic Books, 1971); Seymour
Martin Lipset and Earl Raab, The Politics of Unreason: Right-
wing Extremism in America, 1790-1970 (New York: Harper Torch-
books, 1973 edition, originally published in 1970); Lionel
Rubinoff, The Pornography of Power (Chicago: Quadrangle Books,
1968); Daniel Bell (ed.), The Radical Right (Garden City, N.Y.:
Doubleday Anchor Books, expanded and updated edition, 1964).

7. See John H. Bunzel, Anti-Politics in America: Reflections on the Anti-Political Temper and Its Distortions of the
Democratic Process (New York: Alfred A. Knopf, 1967): "The extreme right wing is angry at almost everything that has happened to the United States in the last thirty-five years because it is violently at odds with the main drift of the world
of the twentieth century..." (p. 63)
   See also Louis J. Halle, The Ideological Imagination (Chicago: Quadrangle Books, 1972): "All movements of right-wing
radicalism have in common the impulse to restore a past, real
or legendary, in which life was simply, in which an austere
morality prevailed, in which people accepted their respective
places in a hierarchical order that represented nature's intention, and in which all were under the discipline of the
common purpose to uphold this state of things." (p. 107)

8. See Lillian Hellman, Scoundrel Time (Boston: Little,
Brown & Co., 1976), including the Introduction by Garry Wills,
where he places the problem in historical perspective: "An element in America's sense of mission has always been the belief
that close foreign ties might sully the purity of republican
doctrine, a fear expressed by Jefferson himself. It was not
enough to be American in citizenship or residence—one must be
American in one's thoughts. There was such a things as Americanism. And lack of right thinking could make an American
citizen un-American. The test was ideological. That is why
we had such a thing as an Un-American Activities Committee in
the first place. Other countries do not think in terms of,
say, Un-British Activities as a political category. But ours
was the first of the modern ideological countries, born of
revolutionary doctrine, and it has maintained a belief that
return to doctrinal purity is the secret of national strength
for us." (pp. 18-19)

9. See Lipset & Raab, The Politics of Unreason, op. cit.:
"Extremist movements are not primarily the product of extremists. The critical ranks in extremist movements are not composed of evil-structured types called 'extremists,' but rath-

er of ordinary people caught in certain kinds of stress. Some of the more dramatically diabolic aspects of extremism, such as bigotry and conspiracy theory, are not so much the source of extremism as its baggage...Right-wing extremist movements in America have all risen against the background of economic and social changes which have resulted in the displacement of some population groups from former positions of dominance..." (pp. 484-485)

See also Martin Duberman, The Uncompleted Past (New York: E.P. Dutton & Co., 1971 paperback edition).

10. See Levin, Political Hysteria in America, op. cit.: "The nativism and anti-Semitism and anti-intellectualism and anti-radicalism of America become resources with which super-patriots can work. America feeds the hysteria, because the facts tap deep American roots." (p. 98)

11. See Charles Hampden-Turner, Radical Man: The Process of Psycho-Social Development (Cambridge, Mass.: Schenkman Pub. Col, 1970): "Authoritarianism is the logical outcome of conservative philosophy. If the Good is apart from man and man can only approach it by keeping to the straight and narrow path to virtue, then deviation from the path is as wrong as the path itself is right. Compromise between man's devious ways and the 'right path' is therefore less satisfactory than the total victory of 'rightness.'" (p. 259)

See also Meyer A. Zeligs, Friendship & Fratricide: An Analysis of Whittaker Chambers and Alger Hiss (New York: The Viking Press, 1967): "It would appear that Chambers joined the Communist Party at the age of twenty-four not to save the world but to save himself. It provided him with an appropriate milieu, a forum in which he could act out his private fantasies. His main obsession in life centered in the idea of establishing an existence. His concern did not originate as a real threat from external reality (as, for example, his fear of the Soviet Secret Police), but was primarily a fear of loss childhood. As a defense against his sense of guilt about the death of his brother, he was in constant flight, a fugitive from himself. He felt pursued, hid from secret police, was constantly harassed by what he was convinced was 'a concealed enemy.' Such a harried existence was for him less anxiety-producing than introspectively confronting his fratricidal guilt. These are the paradoxical and costly economics of mental illness." (p. 98)

12. See Lipset & Raab, The Politics of Unreason, op. cit.: "And the operational heart of extremism is the repression of difference and dissent, the closing down of the market place of ideas. More precisely, the operational essence of extremism, or monism, is the tendency to treat cleavage and ambivalence as illegitimate. This is a critical aspect of extremism because of certain premises that underlie the concept of "the open market place.'" (p. 6)

See also Richard Hofstadter, "Pseudo-Conservatism Revisited (1962)," in Daniel Bell, (ed.) The Radical Right, op. cit.: "The right-wing tolerates no compromise, accepts no half-measures, understands no defeats. In this respect, it stands psychologically outside the frame of normal democratic politics, which is largely an affair of compromise. One of the most fundamental qualities, then, in the right-wing mentality of our time is its implicit utopianism. I can think of no more economical way of expressing its fundamental difference from the spirit of genuine conservatism." (p. 102)

13. See Sheilah R. Koeppen, "The Republican Right," The Annals, March, 1969: "Yet, the support of the Radical Right is valuable to a political party, less in the numbers of right-ists than in the time and money which they are willing to de-vote to Republican activities. The result has been an uneasy alliance between the Radical Right and the Republican party. Republican party leaders have denounced political extremism in general terms, but have usually refrained from singling out for attack a particular radical-right organization." (p. 81)
    See also Michael Paul Rogin, The Intellectuals and Mc-Carthy: The Radical Spector (Cambridge, Mass.: MIT Press paper-back, 1967): "Leaders of the GOP saw in McCarthy a way back to national power after twenty years in the political wilderness (p. 216)...It is tempting to explain the hysteria with which McCarthy infected the country by the hysterical preoccupations of masses of people. But the masses did not levy an attack on their political leaders; the attack was made by a section of the political elite against another and was nurtured by the very elites under attack. The populace contributed to McCarth-y's power primarily because it was worried about communism, Korea, and the cold war (p. 217)...McCarthyism fed into an ex-isting conservative tradition at the elite level, very conser-vative on both domestic and foreign questions (p.225)...Mc-Carthy came out of an old American Right. What was in part new was the intensity and hysteria he provoked. This in turn is largely explained by changes in American society and poli-tics that agitated the conservatives and by the new importance of foreign policy (p. 227)...But perhaps the single most im-portant characteristic of supporters of McCarthy in the na-tional opinion polls was their party affiliation: Democrats opposedMcCarthy, and Republicans supported him (p. 233)."

14. See George F. Kennan, Memoirs 1925-1950, vol. I (Bos-ton: Little, Brown & Co., 1967), p. 322).

15. See Richard H. Rovere, Senator Joe McCarthy (New York: The World Publishing Co., Meridian Books, 1959 edition).

16. Ibid., p. 125.

17. Ibid., p. 130.

18. Robert Griffith, The Politics of Fear: Joseph R. Mc-Carthy and the Senate (New York: Hayden Book Co., 1970 paper-back edition), p. 66.

19. Ibid., pp. 67-68.

20. Ibid., p. 101.

21. Ibid., p. 107.

    See also Daniel P. Moynihan, "The Presidency and the

Press," <u>Commentary</u>, March, 1971: "The American style of objective journalism made McCarthy. He would not, I think, have gotten anywhere in Great Britain where, because it would have been judged he was lying, the stories would simply not have been printed...McCarthy was nominally searching out Communists, but his preferred targets were Eastern patricians, while his supporters were to an alarming degree, members of the Catholic working class."

22. See David Rees, <u>Harry Dexter White: A Study of Paradox</u> (New York: Coward, McCann & Geoghegan, 1973). Mr. Rees, in his careful biography of Harry Dexter White, seems to feel that the evidence, although more circumstantial than provable, does implicate White as part of a government based Communist espionage group involving Alger Hiss, Whittaker Chambers, and others. Although White died of a heart attack shortly after an apprently successful (for him) appearance before a Congressional committee investigating the matter: "The writer considers that the arguments against the credibility of Miss Bentley and Chambers on the central issue regarding White are not sustained..." (p. 425)

See also George F. Kennan, <u>Memoirs 1950-1963</u>, vol. II (Boston: Little, Brown & Co., 1972): "What the phenomenon of McCarthyism did do, in my case, was to implant in my consciousness a lasting doubt as to the adequacy of our political system, and the level of public understanding on which it rested, to the role of a great power in the modern age. A political system and a public opinion, it seemed to me, that could be so easily disoriented by this sort of challenge in one epoch would be no less vulnerable to similar ones in another. I could never recapture, after these experiences of the late 1940s and 1950s, quite the same faith in the American system of government and in traditional American outlooks that I had had, despite all the discouragements of official life, before that time." (p. 228)

See also E.J. Kahn, Jr., <u>The China Hands: America's Foreign Service Officers and What Befell Them</u> (New York: Penguin Books, 1976): "In the fall of 1960, when so much of what was happening in the United States was influenced by attitudes toward China, Everett F. Drumright was the American ambassador at Taipei, and Edward E. Riche, who a year after Kennedy won would become deputy assistant secretary of state for Far Eastern affairs, was a member of that department's Policy Planning Staff. Drumright and Rice were largely unknown, except to people whose thoughts were almost exclusively focused on China, but that they were where they were was significant. For they were the only two China-language experts in the Foreign Service with pre-Second-World-War experience in their field who still had anything to do with China. At the outbreak of the war, there had been more than a score of specialists like them in the service. But in the fifteen years that had elapsed since V-J Day—and the eleven years since Mao Tse-tung had displaced Chiang in China—the rest of the 'Old China Hands' of the Foreign Service had been eased out, or thrown out, of any consequential participation in Chinese affairs, on the ground that they had had a hand in 'losing' China." (p. 1)

See also Allen Weinstein, <u>Perjury: The Hiss-Chambers Case</u> (New York: Alfred A. Knopf, 1978), a well-documented, highly persuasive historical review of the famous Hiss-Chambers case, wherein the author concludes that Hiss was guilty of lying repeatedly about his relationship with Whittaker Chambers and was almost certainly involved in a Soviet engineered and directed espionage group of a dozen or so American officials who transmitted secret information to Soviet KGB agents in the United States in the 1930s and 40s. So there was some justification for public concern about "internal subversion" if Weinstein and others are correct.

23. (New York: Atheneum, 1969 paperback edition).

24. <u>The Politics of Fear</u>, <u>op</u>. <u>cit</u>., p. 241.

25. James F. Simon, <u>In His Own Image: The Supreme Court in Richard Nixon's America</u> (David McKay Co., 1973 paperback edition), pp. 30-31.

26. See William F. Buckley, Jr., and Brent L. Bozell, <u>McCarthy and His Enemies: The Record and Its Meaning</u> (Chicago: Henry Regnery Co., 1954).

27. Besides the books previously cited by Rovere, Rogin, Hofstadter, Griffith, Latham, Caute, see also Athan Theoharis, <u>Seeds of Repression: Harry S. Truman and the Origins of McCarthyism</u> (Chicago: Quadrangle Books, 1971).

28. See also the essay by Daniel Bell, "The Dispossessed (1962)," in Bell (ed.), <u>The Radical Right</u>, <u>op</u>. <u>cit</u>.: "Today the politics of the radical right is the politics of frustration—the sour impotence of those who find themselves unable to understand, let alone command, the complex mass society that is the polity today. In our time, insofar as there is no real left to counterpoise to the right, the liberal has become the psychological target of that frustration..." (p. 42)

29. <u>Ibid</u>., p. 24.

30. <u>Op</u>. <u>cit</u>., p. 268.

31. Latham, <u>The Communist Controversy in Washington</u>, <u>op</u>. <u>cit</u>., p. 423.

32. <u>The Politics of Fear</u>, <u>op</u>. <u>cit</u>., p. 319.

33. Theoharis, <u>Seeds of Repression</u>, <u>op</u>. <u>cit</u>., pp. 5-6.

34. Robert Griffith and Athan Theoharis (eds.), <u>The Specter: Original Essays on the Cold War and the Origins of McCarthyism</u> (New York: Franklin Watts, New Viewpoints Book, 1974).

35. <u>Ibid</u>., p. xii.

36. <u>Ibid</u>., p. 16.

37. <u>Ibid</u>., pp. 43-44.

38. Levin, <u>Political Hysteria in America</u>, <u>op</u>. <u>cit</u>., p. 210.

39. See Norman H. Nie, Sidney Verba and John R. Petrocik, The Changing American Voter (Cambridge, Mass.: Harvard University Press paperback edition, 1976): "Issues play a role in an election if one or both of the candidates takes an outlying position on the issue scale. If each candidate takes a position at the opposite end of the issue spectrum, the election is 'balanced' and they divide the vote—the leftist candidate taking most of those votes to the left of the scale; the rightist taking the right votes. But if one candidate is close to the center, while the other candidate is closer to the extreme, more voters find themselves closer to the centrist than to the outlier, and the vote tilts in favor of the former." (p. 325)

40. See Erwin C. Hargrove, The Power of the Modern Presidency (New York: Alfred A. Knopf, 1974 paperback edition): "The nation badly needs a sophisticated, politically skillful conservative tradition in the Presidency to make constructive use of the waiting periods between the cycles of reform...The conspicuous deficiency of leaders of the American conservative tradition has been their lack of public purpose and political skill. They have not had the tradition of a governing class to draw on." (p. 181)

41. See Philip E. Converse, Aage R. Clausen, and Warren E. Miller, "Electoral Myth and Reality: the 1964 Election," The American Political Science Review, vol. LIX, no. 2, June, 1965, pp. 321-336.

42. A recent study finds a marked transformation in the public's electoral behavior, and predicts increased commitment to issues and ideology, leading to greater rationality and responsibility in voting behavior than has been the case in the recent past. See Gerald M. Pomper, Voters' Choice: Varieties of American Electoral Behavior (New York: Dodd, Mead & Co., 1975), p. 182. For a critique of this position, see John Wettergreen, "The American Voter and His Surveyors," The Political Science Reviewer, vol. VII, Fall, 1977, pp. 181-227.

43. (New York: A MacFadden Capitol Hill Book, 1964 paperback edition; originally published 1960).

44. Ibid; see Forward.

45. Ibid., p. 10.

46. Ibid., pp. 13-14.

47. Ibid., p. 19.

48. Ibid., p. 37.

49. Ibid., p. 38.

50. Ibid., p. 40.

51. Ibid., p. 50.

52. Ibid., p. 61.

53. Ibid., p. 63.

54. Ibid., p. 64.

55. _Ibid_., pp. 68-69.

56. _Ibid_., pp. 75-76.

57. _Ibid_., p. 84.

58. _Ibid_., pp. 122-126.

59. Barry Goldwater, _The Conscience of a Majority_ (New York: Pocket Books, 1971 edition, originally published by Prentice-Hall, 1970), p. 80.

60. _Ibid_., p. 39.

61. _Ibid_.

62. _Ibid_.

63. _Ibid_., p. 45.

64. See Richard J. Whalen, _Taking Sides: A Personal View of America from Kennedy to Nixon to Kennedy_ (Boston: Houghton Mifflin Co., 1974): "The most cogent conservative arguments imaginable would have fallen on deaf ears among the influential intellectuals who were determined to defend the accomplishments of the New Deal against 'reactionaries.' During a decade in power, liberalism hardened into an ideology, intolerant of unorthodox opinions." (p. 105)

65. _The Making of the President 1964_ (New York: Atheneum, 1965), p. 329.

66. Barry Goldwater, _The Conscience of a Majority_, _op. cit_., p. xv.

67. Converse, Clausen and Miller, "Electoral Myth and Reality: the 1964 Election," _op. cit_., p. 331.

68. _The Blue Book of the John Birch Society_ (Belmont: Western Islands Publishers, 1959).

69. _Ibid_., p. 163.

70. _Ibid_., pp. 164-165.

71. _Ibid_., p. 21.

72. _Ibid_., p. 22.

73. _Ibid_.

74. _Ibid_., pp. 74-75.

75. _Ibid_., p. 28.

76. _Ibid_., p. 44.

77. _Ibid_., pp. 61-63.

78. _Ibid_., pp. 72-73.

79. _Ibid_., pp. 81-82.

80. _Ibid_., p. 80.

81. _Ibid_., p. 88.

82. _Ibid_., p. 94.

83. Ibid., pp. 103-115.

84. Ibid., p. 120.

85. Ibid., p. 120.

86. Ibid., p. 122.

87. Ibid., p. 125.

88. Ibid., pp. 134-138.

89. Ibid., p. 149.

90. Ibid., p. 151.

91. Ibid., p. 152.

92. Ibid., p. 156.

93. (Belmont: Belmont Publishing Co., 1964).

94. Ibid., p. 20.

95. Ibid., pp. 42-44.

96. Ibid., p. 59.

97. Ibid., p. 60.

98. Ibid., p. 83.

99. Ibid., p. 133.

100. Ibid., p. 152.

101. Ibid., pp. 22-23.

102. See especially American Opinion, June, 1973 issue.

103. American Opinion, March, 1973.

104. The Paranoid Style in American Politics, op. cit., p. ix.

105. Ibid., p. 39.

106. Ibid., p. 51.

107. (New York: Basic Books, 1960 paperback edition), p. 6.

108. See Gilbert Abcarian and Sherman M. Stanage, "Alienation and the Radical Right," The Journal of Politics, vol. 27, no. 4, November, 1965: "Rightwing emphasis on individualism reflects anxiety over the individual's apparent inability to make autonomous or free decisions that affect public and private life. Increased collectivism is held to have violated the political, moral, economic and other 'laws' of nature, creating a hostile, normless world which the individual faces with a sense of dread and shame...The rightwing admonition to forsake democracy and return to republicanism is partly generated by hostility to prevailing currents of equalitarianism and social welfare..." (p. 790)

109. See the essay by Raymond E. Wolfinger, Barbara Kaye Wolfinger, Kenneth Prewitt and Sheilah Rosenhack, "America's Radical Right: Politics and Ideology," in David Apter (ed.), Ideology and Discontent (New York: The Free Press, 1964), p. 186.

110. "The John Birch Society: A Profile," _The Journal of Politics_, vol. 36, no. 1, February, 1974, p. 193.

111. _The Radical Right_, op. cit., p. 42.

112. _Anti-Politics in America_, op. cit., p. 63.

113. See Benjamin R. Epstein and Arnold Foster, _The Radical Right: Report on the John Birch Society and its Allies_ (New York: Random House Vintage Books, 1967).

114. _The Farther Shores of Politics: The American Political Fringe Today_ (New York: Simon & Schuster Clarion Book, 1968), p. 550.

115. "The John Birch Society: A Profile," op. cit., p. 194.

116. "The John Birch Society: Its Aims, Structure, and Methods," Masters Degree Thesis presented to the Graduate Faculty of Danbury State College, May, 1967, p. 7.

117. _The American Far Right: A Case Study of Billy James Hargis and Christian Crusade_ (Grand Rapids: William Berdmas Publishing Co., 1968), p. 105.

118. See Rogin, _The Intellectuals and McCarthy_, op. cit., p. 233.

119. Lipset & Raab, _The Politics of Unreason_, op. cit., p. 449.

120. See Charles R. Adrian and Charles Press, _American Politics Reappraised: The Enchantment of Camelot Dispelled_ (New York: McGraw-Hill, 1974 paperback edition): "The reactionaries of the far right live in a dream world, imagining that America has somehow bypassed the ideal society that might have been and is so bogged down in a morass of foreign and domestic policy which they see as being dysfunctional for the Republic, and as keeping us from returning to the point where we went astray and picking up once again the path toward the true American dream. Their politics is a politics of nostalgia. The reactionary shares many characteristics with the radical of the left, as both tend to advocate politically unfeasible policies and procedures and in many cases their means are dysfunctional toward their ends even if they could be carried out; both are extremely impatient with those who disagree with them or who would resort to political compromise. This is because they are 'true believers' who feel certain that they have proper solutions to the nation's ills. Characteristically, they truly believe that there is a mammouth conspiracy by the Establishment to run the nation as it is being run and to keep their 'truths' from becoming known or accepted." (pp. 73-74)

NOTES AND REFERENCES

Chapter 7

1. See William F. Buckley Jr.,"Notes Towards an Empirical Definition of Conservatism," in Frank S. Meyer (ed.) What is Conservatism? (New York: Holt, Rinehart & Winston, 1964), pp. 211-226.

2. For a comprehensive, well documented intellectual history of the National Review see Nash, The Conservative Intellectual Movement in America, op. cit.; a more critical appraisal will be found in Diggins, Up From Communism, op. cit. See also the 20th Anniversary issue of the National Review, December 5, 1975.

3. The American Dissent: A Decade of Modern Conservatism (Garden City, N.Y.: Doubleday, 1966), p. 252.

4. See Meyer, What is Conservatism? op. cit.

5. Ibid., pp. 3-4

6. James Burnham, The Managerial Revolution (Bloomington: Indiana University Press, 1966 paperback edition, originally published in 1941).

7. Ibid., p. vii.

8. Ibid., p. 41.

9. Ibid., p. 11.

10. Ibid., p. 118.

11. Ibid., p. 126.

12. Ibid., p. 130.

13. Ibid., p. 138.

14. Ibid., p. 157.

15. Ibid., p. 225.

16. Ibid., p. 273.

17. Ibid., pp. 180-181.

18. See Milovan Djilas, The New Class (New York: Frederick A. Praeger, 1957).
See also John P. Diggins, "Four Theories in Search of Reality: James Burnham, Soviet Communism, and the Cold War," The American Political Science Review, vol. LXX, no. 2, June, 1976, pp. 492-508: "Bureaucracy had not been a problem in orthodox Marxist political thought, and technological elites had not been foreseen even by Lenin, who elevated party control to an Archimedean principle of power only to blind himself to the ultimate authoritarian consequences of his own creation. Burnham was not the first writer to discern in the emergence of bureaucracy a refutation of Marx's class analysis, nor was he the first to see the hidden oligarchical tend-

encies that are potential in all political organizations.   But
Burnham was the first to carry Marxism to its logical conclusion in order to turn it back upon itself...As a sociological
phenomenon, managerial rule, technological authority, and bureaucratic domination could be traced back to the mode of production, the ownership of which Marx had regarded as the sole
source of power and freedom.   Burnham may have indiscriminately
equated ownership with control; he may have narrowly identified
economic power with political authority and class domination;
and he may have valsely stressed property rather than income
as the criterion of class membership.   The point is, however,
that it was perfectly Marxian to make all three assumptions."
(pp. 494-495)

19. (Chicago: Henry Regnery Co., pp. 19-59).

20. _Ibid._, p. 114.

21. _Ibid._, p. 296.

22. _Ibid._, p. 309.

23. _Ibid._, pp. 327-328.

24. _Ibid._, p. 336.

25. Suicide of the West: An Essay on the Meaning and Destiny of Liberalism (New York: The John Day Co., 1964).

26. _Ibid._, p. 26.

27. _Ibid._, p. 42.

28. _Ibid._, p. 59.

29. _Ibid._, p. 178.

30. _Ibid._, p. 287.

31. _Ibid._, p. 294.

32. See In Front of Your Nose 1945-1950, vol. 4, The Col-
lected Essays, Journalism, and Letters of George Orwell by
Sonia Orwell and Ian Angus (eds.) (New York: Harcourt, Brace
& World, 1968), pp. 160-181 and pp. 313-326.

33. _Ibid._, p. 169.

34. _Ibid._, pp. 172-174: "Power worship blurs political
judgment because it leads, almost unavoidably, to the belief
that present trends will continue.   Whoever is winning at the
moment will always seem to be invincible." (p. 174)

35. _Ibid._, p. 181.

36. _Ibid._, p. 321.

37. _Ibid._, pp. 324-325.

38. The Conservative Mind: From Burke to Eliot (New York:
Avon Books, 1973 Equinox Edition, Fourth Revised Edition).

39. (La Salle: Open Court, 1974).

40. (Chicago: Henry Regnery Co., 1954).

41. _Ibid._, p. 6.

42. _Ibid._, p. 10.

43. _Ibid._, p. 21.

44. _Ibid._, pp. 22-23.

45. _Ibid._, pp. 34-35.

46. _Ibid._, p. 41.

47. _Ibid._, p. 47.

48. _Ibid._, p. 50.

49. _Ibid._, p. 66.

50. _Ibid._, pp. 66-67.

51. _Ibid._, p. 117.

52. _Ibid._, pp. 120-121.

53. _Ibid._, p. 134.

54. _Ibid._, p. 184.

55. _Ibid._, p. 240.

56. _Ibid._, p. 259.

57. _Ibid._, pp. 264-265.

58. _Ibid._, p. 288.

59. _Ibid._, p. 301.

60. _Ibid._, p. 303.

61. _Ibid._, p. 305.

62. _Beyond the Dreams of Avarice: Essays of a Social Critic_ (Chicago: Henry Regnery Co., 1956), p. 11.

63. _Ibid._, p. 13.

64. _Ibid._, p. 35.

65. _Ibid._, p. 37.

66. _Ibid._, p. 56.

67. _Ibid._, pp. 101-132.

68. _Ibid._, p. 138.

69. _Ibid._, p. 141.

70. _Ibid._, p. 166.

71. _Ibid._, p. 172.

72. _Op. cit._, p. 409.

73. _Ibid._, p. 416.

74. See Chapter XIII, _The Conservative Mind_, _op. cit._

75. _Ibid._, pp. 436-437.

76. Ibid., pp. 437-439.

77. _Ibid._, p. 443.

78. _Ibid._, p. 444.

79. See "Prescription, Authority, and Ordered Freedom," in Frank S. Meyer (ed.), _What is Conservatism?_, _op. cit._, pp. 23-64.

80. (Chicago: Henry Regnery Co., 1951 paperback edition).

81. _Ibid._; See Forward

82. _Ibid._, p. 175.

83. See especially William Buckley, Jr., _Up From Liberalism_ (New Yorchelle, N.Y.: Arlington House, 1968 edition, originally published in 1959): "Liberalism is powerful but decadent...conservatism is weak but viable." (p. xviii)

84. See collections of his newspaper columns and varied essays: _Inveighing We Will Go_ (New York: G.P. Putnam, Berkley Medallion Book, 1973); _The Jeweler's Eye_ (New York: G.P. Putnam, Berkley Medallion Book, 1969); _Cruising Speed—A Documentary_ (New York: Bantam Books, 1972 edition).

85. _Inveighing We Will Go_, _op. cit._, p. 33.

86. William Buckley, Jr., _The Governor Listeth: A Book of Inspired Political Revelations_ (New York: G.P. Putnam's Sons, 1970), p. 30.

87. _Ibid._, p. 100.

88. _New York Post_ column, August 8, 1974.

89. (New York: G.P. Putnam's Sons, Berkley Medallion Book, 1975).

90. _Ibid._, p. 6.

91. _Ibid._, p. 24.

92. _Ibid._, p. 26.

93. _Ibid._, p. 33.

94. _Ibid._, p. 50.

95. _Ibid._, pp. 63-64.

96. _Ibid._, p. 80.

97. _Ibid._, p. 89.

98. _Ibid._, p. 101.

99. _Ibid._, p. 121.

100. _Ibid._, p. 124.

101. _Ibid._, p. 153.

102. The term neo-conservatism was widely applied to conservative thinkers who achieved a certain popular renown in the post World War II period. Recently, however, the term has been used by liberals and socialists to designate the thinkers who are featured in Chapter 8 of this study. My own preference,

if a label is necessary, is "liberal-conservative" in regard
to the latter group, and the label I feel is more appropriate
to the earlier group of so-called neo-conservatives (except-
ing Peter Viereck) is "ideological conservatism." In my judgment, this is a more precise and accurate way of describing
the matter.

103. Marie Henault, Peter Viereck (New York: Twayne Publishers, 1969), pp. 17-22.

104. Peter Viereck, Conservatism Revisited, revised and en-
larged edition, with the addition of The New Conservatism—
What Went Wrong? (New York: The Free Press, 1965 paperback
edition), p. 18.

105. Ibid., p. 38.

106. Ibid., p. 32.

107. Ibid., p. 110.

108. Peter Viereck, The Unadjusted Man: A New Hero for Americans (New York: Capricorn Books, 1962, originally published
in 1956), p. 40.

109. Ibid., p. 161.

110. Peter Viereck, "The Revolt Against the Elite (1955)"
in Bell, The Radical Right, op. cit., p. 171.

111. The Unadjusted Man, op. cit., p. 173.

112. Shame and Glory of the Intellectuals: Babbitt Jr. vs.
The Rediscovery of Values (Boston: The Beacon Press, 1953),
p. 262.

113. Ibid., p. 248.

114. Ibid.

115. Ibid., p. 221.

116. Conservatism Revisited, op. cit., p. 123.

117. Ibid., pp. 125-126.

118. Ibid., p. 138.

119. Ibid., pp. 145-150.

120. Ibid., p. 153.

121. See Diggins, Up From Communism, op. cit.: "Ultimately
what vitiates American conservatism is not so much a lack of
unity as a lack of historical continuity. To be a conservative means to become aware of the historical dimension of
knowledge, to nurture, revere, and defend those values and institutions that belong to the past. Knowledge of the American
past, however, is precisely the paradox of American conservatism. The same problem of American 'exceptionalism' that confronted the Old Left in the thirties confronted the New Right
in the fifties. For the same country that failed to produce
a revolutionary proletariat failed to produce a conservative
aristocracy. The Right, no less than the Left, must come to

terms with the bourgeois ethos of Lockian individualism that
resounds throughout American history like a choral fugue on
the theme of liberal 'consensus.' Indeed, the dilemma is
greater for the neo-conservative, for even while attacking
contemporary liberalism and radicalism he is forced to defend America in terms of its liberal tradition." (p. 453)

122. See <u>New York Times</u>, February 15, 1975.

123. See the essays in Coser and Howe, <u>The New Conservatives:
A Critique from the Left</u>, <u>op</u>. <u>cit</u>.; in this book the term neo-
conservative is applied to those thinkers featured in Chapter
8 of this book—all of whom were once certified on the Left of
the political spectrum. I feel that the term liberal-conservative is a much more precise rendering of their political outlook, because they tend still to be liberal in their values and
ends but conservative in regard to means. In this regard, they
are much more receptive to change than is the case with the
"conservatives" dealt with in this chapter.
    See also William J. Newman, <u>The Futilitarian Society</u> (New
York: George Braziller, 1961), wherein the term "neo-conservative" is applied to historians and political philosophers such
as Peter Viereck, Russell Kirk, Clinton Rossiter, Walter Lippmann, Louis Hartz, Daniel Boorstin, and Daniel Bell, while
"old conservative" is used to designate more libertarian conservatives such as William H. Chamberlin, Felix Morley, James
Burnham, and Senator Goldwater. This is a highly provocative
study which is most critical of, and unsympathetic toward, all
varieties of conservatism. Although parts of the analysis dealing with individual thinkers is quite sharp and valuable, the
book is seriously flawed, since its pervasively anti-conservative bias frequently degenerates into polemics and superficiality.
    See also the first rate essay, "New Conservatism in Amer-
ica," originally published in 1956, in Horowitz, <u>Ideology and
Utopia in the United States 1956-1976</u>, <u>op</u>. <u>cit</u>, wherein he
stresses the discontinuity between earlier American conservatism of the constitution-building period and contemporary conservatism: "Russell Kirk or Peter Viereck...are very much out-
siders looking in. Twentieth-century conservatives, as an organized body, are outside the power system. The conservative
rhetoric has not penetrated the halls of power, and furthermore the conservative point of view is no longer a consequence
of holding power. In its classic form, conservatism represents
a position of dominance; in its modern form, it is in a subordinate, external, alienated position. An analysis of conservatism shows that while in terms of doctrine there may be lines
of continuity between its classical and modern forms, function-
ally and politically there is incredible discontinuity..." (p.
134) Needless to add, developments since this essay was written in 1956 might require some revision of this interesting
analysis.

Chapter 8

1. "What is the Public Interest?" The Public Interest, No. 1, Fall, 1965, p. 3.

2. Ibid., p. 4.

3. Op. cit.

4. Thomas Sowell, "Black Excellence—The Case of Dunbar High School," The Public Interest, No. 35, Spring, 1974, pp. 3-4.

5. David J. Armor, "The Evidence of Busing," The Public Interest, No. 28, Summer, 1972, pp. 90-124.

6. Robert Martinson, "What Works?—Questions and Answers About Prison Reform," The Public Interest, No. 35, Spring, 1974, pp. 22-54.

7. Brigitte Berger, "People Work—The Youth Culture and the Labor Market," Ibid., pp. 55-66.

8. Daniel J. Elazer, "The 'New Federalism': Can the States be Trusted?" Ibid., pp. 89-102.

9. Iriving Kristol, "Of Populism and Taxes," The Public Interest, No. 28, Summer, 1972, pp. 3-11; Irving Kristol, "Taxes, Poverty, and Equality," No. 37, The Public Interest, Fall, 1974, pp. 3-18.

10. Hon. Edith Green, "The Educational Entrepreneur—a Portrait," No. 28, The Public Interest, Summer, 1972, pp. 12-25.

11. Daniel P. Moynihan, "Equalizing Education: in whose benefit?" No. 29, The Public Interest, Fall, 1972, pp. 69-89.

12. Lester C. Thurow, "Education and Economic Equality," The Public Interest, No. 28, Summer, 1972, pp. 66-81.

13. Nathan Glazer, "On 'Opening Up' the Suburbs," The Public Interest, No. 37, Fall, 1974, pp. 89-111.

14. Marc F. Plattner, "Campaign Financing: the Dilemmas of Reform," Ibid., pp. 112-130.

15. Irving Kristol, "Capitalism, Socialism, and Nihilism," The Public Interest, No. 31, Spring, 1973, pp. 3-16.

16. See "The Welfare State and Its Neoconservative," in Lewis A. Coser and Irving Howe, The New Conservatism, op. cit., pp. 29-63.

17. Michael Walzer, "In Defense of Equality," Ibid., pp. 107-123.

18. David Spitz, "A Grammar of Equality," ibid., pp. 124-150.

19. Mark Kelman, "The Social Costs of Inequality," ibid., pp. 151-164; quotation is from p. 163.

20. David K. Cohen, "Does I.Q. Matter?" *ibid*., pp. 297-227.

21. John H. Goldthorpe, "Theories of Industrial Society: on the Recrudescence of Historicism and the Future of Futurity," *ibid*., pp. 289-316.

22. Robert A. Nisbet, *Community and Power* (New York: Oxford University Press Galaxy Book, 1967), p. xii.

23. *Ibid*., p. 14.

24. *Ibid*., p. 15.

25. *Ibid*., p. 49.

26. *Ibid*., p. 112.

27. *Ibid*., pp. 268-270.

28. Robert A. Nisbet, *The Social Bond: An Introduction to the Study of Society* (New York: Alfred A. Knopf, 1970 paperback edition).

29. See especially Robert A. Nisbet, *The Sociological Tradition* (New York: Basic Books, 1966), p. 154.

30. (New York: Oxford University Press, 1974), p. 95.

31. Robert A. Nisbet, *Social Change and History: Aspects of the Western Theory of Development* (New York: Oxford University Press, 1969), p. 271.
For a negative evaluation of Nisbet's book based upon its purported preference for conservative stability over liberal change, see Gerhard Lenski, "History and Social Change," *American Journal of Sociology*, vol. 82, No. 3, November, 1976, pp. 548-563, where he makes this point: "Available evidence indicates that the rate of change for humanity as a whole has been steadily rising at an accelerating rate. Thus, Nisbet's assertion that fixity is more normal than change fits the facts rather well for the Lower and Middle Paleolithic. On the other hand, the assertion that change is normal and natural is probably closer to the truth for more recent times. But change and continuity alike have been lements in the fabric of life from time immemorial, and it does not serve the cause of social theory to raise questions which, by their very formulation, obscures this fact." (p. 553)

32. Robert A. Nisbet, The Degradation of the Academic Dogma: the University in America 1945-1970 (New York: Basic Books, 1971), pp. 72-73.

33. *Ibid*., p. 98.

34. *Ibid*., p. 100.

35. *Ibid*., p. 199.

36. *Ibid*., p. 207.

37. Robert A. Nisbet, "The Twilight of Authority," *The Public Interest*, No. 15, Spring, 1969, p. 5.

38. *Ibid*., p. 9.

39. Robert Nisbet, "The Pursuit of Equality," _The Public Interest_, No. 35, Spring, 1974, p. 105.

40. _Ibid._, p. 109.

41. _Ibid._, pp. 118-119.

42. Robert A. Nisbet, _The Social Philosophers: Community and Conflict in Western Thought_ (New York: Thomas Y. Crowell, 1973 paperback edition), p. 7.

43. See Robert A. Nisbet, _The Sociological Tradition, op. cit._

44. See especially Robert Nisbet, _Sociology as an Art Form_ (New York: Oxford University Press, 1976 paperback edition).

45. Daniel P. Moynihan, _Maximum Feasible Misunderstanding: Community Action in the War on Poverty_ (New York: The Free Press, 1970 paperback edition), p. 194.

46. _Ibid._, p. 193.

47. _Ibid._, p. lv.

48. One notable exception, however, is Sar A. Levitan and Robert Taggart, _The Promise of Greatness_ (Cambridge, Mass.: Harvard University Press, 1976); this work presents a strong, empirically based defense of "Great Society" liberalism.

49. Nathan Glazer and Daniel P. Moynihan, _Beyond the Melting Pot: The Negroes, Puerto Ricans, Jews, Italians, and Irish of New York City_ (Cambridge, Mass.: MIT Press, 1974 revised paperback edition, originally published 1963), p. lxxxvi.

50. See also Nathan Glazer and Daniel P. Moynihan, (eds.) _Ethnicity: Theory and Experience_ (Cambridge, Mass.: Harvard University Press, 1975 paperback edition).

51. Daniel P. Moynihan, _The Politics of a Guaranteed Income: The Nixon Administration and the Family Assistance Plan_ (New York: Random House Vintage Book, 1973).

52. _Ibid._, p. 5.

53. _Ibid._, p. 440.

54. _Ibid._, p. 551.

55. Daniel P. Moynihan, _Coping: On the Practice of Government_ (New York: Random House, 1973).

56. _Ibid._, p. 13.

57. _Ibid._, p. 21.

58. _Ibid._, p. 22.

59. _Ibid._, p. 25.

60. _Ibid._, p. 27.

61. _Ibid._, p. 35.

62. _Ibid._, p. 47.

63. _Ibid._, p. 132.

64. Coser and Howe, _The New Conservatism_, op. cit., p. 187.

65. See Daniel Bell, _The End of Ideology: On the Exhaustion of Political Ideas in the Fifties_ (New York: The Free Press, 1965 revised paperback edition, originally published in 1962).
For a critique of the "End of Ideology" thesis, see Benjamin S. Kleinberg, _American Society in the Post-industrial Age: Technology, Power, and the End of Ideology_ (Columbus, Ohio: Charles E. Merrill Pub. Co., 1973 paperback edition): "In the past, ideology has reflected present crisis and projected future prospects, while the body of the culture stood as the fixed ground of established social understandings, against which contending ideologies traced the figures of conflict and change. This historical function of ideology, however, is essentially ignored by the end-of-ideologists..." (p. 227)
See also Chaim I. Waxman,(ed.) _The End of Ideology Debate_ (New York: Funk & Wagnalls, 1968).
For a defense of Bell's thesis, see Seymour Martin Lipset, "Ideology & No End," _Encounter_, December, 1972, pp. 17-22: "Much of the debate concerning the concept of the end of ideology has obviously involved ideological differences. Yet the idea in its modern format was advanced as an empirical hypothesis about the consequences of social development on the character of class-related partisan controversy by a number of sociologists and historians. For the most part, the radical critics have ignored the issue of the validity of the hypothesis; they usually have taken its falseness as prima facie, as self evident..." (p. 21)

66. See Daniel Bell, "The End of Ideology in the West: An Epilogue," in _The End of Ideology_, op. cit., pp. 393-407.

67. Daniel Bell, _The Coming of Post-Industrial Society: A Venture in Social Forecasting_ (New York: Basic Books, Inc., 1973), p. 14.

68. _Ibid._, p. 28.

69. _Ibid._, p. 34.

70. _Ibid._, p. 43.

71. _Ibid._, p. 79.

72. _Ibid._, p. 100.

73. _Ibid._, p. 114.

74. _Ibid._, p. 119.

75. _Ibid._, p. 128.

76. _Ibid._, pp. 147-157.

77. _Ibid._, p. 159.

78. _Ibid._, p. 212.

79. _Ibid._, p. 214.

80. _Ibid._, pp. 245-246.

81. _Ibid._, p. 246.

82. _Ibid._, p. 289.

83. <u>Ibid</u>., p. 298.

84. <u>Ibid</u>., p. 324.

85. <u>Ibid</u>., pp. 264-265.

86. <u>Ibid</u>., p. 402.

87. <u>Ibid</u>., p. 453.

88. <u>Ibid</u>., p. 481.

89. Daniel Bell, <u>The Cultural Contradictions of Capitalism</u> (New York: Basic Books, Inc., 1976), p. 10.

90. <u>Ibid</u>., p. 14.

91. <u>Ibid</u>., p. 21.

92. <u>Ibid</u>., p. 24.

93. <u>Ibid</u>., p. 26.

94. <u>Ibid</u>., p. 41.

95. <u>Ibid</u>., p. 71.

96. <u>Ibid</u>., pp. 80-84.

97. <u>Ibid</u>., p. 84.

98. <u>Ibid</u>., p. 95.

99. <u>Ibid</u>., p. 132.

100. <u>Ibid</u>., p. 145.

101. <u>Ibid</u>., p. 245.

102. <u>Ibid</u>., p. 276.

103. See Norman Birnbaum, <u>Toward a Critical Sociology</u> (New York: Oxford University Press, 1971): "Those who command concentrations of power and property are able to employ technical experts—for good or for ill. That expertise is bought, either in the form of bureaucratic organizations producing knowledge, or in the services of individual technical experts. When technicians do rise to actual command positions, they cease to function solely as technicians but function as men in command, men with power." (p. 403)
For a view that appears to coincide more with the Bell thesis, see John Kenneth Galbraith, <u>The New Industrial State</u> (Boston: Houghton Mifflin Co., 1967): "Thus to know how and to what ends we are governed it is necessary to know the goals of the technostructure. These are no longer confined to profit maximization; there is a choice. Depending upon this choice prices, production and income will be different. In none of these matters does the corporation have plenary power; but neither do politicians have absolute power, and interest in their intentions does not for that reason diminish." (p. 111)

104. <u>The Cultural Contradictions of Capitalism</u>, <u>op</u>. <u>cit</u>., p. 15.

105. For a dissenting view, see Richard Sennett & Jonathan Cobb,

<u>The Hidden Injuries of Class</u> (New York: Vintage Books, 1973):
"The increase in low-level white-collar work, jobs which in
many cases demand less skill, allow less independence, and offer less pay than skilled manual labor, is partially dissolving
the traditional symbolic meaning of 'moving up' to the office
from the factory. In the nineteenth and early-twentieth centuries the distinction between blue-and white-collar workers made
a great deal more sense than it does today." (p. 175)

106. (New York: Coward, McCann, & Geoghegan, Inc., 1974),
p. 13.

107. <u>Ibid</u>., p. 26.

108. <u>Ibid</u>., p. 21.

109. <u>The Cultural Contradictions of Capitalism</u>, <u>op</u>. <u>cit</u>.,
p. 273.

110. <u>The Public Interest</u>, No. 1, Fall, 1965, p. 71.

111. <u>Ibid</u>., p. 75.

112. Nathan Glazer, "Housing Problems and Housing Policies,"
<u>The Public Interest</u>, No. 7, Spring, 1967, p. 23.

113. See Nathan Glazer, "On 'Opening Up' the Suburbs," <u>The
Public Interest</u>, No. 37, Fall, 1974, pp. 89-111; "Paradoxes of
Health Care," <u>The Public Interest</u>, No. 22, Winter, 1971, pp.
62-77.

114. Nathan Glazer, "'Regulating' the Poor—or Ruining Them,"
<u>New York Magazine</u>, October 11, 1971, pp. 55-58.

115. <u>Affirmative Discrimination: Ethnic Inequality and Public Policy</u> (New York: Basic Books, 1975).

116. See Ibid., pp. 218-219: "Blacks made progress as discrimination declined in the 1960's under the impact of law and
changing attitudes." He doesn't mention, however, how important
the Montgomery bus boycott, sit-ins, and other forms of a new
black militancy were in creating the climate by which such changes
could occur.

117. <u>Ibid</u>., p. 45.

118. <u>Ibid</u>., p. 58.

119. <u>Ibid</u>., p. 61.

120. <u>Ibid</u>., p. 68.

121. <u>Ibid</u>., pp. 155-167.

122. <u>Ibid</u>., pp. 166-167.

123. <u>Ibid</u>., p. 168.

124. <u>Ibid</u>., pp. 196-197.

125. <u>Ibid</u>., p. 201.

126. "On Being Deradicalized," October, 1970, pp. 74-80.

127. See Nathan Glazer, <u>Remembering the Answers: Essays on</u>

the American Student Revolt (New York: Basic Books, 1970).

128. See Martin Seliger, Ideology and Politics (New York: The Free Press, 1976): "Opinions are also divided as to whether ideology is a mere reflection or rationalization of social conditions, whether it incorporates or derives from ideals, is exclusively linked to social action, or is a belief system or a dimension of one." (p. 13)

129. (New York: Harper Torchbooks, 1972), pp. 12-13.

130. Ibid., p. iv, Preface.

131. Ibid., p. 21.

132. Ibid., p. 144.

133. "The Suburbanized World: Countries that become more equal don't necessarily become happier," by Robert W. Glasgow, February, 1974, pp. 71-80.

134. Irving Kristol, "New Right, New Left," The Public Interest, No. 4, Summer, 1966, pp. 3-7.

135. Irving Kristol, "'When Virtue Loses All Her Loneliness'— Some Reflections on Capitalism and 'the free society,'" The Public Interest, No. 21, Fall, 1970, pp. 3-15.

136. Peter F. Drucker, The Age of Discontinuity: Guidelines to Our Changing Society (New York: Harper & Row, 1968), p. 40.

137. Ibid., p. 56.

138. Ibid., pp. 33-65.

139. Ibid., pp. 68-69.

140. Ibid., pp. 79-81.

141. Ibid., p. 99.

142. Ibid., p. 104.

143. Ibid., p. 124.

144. Ibid., p. 125.

145. Ibid., p. 136.

146. Ibid., p. 179.

147. Ibid., p. 189.

148. Ibid., p. 204.

149. Ibid., p. 212.

150. Ibid., p. 240.

151. Ibid., pp. 241-242.

152. Ibid., p. 288.

153. James Q. Wilson, Political Organization (New York: Basic Books, 1973), p. 14.

154. See James Q. Wilson, Thinking About Crime (New York:

Vintage Books, 1977): "Though intellectually rewarding from a practical point of view it is a mistake to think about crime in terms of its 'causes' and then to search for ways to alleviate those causes. We must think instead of what it is feasible for a government or a community to do, and then try to discover, by experimentation and observation, which of those things will produce, at acceptable costs, desirable changes in the level of criminal victimization." (p. 233)

155. See James Q. Wilson and Edward C. Banfield, City Politics (Cambridge, Mass.: Harvard University Press, 1963), especially chapters 3 and 16. See also James Q. Wilson and Edward C. Banfield, "Political Ethos Revisited," The American Political Science Review, vol. LXV, No. 4, December, 1971, pp. 1048-1062.

156. See "The Urban Unease: Community vs. City," The Public Interest, No. 12, Summer, 1968, pp. 25-39.

157. The Public Interest, No. 39, Spring, 1975, p. 129.

158. Edward C. Banfield, The Unheavenly City Revisited (Boston: Little, Brown & Co., 1973 edition), pp. 1-3.

159. Ibid., p. 54.

160. Ibid., p. 84.

161. Ibid., p. 165.

162. Ibid., p. 184.

163. Ibid., pp. 125-127.

164. Ibid., p. 234.

165. Ibid., pp. 236-237.
See also Edward C. Banfield's contribution to "A Symposium: Nixon, the Great Society, and the Future of Social Policy," Commentary, May, 1977: "In my judgment a sound program in the area of social policy would involve a radical devolution of federal activities to state and local government and, beyond that, of many public ones to competitive markets. Such a program is, however, incompatible with the nature of our political system, which is energized by the pressures that interests exert to get things from government..." (p. 34)

166. See T.R. Marmor, "Banfield's 'Heresy,'" Commentary, July, 1972, pp. 86-88.

167. Political Man: The Social Bases of Politics (Garden City, N.Y.: Doubleday & Co., 1960), pp. 101-102.

168. Ibid., p. 115.

169. Seymour Martin Lipset, The First New Nation: The United States in Historical and Comparative Perspective (Basic Books, 1963), p. 136.

170. Ibid., p. 208.

171. Seymour Martin Lipset and Gerald M. Schaflander, Passion & Politics: Student Activism in America (Boston: Little, Brown &

Co., 1971), p. 41.

172. _Ibid._, p. 75.

173. Seymour Martin Lipset, _Revolution and Counterrevolution: Change and Persistence in Social Structures_ (Garden City, N.Y.: Anchor Books, Revised & Updated edition, 1970), p. 62.

174. _Ibid._, p. 71.

Chapter 9

1. See Donald Atwell Zoll, <u>Twentieth Century Political Philosophy</u> (Englewood Cliffs, N.J.: Prentice-Hall, 1974 paperback edition), especially Chapter Seven, pp. 118-134: "To the conservative, value relativism is anathema. Not only are values independent of human will, but they are binding, in one way or another, and most contemporary conservatives believe that the natural order, societies, and other communal organisms are themselves actualizations of the moral order or that they contain an ethical component." (p. 124)

2. See Erwin C. Hargrove, <u>The Power of the Modern Presidency</u> (New York: Alfred A. Knopf, 1974 paperback edition): "The expanding American fronteir was hospitable to the ideas of English middle-class liberalism but not to either hierarchical conservatism or radical egalitarianism. The social conditions necessary to support an aristocracy and European conservatism emphasizing rank, title, and noblesse oblige or a proletariat that might be converted to revolutionary ideologies simply did not exist. All men had hope that they too might rise. The result is that our conservatives are optimists and rationalists who hope for a productive economy and believe in the free enterprise system to create opportunities for all. And our progressives are reformers who accept capitalism and seek governmental action and social reform only against its excesses. Both operate within a basically liberal framework." (p. 177)

3. See Hans Rogger and Eugene Weber (eds.), <u>The European Right: A Historical Profile</u> (Berkeley: University of California Press, 1966 paperback edition; originally published in 1965).

4. See "Eric Voegelin: The In-Between of Human Life," in Anthony de Crespigny and Kenneth Minogue (eds.), <u>Contemporary Political Philosophy</u> (New York: Dodd, Mead & Co., 1975 paperback edition), p. 119.

5. See Dante Germino, <u>Beyond Ideology: The Revival of Political Theory</u> (New York: Harper & Row, 1967).

6. See Eugene Webb, "Eric Voegelin's Interpretation of Revelation," Paper prepared for delivery at the 1976 Annual Meeting of the American Political Science Association, The Palmer House, Chicago, Ill., Sept. 2-5, 1976.

7. Eric Voegelin, <u>The New Science of Politics</u> (Chicago: University of Chicago Press, 1971 paperback edition; originally published in 1952), p. 1.

8. <u>Ibid</u>., p. 3.

9. <u>Ibid</u>., p. 22.

10. <u>Ibid</u>., p. 26.

11. <u>Ibid</u>., p. 61.

12. <u>Ibid</u>., p. 60.

13. _Ibid._, p. 69.

14. _Ibid._, p. 78.

15. _Ibid._, p. 106.

16. _Ibid._, p. 131.

17. _Ibid._, p. 163.

18. Eric Voegelin, edited by John H. Hallowell (Durham, North Carolina: Duke University Press, 1975), pp. 13-14.

19. _Ibid._, p. 211.

20. _Ibid._, p. 52.

21. _Ibid._, p. 70.

22. _Ibid._, p. 158.

23. _Ibid._, p. 233.

24. Eric Voegelin, _Order and History_, vol. one, _Israel and Revelation_ (Baton Rouge: Louisiana State University Press, 1958 edition, originally published in 1956), p. ix.

25. _Ibid._, p. ix.
See also David J. Walsh, "Philosophy in Voegelin's Work," Paper prepared for delivery at the 1976 Annual Meeting of the American Political Science Association, The Palmer House, Chicago, Ill., Sept. 2-5, 1976.

26. See Eric Voegelin's Introduction to volume four of _Order and History_, _The Ecumenic Age_ (Baton Rouge: Louisiana State University Press, 1974).

27. See Eric Voegelin, _Order and History_, vol. two, _The World of the Polis_ (Baton Rouge: Louisiana State University Press, 1957), p. 22.

28. _Ibid._, p. 2.

29. _Ibid._, p. 22.

30. Eric Voegelin, _Order and History_, vol. three, _Plato and Aristotle_ (Baton Rouge: Louisiana State University Press, 1957), p. 161.

31. _Ibid._, p. 187.

32. Eric Voegelin, _The Ecumenic Age_, _op. cit._, p. 6.

33. _Ibid._, p. 71.

34. _Ibid._, p. 72.

35. _Ibid._, p. 242.

36. _Ibid._, p. 78.

37. _Ibid._, p. 350.

38. _Ibid._, p. 365.

39. _Ibid._, p. 309.

40. _Ibid._, p. 6.

41. According to Voegelin, science is not really science if it does not also aim to become a science of being itself; ontology is indispensable to true science. Yet during the course of this multi-volume study, Voegelin has turned away from the quest for an ontology to a quest for a better understanding of human consciousness. I think that he came to recognize the excessive abstractness and aridity of his philosophical reflections on history and has in the later phase of his thought tried to find a more relevant approach, but with little success. Knowledge, in other words, is less a matter of universality then of concreteness. Yet Voegelin has not given up the quest for a comprehension of divine reality. This still represents the centerpiece of his philosophical endeavors. And divinity, according to Voegelin, can be apprehended through symbols. This is the connection between human consciousness and historical reality: symbolization.

42. Bertrand de Jouvenel, _Sovereignty: An Inquiry into the Political Good_, translated by J.F. Huntington (Chicago: University of Chicago Press, 1957), p. 33.

43. _Ibid._, p. 53.

44. _Ibid._, p. 123.

45. _Ibid._, p. 127.

46. _Ibid._, p. 165.

47. _Ibid._, p. 212.

48. _Ibid._, p. 262.

49. _Ibid._, p. 302.

50. trans. by J.F. Huntington (New York: The Viking Press, 1949).

51. _Ibid._, p. 21.

52. _Ibid._, p. 114.

53. _Ibid._, p. 195.

54. _Ibid._, p. 218.

55. _Ibid._, p. 256.

56. _Ibid._, p. 327.

57. _Ibid._, p. 334.

58. _Ibid._, p. 368.

59. Bertrand de Jouvenel, _The Pure Theory of Politics_ (New Haven: Yale University Press, 1963), pp. 71-74.

60. _Ibid._, p. 51.

61. _Ibid._, p. 207.

62. (London: Cambridge University Press, 1952).

63. _Ibid._, p. 25.

64. _Ibid._, p. 26.

65. _Ibid._, p. 38.

66. _Ibid._, p. 42.

67. _Ibid._, p. 59.

68. _Ibid._, p. 65.

69. _Ibid._, p. 73.

70. Jose Ortega y Gasset, _The Revolt of the Masses_ (New York: W.W. Norton & Co., 1957 paperback edition; originally published in 1930), pp. 13-15.

71. _Ibid._, p. 12.

72. _Ibid._, p. 52.

73. _Ibid._, p. 18.

74. _Ibid._, p. 63.

75. _Ibid._, p. 109.

76. Jose Ortega y Gasset, _History as a System: And Other Essays Toward a Philosophy of History_ (New York: W.W. Norton & Co., 1962 paperback edition; oroginally published in 1941), p. 51.

77. _Ibid._, p. 151.

78. _Ibid._, p. 228.

79. Jose Ortega y Gasset, _Concord and Liberty_ (New York: W.W. Norton & Co., 1963 paperback edition; originally published in 1946), p. 11.

80. _Ibid._, p. 20.

81. Jose Ortega y Gasset, _Man and Crisis_ (New York: W.W. Norton & Co., 1962 paperback edition; originally published in 1958).

82. Jose Ortega y Gasset, _Concord and Liberty, op. cit._, p. 24.

83. Jose Ortega y Gasset, _Man and People_ (New York: W.W. Norton & Co., 1963 paperback edition; originally published in 1957), p. 40.

84. _Ibid._, p. 102.

85. Ortega, _Man and Crisis, op. cit._, p. 99.

86. Jose Ortega y Gasset, _Some Lessons in Metaphysics_ (W.W. Norton & Co., 1966 paperback edition; originally published in 1959), p. 153.

87. _Ibid._, p. 38.

88. _Ibid._, p. 23.

89. Oliver W. Holmes, _Human Reality and the Social World: Ortega's Philosophy of History_ (Amherst: University of Mass.

Press, 1975): "...he succeeded in fusing the philosophical perspectives of phenomenology, historicism, and existentialism into a systematic philosophy of man, society, and history." (p. 68)

90. Jacques Ellul, translated by John Wilkinson, with an Introduction by Robert K. Merton (New York: Vintage Books, 1964), pp. 4-6.

91. Ibid., p. 14.

92. Ibid., p. 79.

93. Ibid., p. 119.

94. Ibid., p. 123.

95. Ibid., p. 184.

96. Ibid., p. 194.

97. Ibid., p. 209.

98. Ibid., p. 198.

99. Ibid., p. 403.

100. See William Kuhns, The Post-Industrial Prophets: Interpretations of Technology (New York: Harper Colophon Books, 1971), p. 116.

101. See Jacques Ellul, The Political Illusion, trans. by Konrad Kellen (New York: Vintage Books, 1972 edition; originally published in 1967).

102. Ibid., p. 81.

103. Jacques Ellul, A Critique of the New Commonplaces (New York: Alfred A. Knopf, 1968), p. 18.

104. Ibid., p. 104.

105. Ibid., p. 114.

106. Jacques Ellul, Autopsy of Revolution, trans. by Patricia Wolf (New York: Alfred A. Knopf, 1971): "Our society is basically technological and statist; all its characteristics point to that, and therefore if a necessary revolution is to be brought about, it will have to be founded upon the realities of technology and the state." (p. 267)

107. Ibid., pp. 268-269.

108. Jacques Ellul, Propaganda: The Formation of Men's Attitudes, trans. by Jean Lerner (New York: Vintage Books, 1973 edition; originally published in 1965), p. xiv.

109. Ibid., p. 25.

110. Ibid., p. 20.

111. Ibid., p. 50.

112. Ibid., p. 86.

113. Ibid., p. 105.

114. <u>Ibid</u>., p. 111.

115. <u>Ibid</u>., p. 121.

116. <u>Ibid</u>., p. 138.

117. <u>Ibid</u>., p. 147.

118. <u>Ibid</u>., p. 158.

119. <u>Ibid</u>., p. 159.

120. <u>Ibid</u>., p. 177.

121. <u>Ibid</u>., p. 180.

122. "The World of Michael Oakeshott," <u>Encounter</u>, June, 1963, pp. 65-74.

123. Michael Oakeshott, <u>Rationalism in Politics: And Other Essays</u> (New York: Basic Books, 1962), p. 127.

124. <u>Ibid</u>., pp. 1-2.

125. <u>Ibid</u>., p. 5.

126. <u>Ibid</u>., p. 18.

127. <u>Ibid</u>., p. 32.

128. <u>Ibid</u>., p. 39.

129. <u>Ibid</u>., p. 41.

130. <u>Ibid</u>., p. 51.

131. <u>Ibid</u>., p. 58.

132. <u>Ibid</u>., p. 67.

133. <u>Ibid</u>., p. 79.

134. <u>Ibid</u>., p. 101.

135. <u>Ibid</u>., p. 109.
See also Michael Oakeshott, <u>On Human Conduct</u> (London: Oxford University Press, 1975). In a review of this book by Josiah Lee Auspitz, <u>Commentary</u>, May, 1976, pp. 89-94, the reviewer states the following: "<u>On Human Conduct</u> is the most important book in the philosophy of politics to have been published in a long time. It will need to be taken into account in any future discussions of the theory of justice, the development of the modern state, the nature of historical explanation, the basis of political experience, the general theory of human action, and the character and practical relevence of theoretical inquiry itself." (p. 89) On the other hand, a recent issue of <u>Political Theory</u>, vol. 4, no. 3, August, 1976, has several critical essays on Michael Oakeshott, especially in regard to <u>On Human Conduct</u>, which find much less value in his theoretical efforts. Sheldon S. Wolin, for example, in his essay "The Politics of Self-Disclosure," accuses Oakeshott of divorcing political theory from politics. (p. 322) David Spitz, in his essay "A Rationalist Malgre Lui: The Perplexities of Being Michael Oakeshott," finds Oakeshott to be an aberrant con-

servative "at odds with, and not a complement to, conceptions of conservatism that seek in God or natural law or natural right absolute standards of morality by which to judge and to guide human conduct and social arrangements and practices." (p. 339) Hannah Fenichel Pitkin, in an essay entitled "Inhuman Conduct and Apolitical Theory," finds On Human Conduct "rigidly dogmatic, assertive, and idiosyncratic almost to the point of being crotchety." (p. 302)

136. Michael Oakeshott, Rationalism in Politics, op. cit., p. 28.

137. Ibid., p. 121.

138. Ibid.., p. 123. For a different view on this point, see Gertrude Himmelfarb, "The Conservative Imagination: Michael Oakeshott," The American Scholar, Spring, 1975, pp. 405-420: "Nor is the conservative, as Oakeshott describes him, averse to change. The question is how to accommodate change. The conservative proposes to do so my small doses rather than large, out of necessity rather than ideology, with a minimum disruption of life." (p. 411)

139. Michael Oakeshott, Rationalism in Politics, op. cit., p. 169.

140. Hobbes on Civil Association (Berkeley: University of California Press, 1975), p. 3.

141. Ibid., p. 17.

142. Ibid., pp. 18-26.

143. Ibid., p. 42.

144. Ibid., p. 58.

145. Ibid., p. 61.

146. Ibid., p. 63.

147. Ibid., p. 117.

148. Ibid., p. 119.

149. Ibid., p. 131.

Chapter 10

1. See Donald J. Devine, <u>The Political Culture of the United States</u>, <u>op</u>. <u>cit</u>. See also George C. Lodge, <u>The New American Ideology</u>, <u>op</u>. <u>cit</u>.

2. See "Harris Poll: Is the U.S. Moving to the Right," <u>New York Post</u>, January 5, 1977.
It should be noted, however, that one recent empirical voting study indicates a change toward more issue oriented, ideological politics when comparing 1956 data to a 1973 portrait of the American voter. See Norman H. Nie, Sidney Verba, and John R. Petrocik, <u>The Changing American Voter</u>, <u>op</u>. <u>cit</u>., p. 143, as follows:

	1956	1973
Leftist	12%	21%
Moderate Leftist	19%	12%
Centrist	41%	27%
Moderate Rightist	15%	17%
Rightist	13%	23%

This "conventional wisdom," however, has been severely criticized by James E. Piereson, "Issue Alignment and the American Party System, 1956-1976," <u>American Politics Quarterly</u>, vol. 6, no. 3, July, 1978: "...contrary to what might have been expected on the basis of previous studies, issue alignment was at a peak on all issues in 1956, after which it declined across the board until 1960 or 1964, and then followed a scattered path thereafter." (p. 290)
See also Seymour Martin Lipset and Earl Raab, "The Message of Proposition 13," <u>Commentary</u>, vol. 66, no. 3, September, 1978, pp. 42-46: "...ideological conservatism has been growing as a partner to a continuingly dominant operational liberalism. This orientation is often described as neo-conservatism, but it might just as likely be called neo-liberalism." (p. 45)

3. <u>Ideologies and Attitudes</u>, <u>op</u>. <u>cit</u>., p. 12.

4. <u>The Nature of Human Values</u> (New York: The Free Press, 1973), p. 13.

5. See H.J. Eysenck, <u>The Psychology of Politics</u> (New York: Frederick A. Praeger, 1954). See also Paul M. Sniderman and Jack Citrin, "Psychological Sources of Political Belief: Self-Esteem and Isolationist Attitudes," <u>The American Political Science Review</u>, vol. LXV, No. 2, June, 1971. See also Robert E. Lane, <u>Political Thinking and Consciousness: The Private Life of the Political Mind</u> (Chicago: Markham Pub. Co., 1969). See also James MacGregor Burns, <u>Leadership</u> (New York: Harper & Row, 1978): "To take the lead is to act in terms of certain values and purposes; leaders assume initiatives and organize support on the basis of the structure of wants, needs, expectations, and demands that lies beneath value and purpose." (p. 408)

6. Rokeach, The Nature of Human Values, op. cit., p. 21.

7. "Conservatism and Personality," in Gordon J. DiRenzo (ed.) Personality and Politics, op. cit., pp. 269-270.

8. Ibid., p. 269.

9. See Jeanne W. Knutson, "Personality Correlates of Political Beliefs: Left, Right and Center," Paper presented at the 67th Annual Meeting of the American Political Science Association, Chicago, Ill., 1971: "A major criticism of the McCloskey study has been that the conservative scale employed by McCloskey enlists the acceptance of only those conservatives who could be defined as feeling threatened and insecure." (p. 38)

10. See Thomas R. Dye and Harmon L. Zeigler, The Irony of Democracy: An Uncommon Introduction to American Politics, 3rd edition, (North Scituate, Mass.: Duxbury Press, 1975): "It is the irony of democracy in America that elites, not masses, are most committed to democratic values...Social science research reveals that the common man is not attached to the causes of liberty, fraternity, or equality. On the contrary, support for free speech and press, for freedom of dissent, and for equality of opportunity for all is associated with high educational levels, prestigious occupations, and high social status." (p. 14)

11. See Hartz, The Liberal Tradition in America, op. cit.

12. "The Trouble With Being in the Middle," Time, July 1, 1974.

13. See Alan D. Monroe, Public Opinion in America (New York: Dodd, Mead, & Co., 1975 paperback edition), pp. 12-13.

14. See Lloyd A. Free and Hadley Cantril, The Political Beliefs of Americans: A Study of Public Opinion (New York: Simon & Schuster Clarion Book, 1969 paperback edition), pp. 5-6.

15. New York Times, November 4, 1972.

16. "The America Inherited by Gerald Ford," Time, August 26, 1974.

17. See William A. Rusher, The Making of the New Majority Party (Ottawa, Ill.: Green Hill Publishers, 1975 paperback edition). See also David S. Broder, The Party's Over: The Failure of Politics in America (New York: Harper & Row Colophon Books, 1972). See also Robert Novak, "Producer's Party," National Review, June 6, 1975. Following the narrow defeat of Gerald Ford by Jimmy Carter in the 1976 presidential election, but continuing poor showing of Republican Party candidates running for Congress and state governorships, there has been a considerable dampening of this prospect of a conservative party political revival. See, for instance, the March 18, 1977 issue of National Review, and the symposium by Clare Boothe Luce, Jeffrey Hart, and Er-

nest Van Den Haag, "Is the Republican Party Dead?" As Clare
Boothe Luce remarked in her opening statement: "The Republican
Party has won four of the last 12 presidential races, and controlled two of the last 24 Congresses. It emerged from the
elections last November with only 12 of the fifty governorships, and 180 of the 535 seats in Congress. With less than
24 per cent of the voters registered as Republicans, it is now
at the lowest point in its 123 year history." (p. 326)

18. See Bruce H. Russett and Elizabeth C. Hanson, Interest
and Ideology: The Foreign Policy Beliefs of American Businessmen (San Francisco: W.H. Freeman Co., 1975 paperback edition):
"Economic interest and ideology—whether of the 'liberal mess-
ianist' variety or of a conservative anticommunist sort—might
therefore combine, in the American case, to produce a more powerful impetus to an assertive, activist foreign policy than
either could produce alone. If perception rather than 'objective' interests determine behavior, then surely ideology is a
key contributor to perception." (p. 52)

19. (New York: John Wiley & Sons, 1964 paperback edition,
2 vols.)

20. See Fred I. Greenstein, Personality and Politics: Problems of Evidence, Inference, and Conceptualization (Chicago:
Markham Publishing Co., 1969): "The Authoritarian Personality
is a book dealing more with prejudice than with the problem
suggested by its title—psychological dispositions toward authority." (p. 97)
   See also Rupert Wilkinson, The Broken Rebel: A Study of
Culture, Politics and Authoritarian Character (New York: Harper & Row, 1972): "It follows, then, that the authoritarian
type can be made a psychiatric scapegoat for much more of man's
cruelty and intolerance than in fact it is responsible for."
(p. 4)

21. T. W. Adorno, et al., The Authoritarian Personality,
vol. 1, op. cit., p. 1.

22. Ibid., p. 147.

23. Ibid., p. 152.

24. Ibid., p. 233.

25. Ibid., p. 235.

26. Ibid., p. 237.

27. Ibid., p. 238.

28. Breach of Faith: The Fall of Richard Nixon (New York:
Atheneum & Readers' Digest Press Book, 1975), p. 13.

29. See Bruce Mazlish, In Search of Nixon: A Psychohistor-
ical Inquiry (Baltimore, Md.: Penguin Books, 1973 paperback
edition). See David Abrahamsen, Nixon v. Nixon: An Emotional
Tragedy (New York: New American Library Signet Book, 1978)
   See also James David Barber, "The Nixon Brush With Tyr-

anny," <u>Political Science Quarterly</u>, vol. 92, No. 4, Winter 1977-8, pp. 581-605.

30. James David Barber, "President Nixon and Richard Nixon: Character Trap," <u>Psychology Today</u>, Oct. 1974; see also James David Barber, <u>The Presidential Character</u> (Englewood Cliffs, N.J.: Prentice-Hall, 1972).

31. "Column," signed "R", April, 1975.

32. See Glenn D. Wilson (ed.), <u>The Psychology of Conservatism</u> (London: Academic Press, 1973), pp. 261-264.

33. William T. Bluhm, <u>Ideologies and Attitudes</u>, <u>op. cit.</u>, p. 117.

34. <u>Ibid.</u>

35. <u>Ibid.</u>

36. <u>Ideology in America: Change and Response in a City, a Suburb, and a Small Town</u> (New York: W.W. Norton, 1972 paperback edition; originally published in 1969), p. xxix, Preface.

37. "Mass Belief Systems Revisited: Political Change and Attitude Structure," <u>The Journal of Politics</u>, vol. 36, no. 3, August, 1974, p. 580.

38. <u>The Vital Center: The Politics of Freedom</u> (London: Andre Deutch, Ltd., 1970 edition; originally published in 1950).

39. <u>Power and Politics in America</u>, 2nd edition (North Scituate, Mass.: Duxbury Press, 1974), p. 5.

40. See William F. Stone, <u>The Psychology of Politics</u> (New York: The Free Press, 1974 paperback edition), p. 174.

41. <u>Ibid.</u>, pp. 175-176.

42. See Garry Wills, <u>Nixon Agonistes: The Crisis of the Self-Made Man</u> (Boston: Houghton-Mifflin Co., 1970).

43. See Joan Huber and William H. Form, <u>Income and Ideology: An Analysis of the American Political Formula</u> (New York: The Free Press, 1973). See also Harold L. Wilensky, <u>The Welfare State and Equality: Structural and Ideological Roots of Public Expenditures</u> (Berkeley: University of California Press, 1975 paperback edition).

44. The following is a chart that is a suggestive outline of the main differences at the present time in regard to major policy-orientations:

LIBERALISM	CONSERVATISM
1. Maximum service state	1. Minimal service state
2. Minimal warfare state	2. Maximum warfare state
3. Individual rights takes precedence over national security considerations	3. National security takes precedence over individual rights
4. What's best for big business is not necessarily best for the country	4. What's best for big business is generally best for the country

<table>
<tr><td>5. Supports delegation of more power to the central government to promote more uniform standards of equity</td><td>5. Shift more power back to the states and local governments and let each community decide on its own what its own best interests are</td></tr>
<tr><td>6. More effective regulation of the private sector</td><td>6. Less regulation of the private sector</td></tr>
<tr><td>7. Pro-reform</td><td>7. Pro status-quo</td></tr>
<tr><td>8. Liberty depends on greater equality and a fairer distribution of the nation's total wealth and assets</td><td>8. Equality depends upon safeguarding the rights of the individual, especially the rights of property</td></tr>
</table>

45. See "Conservatives, Liberals and the Constitution," in Robert A. Goldwin, Left, Right and Center, op. cit., p. 86.

46. See David Riesman, with Nathan Glazer and Rauel Denny, The Lonely Crowd: A Study of the Changing American Character, abridge edition, (New Haven: Yale University Press, 1961 paperback edition).

47. Perhaps one way of characterizing the difference is to contrast two concepts, "Equality of Opportunity" and "Equality of Result," with conservatives favoring the former, and liberals the latter, with varying degrees of emphasis. Here are suggestive definitions of these contrasting views of "equality":

(1) The Conservative View: Equality of Opportunity—
Every individual has a fair and competitive chance to make the most of himself; it is an individual matter whether or not one succeeds. The achievement ethic is open-ended; everyone has a reasonable chance of getting his/her piece of the American dream of material success.

(2) The Liberal View: Equality of Result—As a result of disadvantages inherent in a basically unequal socioeconomic system, it should be the responsibility of government to correct inequities and provide remedial assistance to those who have not had the advantages that others have had. Failure and lack of success are due primarily to an inequitable socioeconomic system where power favors the better off at the expense of the less well-off, and only government can correct such injustices.

48. The Nature of Human Values, op. cit., p. 181.

Chapter 11

1. Lodge, *The New American Ideology*, op. cit., p. 6.

2. *Ibid.*, p. 96.

3. See "America Now: A Failure of Nerve?" Symposium, *Commentary*, July, 1975. See also The Twentieth Anniversary issue of *The Public Interest*, No. 41, Fall, 1975.

4. See James A. Nuechterlein, "The People vs. the Interests," *Commentary*, March, 1975, pp. 66-73: "The confused state of contemporary liberal thought and strategy, manifested most obviously in recent years in the struggles for self-definition within the Democratic party, reflects an inability among liberals not only clearly to define a usable philosophy, but even to specify precisely their proper constituency; they are no longer certain, in other words, just who are the People in whose name they can or should presume to speak." (p. 68)

5. "A Remembrance of Alex Bickel," *The New Republic*, October 18, 1975, pp. 21-23. See also Nelson W. Polsby, "In Praise of Alexander M. Bickel," *Commentary*, January, 1976, pp. 50-54.

6. Alexander M. Bickel, *The Morality of Consent* (New Haven: Yale University Press, 1975), p. 5.

7. *Ibid.*, p. 6.

8. *Ibid.*, p. 8.

9. *Ibid.*, p. 12.

10. *Ibid.*, p. 19.

11. *Ibid.*, p. 21.

12. See Alexander M. Bickel, *The Supreme Court and the Idea of Progress* (New York: Harper Torchbooks, 1970 edition).

13. Bickel, *The Morality of Consent*, op. cit., pp. 28-29.

14. *Ibid.*, p. 57.

15. *Ibid.*, p. 123.

16. See chapter 8 of this book.

17. Robert Nisbet, *Twilight of Authority* (New York: Oxford University Press, 1975), p. 10.

18. *Ibid.*, p. 49.

19. *Ibid.*, p. 47.

20. *Ibid.*, p. 51.

21. *Ibid.*, p. 74.

22. *Ibid.*

23. *Ibid.*, pp. 118-119.

24. _Ibid._, p. 149.

25. _Ibid._

26. _Ibid._, p. 212.

27. _Ibid._, p. 246.

28. See Robert Nisbet, "Many Tocquevilles," _The American Scholar_, Winter, 1976-77, pp. 59-75. It must be said that Robert Nisbet certainly appreciates the importance and complexity of this concept both in Tocqueville's writings and in his own work. What I am alluding to is that Nisbet carries Tocqueville's ambiguous view of equality to the point of clearly emphasizing and preferring the negative implications of this crucial value concept. See especially p. 74 of _The American Scholar_ essay.

29. See review of _Twilight of Authority_ by J. Peter Euben, _Political Theory_, vol. 5, no. 1, February, 1977: "The tone of the entire book is impatient and judgmental. It tends to over-state and under-argue, to rely on exclamation points (thirty of them) rather than analysis. One looks in vain for the conservative graces of proportion, wit, and irony or the careful attention to the texture of texts, arguments, and life." (p. 123)

30. M. Stanton Evans, _Clear and Present Dangers: A Conservative View of America's Government_ (New York: Harcourt Brace Jovanovich, Inc., 1975 paperback edition), p. 14.

31. _Ibid._, p. 26.

32. _Ibid._, p. 34.

33. _Ibid._, p. 45.

34. _Ibid._, p. 52.

35. _Ibid._, p. 55.

36. _Ibid._, p. 63.

37. _Ibid._, p. 96.

38. _Ibid._, p. 115.

39. _Ibid._, p. 128.

40. _Ibid._, p. 141.

41. _Ibid._, pp. 151-154.

42. _Ibid._, p. 190.

43. _Ibid._, p. 200.

44. _Ibid._; see "What is to be Done," Epilogue, pp. 389-405.

45. See J.L. Talmon, "Grevious Sources of Puzzlement: An Historical Perspective," _Encounter_, March, 1977, pp. 23-28: "In the Western highly industrialized and urbanized societies, the welfare state has by now become generally accepted to the point of considerably blunting the differences between liberal-democratic and social-democratic attitudes on social policy. But the relationship between the public and the private sector—state

control and individual initiative, personal incentives and the general good, the ravages which the insatiable urge to consume (with runaway inflation as its inevitable consequences) is visiting upon society as a whole, upon the quality of life, the environment, and the future prospects of mankind—continues to cause deep and often bewildered concern, and to revive Malthusian fears." (p. 25)

46. (Garden City, N.Y.: Doubleday Anchor Books, 1970).

47. (Garden City, N.Y.: Doubleday & Co., 1975).

48. See Walter Dean Burnham, <u>Critical Elections and the Mainsprings of American Politics</u> (New York: W.W. Norton & Co., 1970).

49. Kevin P. Phillips, <u>Mediacracy</u>, <u>op</u>. <u>cit</u>., pp. 1-2.

50. <u>Ibid</u>., p. 15.

51. <u>Ibid</u>., pp. 17-24.

52. <u>Ibid</u>., p. 29.

53. <u>Ibid</u>., p. 52.

54. <u>Ibid</u>., p. 32.

55. <u>Ibid</u>., p. 33.

56. <u>Ibid</u>., p. 39.

57. <u>Ibid</u>., p. 62.

58. <u>Ibid</u>., pp. 64-65.

59. <u>Ibid</u>., pp. 78-79.

60. <u>Ibid</u>., p. 129.
For a similar analysis of changing electoral politics but with a somewhat different evaluation and conclusion, see Everett Carll Ladd, Jr., "Liberalism Upside Down: The Inversion of the New Deal Order," <u>Political Science Quarterly</u>, vol. 91, no. 4, Winter, 1976-77, pp. 577-600: "A new class-ideology alignment has taken form over the past decade as part of the transformation of political conflict and hence of the American party system. Since the mid-1960s, there has been an inversion of the relationship of class to electoral choice from that prevailing in the New Deal era. Broadly interpreted, the New Deal experience sustained the proposition that liberal programs and candidates would find their greatest measure of support among lower-class voters and that conservatives would be strongest within the higher socio-economic strata. Now, in many although not all instances, groups at the top are more supportive of positions deemed liberal and more Democratic than those at the bottom. We also see some evidence of an emergent curvilinear pattern, with the top more Democratic than the middle but the middle less Democratic than the bottom." (p. 577)

61. <u>Ibid</u>., p. 130.

62. <u>Ibid</u>., p. 208.

63. _Ibid._, pp. 225-228.

64. See Eric Hoffer, _The True Believer: Thoughts on the Nature of Mass Movements_ (New York: The New American Library Mentor Book, 1958 edition; originally published in 1951); see also Eric Hoffer, _The Ordeal of Change_ (New York: Harper & Row Perennial Library, 1967 edition; originally published in 1963).

65. (New York: The New American Library Mentor Book, 1959 paperback edition; originally published in 1952).

66. See George F. Kennan, _Russia and the West Under Lenin and Stalin_ (Boston: Little, Brown & Co., 1961); George F. Kennan, _Soviet-American Relations 1917-20_, 2 volumes, (Boston: Little, Brown & Co., 1956 and 1958).

67. See George F. Kennan, _Memoirs: 1925-1950_ (Boston: Little, Brown & Co., 1967); George F. Kennan, _Memoirs: 1950-1963_ (Boston: Little, Brown & Co., 1972).

68. For a negative appraisal of Kennan's recent writings, see Leopold Labedz, "The Two Minds of George Kennan: How to Unlearn from Experience," _Encounter_, April, 1978, pp. 78-86: "The Preacher and the Machiavellian, the diplomat and the intellectual, the official and the non-conformist, the nostalgic conservative and the liberal 'progressive', the sophisticated cosmopolitan and the embarrassed isolationist—all these and other dualities have created an imbalance in his political judgment." (p. 86)
See also Richard Pipes, "Mr. X Revises: A Reply to George F. Kennan," _Encounter_, April, 1978, pp. 18-21.
For a defense of Kennan, see Richard Lowenthal, "Dealing with Soviet-Global Power," _Encounter_, June, 1978, pp. 88-91.

69. "Mr. X...30 Years On," interview conducted by George Urban, _Encounter_, September, 1976, pp. 10-43.

70. _Ibid._, p. 11.

71. See George F. Kennan, _The Cloud of Danger: Current Realities of American Foreign Policy_ (Boston: Little, Brown & Co, 1977). In this book, Kennan recommends a strategic withdrawal from American globalism and a more selective view of what constitutes a vital national interest in U.S. relations with the rest of the world.

72. Kennan, _Memoirs: 1950-1963_, vol. 2, _op. cit._, p. 13.

73. _Ibid._, p. 52.

74. _Ibid._, p. 58.

75. _Ibid._, p. 71.

76. _Ibid._, p. 95.

77. _Ibid._, p. 137.

78. See Chapter 9, "McCarthyism," pp. 190-228, _op. cit._

79. _Ibid._, p. 228.

80. "Mr. X...30 Years On," _Encounter_, _op. cit._, p. 23.

Chapter 12

1. Sidney Verba and Norman H. Nie, _Participation in America: Political Democracy and Social Equality_ (New York: Harper & Row, 1972), p. 4.

2. (New York: John Wiley & Sons, 1965).

3. Verba and Nie, _Participation in America, op. cit._, p. 338.

4. _Ibid._, p. 342.

5. See _The Image: Or What Happened to the American Dream_ (New York: Atheneum, 1962).

6. See news article, "Califano Says Quotas are Necessary to Reduce Bias in Jobs and Schools," _The New York Times_, Friday, March 18, 1977, pp. 1 and A16, column 3: "Employment quotas can and do work in reversing patterns of job discrimination, Joseph A. Califano Jr., Sec. of Health, Education and Welfare, said today. In an interview with _The New York Times_, Mr. Califano said that, based on his experience in the practice of law and in recruiting policy makers for the department, it was possible and necessary to endorse preferential hiring for jobs and admissions policies in higher education."
In a rejoinder to this position, Sidney Hook wrote an article a few days later which appeared in the _New York Daily News_, March 27, 1977, under the heading "Racial & Sexual Quotas: They're not only Illegal; They're Immoral": "The only way to counteract past and present racial and sexual discrimination is by applying a single fair standard to all, and not by reverse discrimination that unfairly punishes some individuals today for the evils of previous generations. Those evils flowed precisely from the same immoral principle that Mr. Califano now endorses—judging persons not by their specific capacities but by their color or sex." (p. C15)

7. See Robert A. Nisbet, "The New Despotism," _Commentary_, June, 1975, pp. 31-45. See also Charles Frankel, "The New Egalitarianism and the Old," _Commentary_, Sept., 1973, pp. 54-61. Frankel refers to this new version of equalitarianism as "redemptive egalitarianism" and rejects it utterly. One might also recall that Charles Frankel is a liberal in the John Dewey pragmatic mold. For example, this is how he defines the problem: "Redemptive egalitarianism is only indirectly concerned with removing specific inequalities. Its deeper concern is to restore things to their original Design, to remove the blight of Accident from the world, and make obtuse Matter lie down and be obedient to God's plan...(p. 59)
For a defense of the "new egalitarianism," see John Rawls, _A Theory of Justice, op. cit._, and Herbert J. Gans, _More Equality, op. cit._: "Moreover, when race and sex have been used for over a century as criteria for not hiring people, it is hypocritical to argue that they should not be used as criteria for

hiring because this would be 'reverse discrimination.' In terms of equality of results, this simply means the continuation of the traditional discrimination, albeit for a different reason." (p. 72)

8. See Seymour Martin Lipset and Earl Raab, "The Election and the National Mood," Commentary, January, 1975, pp. 39-47.

9. Op. cit., p. 269.

10. See Thomas L. Hartshorne, The Distorted Image, op. cit.: "Just as American liberalism had a strong conservative component, so American conservatism had strong overtones of the dominant liberal philosophy. American conservatism differed from that of other countries in that it was more optimistic, more materialistic, and more individualistic. In these respects, it was simply an American conservatism, partaking of the national characteristics. It was distinctively American because it had accepted, as other conservatism had not, the triumph of democracy and industrialism." (p. 163)

11. See Robert H. Wiebe, The Segmented Society: An Historical Preference to the Meaning of America (New York: Oxford University Press, 1975).

12. See Robert Green McCloskey, American Conservatism in the Age of Enterprise 1865-1910, op. cit.

13. Conservatism in America, op. cit., p. 237.

14. A confirmation of this thesis will be found in a recent book on conservatism which is a critique from within the family, for the author is proud of his status as a "true-believer," although he deplores what he feels is an unnecessary and inexcusable lack of larger public acceptance for conservative ideas and principles. See Craig Schiller, The (Guilty) Conscience of a Conservative (New Rochelle, N.Y.: Arlington House Publishers, 1978): "...the rightist attachment to laissez-faire and belligerent foreign-policy rhetoric has become unpalatable to the average contemporary American." (p. 132)

15. The Age of Reform: From Bryan to FDR (New York: Alfred A. Knopf, 1955), p. 20.

16. Ibid., p. 89.

17. Ibid., p. 20.

18. See Robert Justin Goldstein, Political Repression in Modern America: 1870 to the Present (New York: Schenkman & Two Continents Publishing Group, Ltd., 1978 paperback edition). This is an impressive historical analysis and a damning indictment of the "dark side" of American democracy.

19. See Alan Wolfe, The Seamy Side of Democracy, op. cit.

20. See Irving Babbitt, Democracy and Leadership (Boston: Houghton Mifflin, 1924); Paul Elmer More, Shelburne Essays on American Literature, selected and edited by Daniel Aaron (New York: Harcourt, Brace & World Harbinger Book, 1963); T.S.

Eliot, <u>Christianity and Culture: The Idea of a Christian Society</u> and <u>Notes Towards the Definition of Culture</u> (New York: Harcourt, Brace & World Harvest Book, 1949). See also John R. Harrison, <u>The Reactionaries: A Study of the Anti-Democratic Intelligentsia</u> (New York: Schocken Books, 1967).

21. See Joan Hoff Wilson, <u>Herbert Hoover: Forgotten Progressive</u> (Boston: Little, Brown & Co., 1975 paperback edition). See also James T. Patterson, <u>Mr. Republican: A Biography of Robert A. Taft</u> (Boston: Houghton Mifflin Co., 1972).

22. See William Appleman Williams, <u>The Contours of American History</u>, op. cit.

23. (New York: Simon & Schuster, 1975), pp. 194-195.

24. See Richard Hofstadter, <u>The American Political Tradition and the Men Who Made It</u> (New York: Vintage paperback, 1948 edition); chapter 11, "Herbert Hoover and the Crisis of American Individualism."

25. Wilson, <u>Herbert Hoover: Forgotten Progressive</u>, op. cit.

26. See Elliott White, "Genetic Diversity and Political Life," <u>The Journal of Politics</u>, vol. 34, No. 4, November, 1972, pp. 1203-1248.

27. <u>Social Structure and Social Problems</u> (Boston: Allyn & Bacon, 1974), pp. 147-148.

28. See Ben L. Martin, "Experts in Policy Processes: A Contemporary Perspective," <u>Polity</u>, vol. VI, no. 2, Winter, 1973, pp. 149-173.

29. "The Presidency: Shifting Conservative Perspective?" <u>National Review</u>, November 22, 1974.

30. "Republicans, Democrats, and Public Policy Competence," <u>The Yale Review</u>, Summer, 1975, pp. 481-495.

31. <u>Ibid.</u>, p. 485.

32. See Paul N. Goldstene, <u>The Collapse of Liberal Empire: Science and Revolution in the Twentieth Century</u> (New Haven: Yale University Press, 1977). This is a critique of liberalism from a radical perspective which provides an eloquent, if fairly abstract, analysis of the inability of liberal theory to accommodate to contemporary power realities, especially the concentration of economic power in the corporate world and its monopolization of technology.
See also Roberto Mangabeira Unger, <u>Knowledge and Politics</u> (New York: The Free Press, 1975): "The liberal doctrine fails to provide a coherent view of knowledge, personality, and society, a failure evidenced by its antinomies..." (p. 192)

INDEX

(Strauss), 96
White, Elliott, 410
White House, 43, 154
White, Morton, 61, 83, 340
White, Theodore H., 166, 168
Who Governs? (Dahl), 349
Wiebe, Robert H., 334
Wildavsky, Aaron, 327
Wilensky, Harold L., 339,
  402
Wilkinson, Ruphert, 401
Will, George F., 24, 177
Wills, Garry, 270, 318, 368
Williams, William Appleman,
  410
Wilson, Glen D., 402
Wilson, Francis Graham, 352
Wilson, James Q., 24, 227-
  228, 309, 390
Wilson, Joan Hoff, 301-302
Wilson, Woodrow, 1, 37
Wise, David, 367
Witonski, Philip P., 365
Witowski, Peter P., 72,
  328
World War I, 24, 78, 294
World War II, 1, 24, 96,
  101, 109, 116, 133, 151,
  156, 168, 194, 200
Wolfe, Alan, 409
Wolff, Robert Paul, 18,
  320-321
Wolfinger, Raymond E.,
  318, 328
Wolin, Sidney, 14, 364,
  397
Wood, Gordon S., 333
Working-class Majority
  The, (Levison), 218
Works of John Adams, The
  (C.F. Adams, ed.), 333
Wright, Benjamin F., 83

Xenophon, 95

Yale University, 188
Young, James P., 319
Youth and Dissent (Kenis-
  ton), 367

Zeigler, L. Harmon, 354,
  400

Zeligs, Meyer A., 369
Zinkler, Leon, 174
Zoll, Donald Atwell, 326, 392

About the Author

Russell G. Fryer has been a Professor of Political Science and History at Western Connecticut State College (Danbury, Conn.) since 1963. Previous to this he taught for 10 years in New Jersey public schools. He served 5 years in the United States Navy during World War II. He was born in 1923, in Jersey City, N.J. He is the author of an unpublished Ph.D. thesis (New York University, 1964), <u>Power and Human Nature in Western Political Theory</u>. He is married, has three children, and lives in Brookfield, Conn.

555/3